W9-CLL-287

THE WORLD'S CLASSICS

496

DEMOCRACY IN AMERICA

Oxford University Press

ELY HOUSE, LONDON W.I

GLASGOW NEW YORK TORONTO MELBOURNE WELLINGTON
CAPE TOWN SALISBURY IBADAN NAIROBI DAR ES SALAAM
LUSAKA ADDIS ABABA
BOMBAY CALCUTTA MADRAS KARACHI LAHORE DACCA
KUALA LUMPUR SINGAPORE HONG KONG TOKYO

DEMOCRACY
IN AMERICA

By

ALEXIS DE TOCQUEVILLE

Translated by HENRY REEVE

Abridged and edited with an Introduction by

HENRY STEELE COMMAGER

LONDON
OXFORD UNIVERSITY PRESS

ALEXIS DE TOCQUEVILLE
Born : Verneuil, Paris, 29 July 1805
Died : Cannes, 16 April 1859

The first part of De la démocratie en Amérique
was published in 1835 ; *the second part in* 1840.
*Henry Reeve's translation was first published in two
volumes,* 1835 *and* 1840. *This abridgement was
first included in* The World's Classics *in* 1946
and reprinted in 1952, 1953, 1955, 1959, 1961,
1965, *and* 1971

SBN 19 250496 7

PRINTED IN GREAT BRITAIN
BY R. & R. CLARK, LIMITED, EDINBURGH

EXPLANATORY NOTE

IN this edition of *Democracy in America* the text has been reduced to approximately half its original length. An explanation, if not an apology, for what may seem high-handed is called for. *Democracy in America* had been, for some time, unavailable except as part of a large and expensive series of volumes. Happily the complete text, edited and annotated by Mr. Phillips Bradley, has now been published. The present edition is designed to meet the needs of the general reader rather than of the scholar. Experience has suggested that students will not read—or will read with reluctance amounting to animosity—the eight hundred or more large pages of the complete edition. It must be admitted that their recalcitrance is not inexcusable. Much that Tocqueville thought necessary to include by way of description and explanation is now quite useless for all practical purposes. There is no need, now, to preserve the rather tiresome account of the geography, native races, colonial history, local and state government of the United States, and we can, too, easily dispense with the numerous digressions on contemporary France and the speculations on the future of the three races in the United States. It is hoped, and believed, that the present edition sacrifices nothing that is essential, and presents what is essential in more succinct and palatable form.

There has been, needless to say, no tampering with the text. Where entire chapters have been omitted —as with the chapters on Political Jurisdiction and on the Causes of Commercial Prosperity in the United States—the remaining chapters have been numbered consecutively : as the chapter arrangement varies considerably in the different editions this renumbering

constitutes no serious breach of literary etiquette.
The translation by Henry Reeve has been used, and
no attempt has been made to check it with the
French. Tocqueville's original division of the two
parts—abandoned in some later editions—has here
been restored. Editorial comment has been kept to
a minimum, for the editor has not thought it incumbent upon him either to point out or to correct
Tocqueville's errors of fact or judgment. Students
anxious to study in detail the circumstances attending
the composition of *Democracy in America* are referred
to the masterly study by George Pierson, *Tocqueville
and Beaumont in America*.

HENRY STEELE COMMAGER

INTRODUCTION

I

FOR over three centuries the New World has been an object of curiosity to the Old, and for half that time the United States, particularly, has been called upon to point a moral or adorn a tale. Literally thousands of travelers—British, French, and German predominating—have visited here and rushed home to transcribe their impressions : sometimes they have not waited to return but have given a palpitating world their conclusions in advance, as it were. The roll-call of British commentators is long and distinguished : it includes, to name only a few of the more prominent, the Trollopes, mother and son, Harriet Martineau, Dickens, Lyell, Grattan, Marryat, Freeman, Spencer, Bryce, and, in our own day, Wells, Bennett, Joad, Chesterton, and Belloc. French visitors and interpreters are less familiar but scarcely less numerous : one bibliography lists some 1500 volumes by French travelers, and the list includes books by Crèvecœur, Talleyrand, Barbe-Marbois, Chastellux, Chateaubriand, Brissot de Warville, Tocqueville, Considérant, Chevalier, Clemenceau, Jusserand, Tardieu, and Siegfried. No other nation, assuredly, has been subjected to such a literary barrage, exposed to so many million words of praise, blame, and admonition. Only a tough people could have survived.

What is the explanation of this persistent and passionate curiosity about America ?—a curiosity whose only parallel in modern history is the contemporary interest in Russia ? The interest was not fortuitous. Americans are beginning to realize, now, that their country has never been isolated, but Europeans have always known this, for throughout its history America has troubled the Old World. In the sixteenth and seventeenth centuries it was El Dorado, and the nations of Europe fought for the rich prize. In the eighteenth century it became something new under the sun, a republic, a democracy, a federal union, the hope (as Turgot put it) of the human race. Throughout the nineteenth it was a blessing and a menace—and a curiosity. To the poor and oppressed it was the promised land ; to the rich and privileged a standing threat ; while diplomats everywhere had to reckon with in it their plans and intrigues. Its vast distances and shaggy beauty fired the imagination ; its youthful vitality and convulsive growth inspired wonder and respect ; its democracy was a challenge, its social equality a rebuke, its toleration a model. If laws of history or of the evolution of society were to be formulated, they must be based in large part upon the American experiment ; if new political institutions were to be fashioned, they must be modelled in part upon those of the United States. No statesman could be indifferent to the new nation on the western shores of the Atlantic ; no economist could omit it from his calculations ; even philosophers and moralists were required to accommodate their speculations to its experience.

And everything about America was astonishing : its broad prairies and majestic rivers ; its native peoples, so romantic in prospect, so malevolent in reality ; its restless frontier, sweeping across the continent like the tides at St. Michael ; the villages that mushroomed overnight into cities ; the babel of languages ; the Negroes who, slave or free, moulded society into their own pattern ; the farms large as Old World counties ; the democracy of manners so often mistaken for vulgarity ; the spectacle of Catholics and Protestants living amicably side by side, and of scores and hundreds of queer sects ; the singular notion of free public education and the confusion of schools and colleges ; the disconcerting freedom of women and the purity of morals ; the town meeting, the state legislature, the political party, the popular election of a chief magistrate ; the disparity of wealth and the blurring of class distinctions ; the fabulous prosperity, the buoyant confidence, the latent power. No wonder it took a thousand essays to penetrate to the truth about America.

And Americans themselves gave little help. Notwithstanding that nervous boastfulness which impressed so many visitors, Americans, on the whole, gave but a poor account of themselves,—certainly a confusing one. Their newspapers played up the sensational and the eccentric ; their literature reflected an unfamiliar local color or, more recently, mirrored a society incredibly violent and rude ; their politicians indulged in antics that seemed, and often were, preposterous ; and that somehow the political machine worked smoothly enough seemed rather a dispensation of Providence than a tribute to common sense. And, in our own day, the moving pictures, easily the most influential of interpreters, gave a fabulous picture of wealth, crime, vulgarity, speed, excitement, salacity, and abnormality. In Britain nature seemed to conform to art, and from the days of Fielding and Smollett to those of Wells and Bennett, the library was a not unsatisfactory substitute for travel, but it was inconceivable that America could be what, on her many surfaces, she appeared to be. The picture was diverse and contradictory, and the least perspicacious foreigner could confidently predict that America would be unpredictable.

It must be admitted that European visitors did little to resolve the confusion. Most of the literature of description and interpretation, English as well as continental, is pretty shoddy stuff. The interpretation of national character is difficult enough in the most auspicious of circumstances : the circumstances attending the lucubrations of European visitors were rarely auspicious. Of all the thousands of books on America, perhaps less than two score are of lasting value.

Why is the average so low, why is so much of the stuff mediocre or worse ? Why, especially, have men and women otherwise thoughtful, learned, and observant, failed so signally to understand and interpret the United States ? The question is not relevant to the works of a Grattan, a Münsterberg, a Bryce, but it is properly directed to the overwhelming majority of the commentators, British and continental. Only a partial explanation can be submitted here. Many, if not most, of those who wrote about America, came here with a closed mind, came not to learn but to confirm preconceived notions. They assumed—naturally enough—that the Old World was the norm and interpreted every deviation from that norm as quaint, vulgar, or eccentric. That Americans, who had inherited admirable political, legal, religious, and social institutions, preferred to fashion new ones appeared to them faintly perverse. Few of those who wrote so glibly on America saw the whole of it, or saw any part of it thoroughly : altogether too many got their impressions of the American countryside from the windows of a train, their impression of cities from hotel lobbies or dining-rooms. Others, overwhelmed with the vastness and variety of American life, took refuge in anecdotes or in exclamatory descriptions of the picturesque and the exceptional. Some visitors were inspired by purely business considerations—the search for land, for business openings, for investment opportunities. Still others, with their eye on royalties, made a book the excuse for their visit rather than the visit the justification for their book; what they wrote, therefore, was designed to titillate or flatter a British or European audience—an audience notoriously uncritical and credulous in everything concerning America. And, finally, of all those who attempted to interpret America, only a handful were intellectually competent to the task: of most of them it could be said, as the sage Franklin said in another connection, ' their poor noddles were distracted '.

These observations apply with less force, perhaps, to French than to British visitors and commentators. The French had, to be sure, a clearer field, an easier task. There was no tradition of enmity to embarrass relations between Americans and French, but one of friendship: Lafayette proved as immortal as George III. From America France had neither so much to fear nor so much to hope as Britain. Its relation was avuncular rather than maternal, and it could regard the new nation with an objectivity scarcely possible to the mother-country. Then, too, France had had her Revolution, and needed neither to borrow nor to resist American radicalism; nor was America draining France of her population, or threatening her supremacy in commerce, manufacturing, or business. Nor were the two peoples divided—to adapt Shaw's hackneyed phrase—by the barrier of a common language and common institutions. The British were inclined to regard any departure from English ways as a reflection upon themselves, and, at the same time, to resent imitations as the possessors of the genuine commonly resent those who urge the merits of the counterfeit: the French, who were not looking for a New France, were not outraged when they failed to find a New Britain.

To most of these melancholy generalizations, as well as to their Gallic qualifications, Alexis de Tocqueville is an exception. He was thorough and indefatigable in his search for facts, patient and skilful in their organization, sympathetic and perspicacious in their interpretation, luminous in their presentation. His purpose was lofty, his learning solid, his understanding profound. By common consent his *Democracy in America* is the most illuminating commentary on American character and institutions ever penned by a foreigner, the one which, a century after its appearance, seems best assured of immortality.

II

'I confess that in America, I saw more than America ; I sought the image of democracy itself, with its inclinations, its character, its prejudices, and its passions, in order to learn what we have to fear or to hope from its progress.' So wrote Tocqueville, and the confession is basic to an understanding of his work. America, in short, was not the primary object of his investigation, but rather democracy— a word which Tocqueville used much as we use it today to embrace social and economic as well as political practices and institutions. The inspiration of the inquiry was not so much curiosity about America as concern for France especially, and for the Old World in general. America was, it seemed, merely the laboratory ; the findings were designed for application abroad.

For democracy, Tocqueville was persuaded, was inevitable and irresistible, its doctrines and practices destined to spread over the western world. The invasion of England was already under way : Tocqueville's brief visit there had persuaded him of that, and every letter from J. S. Mill or from Nassau Senior strengthened the persuasion. France could not escape, France whose tradition of liberty and equality made her peculiarly susceptible ; before long the ferment of democracy would be at work in all the nations of Europe. 'The question here discussed,' said Tocqueville, 'is interesting not only to the United States, but to the whole world ; it concerns not a nation, but all mankind.'

Yet if democracy was inevitable, would not mere description suffice ? And here we come to the heart of Tocqueville's thought. Democracy was, indeed, inevitable, but democracy was no simple thing but infinitely complex, not a rigid system or an implacable doctrine but an attitude of mind and a habit of conduct. It was a mixture of good and evil—Tocqueville was not always sure which was predominant— but it was possible to separate the good from the evil. It was possible, above all, to separate the natural from the artificial, the universal from the particular, to accommodate democracy to its various environments.

Tocqueville was one of the first students of politics to discern the truth—so often ignored or contemned in our own day—that the great forces of history do not operate uniformly and automatically in every society, but are naturalized, as it were, wherever they appear. He proposed, for France, a reconciliation of fatalism and free will, of the iron forces of history and the genius of the nation. 'The more I study the former condition of the world,' he wrote, ' and see the world of our own day in greater detail, the more I consider the prodigious variety to be met with, not only in laws, but in the principles of law, the more I am tempted to believe that what we call necessary institutions are often no more than institutions to which we have grown accustomed, and that in matters of social constitution, the field of possibilities is much more extensive than men living in their various societies are ready to imagine.'

The field of possibilities was more extensive than men imagined ! Here was the real justification for the study of democracy in America. Democracy was on the march, but the manner in which it was to come, the form it was to take, the consequences it was to have, were all matters over which men might exercise control. And for everything that concerned democracy America was not only the most convenient but the most elaborate laboratory. It held the answer to the questions which were bound to trouble the Old World. Can men govern themselves ? Is it possible to reconcile liberty and order, the individual and the state ? Does democracy but substitute the tyranny of the majority for the tyranny of the few ? Can any government tolerate free speech and a free press, or will liberty inevitably degenerate into license ? Can men of different races, tongues, and faiths live amicably side by side? Will the melting-pot, with its fusing of peoples, produce an inferior race ? Will universal education be accompanied by a vulgarization of culture ? Can art, literature, and philosophy flourish in a society which substitutes the verdict of the majority for the judgment of training and tradition ? Is democracy synonymous with mediocrity, and is the well-being of the many worth the sacrifice of beauty and grace ? Will democracy so depreciate the military virtues as to expose itself to enervation from within and destruction from without ?

No scholar could hope to find conclusive answers to questions so profound and so complex, but that the American experience might illuminate the problem was apparent, for America was the proving ground of history. Here, as James Russell Lowell was shortly to observe, 'the elements are all in solution, and we have only to look to see how they will combine. History, which every day makes less account of governors and more of man, must find here the compendious key to all that picture writing of the Past.'

It was, to be sure, the key to the future rather than to the past that Tocqueville sought, but that America held the key to this, too, was clear. It was clear, at least, to young Tocqueville—who was the first to appreciate the scientific possibilities of the New World —and *Democracy in America* vindicated his judgment and his vision.

III

It is just over one hundred years, now, since young Tocqueville—he was barely thirty—brought out the first two volumes of *Democracy in America*. He was filled with misgivings—and so was his publisher, M. Gosselin. But soon the book was acclaimed in two continents and crowned by the French Academy, and M. Gosselin was delighted. ' So it appears that your book is a masterpiece,' he boasted, rubbing his hands together. It was the comment of a tradesman, said Tocqueville with a sneer. But it was, too, the verdict of posterity.

What explains the fame, the longevity, of *Democracy in America* ? No other book of its kind has weathered so well, none has been so frequently reprinted, and without misgivings even by publishers. The book, certainly, is not without faults. It is, for all its sharpness and spareness, over-long—two more volumes appeared in 1840, making four in all. It makes no concessions to the reader, either in analysis or in interpretation, it has no narrative quality, it is devoid of humor. It includes much that is merely descriptive ; it omits much that is important.

It is, indeed, no difficult task to draw up a general indictment and itemize a bill of particulars. Tocqueville came not to observe America as a whole, but to observe the operations of democracy, and democracy, rather than America, it must never be forgotten, was his primary concern. He tended to substitute his own reflections for facts, or, where the facts were stubborn, to force them into his own preconceived pattern. When he wrote the second—and best—part of *Democracy in America* the sharp impact of personal experience was fading, the pressure of France was strong, and Tocqueville indulged himself more readily in rationalization, yielded increasingly to the temptations of *a priori* reasoning. He did not sufficiently check what he felt was bound to happen with what actually was happening, and where history ran counter to his predictions he was inclined to give the impression that history was somehow at fault. Thus he could write at length, and ominously, of the tyranny of the majority without once citing a convincing example of such tyranny ; thus he could insist upon the inherent weakness of the executive authority at a time when the strongest of American Presidents occupied the White House. His acquaintance with America was limited ; he knew the East better than the West, the North better than the South. His investigations were haphazard rather than systematic, his sources of information inadequate and often misleading. He made it a point to meet the best people, and the best people, then as now, were inclined to deprecate democracy : Justice Story complained, with reason, that Tocqueville had borrowed liberally from his Commentaries, and Story was a high federalist. An aristocrat, Tocqueville exaggerated the importance of manners, and was capable of the observation that 'nothing is more prejudicial to democracy than its outward forms of behaviour; many men would willingly endure its vices who cannot support its manners'. He was not sufficiently familiar with the English background of American institutions, and frequently mistook for peculiarly American or peculiarly democratic what was merely Anglo-American. He missed many things that less perspicacious observers saw, possibly because the obvious did not always accommodate itself to his philosophical pattern; in his anxiety to get below the surface he failed to appreciate things that were on the surface. Thus he could argue the ultimate disintegration of the Union because he failed to notice economic developments or to comprehend the nationalizing effect of the industrial revolution. He missed the abolition movement, and transcendentalism, and his interest in penal and prison reform—the ostensible ground for his visit to America—did not persuade him to study the reform movement in general. For all his concern with democracy, he seemed singularly uninterested in its immediate political manifestations, and the casual reader of his book would scarcely realize that while Tocqueville was traversing America, Andrew Jackson was President.

These are serious defects, defects that would guarantee oblivion to most volumes of description or interpretation. Yet *Democracy in America* has not only survived oblivion; it has earned for itself a place as a classic. For the faults of the book are, after all, superficial rather than fundamental; they are grievous only with reference to the standards which Tocqueville himself set, and those standards were incomparably high. The omissions, the inadequacies, the misconceptions of the book can easily be supplied or corrected by other books ; for its shining merits there is no substitute.

What are these merits ? First, it can be said, Tocqueville chose a great and noble theme and handled it with dignity. That theme was the adjustment of the civilizations of Western Christendom to democracy. Others had written about America ; Tocqueville undertook to relate American to world history, to fix the significance of America in history. His subject, he wrote in all humility, ' is interesting . . . to the whole world ; it concerns, not a nation, but all mankind'. His purpose was to prepare men everywhere for the ' providential fact ' of equality ; to dissipate fears, quiet excessive hopes, encourage accommodation ; to lift men above narrow and selfish and persuade them to broad and generous views. There is almost a Periclean quality about his own statement of his grand design :

> I have sought to show what a democratic people is in our days, and by this delineation, executed with rigorous accuracy, my design has been to produce a twofold effect on my contemporaries. To those who make to themselves an ideal democracy, a brilliant vision which they think it easy to realize, I undertake to show that they have arrayed their future in false colours ; that the democratic government they advocate, if it be of real advantage to those who can support it, has not the lofty features they ascribe to it ; and moreover, that this government can only be maintained on certain conditions of intelligence, private morality, and religious faith, which we do not possess ; and that its political results are not to be obtained without labour.
>
> To those for whom the word ' democracy ' is synonymous with disturbance, anarchy, spoliation, and murder, I have attempted to show that the government of democracy may be reconciled with

respect for property, with deference for rights, with safety to freedom, with reverence to religion ; that if democratic government is less favorable than another to some of the finer parts of human nature, it has also great and noble elements ; and that perhaps, after all, it is the will of God to shed a lesser grade of happiness on the totality of mankind, not to combine a greater share of it on a smaller number, or to raise the few to the verge of perfection. I have undertaken to demonstrate to them that, whatever their opinion on this point may be, it is too late to deliberate, that society is advancing and dragging them along with itself towards equality of conditions ; that the sole remaining alternative lies between evils henceforth inevitable ; that the question is not whether aristocracy or democracy can be maintained, but whether we are to live under a democratic society, devoid indeed of poetry and greatness, but at least orderly, moral, or under a democratic society, lawless and depraved, abandoned to the frenzy of revolution or subjected to a yoke heavier than any of those which have crushed mankind since the fall of the Roman Empire. I have sought to calm the ardour of the former class of persons, and, without discouragement, to point out the only path before them. I have sought to allay the terrors of the latter, and to bend their minds to the idea of an inevitable future, so that with less impetuosity on the one hand, and less resistance on the other, the world may advance more peaceably to the necessary fulfilment of its destiny. This is the fundamental idea of the book ; an idea which connects all its other ideas in a single web.

And to his friend, Kergolat, he confessed, ' To labour in this direction is in my eyes a *sainte occupation*, and one in which one must spare neither one's money nor one's time, nor one's life.'

Tocqueville chose a great subject, and he measured

up to its greatness. He was the first philosophical historian to write of the American experiment ; the first political scientist to make democracy the primary object of realistic investigation. And it must be accounted a capital merit in Tocqueville that he had not only a philosophy, but the right philosophy. He saw that the significance of America in history was to be found in the opportunity which it afforded as a laboratory of social, economic, and political democracy, and he fastened his attention on that aspect of America to the exclusion of the merely picturesque or sensational. He had an instinct for the jugular vein in history.

Other observers had lost themselves in the trivial, the irrelevant, the inconsequential ; they maundered on about hotel service, the litter on the streets of cities, the hardships of railroad travel, the table manners of their hosts. Tocqueville, too, noted these things, but he did not suppose they were important in themselves or permit them to distract his attention from the object of his investigation—the effect of democracy on manners and morals, politics and religion, business and labor, literature and art, family and social relations. He was concerned, throughout, with fundamental causes and ultimate consequences.

And on almost every page of his book we discern the play of an alert, inquisitive, and critical mind. It is a tribute to the triumph of Tocqueville's method that we are, throughout, more interested in what he has to say about a subject than we are in the subject itself. He had, that is, not only a philosophical but an eminently reflective mind ; he had not only a philosophy of history, in the grand manner, but perspicacity and penetration ; he was as illuminating in his particular as in his general observations. We are constantly gratified by his shrewd insights and his happy prophecies. Who, after all, has better comprehended the American character than this French stranger who arrived at his understanding almost as by a mathematical formula, so rigorous was his analysis, so logical his conclusions. In his day our literature was still strongly colonial, but Tocqueville foresaw with astonishing perspicuity the effect that democracy would have upon it in the future. He saw, too, that democracy must have its own History, one in which the individual was subordinate to the mass, fortuity to great sweeping movements ; and from George Bancroft to Henry Adams and Charles Beard, American historical literature has conformed to Tocqueville's formula. He penetrated to the gnawing uncertainty of many Americans about social democracy, the pretentiousness and insincerity of much of the talk about the common man by men who invariably made it clear that they themselves were uncommon men. He understood, as have few foreigners and not many Americans, the combination—peculiarly prominent in the realm of politics—of extravagance of language and prudence of conduct. He noted, as had others, the American passion for change, and found it the natural consequence of the restless search for the ideal and the opportunities afforded all Americans to achieve that ideal. He grasped the fact, as yet concealed from many of our agitated Bourbons, that democracy makes for conservatism and that the surest guaranty of stability is the wide distribution of property. He was the first foreign observer to appreciate the significance of the dominance of the American political scene by men trained to the law, and described in terms still relevant that aristocracy of the robe which Americans take for granted but which other democratic peoples look upon with astonishment. He saw the significance of the inter-action of democracy and religion and emphasized throughout his study the place of the church in American life. He discerned the natural hostility to the military in a democracy, but foresaw with startling accuracy the effect of prolonged war on American society and economy and psychology. There was little, indeed, in the American character that his penetrating eye did not see, his luminous mind com-prehend.

And Tocqueville's interpretation, for all his aristo-cratic and alien background, was almost unfailingly judicious. He was misled, at times, by the men he consulted, the books he read, but his errors were never malicious. His view of democracy was often pessimistic, but never jaundiced, and it is gratifying that America has confounded its most astute critic where he was pessimistic rather than where he was optimistic. No other interpreter of America, not Grattan nor Bryce not Munsterberg nor Brogan, has achieved the aloofness, the objectivity, the serene impersonality, that came naturally to Tocqueville. The explanation is, largely, in Tocqueville's own character ; it is, in part, that Tocqueville was con-cerned to instruct his own people rather than to edify the Americans, and that patriotism and morality inexorably required the most scrupulous objectivity.

And, finally, it must be counted among the great merits of *Democracy in America* that its style is felicitous and even brilliant. There are no purple patches, there are few epigrams, but there is, throughout, a luminous clarity, a resiliency, a masculine toughness, that contrasts sharply with the rhetoric of Trollope or Martineau, the verbosity of Bryce, the strained brilliance of Siegfried or Maurois. Tocqueville has, above all others who have written about America, the magisterial style.

It is this happy combination of a great theme with a philosophy profound enough to comprehend it, a temperament judicious enough to interpret it, an intelligence acute enough to master it, a style adequate to its demands, that makes *Democracy in America* one of the great and enduring works of political literature. As a young man Tocqueville confessed, ' I do not know any way of life more honourable or more attractive than to write with such honesty about the great truths that one's name becomes known to the civilized world '. It is a safe prophecy that as long as democracy itself endures Tocqueville's name will be known to the civilized world.

HENRY STEELE COMMAGER

Rye, New York,
January 1945

CONTENTS

CHAPTER VIII

CHAPTER IX

CHAPTER X

CHAPTER XI

CHAPTER XII

CHAPTER XIII

CHAPTER XIV

CHAPTER XV

CHAPTER XVI

CHAPTER XVII

CHAPTER XVIII

CHAPTER XIX

PART TWO

CHAPTER XX

CHAPTER XXI

CHAPTER XXII

CHAPTER XXIII

CHAPTER XXIV

THE AUTHOR'S PREFACE TO THE FIRST PART

AMONG the novel objects that attracted my attention during my stay in the United States, nothing struck me more forcibly than the general equality of conditions. I readily discovered the prodigious influence which this primary fact exercises on the whole course of society, by giving a certain direction to public opinion, and a certain tenor to the laws ; by imparting new maxims to the governing powers, and peculiar habits to the governed. I speedily perceived that the influence of this fact extends far beyond the political character and the laws of the country, and that it has no less empire over civil society than over the Government ; it creates opinions, engenders sentiments, suggests the ordinary practices of life, and modifies whatever it does not produce. The more I advanced in the study of American society, the more I perceived that the equality of conditions is the fundamental fact from which all others seem to be derived, and the central point at which all my observations constantly terminated.

I then turned my thoughts to our own hemisphere, where I imagined that I discerned something analogous to the spectacle which the New World presented to me. I observed that the equality of conditions is daily progressing toward those extreme limits which it seems to have reached in the United States, and that the democracy which governs the American communities appears to be rapidly rising into power in Europe. I hence conceived the idea of the book which is now before the reader.

It is evident to all alike that a great democratic revolution is going on among us ; but there are two opinions as to its nature and consequences. To some it appears to be a novel accident, which as such may still be checked ; to others it seems irresistible, because it is the most uniform, the most ancient, and the most permanent tendency which is to be found in history. Let us recollect the situation of France seven hundred years ago, when the territory was divided among a small number of families, who were the owners of the soil and the rulers of the inhabitants ; the right of governing descended with the family inheritance from generation to generation ; force was the only means by which man could act on man, and landed property was the sole source of power. Soon, however, the political power of the clergy was founded, and began to exert itself : the clergy opened its ranks to all classes, to the poor and the rich, the villain and the lord ; equality penetrated into the Government through the Church, and the being who as a serf must have vegetated in perpetual bondage took his place as a priest in the midst of nobles, and not unfrequently above the heads of kings.

The different relations of men became more complicated and more numerous as society gradually became more stable and more civilized. Thence the want of civil laws was felt ; and the order of legal functionaries soon rose from the obscurity of the tribunals and their dusty chambers, to appear at the court of the monarch, by the side of the feudal barons in their ermine and their mail. While the kings were ruining themselves by their great enterprises, and the nobles exhausting their resources by private wars, the lower orders were enriching themselves by commerce. The influence of money began to be perceptible in State affairs. The transactions of business opened a new road to power, and the financier rose to a station of political influence in which he was at once flattered and despised. Gradually the spread of mental acquirements, and the increasing taste for literature and art, opened chances of success to talent; science became a means of government, intelligence led to social power, and the man of letters took a part in the affairs of the State. The value attached to the privileges of birth decreased in the exact proportion in which new paths were struck out to advancement. In the eleventh century nobility was beyond all price; in the thirteenth it might be purchased; it was conferred for the first time in 1270; and equality was thus introduced into the Government by the aristocracy itself.

In the course of these seven hundred years it sometimes happened that in order to resist the authority of the Crown, or to diminish the power of their rivals, the nobles granted a certain share of political rights to the people. Or, more frequently, the king permitted the lower orders to enjoy a degree of power, with the intention of repressing the aristocracy. In France the kings have always been the most active and the most constant of levellers. When they were strong and ambitious they spared no pains to raise the people to the level of the nobles; when they were temperate or weak they allowed the people to rise above themselves. Some assisted the democracy by their talents, others by their vices. Louis XI and Louis XIV reduced every rank beneath the throne to the same subjection; Louis XV descended, himself and all his Court, into the dust.

As soon as land was held on any other than a feudal tenure, and personal property began in its turn to confer influence and power, every improvement which was introduced in commerce or manufacture was a fresh element of the equality of conditions. Henceforward every new discovery, every new want which it engendered, and every new desire which craved satisfaction, was a step toward the universal level. The taste for luxury, the love of war, the sway of fashion, and the most superficial as well as the deepest passions of the human heart, co-operated to enrich the poor and to impoverish the rich.

From the time when the exercise of the intellect became the source of strength and of wealth, it is impossible not to consider every addition to science, every fresh truth, and every new idea as a germ of power placed within the reach of the people. Poetry, eloquence, and memory, the grace of wit, the glow of imagination, the depth of thought, and all the gifts which are bestowed by Providence with an equal hand, turned to the advantage of the democracy ; and even when they were in the possession of its adversaries they still served its cause by throwing into relief the natural greatness of man ; its conquests spread, therefore, with those of civilization and knowledge, and literature became an arsenal where the poorest and the weakest could always find weapons to their hand.

In perusing the pages of our history, we shall scarcely meet with a single great event, in the lapse of seven hundred years, which has not turned to the advantage of equality. The Crusades and the wars of the English decimated the nobles and divided their possessions ; the erection of communities introduced an element of democratic liberty into the bosom of feudal monarchy ; the invention of fire-arms equalized the villain and the noble on the field of battle ; printing opened the same resources to the minds of all classes ; the post was organized so as to bring the same information to the door of the poor man's cottage and to the gate of the palace ; and Protestantism proclaimed that all men are alike able to find the road to heaven. The discovery of America offered a thousand new paths to fortune, and placed riches and power within the reach of the adventurous and the obscure. If we examine what has happened in France at intervals of fifty years, beginning with the eleventh century, we shall invariably perceive that a twofold revolution has taken place in the state of society. The noble has gone down on the social ladder, and the *roturier* has gone up; the one descends as the other rises. Every half-century brings them nearer to each other, and they will very shortly meet.

Nor is this phenomenon at all peculiar to France. Whithersoever we turn our eyes we shall witness the same continual revolution throughout the whole of Christendom. The various occurrences of national existence have everywhere turned to the advantage of democracy; all men have aided it by their exertions: those who have intentionally laboured in its cause, and those who have served it unwittingly; those who have fought for it and those who have declared themselves its opponents, have all been driven along in the same track, have all laboured to one end, some ignorantly and some unwillingly; all have been blind instruments in the hands of God.

The gradual development of the equality of conditions is therefore a providential fact, and it possesses all the characteristics of a Divine decree: it is universal, it is durable, it constantly eludes all human interference, and all events as well as all men contribute to its progress. Would it, then, be wise to imagine that a social impulse which dates from so far back can be checked by the efforts of a generation? Is it credible that the democracy which has annihilated the feudal system and vanquished kings will respect the citizen and the capitalist? Will it stop now that it has grown so strong and its adversaries so weak? None can say which way we are going, for all terms of comparison are wanting : the equality of conditions is more complete in the Christian countries of the present day than it has been at any time or in any part of the world ; so that the extent of what already exists prevents us from foreseeing what may be yet to come.

The whole book which is here offered to the public has been written under the impression of a kind of religious dread produced in the author's mind by the contemplation of so irresistible a revolution, which has advanced for centuries in spite of such amazing obstacles, and which is still proceeding in the midst of the ruins it has made. It is not necessary that God himself should speak in order to disclose to us the unquestionable signs of his will ; we can discern them in the habitual course of nature, and in the invariable tendency of events : I know, without a special revelation, that the planets move in the orbits traced by the Creator's finger. If the men of our time were led by attentive observation and by sincere reflection to acknowledge that the gradual and progressive development of social equality is at once the past and future of their history, this solitary truth would confer the sacred character of a Divine decree upon the change. To attempt to check democracy would be in that case to resist the will of God ; and the nations would then be constrained to make the best of the social lot awarded to them by Providence.

The Christian nations of our age seem to me to present a most alarming spectacle ; the impulse which is bearing them along is so strong that it cannot be stopped, but it is not yet so rapid that it cannot be guided : their fate is in their hands ; yet a little while and it may be so no longer. The first duty which is at this time imposed upon those who direct our affairs is to educate the democracy ; to warm its faith, if that be possible ; to purify its morals ; to direct its energies ; to substitute a knowledge of business for its inexperience, and an acquaintance with its true interests for its blind propensities ; to adapt its government to time and place, and to modify it in compliance with the occurrences and the actors of the age. A new science of politics is indispensable to a new world. This, however, is what we think of least ; launched in the middle of a rapid stream, we obstinately fix our eyes on the ruins which may still be descried upon the shore we have left, while the current sweeps us along, and drives us backward toward the gulf.

In no country in Europe has the great social revolution which I have been describing made such rapid progress as in France ; but it has always been borne on by chance. The heads of the State have never had any forethought for its exigencies, and its victories have been obtained without their consent or without their knowledge. The most powerful, the most intelligent, and the most moral classes of the nation have never attempted to connect themselves with it in order to guide it. The people has consequently been abandoned to its wild propensities, and it has grown up like those outcasts who receive their education in the public streets, and who are unacquainted with aught but the vices and wretchedness of society. The existence of a democracy was seemingly unknown, when on a sudden it took possession of the supreme power. Everything was then submitted to its caprices ; it was worshipped as the idol of strength ; until, when it was enfeebled by its own excesses, the legislator conceived the rash project of annihilating its power, instead of instructing it and correcting its vices ; no attempt was made to fit it to govern, but all were bent on excluding it from the government.

The consequence of this has been that the democratic revolution has been effected only in the material parts of society, without that concomitant change in laws, ideas, customs, and manners which was necessary to render such a revolution beneficial. We have obtained a democracy, but without the conditions which lessen its vices and render its natural advantages more prominent ; and although we already perceive the evils it brings, we are ignorant of the benefits it may confer.

While the power of the Crown, supported by the aristocracy, peaceably governed the nations of Europe, society possessed, in the midst of its wretchedness, several different advantages which can now scarcely be appreciated or conceived. The power of a part of his subjects was an insurmountable barrier to the tyranny of the prince ; and the monarch, who felt the almost divine character which he enjoyed in the eyes of the multitude, derived a motive for the 'ust use of his power from the respect which he inspired. High as they were placed above the people, the nobles could not but take that calm and benevolent interest in its fate which the shepherd feels toward his flock ; and without acknowledging the poor as their equals, they watched over the destiny of those whose welfare Providence had intrusted to their care. The people never having conceived the idea of a social condition different from its own, and entertaining no expectation of ever ranking with its chiefs, received benefits from them without discussing their rights. It grew attached to them when they were clement and just, and it submitted without resistance or servility to their exactions, as to the inevitable visitations of the arm of God. Custom, and the manners of the time, had moreover created a species of law in the midst of violence, and established certain limits to oppression. As the noble never suspected that any one would attempt to deprive him of the privileges which he believed to be legitimate, and as the serf looked upon his own inferiority as a consequence of the immutable order of Nature, it is easy to imagine that a mutual exchange of good-will took place between two classes so differently gifted by fate. Inequality and wretchedness were then to be found in society ; but the souls of neither rank of men were degraded. Men are not corrupted by the exercise of power or debased by the habits of obedience, but by the exercise of a power which they believe to be illegal and by obedience to a rule which they consider to be usurped and oppressive. On one side was wealth, strength, and leisure, accompanied by the refinements of luxury, the elegance of taste, the pleasures of wit, and the religion of art. On the other was labour and a rude ignorance ; but in the midst of this coarse and ignorant multitude it was not uncommon to meet with energetic passions, generous sentiments, profound religious convictions, and independent virtues. The body of a State thus organized might boast of its stability, its power, and, above all, of its glory.

But the scene is now changed, and gradually the two ranks mingle ; the divisions which once severed mankind are lowered ; property is divided, power is held in common, the light of intelligence spreads, and the capacities of all classes are equally cultivated ; the State becomes democratic, and the empire of democracy is slowly and peaceably introduced into the institutions and the manners of the nation. I can conceive a society in which all men would profess an equal attachment and respect for the laws of which they are the common authors ; in which the authority of the State would be respected as necessary, though not as divine ; and the loyalty of the subject to the chief magistrate would not be a passion, but a quiet and rational persuasion. Every individual being in the possession of rights which he is sure to retain, a kind of manly reliance and reciprocal courtesy would arise between all classes, alike removed from pride and meanness. The people, well acquainted with its true interests, would allow that in order to profit by the advantages of society it is necessary to satisfy its demands. In this state of things the voluntary association of the citizens might supply the individual exertions of the nobles, and the community would be alike protected from anarchy and from oppression.

I admit that, in a democratic State thus constituted, society will not be stationary ; but the impulses of the social body may be regulated and directed forward ; if there be less splendour than in the halls of an aristocracy, the contrast of misery will be less frequent also ; the pleasures of enjoyment may be less excessive, but those of comfort will be more general ; the sciences may be less perfectly cultivated, but ignorance will be less common ; the impetuosity of the feelings will be repressed, and the habits of the nation softened ; there will be more vices and fewer crimes. In the absence of enthusiasm and of an ardent faith, great sacrifices may be obtained from the members of a commonwealth by an appeal to their understandings and their experience ; each individual will feel the same necessity for uniting with his fellow-citizens to protect his own weakness ; and as he knows that if they are to assist him must co-operate, he will readily perceive that his personal interest is identified with the interest of the community. The nation, taken as a whole, will be less brilliant, less glorious, and perhaps less strong ; but the majority of the citizens will enjoy a greater degree of prosperity, and the people will remain quiet, not because it despairs of amelioration, but because it is conscious of the advantages of its condition. If all the consequences of this state of things were not good or useful, society would at least have appropriated all such as were useful and good ; and having once and for ever renounced the social advantages of aristocracy, mankind would enter into possession of all the benefits which democracy can afford.

But here it may be asked what we have adopted in the place of those institutions, those ideas, and those customs of our forefathers which we have abandoned. The spell of royalty is broken, but it has not been succeeded by the majesty of the laws ; the people has learned to despise all authority, but fear now extorts a larger tribute of obedience than that which was formerly paid by reverence and by love.

I perceive that we have destroyed those independent beings which were able to cope with tyranny single-handed ; but it is the Government that has inherited the privileges of which families, corporations, and individuals have been deprived ; the weakness of the whole community has therefore succeeded that influence of a small body of citizens, which, if it was sometimes oppressive, was often conservative. The division of property has lessened the distance which separated the rich from the poor ; but it would seem that the nearer they draw to each other, the greater is their mutual hatred, and the more vehement the envy and the dread with which they resist each other's claims to power ; the notion of right is alike insensible to both classes, and force affords to both the only argument for the present, and the only guarantee for the future. The poor man retains the prejudices of his forefathers without their faith, and their ignorance without their virtues ; he had adopted the doctrine of self-interest as the rule of his actions, without understanding the science which controls it, and his egotism is no less blind than his devotedness was formerly. If society is tranquil, it is not because it relies upon its strength and its well-being, but because it knows its weakness and its infirmities ; a single effort may cost it its life ; everybody feels the evil, but no one has courage or energy enough to seek the cure ; the desires, the regrets, the sorrows, and the joys of the time produce nothing that is visible or permanent, like the passions of old men which terminate in impotence.

We have, then, abandoned whatever advantages the old state of things afforded, without receiving any compensation from our present condition ; we have destroyed an aristocracy, and we seem inclined to survey its ruins with complacency, and to fix our abode in the midst of them.

The phenomena which the intellectual world presents are not less deplorable. The democracy of France, checked in its course or abandoned to its lawless passions, has overthrown whatever crossed its path, and has shaken all that it has not destroyed. Its empire on society has not been gradually introduced or peaceably established, but it has constantly advanced in the midst of disorder and the agitation of a conflict. In the heat of the struggle each partisan is hurried beyond the limits of his opinions by the opinions and the excesses of his opponents, until he loses sight of the end of his exertions, and holds a language which disguises his real sentiments or secret instincts. Hence arises the strange confusion which we are witnessing. I cannot recall to my mind a passage in history more worthy of sorrow and of pity than the scenes which are happening under our eyes; it is as if the natural bond which unites the opinions of man to his tastes and his actions to his principles was now broken; the sympathy which has always been acknowledged between the feelings and the ideas of mankind appears to be dissolved, and all the laws of moral analogy to be abolished.

Zealous Christians may be found among us whose minds are nurtured in the love and knowledge of a future life, and who readily espouse the cause of human liberty as the source of all moral greatness. Christianity, which has declared that all men are equal in the sight of God, will not refuse to acknowledge that all citizens are equal in the eye of the law. But, by a singular concourse of events, religion is entangled in those institutions which democracy assails, and it is not unfrequently brought to reject the equality it loves, and to curse that cause of liberty as a foe which it might hallow by its alliance.

By the side of these religious men I discern others whose looks are turned to the earth more than to Heaven; they are the partisans of liberty, not only as the source of the noblest virtues, but more especially as the root of all solid advantages; and they sincerely desire to extend its sway, and to impart its blessings to mankind. It is natural that they should hasten to invoke the assistance of religion, for they must know that liberty cannot be established without morality, nor morality without faith; but they have seen religion in the ranks of their adversaries, and they inquire no further; some of them attack it openly, and the remainder are afraid to defend it.

In former ages slavery has been advocated by the venal and slavish-minded, while the independent and the warm-hearted were struggling without hope to save the liberties of mankind. But men of high and generous characters are now to be met with, whose opinions are at variance with their inclinations, and who praise that servility which they have themselves never known. Others, on the contrary, speak in the name of liberty, as if they were able to feel its sanctity and its majesty, and loudly claim for humanity those rights which they have always disowned. There are virtuous and peaceful individuals whose pure morality, quiet habits, affluence, and talents fit them to be the leaders of the surrounding population ; their love of their country is sincere, and they are prepared to make the greatest sacrifices to its welfare, but they confound the abuses of civilization with its benefits, and the idea of evil is inseparable in their minds from that of novelty.

Not far from this class is another party, whose object is to materialize mankind, to hit upon what is expedient without heeding what is just, to acquire knowledge without faith, and prosperity apart from virtue ; assuming the title of the champions of modern civilization, and placing themselves in a station which they usurp with insolence, and from which they are driven by their own unworthiness. Where are we then ? The religionists are the enemies of liberty, and the friends of liberty attack religion ; the high-minded and the noble advocate subjection, and the meanest and most servile minds preach independence ; honest and enlightened citizens are opposed to all progress, while men without patriotism and without principles are the apostles of civilization and of intelligence. Has such been the fate of the centuries which have preceded our own ? and has man always inhabited a world like the present, where nothing is linked together, where virtue is without genius, and genius without honour ; where the love of order is confounded with a taste for oppression, and the holy rites of freedom with a contempt of law ; where the light thrown by conscience on human actions is dim, and where nothing seems to be any longer forbidden or allowed, honourable or shameful, false or true ? I cannot, however, believe that the Creator made man to leave him in an endless struggle with the intellectual miseries which surround us : God destines a calmer and a more certain future to the communities of Europe ; I am unacquainted with his designs, but I shall not cease to believe in them because I cannot fathom them, and I had rather mistrust my own capacity than his justice.

There is a country in the world where the great revolution which I am speaking of seems nearly to have reached its natural limits ; it has been effected with ease and simplicity, say rather that this country has attained the consequences of the democratic revolution which we are undergoing without having experienced the revolution itself. The emigrants who fixed themselves on the shores of America in the beginning of the seventeenth century severed the democratic principle from all the principles which repressed it in the old communities of Europe, and transplanted it unalloyed to the New World. It has there been allowed to spread in perfect freedom, and to put forth its consequences in the laws by influencing the manners of the country.

It appears to me beyond a doubt that sooner or later we shall arrive, like the Americans, at an almost complete equality of conditions. But I do not conclude from this that we shall ever be necessarily led to draw the same political consequences which the Americans have derived from a similar social organization. I am far from supposing that they have chosen the only form of government which a

democracy may adopt ; but the identity of the
efficient cause of laws and manners in the two
countries is sufficient to account for the immense
interest we have in becoming acquainted with its
effects in each of them.

It is not, then, merely to satisfy a legitimate
curiosity that I have examined America ; my wish
has been to find instruction by which we may ourselves profit. Whoever should imagine that I have
intended to write a panegyric will perceive that such
was not my design ; nor has it been my object to
advocate any form of government in particular, for
I am of opinion that absolute excellence is rarely to
be found in any legislation ; I have not even affected
to discuss whether the social revolution, which I
believe to be irresistible, is advantageous or prejudicial to mankind ; I have acknowledged this
revolution as a fact already accomplished or on the
eve of its accomplishment ; and I have selected the
nation, from among those which have undergone it,
in which its development has been the most peaceful
and the most complete, in order to discern its natural
consequences, and, if it be possible, to distinguish the
means by which it may be rendered profitable. I
confess that in America I saw more than America ;
I sought the image of democracy itself, with its
inclinations, its character, its prejudices, and its
passions, in order to learn what we have to fear
or to hope from its progress.

In the first part of this work I have attempted to
show the tendency given to the laws by the democracy
of America, which is abandoned almost without
restraint to its instinctive propensities, and to exhibit
the course it prescribes to the Government and the
influence it exercises on affairs. I have sought to
discover the evils and the advantages which it pro-

duces. I have examined the precautions used by the Americans to direct it, as well as those which they have not adopted, and I have undertaken to point out the causes which enable it to govern society. I do not know whether I have succeeded in making known what I saw in America, but I am certain that such has been my sincere desire, and that I have never, knowingly, moulded facts to ideas, instead of ideas to facts.

Whenever a point could be established by the aid of written documents, I have had recourse to the original text, and to the most authentic and approved works. I have cited my authorities in the notes,[1] and any one may refer to them. Whenever an opinion, a political custom, or a remark on the manners of the country was concerned, I endeavoured to consult the most enlightened men I met with. If the point in question was important or doubtful, I was not satisfied with one testimony, but I formed my opinion on the evidence of several witnesses. Here the reader must necessarily believe me upon my word. I could frequently have quoted names which are either known to him, or which deserve to be so, in proof of what I advance; but I have carefully abstained from this practice. A stranger frequently hears important truths at the fireside of his host, which the latter would perhaps conceal from the ear of friendship; he consoles himself with his guest for the silence to which he is restricted, and the shortness of the traveller's stay takes away all fear of his indiscretion. I carefully noted every conversation of this nature as soon as it occurred, but these notes will never leave my writing-case; I had rather injure the success of my statements than add my name to the list of those strangers who repay the generous hospitality they

[1] Tocqueville's notes are omitted from this abridgment.

have received by subsequent chagrin and annoyance.

I am aware that, notwithstanding my care, nothing will be easier than to criticize this book, if any one ever chooses to criticize it. Those readers who may examine it closely will discover the fundamental idea which connects the several parts together. But the diversity of the subjects I have had to treat is exceedingly great, and it will not be difficult to oppose an isolated fact to the body of facts which I quote, or an isolated idea to the body of ideas I put forth. I hope to be read in the spirit which has guided my labours, and that my book may be judged by the general impression it leaves, as I have formed my own judgment not on any single reason, but upon the mass of evidence. It must not be forgotten that the author who wishes to be understood is obliged to push all his ideas to their utmost theoretical consequences, and often to the verge of what is false or impracticable ; for if it be necessary sometimes to quit the rules of logic in active life, such is not the case in discourse, and a man finds that almost as many difficulties spring from inconsistency of language as usually arise from inconsistency of conduct.

I conclude by pointing out myself what many readers will consider the principal defect of the work. This book is written to favour no particular views, and in composing it I have entertained no designs of serving or attacking any party ; I have undertaken not to see differently, but to look further than parties, and while they are busied for the morrow I have turned my thoughts to the Future.

1835

DEMOCRACY IN AMERICA

PART ONE

Chapter I

EXTERIOR FORM OF NORTH AMERICA

NORTH AMERICA presents in its external form certain general features which it is easy to discriminate at the first glance. A sort of methodical order seems to have regulated the separation of land and water, mountains and valleys. A simple but grand arrangement is discoverable amid the confusion of objects and the prodigious variety of scenes. This continent is divided, almost equally, into two vast regions, one of which is bounded on the north by the Arctic Pole, and by the two great oceans on the east and west. It stretches toward the south, forming a triangle, whose irregular sides meet at length below the great lakes of Canada. The second region begins where the other terminates, and includes all the remainder of the continent. The one slopes gently toward the Pole, the other toward the Equator.

The territory comprehended in the first region descends toward the north with so imperceptible a slope that it may almost be said to form a level plain. Within the bounds of this immense tract of country there are neither high mountains nor deep valleys. Streams meander through it irregularly : great rivers mix their currents, separate and meet again, disperse and form vast marshes, losing all trace of their channels in the labyrinth of waters they have themselves created ; and thus at length, after innumerable

19

windings, fall into the Polar Seas. The great lakes which bound this first region are not walled in, like most of those in the Old World, between hills and rocks. Their banks are flat, and rise but a few feet above the level of their waters ; each of them thus forming a vast bowl filled to the brim. The slightest change in the structure of the globe would cause their waters to rush either toward the Pole or to the Tropical Sea.

The second region is more varied on its surface, and better suited for the habitation of man. Two long chains of mountains divide it from one extreme to the other : the Alleghany ridge takes the form of the shores of the Atlantic Ocean ; the other is parallel with the Pacific. The space which lies between these two chains of mountains contains 1,341,649 square miles. Its surface is therefore about six times as great as that of France. This vast territory, however, forms a single valley, one side of which descends gradually from the rounded summits of the Alleghanies, while the other rises in an uninterrupted course toward the tops of the Rocky Mountains. At the bottom of the valley flows an immense river, into which the various streams issuing from the mountains fall from all parts. In memory of their native land, the French formerly called this river the St. Louis. The Indians, in their pompous language, have named it the Father of Waters, or the Mississippi.

The Mississippi takes its source above the limit of the two great regions of which I have spoken, not far from the highest point of the table-land where they unite. Near the same spot rises another river, which empties itself into the Polar Seas. The course of the Mississippi is at first dubious : it winds several times toward the north, from whence it rose ; and at length, after having been delayed in lakes and marshes, it flows slowly onward to the south. Sometimes quietly gliding along the argillaceous bed which Nature has assigned to it, sometimes swollen by storms, the Mississippi waters 2,500 miles in its course. At the distance of 1,364 miles from its mouth this river attains an average depth of fifteen feet; and it is navigated by vessels of 300 tons burden for a course of nearly 500 miles. Fifty-seven large navigable rivers contribute to swell the waters of the Mississippi; among others, the Missouri, which traverses a space of 2,500 miles, the Arkansas of 1,300 miles, the Red River 1,000 miles, four whose course is from 800 to 1,000 miles in length—viz. the Illinois, the St. Peter's, the St. Francis, and the Moingona—besides a countless multitude of rivulets which unite from all parts their tributary streams.

The valley which is watered by the Mississippi seems formed to be the bed of this mighty river, which, like a god of antiquity, dispenses both good and evil in its course. On the shores of the stream Nature displays an inexhaustible fertility; in proportion as you recede from its banks, the powers of vegetation languish, the soil becomes poor, and the plants that survive have a sickly growth. Nowhere have the great convulsions of the globe left more evident traces than in the valley of the Mississippi; the whole aspect of the country shows the powerful effects of water, both by its fertility and by its barrenness. The waters of the primeval ocean accumulated enormous beds of vegetable mould in the valley, which they levelled as they retired. Upon the right shore of the river are seen immense plains, as smooth as if the husbandman had passed over them with his roller. As you approach the mountains the soil becomes more and more unequal and sterile; the ground is, as it were, pierced in a thousand places by primitive rocks, which appear like the bones of a skeleton whose flesh is partly consumed. The surface of the earth is covered with a granitic sand and huge irregular masses of stone, among which a few plants force their growth, and give the appearance of a green field covered with the ruins of a vast edifice. These stones and this sand discover, on examination, a perfect analogy with those which compose the arid and broken summits of the Rocky Mountains. The flood of waters which washed the soil to the bottom of the valley afterward carried away portions of the rocks themselves ; and these, dashed and bruised against the neighbouring cliffs, were left scattered like wrecks at their feet. The valley of the Mississippi is, upon the whole, the most magnificent dwelling-place prepared by God for man's abode ; and yet it may be said that at present it is but a mighty desert.

On the eastern side of the Alleghanies, between the base of these mountains and the Atlantic Ocean, there lies a long ridge of rocks and sand, which the sea appears to have left behind as it retired. The mean breadth of this territory does not exceed one hundred miles ; but it is about nine hundred miles in length. This part of the American continent has a soil which offers every obstacle to the husbandman, and its vegetation is scanty and unvaried.

Upon this inhospitable coast the first united efforts of human industry were made. The tongue of arid land was the cradle of those English colonies which were destined one day to become the United States of America. The centre of power still remains here ; while in the backwoods the true elements of the great people to whom the future control of the continent belongs are gathering almost in secrecy together.

When the Europeans first landed on the shores of the West Indies, and afterward on the coast of South

America, they thought themselves transported into those fabulous regions of which poets had sung. The sea sparkled with phosphoric light, and the extraordinary transparency of its waters discovered to the view of the navigator all that had hitherto been hidden in the deep abyss. Here and there appeared little islands perfumed with odoriferous plants, and resembling baskets of flowers floating on the tranquil surface of the ocean. Every object which met the sight, in this enchanting region, seemed prepared to satisfy the wants or contribute to the pleasures of man. Almost all the trees were loaded with nourishing fruits, and those which were useless as food delighted the eye by the brilliancy and variety of their colours. In groves of fragrant lemon-trees, wild figs, flowering myrtles, acacias, and oleanders, which were hung with festoons of various climbing plants, covered with flowers, a multitude of birds unknown in Europe displayed their bright plumage, glittering with purple and azure, and mingled their warbling with the harmony of a world teeming with life and motion. Underneath this brilliant exterior death was concealed. But the air of these climates had so enervating an influence that man, absorbed by present enjoyment, was rendered regardless of the future.

North America appeared under a very different aspect ; there everything was grave, serious, and solemn : it seemed created to be the domain of intelligence, as the South was that of sensual delight. A turbulent and foggy ocean washed its shores. It was girt round by a belt of granite rocks, or by wide tracts of sand. The foliage of its woods was dark and gloomy, for they were composed of firs, larches, evergreen oaks, wild olive-trees, and laurels. Beyond this outer belt lay the thick shades of the central forest, where the largest trees which are produced in the two hemispheres grow side by side. The plane, the catalpa, the sugar-maple, and the Virginian poplar mingled their branches with those of the oak, the beech, and the lime. In these, as in the forests of the Old World, destruction was perpetually going on. The ruins of vegetation were heaped upon each other ; but there was no labouring hand to remove them, and their decay was not rapid enough to make room for the continual work of reproduction. Climbing-plants, grasses, and other herbs forced their way through the mass of dying trees ; they crept along their bending trunks, found nourishment in their dusty cavities, and a passage beneath the lifeless bark. Thus decay gave its assistance to life, and their respective productions were mingled together. The depths of these forests were gloomy and obscure, and a thousand rivulets, undirected in their course by human industry, preserved in them a constant moisture. It was rare to meet with flowers, wild fruits, or birds beneath their shades. The fall of a tree overthrown by age, the rushing torrent of a cataract, the lowing of the buffalo, and the howling of the wind were the only sounds which broke the silence of Nature.

To the east of the great river, the woods almost disappeared ; in their stead were seen prairies of immense extent. Whether Nature in her infinite variety had denied the germs of trees to these fertile plains, or whether they once had been covered with forests, subsequently destroyed by the hand of man, is a question which neither tradition nor scientific research has been able to resolve.

These immense deserts were not, however, devoid of human inhabitants. Some wandering tribes had been for ages scattered among the forest shades or the green pastures of the prairie. From the mouth of the St. Lawrence to the Delta of the Mississippi, and from the Atlantic to the Pacific Ocean, these savages possessed certain points of resemblance which bore witness of their common origin ; but at the same time they differed from all other known races of men : they were neither white like the Europeans, nor yellow like most of the Asiatics, nor black like the negroes. Their skin was reddish brown, their hair long and shining, their lips thin, and their cheekbones very prominent. The languages spoken by the North American tribes were various as far as regarded their words, but they were subject to the same grammatical rules. These rules differed in several points from such as had been observed to govern the origin of language. The idiom of the Americans seemed to be the product of new combinations, and bespoke an effort of the understanding of which the Indians of our days would be incapable.

The social state of these tribes differed also in many respects from all that was seen in the Old World. They seemed to have multiplied freely in the midst of their deserts without coming in contact with other races more civilized than their own. Accordingly, they exhibited none of those indistinct, incoherent notions of right and wrong, none of that deep corruption of manners, which is usually joined with ignorance and rudeness among nations which, after advancing to civilization, have relapsed into a state of barbarism. The Indian was indebted to no one but himself ; his virtues, his vices, and his prejudices were his own work ; he had grown up in the wild independence of his nature. . . .

The Indians, although they are ignorant and poor, are equal and free. At the period when Europeans first came among them the natives of North America were ignorant of the value of riches, and indifferent to the enjoyments which civilized man procures to himself by their means. Nevertheless there was nothing coarse in their demeanour; they practised an habitual reserve and a kind of aristocratic politeness. Mild and hospitable when at peace, though merciless in war beyond any known degree of human ferocity, the Indian would expose himself to die of hunger in order to succour the stranger who asked admittance by night at the door of his hut; yet he could tear in pieces with his hands the still quivering limbs of his prisoner. The famous republics of antiquity never gave examples of more unshaken courage, more haughty spirits, or more intractable love of independence than were hidden in former times among the wild forests of the New World. The Europeans produced no great impressions when they landed upon the shores of North America; their presence engendered neither envy nor fear. What influence could they possess over such men as we have described? The Indian could live without wants, suffer without complaint, and pour out his death-song at the stake. Like all the other members of the great human family, these savages believed in the existence of a better world, and adored, under different names, God, the creator of the universe. Their notions on the great intellectual truths were in general simple and philosophical.

Although we have here traced the character of a primitive people, yet it cannot be doubted that another people, more civilized and more advanced in all respects, had preceded it in the same regions.

An obscure tradition which prevailed among the Indians to the north of the Atlantic informs us that these very tribes formerly dwelt on the west side of the Mississippi. Along the banks of the Ohio, and throughout the central valley, there are frequently found, at this day, tumuli raised by the hands of men. On exploring these heaps of earth to their centre, it is usual to meet with human bones, strange instruments, arms and utensils of all kinds, made of metal, or destined for purposes unknown to the present race. The Indians of our time are unable to give any information relative to the history of this unknown people. Neither did those who lived three hundred years ago, when America was first discovered, leave any accounts from which even an hypothesis could be formed. Tradition—that perishable yet ever renewed monument of the pristine world—throws no light upon the subject. It is an undoubted fact, however, that in this part of the globe thousands of our fellow-beings had lived. When they came hither, what was their origin, their destiny, their history, and how they perished, no one can tell. How strange does it appear that nations have existed, and afterward so completely disappeared from the earth that the remembrance of their very names is effaced; their languages are lost; their glory is vanished like a sound without an echo; though perhaps there is not one which has not left behind it some tomb in memory of its passage! The most durable monument of human labour is that which recalls the wretchedness and nothingness of man.

Although the vast country which we have been describing was inhabited by many indigenous tribes, it may justly be said at the time of its discovery by Europeans to have formed one great desert. The Indians occupied it without possessing it. It is by agricultural labour that man appropriates the soil, and the early inhabitants of North America lived by the produce of the chase. Their implacable prejudices, their uncontrolled passions, their vices, and still more perhaps their savage virtues, consigned them to inevitable destruction. The ruin of these nations began from the day when Europeans landed on their shores ; it has proceeded ever since, and we are now witnessing the completion of it. They seem to have been placed by Providence amid the riches of the New World to enjoy them for a season, and then surrender them. Those coasts, so admirably adapted for commerce and industry ; those wide and deep rivers ; that inexhaustible valley of the Mississippi ; the whole continent, in short, seemed prepared to be the abode of a great nation, yet unborn.

In that land the great experiment was to be made, by civilized man, of the attempt to construct society upon a new basis ; and it was there, for the first time, that theories hitherto unknown, or deemed impracticable, were to exhibit a spectacle for which the world had not been prepared by the history of the past.

Chapter II

ORIGIN OF THE ANGLO-AMERICANS, AND ITS IMPORTANCE
IN RELATION TO THEIR FUTURE CONDITION

. . . IF we were able to go back to the elements of
states, and to examine the oldest monuments of their
history, I doubt not that we should discover the primal
cause of the prejudices, the habits, the ruling passions,
and, in short, of all that constitutes what is called the
national character : we should then find the explanation of certain customs which now seem at variance
with the prevailing manners ; of such laws as conflict
with established principles ; and of such incoherent
opinions as are here and there to be met with in
society, like those fragments of broken chains which
we sometimes see hanging from the vault of an edifice,
and supporting nothing. This might explain the
destinies of certain nations which seem borne on by
an unknown force to ends of which they themselves
are ignorant. But hitherto facts have been wanting
to researches of this kind : the spirit of inquiry has
only come upon communities in their latter days ;
and when they at length contemplated their origin,
time had already obscured it, or ignorance and pride
adorned it with truth-concealing fables.

America is the only country in which it has been
possible to witness the natural and tranquil growth
of society, and where the influence exercised on the
future condition of states by their origin is clearly
distinguishable. At the period when the peoples of
Europe landed in the New World their national
characteristics were already completely formed ; each
of them had a physiognomy of its own ; and as they
had already attained that stage of civilization at which
men are led to study themselves, they have transmitted to us a faithful picture of their opinions, their

manners, and their laws. The men of the sixteenth century are almost as well known to us as our contemporaries. America, consequently, exhibits in the broad light of day the phenomena which the ignorance or rudeness of earlier ages conceals from our researches. Near enough to the time when the states of America were founded, to be accurately acquainted with their elements, and sufficiently removed from that period to judge of some of their results, the men of our own day seem destined to see further than their predecessors into the series of human events. Providence has given us a torch which our forefathers did not possess, and has allowed us to discern fundamental causes in the history of the world which the obscurity of the past concealed from them. If we carefully examine the social and political state of America, after having studied its history, we shall remain perfectly convinced that not an opinion, not a custom, not a law, I may even say not an event, is upon record which the origin of that people will not explain. The readers of this book will find the germ of all that is to follow in the present chapter, and the key to almost the whole work.

The emigrants who came, at different periods, to occupy the territory now covered by the American Union differed from each other in many respects; their aim was not the same, and they governed themselves on different principles. These men had, however, certain features in common, and they were all placed in an analogous situation. The tie of language is perhaps the strongest and the most durable that can unite mankind. All the emigrants spoke the same tongue; they were all offsets from the same people.[1] Born in a country which had been agitated

[1] This is not correct. The non-English stock constituted a substantial proportion of the population of the English

for centuries by the struggles of faction, and in which all parties had been obliged in their turn to place themselves under the protection of the laws, their political education had been perfected in this rude school, and they were more conversant with the notions of right and the principles of true freedom than the greater part of their European contemporaries. At the period of their first emigrations the parish system, that fruitful germ of free institutions, was deeply rooted in the habits of the English ; and with it the doctrine of the sovereignty of the people had been introduced into the bosom of the monarchy of the House of Tudor.

The religious quarrels which have agitated the Christian world were then rife. England had plunged into the new order of things with headlong vehemence. The character of its inhabitants, which had always been sedate and reflective, became argumentative and austere. General information had been increased by intellectual debate, and the mind had received a deeper cultivation. While religion was the topic of discussion, the morals of the people were reformed. All these national features are more or less discoverable in the physiognomy of those adventurers who came to seek a new home on the opposite shores of the Atlantic.

Another remark, to which we shall hereafter have occasion to recur, is applicable not only to the English, but to the French, the Spaniards, and all the Europeans who successively established themselves in the New World. All these European colonies contained the elements, if not the development, of a complete democracy. Two causes led to this result.

colonies. The Germans were particularly numerous and it is estimated that one-third of the population of colonial Pennsylvania was German-speaking.—H. S. C.

It may safely be advanced, that on leaving the mother-country the emigrants had in general no notion of superiority over one another. The happy and the powerful do not go into exile, and there are no surer guarantees of equality among men than poverty and misfortune. It happened, however, on several occasions, that persons of rank were driven to America by political and religious quarrels. Laws were made to establish a gradation of ranks ; but it was soon found that the soil of America was opposed to a territorial aristocracy. To bring that refractory land into cultivation, the constant and interested exertions of the owner himself were necessary ; and when the ground was prepared, its produce was found to be insufficient to enrich a master and a farmer at the same time. The land was then naturally broken up into small portions, which the proprietor cultivated for himself. Land is the basis of an aristocracy, which clings to the soil that supports it ; for it is not by privileges alone, nor by birth, but by landed property handed down from generation to generation, that an aristocracy is constituted. A nation may present immense fortunes and extreme wretchedness, but unless those fortunes are territorial there is no aristocracy, but simply the class of the rich and that of the poor.

All the British colonies had then a great degree of similarity at the epoch of their settlement. All of them, from their first beginning, seemed destined to witness the growth, not of the aristocratic liberty of their mother-country, but of that freedom of the middle and lower orders of which the history of the world had as yet furnished no complete example.

In this general uniformity several striking differences were however discernible, which it is necessary to point out. Two branches may be distinguished in the Anglo-American family which have hitherto grown up without entirely commingling ; the one in the South, the other in the North.

Virginia received the first English colony ; the emigrants took possession of it in 1607. The idea that mines of gold and silver are the sources of national wealth was at that time singularly prevalent in Europe ; a fatal delusion, which has done more to impoverish the nations which adopted it, and has cost more lives in America, than the united influence of war and bad laws. The men sent to Virginia were seekers of gold, adventurers without resources and without character, whose turbulent and restless spirit endangered the infant colony, and rendered its progress uncertain. The artisans and agriculturists arrived afterward ; and, although they were a more moral and orderly race of men, they were in nowise above the level of the inferior classes in England. No lofty conceptions, no intellectual system, directed the foundation of these new settlements. The colony was scarcely established when slavery was introduced, and this was the main circumstance which has exercised so prodigious an influence on the character, the laws, and all the future prospects of the South. Slavery, as we shall afterward show, dishonours labour ; it introduces idleness into society, and with idleness, ignorance and pride, luxury and distress. It enervates the powers of the mind, and benumbs the activity of man. The influence of slavery, united to the English character, explains the manners and the social condition of the Southern States.

In the North, the same English foundation was modified by the most opposite shades of character ; and here I may be allowed to enter into some details. The two or three main ideas which constitute the basis of the social theory of the United States were first combined in the Northern English colonies, more generally denominated the States of New England. The principles of New England spread at first to the neighbouring States ; they then passed successively to the more distant ones ; and at length they imbued the whole Confederation. They now extend their influence beyond its limits over the whole American world. The civilization of New England has been like a beacon lit upon a hill, which, after it has diffused its warmth around, tinges the distant horizon with its glow.

The foundation of New England was a novel spectacle, and all the circumstances attending it were singular and original. The large majority of colonies have been first inhabited either by men without education and without resources, driven by their poverty and their misconduct from the land which gave them birth, or by speculators and adventurers greedy of gain. Some settlements cannot even boast so honourable an origin ; St. Domingo was founded by buccaneers ; and the criminal courts of England originally supplied the population of Australia.

The settlers who established themselves on the shores of New England all belonged to the more independent classes of their native country. Their union on the soil of America at once presented the singular phenomenon of a society containing neither lords nor common people, neither rich nor poor. These men possessed, in proportion to their number, a greater mass of intelligence than is to be found in any European nation of our own time. All, without a single exception, had received a good education, and many of them were known in Europe for their talents and their acquirements. The other colonies had been founded by adventurers without family ;

the emigrants of New England brought with them the best elements of order and morality—they landed in the desert accompanied by their wives and children. But what most especially distinguished them was the aim of their undertaking. They had not been obliged by necessity to leave their country ; the social position they abandoned was one to be regretted, and their means of subsistence were certain. Nor did they cross the Atlantic to improve their situation or to increase their wealth ; the call which summoned them from the comforts of their homes was purely intellectual ; and in facing the inevitable sufferings of exile their object was the triumph of an idea.

The emigrants, or, as they deservedly styled themselves, the Pilgrims, belonged to that English sect the austerity of whose principles had acquired for them the name of Puritans. Puritanism was not merely a religious doctrine, but it corresponded in many points with the most absolute democratic and republican theories. It was this tendency which had aroused its most dangerous adversaries. Persecuted by the Government of the mother-country, and disgusted by the habits of a society opposed to the rigour of their own principles, the Puritans went forth to seek some rude and unfrequented part of the world, where they could live according to their own opinions, and worship God in freedom. . . .

It must not be imagined that the piety of the Puritans was of a merely speculative kind, or that it took no cognizance of the course of worldly affairs. Puritanism, as I have already remarked, was scarcely less a political than a religious doctrine. No sooner had the emigrants landed on the barren coast described by Nathaniel Morton than it was their first care to constitute a society, by passing the [Mayflower Compact]. . . .

This happened in 1620, and from that time forward the emigration went on. The religious and political passions which ravaged the British Empire during the whole reign of Charles I drove fresh crowds of sectarians every year to the shores of America. In England the stronghold of Puritanism was in the middle classes, and it was from the middle classes that the majority of the emigrants came. The population of New England increased rapidly ; and while the hierarchy of rank despotically classed the inhabitants of the mother - country, the colony continued to present the novel spectacle of a community homogeneous in all its parts. A democracy, more perfect than any which antiquity had dreamed of, started in full size and panoply from the midst of an ancient feudal society.

The English Government was not dissatisfied with an emigration which removed the elements of fresh discord and of further revolutions. On the contrary, everything was done to encourage it, and great exertions were made to mitigate the hardships of those who sought a shelter from the rigour of their country's laws on the soil of America. It seemed as if New England was a region given up to the dreams of fancy and the unrestrained experiments of innovators.

The English colonies (and this is one of the main causes of their prosperity) have always enjoyed more internal freedom and more political independence than the colonies of other nations ; but this principle of liberty was nowhere more extensively applied than in the States of New England. . . .

In general, charters were not given to the colonies of New England till they had acquired a certain existence. Plymouth, Providence, New Haven, the State of Connecticut, and that of Rhode Island were founded without the co-operation and almost without the knowledge of the mother-country. The new settlers did not derive their incorporation from the seat of the empire, although they did not deny its supremacy ; they constituted a society of their own accord, and it was not till thirty or forty years afterward, under Charles II, that their existence was legally recognized by a royal charter.

This frequently renders it difficult to detect the link which connected the emigrants with the land of their forefathers in studying the earliest historical and legislative records of New England. They exercised the rights of sovereignty ; they named their magistrates, concluded peace or declared war, made police regulations, and enacted laws as if their allegiance was due only to God. . . .

The general principles which are the groundwork of modern constitutions—principles which were imperfectly known in Europe, and not completely triumphant even in Great Britain, in the seventeenth century—were all recognized and determined by the laws of New England : the intervention of the people in public affairs, the free voting of taxes, the responsibility of authorities, personal liberty, and trial by jury, were all positively established without discussion. From these fruitful principles consequences have been derived and applications have been made such as no nation in Europe has yet ventured to attempt.

In Connecticut the electoral body consisted, from its origin, of the whole number of citizens ; and this is readily to be understood, when we recollect that this people enjoyed an almost perfect equality of fortune, and a still greater uniformity of opinions. In Connecticut, at this period, all the executive functionaries were elected, including the Governor of the State. The citizens above the age of sixteen were obliged to bear arms ; they formed a national militia, which appointed its own officers, and was to hold itself at all times in readiness to march for the defence of the country.

In the laws of Connecticut, as well as in all those of New England, we find the germ and gradual development of that township independence which is the life and mainspring of American liberty at the present day. The political existence of the majority of the nations of Europe commenced in the superior ranks of society, and was gradually and imperfectly communicated to the different members of the social body. In America, on the other hand, it may be said that the township was organized before the county, the county before the State, the State before the Union. In New England townships were completely and definitely constituted as early as 1650. The independence of the township was the nucleus round which the local interests, passions, rights, and duties collected and clung. It gave scope to the activity of a real political life most thoroughly democratic and republican. The colonies still recognized the supremacy of the mother-country ; monarchy was still the law of the State ; but the republic was already established in every township. The towns named their own magistrates of every kind, rated themselves, and levied their own taxes. In the parish of New England the law of representation was not adopted, but the affairs of the community were discussed, as at Athens, in the market-place, by a general assembly of the citizens.

In studying the laws which were promulgated in this first era of the American republics, it is impossible not to be struck by the remarkable acquaintance with the science of government and the advanced theory of legislation which they display. The ideas there formed of the duties of society toward its members are evidently much loftier and more comprehensive than those of the European legislators at that time : obligations were there imposed which were elsewhere slighted. In the States of New England, from the first, the condition of the poor was provided for ; strict measures were taken for the maintenance of roads, and surveyors were appointed to attend to them ; registers were established in every parish, in which the results of public deliberations, and the births, deaths, and marriages of the citizens were entered ; clerks were directed to keep these registers ; officers were charged with the administration of vacant inheritances, and with the arbitration of litigated landmarks ; and many others were created whose chief functions were the maintenance of public order in the community. The law enters into a thousand useful provisions for a number of social wants which are at present very inadequately felt in France.

But it is by the attention it pays to Public Education that the original character of American civilization is at once placed in the clearest light. ' It being,' says the law, ' one chief project of the old deluder Satan to keep men from the knowledge of the Scriptures . . . by persuading from the use of tongues, that learning may not be buried in the grave of our fathers, in the church and commonwealth, the Lord assisting our endeavours. . . .' [1] Here follow clauses establishing schools in every township, and obliging the inhabitants, under pain of heavy fines, to support them. Schools of a superior kind were founded in the same manner in the more populous districts. The municipal authorities were bound to enforce the sending of children to school by their parents ; they were empowered to inflict fines upon all who refused

[1] The Massachusetts School Law of 1647.—H. S. C.

compliance ; and in cases of continued resistance society assumed the place of the parent, took possession of the child, and deprived the father of those natural rights which he used to so bad a purpose. The reader will undoubtedly have remarked the preamble of these enactments : in America religion is the road to knowledge, and the observance of the divine laws leads man to civil freedom.

If, after having cast a rapid glance over the state of American society in 1650, we turn to the condition of Europe, and more especially to that of the Continent, at the same period, we cannot fail to be struck with astonishment. On the continent of Europe, at the beginning of the seventeenth century, absolute monarchy had everywhere triumphed over the ruins of the oligarchical and feudal liberties of the Middle Ages. Never were the notions of right more completely confounded than in the midst of the splendour and literature of Europe ; never was there less political activity among the people ; never were the principles of true freedom less widely circulated ; and at that very time those principles, which were scorned or unknown by the nations of Europe, were proclaimed in the deserts of the New World, and were accepted as the future creed of a great people. The boldest theories of the human reason were put into practice by a community so humble that not a statesman condescended to attend to it ; and a legislation without a precedent was produced offhand by the imagination of the citizens. . . .

The remarks I have made will suffice to display the character of Anglo-American civilization in its true light. It is the result (and this should be constantly present to the mind) of two distinct elements, which in other places have been in frequent hostility, but which in America have been admirably incorporated and combined with one another. I allude to the spirit of religion and the spirit of Liberty.

The settlers of New England were at the same time ardent sectarians and daring innovators. Narrow as the limits of some of their religious opinions were, they were entirely free from political prejudices. Hence arose two tendencies, distinct but not opposite, which are constantly discernible in the manners as well as in the laws of the country.

It might be imagined that men who sacrificed their friends, their family, and their native land to a religious conviction were absorbed in the pursuit of the intellectual advantages which they purchased at so dear a rate. The energy, however, with which they strove for the acquirement of wealth, moral enjoyment, and the comforts as well as liberties of the world, is scarcely inferior to that with which they devoted themselves to Heaven.

Political principles and all human laws and institutions were moulded and altered at their pleasure; the barriers of the society in which they were born were broken down before them; the old principles which had governed the world for ages were no more; a path without a term and a field without an horizon were opened to the exploring and ardent curiosity of man: but at the limits of the political world he checks his researches, he discreetly lays aside the use of his most formidable faculties, he no longer consents to doubt or to innovate, but carefully abstaining from raising the curtain of the sanctuary, he yields with submissive respect to truths which he will not discuss. Thus, in the moral world everything is classed, adapted, decided, and foreseen; in the political world everything is agitated, uncertain, and disputed: in the one is a passive, though a voluntary, obedience; in the other an independence scornful of experience and jealous of authority.

These two tendencies, apparently so discrepant, are far from conflicting ; they advance together, and mutually support each other. Religion perceives that civil liberty affords a noble exercise to the faculties of man, and that the political world is a field prepared by the Creator for the efforts of the intelligence. Contented with the freedom and the power which it enjoys in its own sphere, and with the place which it occupies, the empire of religion is never more surely established than when it reigns in the hearts of men unsupported by aught beside its native strength. Religion is no less the companion of liberty in all its battles and its triumphs ; the cradle of its infancy, and the divine source of its claims. The safeguard of morality is religion, and morality is the best security of law and the surest pledge of freedom. . . .

Chapter III

THE STRIKING CHARACTERISTIC OF THE SOCIAL CON-
DITION OF THE ANGLO-AMERICANS IS ITS ESSENTIAL
DEMOCRACY

A SOCIAL condition is commonly the result of circumstances, sometimes of laws, oftener still of these two
causes united ; but wherever it exists, it may justly
be considered as the source of almost all the laws, the
usages, and the ideas which regulate the conduct of
nations ; whatever it does not produce it modifies.
It is therefore necessary, if we would become acquainted with the legislation and the manners of a
nation, to begin by the study of its social condition.

Many important observations suggest themselves
upon the social condition of the Anglo-Americans,
but there is one which takes precedence of all the rest.
The social condition of the Americans is eminently
democratic ; this was its character at the foundation
of the colonies, and is still more strongly marked at
the present day. I have stated in the preceding
chapter that great equality existed among the emigrants who settled on the shores of New England.
The germ of aristocracy was never planted in that
part of the Union. The only influence which obtained
there was that of intellect ; the people were used to
reverence certain names as the emblems of knowledge
and virtue. Some of their fellow-citizens acquired
a power over the rest which might truly have been
called aristocratic, if it had been capable of transmission from father to son.

This was the state of things to the east of the
Hudson : to the south-west of that river, and in the
direction of the Floridas, the case was different. In
most of the States situated to the south-west of the
Hudson some great English proprietors had settled,

who had imported with them aristocratic principles and the English law of descent. . . . In the South, one man, aided by slaves, could cultivate a great extent of country : it was therefore common to see rich landed proprietors. But their influence was not altogether aristocratic as that term is understood in Europe, since they possessed no privileges ; and the cultivation of their estates being carried on by slaves, they had no tenants depending on them, and consequently no patronage. Still, the great proprietors south of the Hudson constituted a superior class, having ideas and tastes of its own, and forming the centre of political action. This kind of aristocracy sympathized with the body of the people, whose passions and interests it easily embraced ; but it was too weak and too short-lived to excite either love or hatred for itself. This was the class which headed the insurrection in the South, and furnished the best leaders of the American Revolution.

At the period of which we are now speaking society was shaken to its centre : the people, in whose name the struggle had taken place, conceived the desire of exercising the authority which it had acquired ; its democratic tendencies were awakened ; and having thrown off the yoke of the mother-country, it aspired to independence of every kind. The influence of individuals gradually ceased to be felt, and custom and law united together to produce the same result.

But the law of descent was the last step to equality. I am surprised that ancient and modern jurists have not attributed to this law a greater influence on human affairs. It is true that these laws belong to civil affairs ; but they ought nevertheless to be placed at the head of all political institutions ; for, while political laws are only the symbol of a nation's condition, they exercise an incredible influence upon its social state. They have, moreover, a sure and uniform manner of operating upon society, affecting, as it were, generations yet unborn. . . .

The law of equal distribution proceeds by two methods : by acting upon things, it acts upon persons ; by influencing persons, it affects things. By these means the law succeeds in striking at the root of landed property, and dispersing rapidly both families and fortunes. . . .

In the United States it has nearly completed its work of destruction, and there we can best study its results. The English laws concerning the transmission of property were abolished in almost all the States at the time of the Revolution. The law of entail was so modified as not to interrupt the free circulation of property. The first generation having passed away, estates began to be parcelled out, and the change became more and more rapid with the progress of time. At this moment, after a lapse of a little more than sixty years, the aspect of society is totally altered ; the families of the great landed proprietors are almost all commingled with the general mass. In the State of New York, which formerly contained many of these, there are but two who still keep their heads above the stream, and they must shortly disappear. The sons of these opulent citizens are become merchants, lawyers, or physicians. Most of them have lapsed into obscurity. The last trace of hereditary ranks and distinctions is destroyed—the law of partition has reduced all to one level.

I do not mean that there is any deficiency of wealthy individuals in the United States ; I know of no country, indeed, where the love of money has taken stronger hold upon the affections of men, and where profounder contempt is expressed for the theory of the permanent equality of property. But wealth circulates with inconceivable rapidity, and experience shows that it is rare to find two succeeding generations in the full enjoyment of it.

This picture, which may perhaps be thought to be overcharged, still gives a very imperfect idea of what is taking place in the new States of the West and South-west. At the end of the last century a few bold adventurers began to penetrate into the valleys of the Mississippi, and the mass of the population very soon began to move in that direction : communities unheard of till then were seen to emerge from the wilds : States whose names were not in existence a few years before claimed their place in the American Union ; and in the Western settlements we may behold democracy arrived at its utmost extreme. In these States, founded offhand, and, as it were, by chance, the inhabitants are but of yesterday. Scarcely known to one another, the nearest neighbours are ignorant of each other's history. In this part of the American continent, therefore, the population has not experienced the influence of great names and great wealth, nor even that of the natural aristocracy of knowledge and virtue. None are there to wield that respectable power which men willingly grant to the remembrance of a life spent in doing good before their eyes. The new States of the West are already inhabited, but society has no existence among them.

It is not only the fortunes of men which are equal in America ; even their requirements partake in some degree of the same uniformity. I do not believe that there is a country in the world where, in proportion to the population, there are so few uninstructed and at the same time so few learned individuals. Primary instruction is within the reach of everybody ; superior instruction is scarcely to be obtained by any.

This is not surprising ; it is, in fact, the necessary consequence of what we have advanced above. Almost all the Americans are in easy circumstances, and can therefore obtain the first elements of human knowledge.

In America there are comparatively few who are rich enough to live without a profession. Every profession requires an apprenticeship, which limits the time of instruction to the early years of life. At fifteen they enter upon their calling, and thus their education ends at the age when ours begins. Whatever is done afterward is with a view to some special and lucrative object ; a science is taken up as a matter of business, and the only branch of it which is attended to is such as admits of an immediate practical application. In America most of the rich men were formerly poor ; most of those who now enjoy leisure were absorbed in business during their youth; the consequence of which is, that when they might have had a taste for study they had no time for it, and when time is at their disposal they have no longer the inclination.

There is no class, then, in America in which the taste for intellectual pleasures is transmitted with hereditary fortune and leisure, and by which the labours of the intellect are held in honour. Accordingly, there is an equal want of the desire and the power of application to these objects.

A middle standard is fixed in America for human knowledge. All approach as near to it as they can ; some as they rise, others as they descend. Of course, an immense multitude of persons are to be found who entertain the same number of ideas on religion, history, science, political economy, legislation, and government. The gifts of intellect proceed directly from God, and man cannot prevent their unequal distribution. But in consequence of the state of things which we have here represented it happens that, although the capacities of men are widely different, as the Creator has doubtless intended they should be, they are submitted to the same method of treatment.

In America the aristocratic element has always been feeble from its birth ; and if at the present day it is not actually destroyed, it is at any rate so completely disabled that we can scarcely assign to it any degree of influence in the course of affairs. The democratic principle, on the contrary, has gained so much strength by time, by events, and by legislation, as to have become not only predominant but all-powerful. There is no family or corporate authority, and it is rare to find even the influence of individual character enjoying any durability.

America, then, exhibits in her social state a most extraordinary phenomenon. Men are there seen on a greater equality in point of fortune and intellect, or, in other words, more equal in their strength, than in any other country of the world, or in any age of which history has preserved the remembrance.

The political consequences of such a social condition as this are easily deducible. It is impossible to believe that equality will not eventually find its way into the political world as it does everywhere else. To conceive of men remaining for ever unequal upon one single point, yet equal on all others, is impossible ; they must come in the end to be equal upon all. Now I know of only two methods of establishing equality in the political world ; every citizen must be put in possession of his rights, or rights must be granted to no one. For nations which are arrived at the same stage of social existence as the Anglo-Americans, it is therefore very difficult to discover a medium between the sovereignty of all and the absolute power of one man : and it would be vain to deny that the social condition which I have been describing is equally liable to each of these consequences.

There is, in fact, a manly and lawful passion for equality which excites men to wish all to be powerful and honoured. This passion tends to elevate the humble to the rank of the great ; but there exists also in the human heart a depraved taste for equality, which impels the weak to attempt to lower the powerful to their own level, and reduces men to prefer equality in slavery to inequality with freedom. Not that those nations whose social condition is democratic naturally despise liberty ; on the contrary, they have an instinctive love of it. But liberty is not the chief and constant object of their desires ; equality is their idol : they make rapid and sudden efforts to obtain liberty, and if they miss their aim resign themselves to their disappointment ; but nothing can satisfy them except equality, and rather than lose it they resolve to perish.

On the other hand, in a State where the citizens are nearly on an equality, it becomes difficult for them to preserve their independence against the aggressions of power. No one among them being strong enough to engage in the struggle with advantage, nothing but a general combination can protect their liberty. And such a union is not always to be found.

From the same social position, then, nations may derive one or the other of two great political results ; these results are extremely different from each other, but they may both proceed from the same cause.

The Anglo-Americans are the first nations who, having been exposed to this formidable alternative, have been happy enough to escape the dominion of absolute power. They have been allowed by their circumstances, their origin, their intelligence, and especially by their moral feeling, to establish and maintain the sovereignty of the people.

Chapter IV

THE PRINCIPLE OF THE SOVEREIGNTY OF THE
PEOPLE IN AMERICA

WHENEVER the political laws of the United States are to be discussed, it is with the doctrine of the sovereignty of the people that we must begin. The principle of the sovereignty of the people, which is to be found, more or less, at the bottom of almost all human institutions, generally remains concealed from view. It is obeyed without being recognized, or if for a moment it be brought to light, it is hastily cast back into the gloom of the sanctuary. "The will of the nation" is one of those expressions which have been most profusely abused by the wily and the despotic of every age. To the eyes of some it has been represented by the venal suffrages of a few of the satellites of power; to others by the votes of a timid or an interested minority; and some have even discovered it in the silence of a people, on the supposition that the fact of submission established the right of command.

In America the principle of the sovereignty of the people is not either barren or concealed, as it is with some other nations; it is recognized by the customs and proclaimed by the laws; it spreads freely, and arrives without impediment at its most remote consequences. If there be a country in the world where the doctrine of the sovereignty of the people can be fairly appreciated, where it can be studied in its application to the affairs of society, and where its dangers and its advantages may be foreseen, that country is assuredly America.

I have already observed that, from their origin, the sovereignty of the people was the fundamental principle of the greater number of British colonies in

America. It was far, however, from then exercising as much influence on the government of society as it now does. Two obstacles, the one external, the other internal, checked its invasive progress. It could not ostensibly disclose itself in the laws of colonies which were still constrained to obey the mother-country : it was therefore obliged to spread secretly, and to gain ground in the provincial assemblies, and especially in the townships.

American society was not yet prepared to adopt it with all its consequences. The intelligence of New England, and the wealth of the country to the south of the Hudson (as I have shown in the preceding chapter), long exercised a sort of aristocratic influence, which tended to retain the exercise of social authority in the hands of a few. The public functionaries were not universally elected, and the citizens were not all of them electors. The electoral franchise was everywhere placed within certain limits, and made dependent on a certain qualification, which was exceedingly low in the North and more considerable in the South.

The American Republic broke out, and the doctrine of the sovereignty of the people, which had been nurtured in the townships and municipalities, took possession of the State : every class was enlisted in its cause ; battles were fought, and victories obtained for it, until it became the law of laws.

A no less rapid change was effected in the interior of society, where the law of descent completed the abolition of local influences.

At the very time when this consequence of the laws and of the Revolution was apparent to every eye, victory was irrevocably pronounced in favour of the democratic cause. All power was, in fact, in its hands, and resistance was no longer possible. The higher orders submitted without a murmur and without a struggle to an evil which was thenceforth inevitable. The ordinary fate of falling powers awaited them ; each of their several members followed his own interests ; and as it was impossible to wring the power from the hands of a people which they did not detest sufficiently to brave, their only aim was to secure its good-will at any price. The most democratic laws were consequently voted by the very men whose interests they impaired ; and thus, although the higher classes did not excite the passions of the people against their order, they accelerated the triumph of the new state of things ; so that by a singular change the democratic impulse was found to be most irresistible in the very States where the aristocracy had the firmest hold. The State of Maryland, which had been founded by men of rank, was the first to proclaim universal suffrage, and to introduce the most democratic forms into the conduct of its government.

When a nation modifies the elective qualification, it may easily be foreseen that sooner or later that qualification will be entirely abolished. There is no more invariable rule in the history of society : the further electoral rights are extended, the greater is the need of extending them ; for after each concession the strength of the democracy increases, and its demands increase with its strength. The ambition of those who are below the appointed rate is irritated in exact proportion to the great number of those who are above it. The exception at last becomes the rule, concession follows concession, and no stop can be made short of universal suffrage.

At the present day the principle of the sovereignty of the people has acquired, in the United States, all the practical development which the imagination can conceive. It is unencumbered by those fictions which have been thrown over it in other countries, and it appears in every possible form according to the exigency of the occasion. Sometimes the laws are made by the people in a body, as at Athens ; and sometimes its representatives, chosen by universal suffrage, transact business in its name, and almost under its immediate control.

In some countries a power exists which, though it is in a degree foreign to the social body, directs it, and forces it to pursue a certain track. In others the ruling force is divided, being partly within and partly without the ranks of the people. But nothing of the kind is to be seen in the United States ; there society governs itself for itself. All power centres in its bosom ; and scarcely an individual is to be met with who would venture to conceive, or, still less, to express, the idea of seeking it elsewhere. The nation participates in the making of its laws by the choice of its legislators, and in the execution of them by the choice of the agents of the executive government ; it may almost be said to govern itself, so feeble and so restricted is the share left to the administration, so little do the authorities forget their popular origin and the power from which they emanate.

Chapter V

TOWNSHIPS AND MUNICIPAL BODIES

IT is proposed to examine in the following chapter
what is the form of government established in America
on the principle of the sovereignty of the people ;
what are its resources, its hindrances, its advantages,
and its dangers. The first difficulty which presents
itself arises from the complex nature of the Constitution of the United States, which consists of two
distinct social structures, connected and, as it were,
incased one within the other ; two governments,
completely separate and almost independent, the one
fulfilling the ordinary duties and responding to the
daily and indefinite calls of a community, the other
circumscribed within certain limits, and only exercising an exceptional authority over the general
interests of the country. In short, there are twenty-
four small sovereign nations, whose agglomeration
constitutes the body of the Union. To examine the
Union before we have studied the States would be to
adopt a method filled with obstacles. The form of
the Federal Government of the United States was the
last which was adopted ; and it is, in fact, nothing
more than a modification or a summary of those
republican principles which were current in the
whole community before it existed, and independently
of its existence. Moreover, the Federal Government
is, as I have just observed, the exception ; the
government of the States is the rule. The author
who should attempt to exhibit the picture as a whole
before he had explained its details would necessarily
fall into obscurity and repetition.

The great political principles which govern
American society at this day undoubtedly took their
origin and their growth in the State. It is therefore

necessary to become acquainted with the State in order to possess a clue to the remainder. The States which at present compose the American Union all present the same features, as far as regards the external aspect of their institutions. Their political or administrative existence is centred in three focuses of action, which may not inaptly be compared to the different nervous centres which convey motion to the human body. The township is the lowest in order, then the county, and lastly the State ; and I propose to devote the following chapter to the examination of these three divisions.

It is not undesignedly that I begin this subject with the township. The village or township is the only association which is so perfectly natural that wherever a number of men are collected it seems to constitute itself.

The town, or tithing, as the smallest division of a community, must necessarily exist in all nations, whatever their laws and customs may be : if man makes monarchies and establishes republics, the first association of mankind seems constituted by the hand of God. But although the existence of the township is coeval with that of man, its liberties are not the less rarely respected and easily destroyed. A nation is always able to establish great political assemblies, because it habitually contains a certain number of individuals fitted by their talents, if not by their habits, for the direction of affairs. The township is, on the contrary, composed of coarser materials, which are less easily fashioned by the legislator. The difficulties which attend the consolidation of its independence rather augment than diminish with the increasing enlightenment of the people. A highly civilized community spurns the attempts of a local independence, is disgusted at its numerous blunders, and is apt to despair of success before the experiment is completed. Again, no immunities are so ill protected from the encroachments of the supreme power as those of municipal bodies in general : they are unable to struggle, single-handed, against a strong or an enterprising government, and they cannot defend their cause with success unless it be identified with the customs of the nation and supported by public opinion. Thus until the independence of townships is amalgamated with the manners of a people it is easily destroyed, and it is only after a long existence in the laws that it can be thus amalgamated. Municipal freedom is not the fruit of human device ; it is rarely created ; but it is, as it were, secretly and spontaneously engendered in the midst of a semibarbarous state of society. The constant action of the laws and the national habits, peculiar circumstances, and above all, time may consolidate it ; but there is certainly no nation on the continent of Europe which has experienced its advantages. Nevertheless local assemblies of citizens constitute the strength of free nations. Town-meetings are to liberty what primary schools are to science ; they bring it within the people's reach, they teach men how to use and how to enjoy it. A nation may establish a system of free government, but without the spirit of municipal institutions it cannot have the spirit of liberty. The transient passions and the interests of an hour, or the chance of circumstances, may have created the external forms of independence ; but the despotic tendency which has been repelled will, sooner or later, inevitably reappear on the surface.

In order to explain to the reader the general principles on which the political organization of the counties and townships of the United States rest, I have thought it expedient to choose one of the States of New England as an example, to examine the mechanism of its constitution, and then to cast a general glance over the country. The township and the county are not organized in the same manner in every part of the Union; it is, however, easy to perceive that the same principles have guided the formation of both of them throughout the Union. I am inclined to believe that these principles have been carried further in New England than elsewhere, and consequently that they offer greater facilities to the observation of a stranger. The institutions of New England form a complete and regular whole; they have received the sanction of time, they have the support of the laws, and the still stronger support of the manners of the community, over which they exercise the most prodigious influence; they consequently deserve our attention on every account.

The township of New England is a division which stands between the commune and the canton of France, and which corresponds in general to the English tithing, or town. Its average population is from two to three thousand; so that, on the one hand, the interests of its inhabitants are not likely to conflict, and, on the other, men capable of conducting its affairs are always to be found among its citizens.

In the township, as well as everywhere else, the people is the only source of power; but in no stage of government does the body of citizens exercise a more immediate influence. In America the people is a master whose exigencies demand obedience to the utmost limits of possibility.

In New England the majority acts by representatives in the conduct of the public business of the State; but if such an arrangement be necessary in general affairs, in the townships, where the legislative and administrative action of the government is in more immediate contact with the subject, the system of representation is not adopted. There is no corporation ; but the body of electors, after having designated its magistrates, directs them in everything that exceeds the simple and ordinary executive business of the State.

This state of things is so contrary to our ideas, and so different from our customs, that it is necessary for me to adduce some examples to explain it thoroughly. The public duties in the township are extremely numerous and minutely divided, as we shall see further on ; but the larger proportion of administrative power is vested in the hands of a small number of individuals, called " the selectmen." The general laws of the State impose a certain number of obligations on the selectmen, which they may fulfil without the authorization of the body they represent, but which they can only neglect on their own responsibility. The law of the State obliges them, for instance, to draw up the list of electors in their townships ; and if they omit this part of their functions, they are guilty of a misdemeanour. In all the affairs, however, which are determined by the town-meeting, the selectmen are the organs of the popular mandate, as in France the Maire executes the decree of the municipal council. They usually act upon their own responsibility, and merely put in practice principles which have been previously recognized by the majority. But if any change is to be introduced in the existing state of things, or if they wish to undertake any new enterprise, they are obliged to refer to the source of their power. If, for instance, a school is to be established, the selectmen convoke the whole body of the electors on a certain day at an appointed place ; they explain the urgency of the case ; they give their opinion on the means of satisfying it, on the probable expense, and the site which seems to be most favourable. The meeting is consulted on these several points ; it adopts the principle, marks out the site, votes the rate, and confides the execution of its resolution to the selectmen.

The selectmen alone have the right of calling a town-meeting, but they may be requested to do so : if ten citizens are desirous of submitting a new project to the assent of the township, they may demand a general convocation of the inhabitants ; the selectmen are obliged to comply, but they have only the right of presiding at the meeting.

The selectmen are elected every year in the month of April or of May. The town-meeting chooses at the same time a number of other municipal magistrates, who are intrusted with important administrative functions. The assessors rate the township ; the collectors receive the rate. A constable is appointed to keep the peace, to watch the streets, and to forward the execution of the laws ; the town-clerk records all the town votes, orders, grants, births, deaths, and marriages ; the treasurer keeps the funds ; the overseer of the poor performs the difficult task of superintending the action of the poor-laws ; committee-men are appointed to attend to the schools and to public instruction ; and the road-surveyors, who take care of the greater and lesser thoroughfares of the township, complete the list of the principal functionaries. They are, however, still further subdivided ; and among the municipal officers are to be found parish commissioners, who audit the expenses of public worship ; different classes of inspectors, some of whom are to direct the citizens in case of fire ; tithing-men, listers, haywards, chimney-viewers, fence-viewers to maintain the bounds of property, timber-measurers, and sealers of weights and measures.

There are nineteen principal offices in a township. Every inhabitant is constrained, on the pain of being fined, to undertake these different functions ; which, however, are almost all paid, in order that the poorer citizens may be able to give up their time without loss. In general the American system is not to grant a fixed salary to its functionaries. Every service has its price, and they are remunerated in proportion to what they have done.

I have already observed that the principle of the sovereignty of the people governs the whole political system of the Anglo-Americans. Every page of this book will afford new instances of the same doctrine. In the nations by which the sovereignty of the people is recognized every individual possesses an equal share of power, and participates alike in the government of the State. Every individual is, therefore, supposed to be as well informed, as virtuous, and as strong as any of his fellow-citizens. He obeys the government, not because he is inferior to the authorities which conduct it, or that he is less capable than his neighbour of governing himself, but because he acknowledges the utility of an association with his fellow-men, and because he knows that no such association can exist without a regulating force. If he be a subject in all that concerns the mutual relations of citizens, he is free and responsible to God alone for all that concerns himself. Hence arises the maxim that every one is the best and the sole judge of his own private interest, and that society has no right to control a man's actions, unless they are prejudicial to the common weal, or unless the common weal demands his co-operation. This doctrine is universally admitted in the United States. I shall hereafter examine the general influence which it exercises on the ordinary actions of life ; I am now speaking of the nature of municipal bodies.

The township, taken as a whole, and in relation to the government of the country, may be looked upon as an individual to whom the theory I have just alluded to is applied. Municipal independence is therefore a natural consequence of the principle of the sovereignty of the people in the United States : all the American republics recognize it more or less ; but circumstances have peculiarly favoured its growth in New England.

In this part of the Union the impulsion of political activity was given in the townships ; and it may almost be said that each of them originally formed an independent nation. When the Kings of England asserted their supremacy, they were contented to assume the central power of the State. The townships of New England remained as they were before ; and although they are now subject to the State, they were at first scarcely dependent upon it. It is important to remember that they have not been invested with privileges, but that they have, on the contrary, forfeited a portion of their independence to the State. The townships are only subordinate to the State in those interests which I shall term social, as they are common to all the citizens. They are independent in all that concerns themselves ; and among the inhabitants of New England I believe that not a man is to be found who would acknowledge that the State has any right to interfere in their local interests. The towns of New England buy and sell, sue or are sued, augment or diminish their rates, without the slightest opposition on the part of the administrative authority of the State.

They are bound, however, to comply with the

demands of the community. If the State is in need of money, a town can neither give nor withhold the supplies. If the State projects a road, the township cannot refuse to let it cross its territory ; if a police regulation is made by the State, it must be enforced by the town. A uniform system of instruction is organized all over the country, and every town is bound to establish the schools which the law ordains. In speaking of the administration of the United States I shall have occasion to point out the means by which the townships are compelled to obey in these different cases : I here merely show the existence of the obligation. Strict as this obligation is, the government of the State imposes it in principle only, and in its performance the township resumes all its independent rights. Thus, taxes are voted by the State, but they are levied and collected by the township ; the existence of a school is obligatory, but the township builds, pays, and superintends it. In France the State-collector receives the local imposts ; in America the town-collector receives the taxes of the State. Thus the French Government lends its agents to the commune ; in America the township is the agent of the Government. This fact alone shows the extent of the differences which exist between the two nations.

In America, not only do municipal bodies exist, but they are kept alive and supported by public spirit. The township of New England possesses two advantages which infallibly secure the attentive interest of mankind, namely, independence and authority. Its sphere is indeed small and limited, but within that sphere its action is unrestrained ; and its independence gives to it a real importance which extent and population may not always insure.

It is to be remembered that the affections of men generally lie on the side of authority. Patriotism is not durable in a conquered nation. The New-Englander is attached to his township, not only because he was born in it, but because it constitutes a social body of which he is a member, and whose government claims and deserves the exercise of his sagacity. In Europe the absence of local public spirit is a frequent subject of regret to those who are in power ; every one agrees that there is no surer guarantee of order and tranquillity, and yet nothing is more difficult to create. If the municipal bodies were made powerful and independent, the authorities of the nation might be disunited and the peace of the country endangered. Yet, without power and independence, a town may contain good subjects, but it can have no active citizens. Another important fact is that the township of New England is so constituted as to excite the warmest of human affections, without arousing the ambitious passions of the heart of man. The officers of the county are not elected, and their authority is very limited. Even the State is only a second-rate community, whose tranquil and obscure administration offers no inducement sufficient to draw men away from the circle of their interests into the turmoil of public affairs. The Federal Government confers power and honour on the men who conduct it ; but these individuals can never be very numerous.[1] The high station of the presidency can only be reached at an advanced period of life, and the other federal functionaries are generally men who have been favoured by fortune, or distinguished in some other career. Such cannot be the permanent aim of the ambitious. But the township serves as a centre for the desire of public esteem, the want of exciting interests, and the taste for authority and

[1] The number of civilian Federal employees in December 1938 was 894,919.—H. S. C.

popularity, in the midst of the ordinary relations of life ; and the passions which commonly embroil society change their character when they find a vent so near the domestic hearth and the family circle.

In the American States power has been disseminated with admirable skill for the purpose of interesting the greatest possible number of persons in the common weal. Independently of the electors who are from time to time called into action, the body politic is divided into innumerable functionaries and officers, who all, in their several spheres, represent the same powerful whole in whose name they act. The local administration thus affords an unfailing source of profit and interest to a vast number of individuals.

The American system, which divides the local authority among so many citizens, does not scruple to multiply the functions of the town officers. For in the United States it is believed, and with truth, that patriotism is a kind of devotion which is strengthened by ritual observance. In this manner the activity of the township is continually perceptible ; it is daily manifested in the fulfilment of a duty or the exercise of a right, and a constant though gentle motion is thus kept up in society which animates without disturbing it.

The American attaches himself to his home as the mountaineer clings to his hills, because the characteristic features of his country are there more distinctly marked than elsewhere. The existence of the townships of New England is in general a happy one. Their government is suited to their tastes, and chosen by themselves. In the midst of the profound peace and general comfort which reign in America the commotions of municipal discord are infrequent. The conduct of local business is easy. The political education of the people has long been complete ; say rather that it was complete when the people first set foot upon the soil. In New England no tradition exists of a distinction of ranks ; no portion of the community is tempted to oppress the remainder ; and the abuses which may injure isolated individuals are forgotten in the general contentment which prevails. If the government is defective (and it would no doubt be easy to point out its deficiencies), the fact that it really emanates from those it governs, and that it acts, either ill or well, casts the protecting spell of a parental pride over its faults. No term of comparison disturbs the satisfaction of the citizen : England formerly governed the mass of the colonies, but the people was always sovereign in the township where its rule is not only an ancient but a primitive state.

The native of New England is attached to his township because it is independent and free : his co-operation in its affairs insures his attachment to its interest ; the well-being it affords him secures his affection ; and its welfare is the aim of his ambition and of his future exertions : he takes a part in every occurrence in the place ; he practises the art of government in the small sphere within his reach ; he accustoms himself to those forms which can alone insure the steady progress of liberty ; he imbibes their spirit ; he acquires a taste for order, comprehends the union or the balance of powers, and collects clear practical notions on the nature of his duties and the extent of his rights. . . .

I have described the townships and the administration ; it now remains for me to speak of the State and the Government. This is ground I may pass over rapidly, without fear of being misunderstood ; for all I have to say is to be found in written forms of the various constitutions, which are easily to be procured.

These constitutions rest upon a simple and rational theory ; their forms have been adopted by all constitutional nations, and are become familiar to us. In this place, therefore, it is only necessary for me to give a short analysis ; I shall endeavour afterward to pass judgment upon what I now describe.

The legislative power of the State is vested in two assemblies, the first of which generally bears the name of the Senate. The Senate is commonly a legislative body ; but it sometimes becomes an executive and a judicial one. It takes a part in the government in several ways, according to the constitution of the different States ; but it is in the nomination of public functionaries that it most commonly assumes an executive power. It partakes of judicial power in the trial of certain political offences, and sometimes also in the decision of certain civil cases. The number of its members is always small. The other branch of the legislature, which is usually called the House of Representatives, has no share whatever in the administration, and only takes a part in the judicial power inasmuch as it impeaches public functionaries before the Senate. The members of the two Houses are nearly everywhere subject to the same conditions of election. They are chosen in the same manner, and by the same citizens. The only difference which exists between them is, that the term for which the Senate is chosen is in general longer than that of the House of Representatives. The latter seldom remain in office longer than a year ; the former usually sit two or three years. By granting to the senators the privilege of being chosen for several years, and being renewed seriatim, the law takes care to preserve in the legislative body a nucleus of men already accustomed to public business, and capable of exercising a salutary influence upon the junior members.

The Americans, plainly, did not desire, by this separation of the legislative body into two branches, to make one House hereditary and the other elective ; one aristocratic and the other democratic. It was not their object to create in the one a bulwark to power, while the other represented the interests and passions of the people. The only advantages which result from the present Constitution of the United States are the division of the legislative power and the consequent check upon political assemblies ; with the creation of a tribunal of appeal for the revision of the laws.

Time and experience, however, have convinced the Americans that if these are its only advantages, the division of the legislative power is still a principle of the greatest necessity. Pennyslvania was the only one of the United States which at first attempted to establish a single House of Assembly, and Franklin himself was so far carried away by the necessary consequences of the principle of the sovereignty of the people as to have concurred in the measure ; but the Pennsylvanians were soon obliged to change the law, and to create two Houses. Thus the principle of the division of the legislative power was finally established, and its necessity may henceforward be regarded as a demonstrated truth. This theory, which was nearly unknown to the republics of antiquity—which was introduced into the world almost by accident, like so many other great truths—and misunderstood by several modern nations, is at length become an axiom in the political science of the present age.

The executive power of the State may with truth be said to be represented by the Governor, although he enjoys but a portion of its rights. The supreme magistrate, under the title of Governor, is the official moderator and counsellor of the legislature. He is armed with a veto or suspensive power, which allows him to stop, or at least to retard, its movements at pleasure. He lays the wants of the country before the legislative body, and points out the means which he thinks may be usefully employed in providing for them ; he is the natural executor of its decrees in all the undertakings which interest the nation at large. In the absence of the legislature, the Governor is bound to take all necessary steps to guard the State against violent shocks and unforeseen dangers. The whole military power of the State is at the disposal of the Governor. He is the commander of the militia, and head of the armed force. When the authority, which is by general consent awarded to the laws, is disregarded, the Governor puts himself at the head of the armed force of the State, to quell resistance, and to restore order. Lastly, the Governor takes no share in the administration of townships and counties, except it be indirectly in the nomination of justices of the peace, which nomination he has not the power to cancel. The Governor is an elected magistrate, and is generally chosen for one or two years only ; so that he always continues to be strictly dependent upon the majority who returned him.

Centralization is become a word of general and daily use, without any precise meaning being attached to it. Nevertheless, there exist two distinct kinds of centralization, which it is necessary to discriminate with accuracy. Certain interests are common to all parts of a nation, such as the enactment of its general laws and the maintenance of its foreign relations. Other interests are peculiar to certain parts of the nation, such, for instance, as the business of different townships. When the power which directs the general interests is centred in one place, or vested in the same persons, it constitutes a central government. In like manner the power of directing partial or local interests, when brought together into one place, constitutes what may be termed a central administration.

Upon some points these two kinds of centralization coalesce ; but by classifying the objects which fall more particularly within the province of each of them, they may easily be distinguished. It is evident that a central government acquires immense power when united to administrative centralization. Thus combined, it accustoms men to set their own will habitually and completely aside ; to submit, not only for once, or upon one point, but in every respect, and at all times. Not only, therefore, does this union of power subdue them compulsorily, but it affects them in the ordinary habits of life, and influences each individual, first separately and then collectively.

These two kinds of centralization mutually assist and attract each other ; but they must not be supposed to be inseparable. It is impossible to imagine a more completely central government than that which existed in France under Louis XIV ; when the same individual was the author and the interpreter of the laws, and the representative of France at home and abroad, he was justified in asserting that the State was identified with his person. Nevertheless, the administration was much less centralized under Louis XIV than it is at the present day.

In England the centralization of the government is carried to great perfection ; the State has the compact vigour of a man, and by the sole act of its will it puts immense engines in motion, and wields or collects the efforts of its authority. Indeed, I cannot conceive that a nation can enjoy a secure or prosperous existence without a powerful centralization of government. But I am of opinion that a central administration enervates the nations in which it exists by incessantly diminishing their public spirit. If such an administration succeeds in condensing at a given moment, on a given point, all the disposable resources of a people, it impairs at least the renewal of those resources. It may insure a victory in the hour of strife, but it gradually relaxes the sinews of strength. It may contribute admirably to the transient greatness of a man, but it cannot insure the durable prosperity of a nation.

If we pay proper attention, we shall find that whenever it is said that a State cannot act because it has no central point, it is the centralization of the government in which it is deficient. It is frequently asserted, and we are prepared to assent to the proposition, that the German Empire was never able to bring all its powers into action. But the reason was, that the State was never able to enforce obedience to its general laws, because the several members of that great body always claimed the right, or found the means, of refusing their co-operation to the representatives of the common authority, even in the affairs which concerned the mass of the people ; in other words, because there was no centralization of government. The same remark is applicable to the Middle Ages ; the cause of all the confusion of feudal society was that the control, not only of local but of general interests, was divided among a thousand hands, and broken up in a thousand different ways ; the absence of a central government prevented the nations of Europe from advancing with energy in any straightforward course.

We have shown that in the United States no central administration and no dependent series of public functionaries exist. Local authority has been carried to lengths which no European nation could endure without great inconvenience, and which has even produced some disadvantageous consequences in America. But in the United States the centralization of the Government is complete; and it would be easy to prove that the national power is more compact than it ever has been in the old nations of Europe. Not only is there but one legislative body in each State; not only does there exist but one source of political authority; but district assemblies and county courts have not in general been multiplied, lest they should be tempted to exceed their administrative duties, and interfere with the Government. In America the legislature of each State is supreme; nothing can impede its authority; neither privileges, nor local immunities, nor personal influence, nor even the empire of reason, since it represents that majority which claims to be the sole organ of reason. Its own determination is, therefore, the only limit to this action. In juxtaposition to it, and under its immediate control, is the representative of the executive power, whose duty it is to constrain the refractory to submit by superior force. The only symptom of weakness lies in certain details of the action of the Government. The American republics have no standing armies to intimidate a discontented minority; but as no minority has as yet been reduced to declare open war, the necessity of an army has not been felt. The State usually employs the officers of the township or the county to deal with the citizens. Thus, for instance, in New England, the assessor fixes the rate of taxes; the collector receives them; the town-treasurer transmits the amount to the public treasury; and the disputes which may arise are brought before the ordinary courts of justice. This method of collecting taxes is slow as well as inconvenient, and it would prove a perpetual hindrance to a Government whose pecuniary demands were large. It is desirable that, in whatever materially affects its existence, the Government should be served by officers of its own, appointed by itself, removable at pleasure, and accustomed to rapid methods of proceeding. But it will always be easy for the central government, organized as it is in America, to introduce new and more efficacious modes of action, proportioned to its wants. . . .

It is undeniable that the want of those uniform regulations which control the conduct of every inhabitant of France is not infrequently felt in the United States. Gross instances of social indifference and neglect are to be met with, and from time to time disgraceful blemishes are seen in complete contrast with the surrounding civilization. Useful undertakings which cannot succeed without perpetual attention and rigorous exactitude are very frequently abandoned in the end ; for in America, as well as in other countries, the people is subject to sudden impulses and momentary exertions. The European who is accustomed to find a functionary always at hand to interfere with all he undertakes has some difficulty in accustoming himself to the complex mechanism of the administration of the townships. In general it may be affirmed that the lesser details of the police, which render life easy and comfortable, are neglected in America ; but that the essential guarantees of man in society are as strong there as elsewhere. In America the power which conducts the Government is far less regular, less enlightened, and less learned, but a hundredfold more authoritative than in Europe. In no country in the world do the citizens make such exertions for the common weal ; and I am acquainted with no people which has established schools as numerous and as efficacious, places of public worship better suited to the wants of the inhabitants, or roads kept in better repair. Uniformity or permanence of design, the minute arrangement of details, and the perfection of an ingenious administration, must not be sought for in the United States; but it will be easy to find, on the other hand, the symptoms of a power which, if it is somewhat barbarous, is at least robust; and of an existence which is checkered with accidents indeed, but cheered at the same time by animation and effort. . . .

It is not the administrative but the political effects of the local system that I most admire in America. In the United States the interests of the country are everywhere kept in view; they are an object of solicitude to the people of the whole Union, and every citizen is as warmly attached to them as if they were his own. He takes pride in the glory of his nation; he boasts of its success, to which he conceives himself to have contributed, and he rejoices in the general prosperity by which he profits. The feeling he entertains toward the State is analogous to that which unites him to his family, and it is by a kind of egotism that he interests himself in the welfare of his country.

The European generally submits to a public officer because he represents a superior force; but to an American he represents a right. In America it may be said that no one renders obedience to man, but to justice and to law. If the opinion which the citizen entertains of himself is exaggerated, it is at least salutary; he unhesitatingly confides in his own powers, which appear to him to be all-sufficient. When a private individual meditates an undertaking, however directly connected it may be with the welfare of society, he never thinks of soliciting the co-operation of the Government, but he publishes his plan, offers to execute it himself, courts the assistance of other individuals, and struggles manfully against all obstacles. Undoubtedly he is often less successful than the State might have been in his position ; but in the end the sum of these private undertakings far exceeds all that the Government could have done.

As the administrative authority is within the reach of the citizens, whom it in some degree represents, it excites neither their jealousy nor their hatred ; as its resources are limited, every one feels that he must not rely solely on its assistance. Thus, when the administration thinks fit to interfere, it is not abandoned to itself as in Europe ; the duties of the private citizens are not supposed to have lapsed because the State assists in their fulfilment, but every one is ready, on the contrary, to guide and to support it. This action of individual exertions, joined to that of the public authorities, frequently performs what the most energetic central administration would be unable to execute. . . .

I believe that provincial institutions are useful to all nations, but nowhere do they appear to me to be more indispensable than among a democratic people. In an aristocracy order can always be maintained in the midst of liberty, and as the rulers have a great deal to lose, order is to them a first-rate consideration. In like manner an aristocracy protects the people from the excesses of despotism, because it always possesses an organized power ready to resist a despot. But a democracy without provincial institutions has no security against these evils. How can a populace, unaccustomed to freedom in small concerns, learn to use it temperately in great affairs ? What resistance can be afforded to tyranny in a country where every private individual is impotent, and where the citizens are united by no common tie ? Those who dread the license of the mob, and those who fear the rule of absolute power, ought alike to desire the progressive growth of provincial liberties. . . .

Chapter VI

JUDICIAL POWER IN THE UNITED STATES, AND ITS
INFLUENCE UPON POLITICAL SOCIETY

I HAVE thought it essential to devote a separate
chapter to the judicial authorities of the United
States, lest their great political importance should be
lessened in the reader's eyes by a merely incidenta
mention of them. Confederations have existed in
other countries besides America, and republics have
not been established upon the shores of the New
World alone ; the representative system of government has been adopted in several States of Europe,
but I am not aware that any nation of the globe has
hitherto organized a judicial power on the principle
now adopted by the Americans. The judicial organization of the United States is the institution which a
stranger has the greatest difficulty in understanding.
He hears the authority of a judge invoked in the
political occurrences of every day, and he naturally
concludes that in the United States the judges are
important political functionaries ; nevertheless, when
he examines the nature of the tribunals, they offer
nothing which is contrary to the usual habits and
privileges of those bodies, and the magistrates seem to
him to interfere in public affairs by chance, but by a
chance which recurs every day.

When the Parliament of Paris remonstrated, or
refused to enregister an edict, or when it summoned
a functionary accused of malversation to its bar, its
political influence as a judicial body was clearly
visible ; but nothing of the kind is to be seen in the
United States. The Americans have retained all the
ordinary characteristics of judicial authority, and have
carefully restricted its action to the ordinary circle of
its functions.

The first characteristic of judicial power in all nations is the duty of arbitration. But rights must be contested in order to warrant the interference of a tribunal ; and an action must be brought to obtain the decision of a judge. As long, therefore, as a law is uncontested, the judicial authority is not called upon to discuss it, and it may exist without being perceived. When a judge in a given case attacks a law relating to that case, he extends the circle of his customary duties, without however stepping beyond it ; since he is in some measure obliged to decide upon the law in order to decide the case. But if he pronounces upon a law without resting upon a case, he clearly steps beyond his sphere, and invades that of the legislative authority.

The second characteristic of judicial power is that it pronounces on special cases, and not upon general principles. If a judge in deciding a particular point destroys a general principle, by passing a judgment which tends to reject all the inferences from that principle, and consequently to annul it, he remains within the ordinary limits of his functions. But if he directly attacks a general principle without having a particular case in view, he leaves the circle in which all nations have agreed to confine his authority, he assumes a more important, and perhaps a more useful, influence than that of the magistrate, but he ceases to be a representative of the judicial power.

The third characteristic of judicial power is its inability to act unless it is appealed to, or until it has taken cognizance of an affair. This characteristic is less general than the other two ; but, notwithstanding the exceptions, I think it may be regarded as essential. The judicial power is by its nature devoid of action ; it must be put in motion in order to produce a result. When it is called upon to repress a crime, it punishes the criminal ; when a wrong is to be redressed, it is ready to redress it ; when an act requires interpretation, it is prepared to interpret it ; but it does not pursue criminals, hunt out wrongs, or examine into evidence of its own accord. A judicial functionary who should open proceedings, and usurp the censorship of the laws, would in some measure do violence to the passive nature of his authority.

The Americans have retained these three distinguishing characteristics of judicial power : an American judge can only pronounce a decision when litigation has arisen, he is only conversant with special cases, and he cannot act until the cause has been duly brought before the court. His position is therefore perfectly similar to that of the magistrate of other nations ; and he is nevertheless invested with immense political power. If the sphere of his authority and his means of action are the same as those of other judges, it may be asked whence he derives a power which they do not possess. The cause of this difference lies in the simple fact that the Americans have acknowledged the right of the judges to found their decisions on the constitution rather than on the laws. In other words, they have left them at liberty not to apply such laws as may appear to them to be unconstitutional.

I am aware that a similar right has been claimed— but claimed in vain—by courts of justice in other countries ; but in America it is recognized by all the authorities ; and not a party, nor so much as an individual, is found to contest it. This fact can only be explained by the principles of the American constitutions. In France the constitution is (or at least is supposed to be) immutable ; and the received theory is that no power has the right of changing any part of it. In England the Parliament has an acknowledged right to modify the constitution ; as, therefore, the constitution may undergo perpetual changes, it does not in reality exist; the Parliament is at once a legislative and a constituent assembly. The political theories of America are more simple and more rational. An American constitution is not supposed to be immutable as in France, nor is it susceptible of modification by the ordinary powers of society as in England. It constitutes a detached whole, which, as it represents the determination of the whole people, is no less binding on the legislator than on the private citizen, but which may be altered by the will of the people in predetermined cases, according to established rules. In America the constitution may therefore vary, but as long as it exists it is the origin of all authority, and the sole vehicle of the predominating force. . . .

In the United States the constitution governs the legislator as much as the private citizen; as it is the first of laws it cannot be modified by a law, and it is therefore just that the tribunals should obey the constitution in preference to any law. This condition is essential to the power of the judicature, for to select that legal obligation by which he is most strictly bound is the natural right of every magistrate.

In France the constitution is also the first of laws, and the judges have the same right to take it as the ground of their decisions, but were they to exercise this right they must perforce encroach on rights more sacred than their own, namely, on those of society, in whose name they are acting. In this case the State-motive clearly prevails over the motives of an individual. In America, where the nation can always reduce its magistrates to obedience by changing its constitution, no danger of this kind is to be feared. Upon this point, therefore, the political and the logical reasons agree, and the people as well as the judges preserve their privileges.

Whenever a law which the judge holds to be unconstitutional is argued in a tribunal of the United States he may refuse to admit it as a rule ; this power is the only one which is peculiar to the American magistrate, but it gives rise to immense political influence. Few laws can escape the searching analysis of the judicial power for any length of time, for there are few which are not prejudicial to some private interest or other, and none which may not be brought before a court of justice by the choice of parties, or by the necessity of the case. But from the time that a judge has refused to apply any given law in a case, that law loses a portion of its moral cogency. The persons to whose interests it is prejudicial learn that means exist of evading its authority, and similar suits are multiplied, until it becomes powerless. One of two alternatives must then be resorted to : the people must alter the constitution, or the legislature must repeal the law. The political power which the Americans have intrusted to their courts of justice is therefore immense, but the evils of this power are considerably diminished by the obligation which has been imposed of attacking the laws through the courts of justice alone. If the judge had been empowered to contest the laws on the ground of theoretical generalities, if he had been enabled to open an attack or to pass a censure on the legislator, he would have played a prominent part in the political sphere ; and as the champion or the antagonist of a party, he would have arrayed the hostile passions of the nation in the conflict. But when a judge contests a law applied to some particular case in an obscure proceeding, the importance of his attack is concealed from the public gaze, his decision bears upon the interest of an individual, and if the law is slighted it is only collaterally. Moreover, although it is censured, it is not abolished ; its moral force may be diminished, but its cogency is by no means suspended, and its final destruction can only be accomplished by the reiterated attacks of judicial functionaries. It readily will be understood that by connecting the censorship of the laws with the private interests of members of the community, and by intimately uniting the prosecution of the law with the prosecution of an individual, legislation is protected from wanton assailants, and from the daily aggressions of party-spirit. The errors of the legislator are exposed whenever their evil consequences are most felt, and it is always a positive and appreciable fact which serves as the basis of a prosecution.

I am inclined to believe this practice of the American courts to be at once the most favourable to liberty as well as to public order. If the judge could only attack the legislator openly and directly, he would sometimes be afraid to oppose any resistance to his will ; and at other moments party-spirit might encourage him to brave it at every turn. The laws would consequently be attacked when the power from which they emanate is weak, and obeyed when it is strong. That is to say, when it would be useful to respect them they would be contested, and when it would be easy to convert them into an instrument of oppression they would be respected. But the American judge is brought into the political arena independently of his own will. He only judges the law because he is obliged to judge a case. The political question which he is called upon to resolve is connected with the interest of the suitors, and he cannot refuse to decide it without abdicating the duties of his post. He performs his functions as a citizen by fulfilling the precise duties which belong to his profession as a magistrate. It is true that upon this system the judicial censorship which is exercised by the courts of justice over the legislation cannot extend to all laws indistinctly, inasmuch as some of them can never give rise to that exact species of contestation which is termed a lawsuit ; and even when such a contestation is possible, it may happen that no one cares to bring it before a court of justice. The Americans often have felt this disadvantage, but they have left the remedy incomplete, lest they should give it an efficacy which might in some cases prove dangerous. Within these limits the power vested in the American courts of justice of pronouncing a statute to be unconstitutional forms one of the most powerful barriers which has ever been devised against the tyranny of political assemblies.

It is perfectly natural that in a free country like America all the citizens should have the right of indicting public functionaries before the ordinary tribunals, and that all the judges should have the power of punishing public offences. The right granted to the courts of justice of judging the agents of the executive government, when they have violated the laws, is so natural a one that it cannot be looked upon as an extraordinary privilege. Nor do the springs of government appear to me to be weakened in the United States by the custom which renders all public officers responsible to the judges of the land. The Americans seem, on the contrary, to have increased by this means that respect which is due to the authorities, and at the same time to have rendered those who are in power more scrupulous of offending public opinion. I was struck by the small number of political trials which occur in the United States, but I had no difficulty in accounting for this circumstance. A lawsuit, of whatever nature it may be, is always a difficult and expensive undertaking. It is easy to attack a public man in a journal, but the motives which can warrant an action at law must be serious. A solid ground of complaint must therefore exist to induce an individual to prosecute a public officer, and public officers are careful not to furnish these grounds of complaint when they are afraid of being prosecuted.

This does not depend upon the republican form of American institutions, for the same facts present themselves in England. These two nations do not regard the impeachment of the principal officers of State as a sufficient guarantee of their independence. But they hold that the right of minor prosecutions, which are within the reach of the whole community, is a better pledge of freedom than those great judicial actions which are rarely employed until it is too late.

. . . .

Chapter VII

THE FEDERAL CONSTITUTION

I HAVE hitherto considered each State as a separate whole, and I have explained the different springs which the people sets in motion, and the different means of action which it employs. But all the States which I have considered as independent are forced to submit, in certain cases, to the supreme authority of the Union. The time is now come for me to examine separately the supremacy with which the Union has been invested, and to cast a rapid glance over the Federal Constitution.

The thirteen colonies which simultaneously threw off the yoke of England toward the end of the last century professed, as I have already observed, the same religion, the same language, the same customs, and almost the same laws; they were struggling against a common enemy; and these reasons were sufficiently strong to unite them one to another, and to consolidate them into one nation. But as each of them had enjoyed a separate existence and a government within its own control, the peculiar interests and customs which resulted from this system were opposed to a compact and intimate union which would have absorbed the individual importance of each in the general importance of all. Hence arose two opposite tendencies, the one prompting the Anglo-Americans to unite, the other to divide their strength. As long as the war with the mother-country lasted the principle of union was kept alive by necessity; and although the laws which constituted it were defective, the common tie subsisted in spite of their imperfections. But no sooner was peace concluded than the faults of the legislation became manifest, and the State seemed to be suddenly dissolved. Each colony became an independent republic, and assumed an absolute sovereignty. The Federal Government, condemned to impotence by its Constitution, and no longer sustained by the presence of a common danger, witnessed the outrages offered to its flag by the great nations of Europe, while it was scarcely able to maintain its ground against the Indian tribes, and to pay the interest of the debt which had been contracted during the war of independence. It was already on the verge of destruction, when it officially proclaimed its inability to conduct the government, and appealed to the constituent authority of the nation. If America ever approached (for however brief a time) that lofty pinnacle of glory to which the fancy of its inhabitants is wont to point, it was at the solemn moment at which the power of the nation abdicated, as it were, the empire of the land. All ages have furnished the spectacle of a people struggling with energy to win its independence ; and the efforts of the Americans in throwing off the English yoke have been considerably exaggerated. Separated from their enemies by three thousand miles of ocean, and backed by a powerful ally, the success of the United States may be more justly attributed to their geographical position than to the valour of their armies or the patriotism of their citizens. . . .

But it is a novelty in the history of society to see a great people turn a calm and scrutinizing eye upon itself, when apprised by the legislature that the wheels of government are stopped ; to see it carefully examine the extent of the evil, and patiently wait for two whole years until a remedy was discovered, which it voluntarily adopted without having wrung a tear or a drop of blood from mankind. At the time when the inadequacy of the first constitution was discovered America possessed the double advantage of that calm which had succeeded the effervescence of the Revolution, and of those great men who had led the Revolution to a successful issue. The assembly which accepted the task of composing the second constitution was small; but George Washington was its President, and it contained the choicest talents and the noblest hearts which had ever appeared in the New World. This national commission, after long and mature deliberation, offered to the acceptance of the people the body of general laws which still rules the Union. All the States adopted it successively. The New Federal Government commenced its functions in 1789, after an interregnum of two years. The Revolution of America terminated when that of France began.

The first question which awaited the Americans was intricate, and by no means easy of solution: the object was so to divide the authority of the different States which composed the Union that each of them should continue to govern itself in all that concerned its internal prosperity, while the entire nation, represented by the Union, should continue to form a compact body, and to provide for the general exigencies of the people. It was as impossible to determine beforehand, with any degree of accuracy, the share of authority which each of two governments was to enjoy, as to foresee all the incidents in the existence of a nation.

The obligations and the claims of the Federal Government were simple and easily definable, because the Union had been formed with the express purpose of meeting the general exigencies of the people; but the claims and obligations of the States were, on the other hand, complicated and various, because those Governments had penetrated into all the details of social life. The attributes of the Federal Government were therefore carefully enumerated, and all that was not included among them was declared to constitute a part of the privileges of the several Governments of the States. Thus the government of the States remained the rule, and that of the Confederation became the exception.

But as it was foreseen that, in practice, questions might arise as to the exact limits of this exceptional authority, and that it would be dangerous to submit these questions to the decision of the ordinary courts of justice, established in the States by the States themselves, a high Federal court was created, which was destined, among other functions, to maintain the balance of power which had been established by the Constitution between the two rival Governments.

The external relations of a people may be compared to those of private individuals, and they cannot be advantageously maintained without the agency of a single head of a Government. The exclusive right of making peace and war, of concluding treaties of commerce, of raising armies, and equipping fleets, was granted to the Union. The necessity of a national Government was less imperiously felt in the conduct of the internal policy of society; but there are certain general interests which can only be attended to with advantage by a general authority. The Union was invested with the power of controlling the monetary system, of directing the post-office, and of opening the great roads which were to establish a communication between the different parts of the country. The independence of the Government of each State was formally recognized in its sphere; nevertheless, the Federal Government was authorized to interfere in the internal affairs of the States in a few predetermined cases, in which an indiscreet abuse of their independence might compromise the security of the

Union at large. Thus, while the power of modifying and changing their legislation at pleasure was preserved in all the republics, they were forbidden to enact *ex post facto* laws, or to create a class of nobles in their community. Lastly, as it was necessary that the Federal Government should be able to fulfil its engagements, it was endowed with an unlimited power of levying taxes.

In examining the balance of power as established by the Federal Constitution ; in remarking on the one hand the portion of sovereignty which has been reserved to the several States, and on the other the share of power which the Union has assumed, it is evident that the Federal legislators entertained the clearest and most accurate notions on the nature of the centralization of government. The United States form not only a republic, but a confederation ; nevertheless the authority of the nation is more central than it was in several of the monarchies of Europe when the American Constitution was formed. . . .

The great difficulty was, not to devise the Constitution to the Federal Government, but to find out a method of enforcing its laws. Governments have in general but two means of overcoming the opposition of the people they govern, viz. the physical force which is at their own disposal, and the moral force which they derive from the decisions of the courts of justice.

A Government which should have no other means of exacting obedience than open war must be very near its ruin, for one of two alternatives would then probably occur : if its authority was small and its character temperate, it would not resort to violence till the last extremity, and it would connive at a number of partial acts of insubordination, in which case the State would gradually fall into anarchy ; if it was enterprising and powerful, it would perpetually have recourse to its physical strength, and would speedily degenerate into a military despotism. So that its activity would not be less prejudicial to the community than its inaction.

The great end of justice is to substitute the notion of right for that of violence, and to place a legal barrier between the power of the Government and the use of physical force. The authority which is awarded to the intervention of a court of justice by the general opinion of mankind is so surprisingly great that it clings to the mere formalities of justice, and gives a bodily influence to the shadow of the law. The moral force which courts of justice possess renders the introduction of physical force exceedingly rare, and is very frequently substituted for it ; but if the latter proves to be indispensable, its power is doubled by the association of the idea of law.

A Federal Government stands in greater need of the support of judicial institutions than any other, because it is naturally weak and exposed to formidable opposition. If it were always obliged to resort to violence in the first instance, it could not fulfil its task. The Union, therefore, required a national judiciary to enforce the obedience of the citizens to the laws, and to repel the attacks which might be directed against them. The question then remained as to what tribunals were to exercise these privileges ; were they to be intrusted to the courts of justice which were already organized in every State ? or was it necessary to create Federal courts ? It may easily be proved that the Union could not adapt the judicial power of the States to its wants. The separation of the judiciary from the administrative power of the State no doubt affects the security of every citizen and the liberty of all. But it is no less important to the existence of the nation that these several powers should have the same origin, should follow the same principles, and act in the same sphere ; in a word, that they should be correlative and homogeneous. No one, I presume, ever suggested the advantage of trying offences committed in France by a foreign court of justice, in order to secure the impartiality of the judges. The Americans form one people in relation to their Federal Government ; but in the bosom of this people divers political bodies have been allowed to subsist which are dependent on the national Government in a few points, and independent in all the rest ; which have all a distinct origin, maxims peculiar to themselves, and special means of carrying on their affairs. To intrust the execution of the laws of the Union to tribunals instituted by these political bodies would be to allow foreign judges to preside over the nation. Nay, more ; not only is each State foreign to the Union at large, but it is in perpetual opposition to the common interests, since whatever authority the Union loses turns to the advantage of the States. Thus to enforce the laws of the Union by means of the tribunals of the States would be to allow not only foreign but partial judges to preside over the nation.

But the number, still more than the mere character, of the tribunals of the States rendered them unfit for the service of the nation. When the Federal Constitution was formed there were already thirteen courts of justice in the United States which decided causes without appeal. That number is now increased to twenty-four. To suppose that a State can subsist when its fundamental laws may be subjected to four-and-twenty different interpretations at the same time is to advance a proposition alike contrary to reason and to experience.

The American legislators therefore agreed to create

a Federal judiciary power to apply the laws of the Union, and to determine certain questions affecting general interests, which were carefully determined beforehand. The entire judicial power of the Union was centred in one tribunal, which was denominated the Supreme Court of the United States. But, to facilitate the expedition of business, inferior courts were appended to it, which were empowered to decide causes of small importance without appeal, and with appeal causes of more magnitude. The members of the Supreme Court are named neither by the people nor the legislature, but by the President of the United States, acting with the advice of the Senate. In order to render them independent of the other authorities, their office was made inalienable ; and it was determined that their salary, when once fixed, should not be altered by the legislature. It was easy to proclaim the principle of a Federal judiciary, but difficulties multiplied when the extent of its jurisdiction was to be determined.

As the Constitution of the United States recognized two distinct powers in presence of each other, represented in a judicial point of view by two distinct classes of courts of justice, the utmost care which could be taken in defining their separate jurisdictions would have been insufficient to prevent frequent collisions between those tribunals. The question then arose to whom the right of deciding the competency of each court was to be referred.

In nations which constitute a single body politic, when a question is debated between two courts relating to their mutual jurisdiction, a third tribunal is generally within reach to decide the difference ; and this is effected without difficulty, because in these nations the questions of judicial competency have no connection with the privileges of the national supremacy. But it was impossible to create an arbiter between a superior court of the Union and the superior court of a separate State which would not belong to one of these two classes. It was therefore necessary to allow one of these courts to judge its own cause, and to take or to retain cognizance of the point which was contested. To grant this privilege to the different courts of the States would have been to destroy the sovereignty of the Union *de facto* after having established it *de jure*; for the interpretation of the Constitution would soon have restored to the States that portion of independence of which the terms of that act deprived them. The object of the creation of a Federal tribunal was to prevent the courts of the States from deciding questions affecting the national interests in their own department, and so to form a uniform body of jurisprudence for the interpretation of the laws of the Union. This end would not have been accomplished if the courts of the several States had been competent to decide upon cases in their separate capacities from which they were obliged to abstain as Federal tribunals. The Supreme Court of the United States was therefore invested with the right of determining all questions of jurisdiction.

This was a severe blow upon the independence of the States, which was thus restricted not only by the laws, but by the interpretation of them; by one limit which was known, and by another which was dubious; by a rule which was certain, and a rule which was arbitrary. It is true the Constitution had laid down the precise limits of the Federal supremacy, but whenever this supremacy is contested by one of the States, a Federal tribunal decides the question. . . .

The Union, as it was established in 1789, possesses, it is true, a limited supremacy; but it was intended that within its limits it should form one and the same people. Within those limits the Union is sovereign. When this point is established and admitted, the inference is easy ; for if it be acknowledged that the United States constitute one and the same people within the bounds prescribed by their Constitution, it is impossible to refuse them the rights which belong to other nations. But it has been allowed, from the origin of society, that every nation has the right of deciding by its own courts those questions which concern the execution of its own laws. To this it is answered that the Union is in so singular a position that in relation to some matters it constitutes a people, and that in relation to all the rest it is a nonentity. But the inference to be drawn is, that in the laws relating to these matters the Union possesses all the rights of absolute sovereignty. The difficulty is to know what these matters are ; and when once it is resolved (and we have shown how it was resolved, in speaking of the means of determining the jurisdiction of the Federal courts) no further doubt can arise ; for as soon as it is established that a suit is Federal—that is to say, that it belongs to the share of sovereignty reserved by the Constitution to the Union—the natural consequence is that it should come within the jurisdiction of a Federal court.

Whenever the laws of the United States are attacked, or whenever they are resorted to in self-defence, the Federal courts must be appealed to. Thus the jurisdiction of the tribunals of the Union extends and narrows its limits exactly in the same ratio as the sovereignty of the Union augments or decreases. . . . The principal aim of the legislators of 1789 was to divide the sovereign authority into two parts. In the one they placed the control of all the general interests of the Union, in the other the control of the special interests of its component States. Their chief solicitude was to arm the Federal Government with sufficient power to enable it to resist, within its sphere, the encroachments of the several States. As for these communities, the principle of independence within certain limits of their own was adopted in their behalf ; and they were concealed from the inspection, and protected from the control, of the central Government. In speaking of the division of authority, I observed that this latter principle had not always been held sacred, since the States are prevented from passing certain laws which apparently belong to their own particular sphere of interest. When a State of the Union passes a law of this kind, the citizens who are injured by its execution can appeal to the Federal courts.

Thus the jurisdiction of the Federal courts extends not only to all the cases which arise under the laws of the Union, but also to those which arise under laws made by the several States in opposition to the Constitution. The States are prohibited from making *ex post facto* laws in criminal cases, and any person condemned by virtue of a law of this kind can appeal to the judicial power of the Union. The States are likewise prohibited from making laws which may have a tendency to impair the obligations of contracts. If a citizen thinks that an obligation of this kind is impaired by a law passed in his State, he may refuse to obey it, and may appeal to the Federal courts.

This provision appears to me to be the most serious attack upon the independence of the States. The rights awarded to the Federal Government for purposes of obvious national importance are definite and easily comprehensible ; but those with which this last clause invests it are not either clearly appreciable or accurately defined. For there are vast numbers of political laws which influence the existence of obligations of contracts, which may thus furnish an easy pretext for the aggressions of the central authority. . . .

When we have successively examined in detail the organization of the Supreme Court, and the entire prerogatives which it exercises, we shall readily admit that a more imposing judicial power was never constituted by any people. The Supreme Court is placed at the head of all known tribunals, both by the nature of its rights and the class of justiciable parties which it controls.

In all the civilized countries of Europe the Government always has shown the greatest repugnance to allow the cases to which it was itself a party to be decided by the ordinary course of justice. This repugnance naturally attains its utmost height in an absolute Government ; and, on the other hand, the privileges of the courts of justice are extended with the increasing liberties of the people : but no European nation has at present held that all judicial controversies, without regard to their origin, can be decided by the judges of common law.

In America this theory has been actually put in practice, and the Supreme Court of the United States is the sole tribunal of the nation. Its power extends to all the cases arising under laws and treaties made by the executive and legislative authorities, to all cases of admiralty and maritime jurisdiction, and in general to all points which affect the law of nations. It may even be affirmed that, although its constitution is essentially judicial, its prerogatives are almost entirely political. Its sole object is to enforce the execution of the laws of the Union ; and the Union only regulates the relations of the Government with the citizens, and of the nation with Foreign Powers : the relations of citizens among themselves are almost exclusively regulated by the sovereignty of the States.

A second and still greater cause of the preponderance of this court may be adduced. In the nations of Europe the courts of justice are only called upon to try the controversies of private individuals ; but the Supreme Court of the United States summons sovereign powers to its bar. When the clerk of the court advances on the steps of the tribunal, and simply says, " The State of New York versus the State of Ohio," it is impossible not to feel that the court which he addresses is no ordinary body ; and when it is recollected that one of these parties represents one million, and the other two millions of men, one is struck by the responsibility of the seven judges whose decision is about to satisfy or to disappoint so large a number of their fellow-citizens.

The peace, the prosperity, and the very existence of the Union are vested in the hands of the seven judges. Without their active co-operation the Constitution would be a dead letter : the Executive appeals to them for assistance against the encroachments of the legislative powers ; the legislature demands their protection from the designs of the Executive ; they defend the Union from the disobedience of the States, the States from the exaggerated claims of the Union, the public interest against the interests of private citizens, and the conservative spirit of order against the fleeting innovations of democracy. Their power is enormous, but it is clothed in the authority of public opinion. They are the all-powerful guardians of a people which respects law, but they would be impotent against popular neglect or popular contempt. The force of public opinion is the most intractable of agents, because its exact limits cannot be defined ; and it is not less dangerous to exceed than to remain below the boundary prescribed.

The Federal judges must not only be good citizens, and men possessed of that information and integrity which are indispensable to magistrates, but they must be statesmen—politicians, not unread in the signs of the times, not afraid to brave the obstacles which can be subdued, nor slow to turn aside such encroaching elements as may threaten the supremacy of the Union and the obedience which is due to the laws.

The President, who exercises a limited power, may err without causing great mischief in the State. Congress may decide amiss without destroying the Union, because the electoral body in which Congress originates may cause it to retract its decision by changing its members. But if the Supreme Court is ever composed of imprudent men or bad citizens, the Union may be plunged into anarchy or civil war.

The real cause of this danger, however, does not lie in the constitution of the tribunal, but in the very nature of Federal Governments. We have observed that in confederated peoples it is especially necessary to consolidate the judicial authority, because in no other nations do those independent persons who are able to cope with the social body exist in greater power or in a better condition to resist the physical strength of the Government. But the more a power requires to be strengthened, the more extensive and independent it must be made ; and the dangers which its abuse may create are heightened by its independence and its strength. The source of the evil is not, therefore, in the constitution of the power, but in the constitution of those States which render its existence necessary. . . .

Chapter VIII

CHARACTERISTICS AND ADVANTAGES OF THE AMERICAN FEDERAL SYSTEM

THE United States of America do not afford either the first or the only instance of confederate States, several of which have existed in modern Europe, without adverting to those of antiquity. Switzerland, the Germanic Empire, and the Republic of the United Provinces either have been or still are confederations. In studying the constitutions of these different countries, the politician is surprised to observe that the powers with which they invested the Federal Government are nearly identical with the privileges awarded by the American Constitution to the Government of the United States. They confer upon the central power the same rights of making peace and war, of raising money and troops, and of providing for the general exigencies and the common interests of the nation. Nevertheless the Federal Government of these different peoples has always been as remarkable for its weakness and inefficiency as that of the Union is for its vigorous and enterprising spirit. Again, the first American Confederation perished through the excessive weakness of its Government ; and this weak Government was, notwithstanding, in possession of rights even more extensive than those of the Federal Government of the present day. But the more recent Constitution of the United States contains certain principles which exercise a most important influence, although they do not at once strike the observer.

This Constitution, which may at first sight be confounded with the Federal constitutions which preceded it, rests upon a novel theory, which may be considered as a great invention in modern political science. In all the confederations which had been formed before the American Constitution of 1789 the allied States agreed to obey the injunctions of a Federal Government ; but they reserved to themselves the right of ordaining and enforcing the execution of the laws of the Union. The American States which combined in 1789 agreed that the Federal Government should not only dictate the laws, but that it should execute its own enactments. In both cases the right is the same, but the exercise of the right is different ; and this alteration produced the most momentous consequences.

In all the confederations which had been formed before the American Union the Federal Government demanded its supplies at the hands of the separate Governments ; and if the measure it prescribed was onerous to any one of those bodies means were found to evade its claims : if the State was powerful, it had recourse to arms ; if it was weak, it connived at the resistance which the law of the Union, its sovereign, met with, and resorted to inaction under the plea of inability. Under these circumstances one of the two alternatives has invariably occurred : either the most preponderant of the allied peoples has assumed the privileges of the Federal authority and ruled all the States in its name, or the Federal Government has been abandoned by its natural supporters, anarchy has arisen between the confederates, and the Union has lost all powers of action.

In America the subjects of the Union are not States, but private citizens : the national Government levies a tax, not upon the State of Massachusetts, but upon each inhabitant of Massachusetts. All former confederate governments presided over communities, but that of the Union rules individuals ; its force is not borrowed, but self-derived ; and it is served by its own civil and military officers, by its own army, and its own courts of justice. It cannot be doubted that the spirit of the nation, the passions of the multitude, and the provincial prejudices of each State tend singularly to diminish the authority of a Federal authority thus constituted, and to facilitate the means of resistance to its mandates ; but the comparative weakness of a restricted sovereignty is an evil inherent in the Federal system. In America, each State has fewer opportunities of resistance and fewer temptations to non-compliance ; nor can such a design be put into execution (if indeed it be entertained) without an open violation of the laws of the Union, a direct interruption of the ordinary course of justice, and a bold declaration of revolt ; in a word, without taking a decisive step which men hesitate to adopt.

In all former confederations the privileges of the Union furnished more elements of discord than of power, since they multiplied the claims of the nation without augmenting the means of enforcing them : and in accordance with this fact it may be remarked that the real weakness of Federal governments has almost always been in the exact ratio of their nominal power. Such is not the case in the American Union, in which, as in ordinary governments, the Federal Government has the means of enforcing all it is empowered to demand.

The human understanding more easily invents new things than new words, and we are thence constrained to employ a multitude of improper and inadequate expressions. When several nations form a permanent league and establish a supreme authority, which, although it has not the same influence over the members of the community as a national government, acts upon each of the confederate States in a body, this government, which is so essentially different from all others, is denominated a Federal one. Another form of society is afterward discovered, in which several peoples are fused into one and the same nation with regard to certain common interests, although they remain distinct, or at least only confederate, with regard to all their other concerns. In this case the central power acts directly upon those whom it governs, whom it rules, and whom it judges, in the same manner as, but in a more limited circle than, a national government. Here the term Federal Government is clearly no longer applicable to a state of things which must be styled an incomplete national government : a form of government has been found out which is neither exactly national nor Federal ; but no further progress has been made, and the new word which will one day designate this novel invention does not yet exist.

The absence of this new species of confederation has been the cause which has brought all Unions to civil war, to subjection, or to a stagnant apathy ; and the peoples which formed these leagues have been either too dull to discern, or too pusillanimous to apply, this great remedy. The American Confederation perished by the same defects.

But the confederate States of America had been long accustomed to form a portion of one empire before they had won their independence ; they had not contracted the habit of governing themselves, and their national prejudices had not taken deep root in their minds. Superior to the rest of the world in political knowledge, and sharing that knowledge equally among themselves, they were little agitated by the passions which generally oppose the extension of Federal authority in a nation, and those passions were checked by the wisdom of the chief citizens.

The Americans applied the remedy with prudent firmness as soon as they were conscious of the evil ; they amended their laws, and they saved their country. . . .

The history of the world affords no instance of a great nation retaining the form of republican government for a long series of years, and this has led to the conclusion that such a state of things is impracticable. For my own part, I cannot but censure the imprudence of attempting to limit the possible and to judge the future on the part of a being who is hourly deceived by the most palpable realities of life, and who is constantly taken by surprise in the circumstances with which he is most familiar. But it may be advanced with confidence that the existence of a great republic will always be exposed to far greater perils than that of a small one.

All the passions which are most fatal to republican institutions spread with an increasing territory, while the virtues which maintain their dignity do not augment in the same proportion. The ambition of the citizens increases with the power of the State ; the strength of parties with the importance of the ends they have in view ; but that devotion to the common weal which is the surest check on destructive passions is not stronger in a large than in a small republic. It might, indeed, be proved without difficulty that it is less powerful and less sincere. The arrogance of wealth and the dejection of wretchedness, capital cities of unwonted extent, a lax morality, a vulgar egotism, and a great confusion of interests, are the dangers which almost invariably arise from the magnitude of States. But several of these evils are scarcely prejudicial to a monarchy, and some of them contribute to maintain its existence. In monarchical States the strength of the government is its own ; it may use, but it does not depend on, the community, and the authority of the prince is proportioned to the prosperity of the nation ; but the only security which a republican government possesses against these evils lies in the support of the majority. This support is not, however, proportionably greater in a large republic than it is in a small one ; and thus, while the means of attack perpetually increase both in number and in influence, the power of resistance remains the same, or it may rather be said to diminish, since the propensities and interests of the people are diversified by the increase of the population, and the difficulty of forming a compact majority is constantly augmented. It has been observed, moreover, that the intensity of human passions is heightened, not only by the importance of the end which they propose to attain, but by the multitude of individuals who are animated by them at the same time. Every one has had occasion to remark that his emotions in the midst of a sympathizing crowd are far greater than those which he would have felt in solitude. In great republics the impetus of political passion is irresistible, not only because it aims at gigantic purposes, but because it is felt and shared by millions of men at the same time.

It may therefore be asserted as a general proposition that nothing is more opposed to the well-being and the freedom of man than vast empires. Nevertheless it is important to acknowledge the peculiar advantages of great States. For the very reason which renders the desire of power more intense in these communities than among ordinary men, the love of glory is also more prominent in the hearts of a class of citizens, who regard the applause of a great people as a reward worthy of their exertions, and an elevating encouragement to man. If we would learn why it is that great nations contribute more powerfully to the spread of human improvement than small States, we shall discover an adequate cause in the rapid and energetic circulation of ideas, and in those great cities which are the intellectual centres where all the rays of human genius are reflected and combined. To this it may be added that most important discoveries demand a display of national power which the Government of a small State is unable to make ; in great nations the Government entertains a greater number of general notions, and is more completely disengaged from the routine of precedent and the egotism of local prejudice ; its designs are conceived with more talent, and executed with more boldness.

In time of peace the well-being of small nations is undoubtedly more general and more complete, but they are apt to suffer more acutely from the calamities of war than those great empires whose distant frontiers may for ages avert the presence of the danger from the mass of the people, which is therefore more frequently afflicted than ruined by the evil.

But in this matter, as in many others, the argument derived from the necessity of the case predominates over all others. If none but small nations existed, I do not doubt that mankind would be more happy and more free ; but the existence of great nations is unavoidable.

This consideration introduces the element of physical strength as a condition of national prosperity. It profits a people but little to be affluent and free if it is perpetually exposed to be pillaged or subjugated ; the number of its manufactures and the extent of its commerce are of small advantage if another nation has the empire of the seas and gives the law in all the markets of the globe. Small nations are often impoverished, not because they are small, but because they are weak ; the great empires prosper less because they are great than because they are strong. Physical strength is therefore one of the first conditions of the happiness and even of the existence of nations. Hence it occurs that, unless very peculiar circumstances intervene, small nations are always united to large empires in the end, either by force or by their own consent : yet I am unacquainted with a more deplorable spectacle than that of a people unable either to defend or to maintain its independence.

The Federal system was created with the intention of combining the different advantages which result from the greater and the lesser extent of nations ; and a single glance over the United States of America suffices to discover the advantages which they have derived from its adoption.

In great centralized nations the legislator is obliged to impart a character of uniformity to the laws which does not always suit the diversity of customs and of districts ; as he takes no cognizance of special cases, he can only proceed upon general principles ; and the population is obliged to conform to the exigencies of the legislation, since the legislation cannot adapt itself to the exigencies and the customs of the population, which is the cause of endless trouble and misery. This disadvantage does not exist in confederations. Congress regulates the principal measures of the national Government, and all the details of the administration are reserved to the provincial legislatures. It is impossible to imagine how much this division of sovereignty contributes to the well-being of each of the States which compose the Union. In these small communities, which are never agitated by the desire of aggrandizement or the cares of self-defence, all public authority and private energy is employed in internal amelioration. The central government of each State, which is in immediate juxtaposition to the citizens, is daily apprised of the wants which arise in society ; and new projects are proposed every year, which are discussed either at town-meetings or by the legislature of the State, and which are transmitted by the press to stimulate the zeal and to excite the interest of the citizens. This spirit of amelioration is constantly alive in the American republics, without compromising their tranquillity ; the ambition of power yields to the less refined and less dangerous love of comfort. It is generally believed in America that the existence and the permanence of the republican form of government in the New World depend upon the existence and the permanence of the Federal system ; and it is not unusual to attribute a large share of the misfortunes which have befallen the new States of South America to the injudicious erection of great republics, instead of a divided and confederate sovereignty.

It is incontestably true that the love and the habits of republican government in the United States were engendered in the townships and in the provincial assemblies. In a small State, like that of Connecticut for instance, where cutting a canal or laying down a road is a momentous political question, where the State has no army to pay and no wars to carry on, and where much wealth and much honour cannot be bestowed upon the chief citizens, no form of government can be more natural or more appropriate than that of a republic. But it is this same republican spirit, it is these manners and customs of a free people, which are engendered and nurtured in the different States, to be afterward applied to the country at large. The public spirit of the Union is, so to speak, nothing more than an abstract of the patriotic zeal of the provinces. Every citizen of the United States transfuses his attachment to his little republic in the

common store of American patriotism. In defending
the Union he defends the increasing prosperity of his
own district, the right of conducting its affairs, and
the hope of causing measures of improvement to be
adopted which may be favourable to his own interests ; and these are motives which are wont to stir
men more readily than the general interests of the
country and the glory of the nation.

On the other hand, if the temper and the manners
of the inhabitants especially fitted them to promote
the welfare of a great republic, the Federal system
smoothed the obstacles which they might have encountered. The confederation of all the American
States presents none of the ordinary disadvantages
resulting from great agglomerations of men. The
Union is a great republic in extent, but the paucity
of objects for which its Government provides assimi-
lates it to a small State. Its acts are important, but
they are rare. As the sovereignty of the Union is
limited and incomplete, its exercise is not incompatible with liberty ; for it does not excite those
insatiable desires of fame and power which have
proved so fatal to great republics. As there is no
common centre to the country, vast capital cities,
colossal wealth, abject poverty, and sudden revolutions are alike unknown ; and political passion,
instead of spreading over the land like a torrent of
desolation, spends its strength against the interests
and the individual passions of every State.

Nevertheless, all commodities and ideas circulate
throughout the Union as freely as in a country
inhabited by one people. Nothing checks the spirit
of enterprise. Government avails itself of the assistance of all who have talents or knowledge to serve
it. Within the frontiers of the Union the profoundest
peace prevails, as within the heart of some great

empire ; abroad, it ranks with the most powerful nations of the earth ; two thousand miles of coast are open to the commerce of the world ; and as it possesses the keys of the globe, its flag is respected in the most remote seas.   The Union is as happy and as free as a small people, and as glorious and as strong as a great nation. . .

Chapter IX

WHY THE PEOPLE STRICTLY MAY BE SAID **TO** GOVERN IN THE UNITED STATES. POLITICAL PARTIES

I HAVE hitherto examined the institutions of the United States ; I have passed their legislation in review, and I have depicted the present character-istics of political society in that country. But a sovereign power exists above these institutions and beyond these characteristic features which may destroy or modify them at its pleasure—I mean that of the people. It remains to be shown in what manner this power, which regulates the laws, acts : its propensities and its passions remain to be pointed out, as well as the secret springs which retard, accelerate, or direct its irresistible course ; and the effects of its unbounded authority, with the destiny which is probably reserved for it.

In America the people appoints the legislative and the executive power, and furnishes the jurors who punish all offences against the laws. The American institutions are democratic, not only in their principle but in all their consequences ; and the people elects its representatives directly, and for the most part annually, in order to insure their dependence. The people is therefore the real directing power ; and although the form of government is representative, it is evident that the opinions, the prejudices, the in-terests, and even the passions of the community are hindered by no durable obstacles from exercising a perpetual influence on society. In the United States the majority governs in the name of the people, as is the case in all the countries in which the people is supreme. This majority is principally composed of peaceable citizens, who, either by inclination or by interest, are sincerely desirous of the welfare of their country. But they are surrounded by the incessant agitation of parties, which attempt to gain their co-operation and to avail themselves of their support. . . .

America has already lost the great parties which once divided the nation ; and if her happiness is considerably increased, her morality has suffered by their extinction. When the War of Independence was terminated, and the foundations of the new Government were to be laid down, the nation was divided between two opinions—two opinions which are as old as the world, and which are perpetually to be met with under all the forms and all the names which have ever obtained in free communities—the one tending to limit, the other to extend indefinitely, the power of the people. The conflict of these two opinions never assumed that degree of violence in America which it frequently has displayed elsewhere. Both parties of the Americans were, in fact, agreed upon the most essential points ; and neither of them had to destroy a traditionary constitution, or to overthrow the structure of society, in order to insure its own triumph. In neither of them, consequently, were a great number of private interests affected by success or by defeat ; but moral principles of a high order, such as the love of equality and of independence, were concerned in the struggle, and they sufficed to kindle violent passions.

The party which desired to limit the power of the people endeavoured to apply its doctrines more especially to the Constitution of the Union, whence it derived its name of Federal. The other party, which affected to be more exclusively attached to the cause of liberty, took that of Republican. America is a land of democracy, and the Federalists were always in a minority ; but they reckoned on their side almost all the great men who had been called forth by

the War of Independence, and their moral influence
was very considerable. Their cause was, moreover,
favoured by circumstances. The ruin of the Confederation had impressed the people with a dread of
anarchy, and the Federalists did not fail to profit by
this transient disposition of the multitude. For ten
or twelve years they were at the head of affairs, and
they were able to apply some, though not all, of their
principles ; for the hostile current was becoming
from day to day too violent to be checked or stemmed.
In 1801 the Republicans got possession of the Government ; Thomas Jefferson was named President ; and
he increased the influence of their party by the weight
of his celebrity, the greatness of his talents, and the
immense extent of his popularity.

The means by which the Federalists had maintained their position were artificial, and their resources
were temporary ; it was by the virtues or the talents
of their leaders that they had risen to power. When
the Republicans attained to that lofty station, their
opponents were overwhelmed by utter defeat. An
immense majority declared itself against the retiring
party, and the Federalists found themselves in so small
a minority that they at once despaired of their future
success. From that moment the Republican or
Democratic party has proceeded from conquest to
conquest, until it has acquired absolute supremacy in
the country. The Federalists, perceiving that they
were vanquished without resource, and isolated in the
midst of the nation, fell into two divisions, of which
one joined the victorious Republicans, and the other
abandoned its rallying-point and its name. . . .

Whether their theories were good or bad, they had
the effect of being inapplicable, as a system, to the
society which they professed to govern, and that
which occurred under the auspices of Jefferson must

therefore have taken place sooner or later. But their Government gave the new republic time to acquire a certain stability, and afterward to support the rapid growth of the very doctrines which they had combated. A considerable number of their principles were in point of fact embodied in the political creed of their opponents ; and the Federal Constitution which subsists at the present day is a lasting monument of their patriotism and their wisdom.

Great political parties are not, then, to be met with in the United States at the present time.[1] . . .

In the absence of great parties, the United States abound with lesser controversies ; and public opinion is divided into a thousand minute shades of difference upon questions of very little moment. The pains which are taken to create parties are inconceivable, and at the present day it is no easy task. In the United States there is no religious animosity, because all religion is respected, and no sect is predominant ; there is no jealousy of rank, because the people is everything, and none can contest its authority ; lastly, there is no public indigence to supply the means of agitation, because the physical position of the country opens so wide a field to industry that man is able to accomplish the most surprising undertakings with his own native resources. Nevertheless, ambitious men are interested in the creation of parties, since it is difficult to eject a person from authority upon the mere ground that his place is coveted by others. The skill of the actors in the political world

[1] It must be remembered that at the time of Tocqueville's visit to the United States the Whig party, successor to the defunct Federalist, had not yet crystallized. The Democratic party, however, had been in continuous existence since the 1790s, and in control of the Government since 1801.—H. S. C.

lies therefore in the art of creating parties. A political aspirant in the United States begins by discriminating his own interest, and by calculating upon those interests which may be collected around and amalgamated with it ; he then contrives to discover some doctrine or some principle which may suit the purposes of this new association, and which he adopts in order to bring forward his party and to secure his popularity ; just as the imprimatur of a king was in former days incorporated with the volume which it authorized, but to which it nowise belonged. When these preliminaries are terminated, the new party is ushered into the political world.

All the domestic controversies of the Americans at first appear to a stranger to be so incomprehensible and so puerile that he is at a loss whether to pity a people which takes such arrant trifles in good earnest, or to envy the happiness which enables it to discuss them. But when he comes to study the secret propensities which govern the factions of America, he easily perceives that the greater part of them are more or less connected with one or the other of those two divisions which have always existed in free communities. The deeper we penetrate into the working of these parties, the more do we perceive that the object of the one is to limit, and that of the other to extend, the popular authority. I do not assert that the ostensible end, or even that the secret aim, of American parties is to promote the rule of aristocracy or democracy in the country ; but I affirm that aristocratic or democratic passions may easily be detected at the bottom of all parties, and that, although they escape a superficial observation, they are the main point and the very soul of every faction in the United States.

To quote a recent example. When the President

attacked the Bank,[1] the country was excited and parties were formed ; the well-informed classes rallied round the Bank, the common people round the President. But it must not be imagined that the people had formed a rational opinion upon a question which offers so many difficulties to the most experienced statesmen. The Bank is a great establishment which enjoys an independent existence, and the people, accustomed to make and unmake whatsoever it pleases, is startled to meet with this obstacle to its authority. In the midst of the perpetual fluctuation of society the community is irritated by so permanent an institution, and is led to attack it in order to see whether it can be shaken and controlled, like all the other institutions of the country.

It sometimes happens in a people among which various opinions prevail that the balance of the several parties is lost, and one of them obtains an irresistible preponderance, overpowers all obstacles, harasses its opponents, and appropriates all the resources of society to its own purposes. The vanquished citizens despair of success and conceal their dissatisfaction in silence and in general apathy. The nation seems to be governed by a single principle, and the prevailing party assumes the credit of having restored peace and unanimity to the country. But this apparent unanimity is merely a cloak to alarming dissensions and perpetual opposition.

This is precisely what occurred in America ; when the Democratic party got the upper hand, it took exclusive possession of the conduct of affairs, and from that time the laws and the customs of society have been adapted to its caprices. At the present day the more affluent classes of society are so entirely

[1] The reference is to Jackson's war on the second Bank of the United States.—H. S. C.

removed from the direction of political affairs in the United States that wealth, far from conferring a right to the exercise of power, is rather an obstacle than a means of attaining to it. The wealthy members of the community abandon the lists, through unwillingness to contend, and frequently to contend in vain, against the poorest classes of their fellow-citizens. They concentrate all their enjoyments in the privacy of their homes, where they occupy a rank which cannot be assumed in public ; and they constitute a private society in the State, which has its own tastes and its own pleasures. They submit to this state of things as an irremediable evil, but they are careful not to show that they are galled by its continuance ; it is even not uncommon to hear them laud the delights of a republican government, and the advantages of democratic institutions when they are in public. Next to hating their enemies, men are most inclined to flatter them.

Mark, for instance, that opulent citizen, who is as anxious as a Jew of the Middle Ages to conceal his wealth. His dress is plain, his demeanour unassuming ; but the interior of his dwelling glitters with luxury, and none but a few chosen guests whom he haughtily styles his equals are allowed to penetrate into this sanctuary. No European noble is more exclusive in his pleasures, or more jealous of the smallest advantages which his privileged station confers upon him. But the very same individual crosses the city to reach a dark counting-house in the centre of traffic, where every one may accost him who pleases. If he meets his cobbler upon the way, they stop and converse ; the two citizens discuss the affairs of the State in which they have an equal interest, and they shake hands before they part.

But beneath this artificial enthusiasm, and these

obsequious attentions to the preponderating power, it is easy to perceive that the wealthy members of the community entertain a hearty distaste for the democratic institutions of their country. The populace is at once the object of their scorn and of their fears. If the maladministration of the democracy ever brings about a revolutionary crisis, and if monarchical institutions ever become practicable in the United States, the truth of what I advance will become obvious.

The two chief weapons which parties use in order to insure success are the public press and the formation of associations.

Chapter X

LIBERTY OF THE PRESS IN THE UNITED STATES

THE influence of the liberty of the press does not affect political opinions alone, but it extends to all the opinions of men, and it modifies customs as well as laws. In another part of this work I shall attempt to determine the degree of influence which the liberty of the press has exercised upon civil society in the United States, and to point out the direction which it has given to the ideas, as well as the tone which it has imparted to the character and the feelings, of the Anglo-Americans, but at present I purpose simply to examine the effects produced by the liberty of the press in the political world. . . .

In the countries in which the doctrine of the sovereignty of the people ostensibly prevails, the censorship of the press is not only dangerous, but it is absurd. When the right of every citizen to co-operate in the government of society is acknowledged, every citizen must be presumed to possess the power of discriminating between the different opinions of his contemporaries, and of appreciating the different facts from which inferences may be drawn. The sovereignty of the people and the liberty of the press may therefore be looked upon as correlative institutions; just as the censorship of the press and universal suffrage are two things which are irreconcilably opposed, and which cannot long be retained among the institutions of the same people. Not a single individual of the twelve millions who inhabit the territory of the United States has as yet dared to propose any restrictions to the liberty of the press.[1] . . .

[1] The Sedition Act of 1798 included far-reaching restrictions on the freedom of the press. It lapsed in March 1801 and was not re-enacted.—H. S. C.

America is perhaps, at this moment, the country of the whole world which contains the fewest germs of revolution; but the press is not less destructive in its principles than in France, and it displays the same violence without the same reasons for indignation. In America, as in France, it constitutes a singular power, so strangely composed of mingled good and evil that it is at the same time indispensable to the existence of freedom, and nearly incompatible with the maintenance of public order. Its power is certainly much greater in France than in the United States; though nothing is more rare in the latter country than to hear of a prosecution having been instituted against it. The reason of this is perfectly simple: the Americans, having once admitted the doctrine of the sovereignty of the people, apply it with perfect consistency. It was never their intention to found a permanent state of things with elements which undergo daily modifications; and there is consequently nothing criminal in an attack upon the existing laws, provided it be not attended with a violent infraction of them. They are, moreover, of opinion that courts of justice are unable to check the abuses of the press; and that as the subtilty of human language perpetually eludes the severity of judicial analysis, offences of this nature are apt to escape the hand which attempts to apprehend them. They hold that to act with efficacy upon the press it would be necessary to find a tribunal, not only devoted to the existing order of things, but capable of surmounting the influence of public opinion; a tribunal which should conduct its proceedings without publicity, which should pronounce its decrees without assigning its motives, and punish the intentions even more than the language of an author. Whosoever should have the power of creating and maintaining a tribunal of this kind would waste his time in prosecuting the liberty of the press ; for he would be the supreme master of the whole community, and he would be as free to rid himself of the authors as of their writings. In this question, therefore, there is no medium between servitude and extreme licence ; in order to enjoy the inestimable benefits which the liberty of the press insures, it is necessary to submit to the inevitable evils which it engenders. To expect to acquire the former and to escape the latter is to cherish one of those illusions which commonly mislead nations in their times of sickness, when, tired with faction and exhausted by effort, they attempt to combine hostile opinions and contrary principles upon the same soil.

The small influence of the American journals is attributable to several reasons, among which are the following :

The liberty of writing, like all other liberty, is most formidable when it is a novelty ; for a people which has never been accustomed to co-operate in the conduct of State affairs places implicit confidence in the first tribune who arouses its attention. The Anglo-Americans have enjoyed this liberty ever since the foundation of the settlements ; moreover, the press cannot create human passions by its own power, however skilfully it may kindle them where they exist. In America politics are discussed with animation and a varied activity, but they rarely touch those deep passions which are excited whenever the positive interest of a part of the community is impaired : but in the United States the interests of the community are in a most prosperous condition. A single glance upon a French and an American newspaper is sufficient to show the difference which exists between the two nations on this head. In France the space allotted to commercial advertisements is very limited, and the intelligence is not considerable, but the most essential part of the journal is that which contains the discussion of the politics of the day. In America three quarters of the enormous sheet which is set before the reader are filled with advertisements, and the remainder is frequently occupied by political intelligence or trivial anecdotes : it is only from time to time that one finds a corner devoted to passionate discussions like those with which the journalists of France are wont to indulge their readers.

It has been demonstrated by observation, and discovered by the innate sagacity of the pettiest as well as the greatest of despots, that the influence of a power is increased in proportion as its direction is rendered more central. In France the press combines a twofold centralization ; almost all its power is centred in the same spot, and vested in the same hands, for its organs are far from numerous. . . .

Neither of these kinds of centralization exists in America. The United States have no metropolis ; the intelligence as well as the power of the country are dispersed abroad, and instead of radiating from a point, they cross each other in every direction ; the Americans have established no central control over the expression of opinion, any more than over the conduct of business. These are circumstances which do not depend on human foresight ; but it is owing to the laws of the Union that there are no licences to be granted to printers, no securities demanded from editors as in France, and no stamp duty as in France and formerly in England. The consequence of this is that nothing is easier than to set up a newspaper, and a small number of readers suffices to defray the expenses of the editor.

The number of periodical and occasional publications which appear in the United States actually surpasses belief. The most enlightened Americans attribute the subordinate influence of the press to this excessive dissemination ; and it is adopted as an axiom of political science in that country that the only way to neutralize the effect of public journals is to multiply them indefinitely. . . .

In America there is scarcely a hamlet which has not its own newspaper. It may readily be imagined that neither discipline nor unity of design can be communicated to so multifarious a host, and each one is consequently led to fight under his own standard. All the political journals of the United States are arrayed indeed on the side of the administration or against it ; but they attack and defend in a thousand different ways. They cannot succeed in forming those great currents of opinion which overwhelm the most solid obstacles. This division of the influence of the press produces a variety of other consequences which are scarcely less remarkable. The facility with which journals can be established induces a multitude of individuals to take a part in them ; but as the extent of competition precludes the possibility of considerable profit, the most distinguished classes of society are rarely led to engage in these undertakings. But such is the number of the public prints that, even if they were a source of wealth, writers of ability could not be found to direct them all. . . . The characteristics of the American journalist consist in an open and coarse appeal to the passions of the populace ; and he habitually abandons the principles of political science to assail the characters of individuals, to track them into private life, and disclose all their weaknesses and errors. . . .

It cannot be denied that the effects of this extreme licence of the press tend indirectly to the maintenance of public order. The individuals who are already in the possession of a high station in the esteem of their fellow-citizens are afraid to write in the newspapers, and they are thus deprived of the most powerful instrument which they can use to excite the passions of the multitude to their own advantage. . . .

But although the press is limited to these resources, its influence in America is immense. It is the power which impels the circulation of political life through all the districts of that vast territory. Its eye is open constantly to detect the secret springs of political designs, and to summon the leaders of all parties to the bar of public opinion. It rallies the interests of the community round certain principles, and it draws up the creed which factions adopt ; for it affords a means of intercourse between parties which hear, and which address each other without ever having been in immediate contact. When a great number of the organs of the press adopt the same line of conduct, their influence becomes irresistible ; and public opinion, when it is perpetually assailed from the same side, eventually yields to the attack. In the United States each separate journal exercises but little authority, but the power of the periodical press is only second to that of the people.

In the United States the democracy perpetually raises fresh individuals to the conduct of public affairs ; and the measures of the administration are consequently seldom regulated by the strict rules of consistency or of order. But the general principles of the Government are more stable, and the opinions most prevalent in society are generally more durable than in many other countries. When once the Americans have taken up an idea, whether it be well or ill founded, nothing is more difficult than to eradicate it from their minds. The same tenacity of opinion has been observed in England, where, for the last century, greater freedom of conscience and more invincible prejudices have existed than in all the other countries of Europe. I attribute this consequence to a cause which may at first sight appear to have a very opposite tendency, namely, to the liberty of the press. The nations among which this liberty exists are as apt to cling to their opinions from pride as from conviction. They cherish them because they hold them to be just, and because they exercised their own free will in choosing them ; and they maintain them not only because they are true, but because they are their own. Several other reasons conduce to the same end. . . .

It has been remarked that in times of great religious fervour men sometimes change their religious opinions ; whereas in times of general scepticism every one clings to his own persuasion. The same thing takes place in politics under the liberty of the press. In countries where all the theories of social science have been contested in their turn, the citizens who have adopted one of them stick to it, not so much because they are assured of its excellence, as because they are not convinced of the superiority of any other. In the present age men are not very ready to die in defence of their opinions, but they are rarely inclined to change them ; and there are fewer martyrs as well as fewer apostates.

Another still more valid reason may yet be adduced: when no abstract opinions are looked upon as certain, men cling to the mere propensities and external interests of their position, which are naturally more tangible and more permanent than any opinions in the world.

It is not a question of easy solution whether aristocracy or democracy is most fit to govern a country.

But it is certain that democracy annoys one part of the community, and that aristocracy oppresses another part. When the question is reduced to the simple expression of the struggle between poverty and wealth, the tendency of each side of the dispute becomes perfectly evident without further controversy.

Chapter XI

POLITICAL ASSOCIATIONS IN THE UNITED STATES

IN no country in the world has the principle of association been more successfully used, or more unsparingly applied to a multitude of different objects, than in America. Besides the permanent associations which are established by law under the names of townships, cities, and counties, a vast number of others are formed and maintained by the agency of private individuals.

The citizen of the United States is taught from his earliest infancy to rely upon his own exertions in order to resist the evils and the difficulties of life ; he looks upon social authority with an eye of mistrust and anxiety, and he only claims its assistance when he is quite unable to shift without it. This habit may even be traced in the schools of the rising generation, where the children in their games are wont to submit to rules which they have themselves established, and to punish misdemeanours which they have themselves defined. The same spirit pervades every act of social life. If a stoppage occurs in a thoroughfare, and the circulation of the public is hindered, the neighbours immediately constitute a deliberative body ; and this extemporaneous assembly gives rise to an executive power which remedies the inconvenience before anybody has thought of recurring to an authority superior to that of the persons immediately concerned. If the public pleasures are concerned, an association is formed to provide for the splendour and the regularity of the entertainment. Societies are formed to resist enemies which are exclusively of a moral nature, and to diminish the vice of intemperance : in the United States associations are established to promote public order, commerce, industry, morality, and religion ; for there is no end which the human will, seconded by the collective exertions of individuals, despairs of attaining.

Hereafter I shall have occasion to show the effects of association upon the course of society, and I must confine myself for the present to the political world. When once the right of association is recognized, the citizens may employ it in several different ways.

An association consists simply in the public assent which a number of individuals give to certain doctrines, and in the engagement which they contract to promote the spread of those doctrines by their exertions. The right of association with these views is very analogous to the liberty of unlicensed writing ; but societies thus formed possess more authority than the press. When an opinion is represented by a society, it necessarily assumes a more exact and explicit form. It numbers its partisans, and compromises their welfare in its cause : they, on the other hand, become acquainted with each other, and their zeal is increased by their number. An association unites the efforts of minds which have a tendency to diverge in one single channel, and urges them vigorously toward one single end which it points out.

The second degree in the right of association is the power of meeting. When an association is allowed to establish centres of action at certain important points in the country, its activity is increased and its influence extended. Men have the opportunity of seeing each other ; means of execution are more readily combined, and opinions are maintained with a degree of warmth and energy which written language cannot approach.

Lastly, in the exercise of the right of political association, there is a third degree : the partisans of an opinion may unite in electoral bodies, and choose delegates to represent them in a central assembly. This is, properly speaking, the application of the representative system to a party. . . .

The more we consider the independence of the press in its principal consequences, the more are we convinced that it is the chief and, so to speak, the constitutive element of freedom in the modern world. A nation which is determined to remain free is therefore right in demanding the unrestrained exercise of this independence. But the unrestrained liberty of political association cannot be entirely assimilated to the liberty of the press. The one is at the same time less necessary and more dangerous than the other. A nation may confine it within certain limits without forfeiting any part of its self-control ; and it may sometimes be obliged to do so in order to maintain its own authority. . . .

It must be acknowledged that the unrestrained liberty of political association has not hitherto produced, in the United States, those fatal consequences which might perhaps be expected from it elsewhere. The right of association was imported from England, and it has always existed in America ; so that the exercise of this privilege is now amalgamated with the manners and customs of the people. At the present time the liberty of association is become a necessary guarantee against the tyranny of the majority. In the United States, as soon as a party is become preponderant, all public authority passes under its control ; its private supporters occupy all the places, and have all the force of the administration at their disposal. As the most distinguished partisans of the other side of the question are unable to surmount the obstacles which exclude them from power, they require some means of establishing themselves upon their own basis, and of opposing the moral authority of the minority to the physical power which domineers over it. Thus a dangerous expedient is used to obviate a still more formidable danger.

The omnipotence of the majority appears to me to present such extreme perils to the American republics that the dangerous measure which is used to repress it seems to be more advantageous than prejudicial. And here I am about to advance a proposition which may remind the reader of what I said before in speaking of municipal freedom : There are no countries in which associations are more needed, to prevent the despotism of faction or the arbitrary power of a prince, than those which are democratically constituted. In aristocratic nations the body of the nobles and the more opulent part of the community are in themselves natural associations, which act as checks upon the abuses of power. In countries in which these associations do not exist, if private individuals are unable to create an artificial and a temporary substitute for them, I can imagine no permanent protection against the most galling tyranny ; and a great people may be oppressed by a small faction, or by a single individual, with impunity. . . .

It cannot be denied that the unrestrained liberty of association for political purposes is the privilege which a people is longest in learning how to exercise. If it does not throw the nation into anarchy, it perpetually augments the chances of that calamity. On one point, however, this perilous liberty offers a security against dangers of another kind ; in countries where associations are free, secret societies are unknown. In America there are numerous factions, but no conspiracies.

The most natural privilege of man, next to the right of acting for himself, is that of combining his exertions with those of his fellow-creatures, and of acting in common with them. I am therefore led to conclude that the right of association is almost as inalienable as the right of personal liberty. No legislator can attack it without impairing the very foundations of society. Nevertheless, if the liberty of association is a fruitful source of advantages and prosperity to some nations, it may be perverted or carried to excess by others, and the element of life may be changed into an element of destruction. A comparison of the different methods which associations pursue in those countries in which they are managed with discretion, as well as in those where liberty degenerates into licence, may perhaps be thought useful both to governments and to parties.

The greater part of Europeans look upon an association as a weapon which is to be hastily fashioned, and immediately tried in the conflict. A society is formed for discussion; but the idea of impending action prevails in the minds of those who constitute it : it is, in fact, an army ; and the time given to parley serves to reckon up the strength and to animate the courage of the host, after which they direct their march against the enemy. Resources which lie within the bounds of the law may suggest themselves to the persons who compose it as means, but never as the only means, of success.

Such, however, is not the manner in which the right of association is understood in the United States. In America the citizens who form the minority associate, in order, in the first place, to show their numerical strength, and so to diminish the moral authority of the majority ; and, in the second place, to stimulate competition, and to discover those arguments which are most fitted to act upon the majority ; for they always entertain hopes of drawing over their opponents to their own side, and of afterward disposing of the supreme power in their name. Political associations in the United States are therefore peaceable in their intentions, and strictly legal in the means which they employ; and they assert with perfect truth that they only aim at success by lawful expedients.

The difference which exists between the Americans and ourselves depends on several causes. In Europe there are numerous parties so diametrically opposed to the majority that they can never hope to acquire its support, and at the same time they think that they are sufficiently strong in themselves to struggle and to defend their cause. When a party of this kind forms an association, its object is, not to conquer, but to fight. In America the individuals who hold opinions very much opposed to those of the majority are no sort of impediment to its power, and all other parties hope to win it over to their own principles in the end. The exercise of the right of association becomes dangerous in proportion to the impossibility which excludes great parties from acquiring the majority. In a country like the United States, in which the differences of opinions are mere differences of hue, the right of association may remain unrestrained without evil consequences. The inexperience of many of the European nations in the enjoyment of liberty leads them only to look upon the liberty of association as a right of attacking the Government. The first notion which presents itself to a party, as well as to an individual, when it has acquired a consciousness of its own strength, is that of violence: the notion of persuasion arises at a later period and is only derived from experience. The English, who are divided into parties which differ most essentially from each other, rarely abuse the right of association, because they have long been accustomed to exercise it. In France the passion for war is so intense that there is no undertaking so mad, or so injurious to the welfare of the State, that a man does not consider himself honoured in defending it, at the risk of his life.

But perhaps the most powerful of the causes which tend to mitigate the excesses of political association in the United States is Universal Suffrage. In countries in which universal suffrage exists the majority is never doubtful, because neither party can pretend to represent that portion of the community which has not voted. The associations which are formed are aware, as well as the nation at large, that they do not represent the majority : this is, indeed, a condition inseparable from their existence : for if they did represent the preponderating power, they would change the law instead of soliciting its reform. The consequence of this is that the moral influence of the Government which they attack is very much increased, and their own power is very much enfeebled.

In Europe there are few associations which do not affect to represent the majority, or which do not believe that they represent it. This conviction or this pretension tends to augment their force amazingly, and contributes no less to legalize their measures. Violence may seem to be excusable in defence of the cause of oppressed right. Thus it is, in the vast labyrinth of human laws, that extreme liberty sometimes corrects the abuses of licence, and that extreme democracy obviates the dangers of democratic government. In Europe, associations consider themselves, in some degree, as the legislative and executive councils of the people, which is unable to speak for itself. In America, where they only represent **a** minority of the nation, they argue and they petition. . . .

The Americans have also established certain forms of government which are applied to their associations, but these are invariably borrowed from the forms of the civil administration. The independence of each individual is formally recognized ; the tendency of the members of the association points, as it does in the body of the community, toward the same end, but they are not obliged to follow the same track. No one abjures the exercise of his reason and his free will ; but every one exerts that reason and that will for the benefit of a common undertaking.

Chapter XII

DEMOCRATIC GOVERNMENT IN AMERICA

I AM well aware of the difficulties which attend this part of my subject, but although every expression which I am about to make use of may clash, upon some one point, with the feelings of the different parties which divide my country, I shall speak my opinion with the most perfect openness.

In Europe we are at a loss how to judge the true character and the more permanent propensities of democracy, because in Europe two conflicting principles exist, and we do not know what to attribute to the principles themselves, and what to refer to the passions which they bring into collision. Such, however, is not the case in America ; there the people reigns without any obstacle, and it has no perils to dread and no injuries to avenge. In America, democracy is swayed by its own free propensities ; its course is natural and its activity is unrestrained ; the United States consequently afford the most favourable opportunity of studying its real character. . . .

I have already observed that universal suffrage has been adopted in all the States of the Union [1] ; it consequently occurs among different populations which occupy very different positions in the scale of society. I have had opportunities of observing its effects in different localities, and among races of men who are nearly strangers to each other by their language, their religion, and their manner of life ; in Louisiana as well as in New England, in Georgia and in Canada. I have remarked that universal

[1] Not, of course, universal suffrage as the term is understood today. Universal white male suffrage had been substantially achieved, though some States still retained minor qualifications.—H. S. C.

suffrage is far from producing in America either all the good or all the evil consequences which are assigned to it in Europe, and that its effects differ very widely from those which are usually attributed to it.

Many people in Europe are apt to believe without saying it, or to say without believing it, that one of the great advantages of universal suffrage is, that it intrusts the direction of public affairs to men who are worthy of the public confidence. They admit that the people is unable to govern for itself, but they aver that it is always sincerely disposed to promote the welfare of the State, and that it instinctively designates those persons who are animated by the same good wishes, and who are the most fit to wield the supreme authority. I confess that the observations I made in America by no means coincide with these opinions. On my arrival in the United States I was surprised to find so much distinguished talent among the subjects, and so little among the heads of the Government. It is a well-authenticated fact, that at the present day the most able men in the United States are very rarely placed at the head of affairs ; and it must be acknowledged that such has been the result in proportion as democracy has outstepped all its former limits. The race of American statesmen has evidently dwindled most remarkably in the course of the last fifty years.[1]

Several causes may be assigned to this phenomenon. It is impossible, notwithstanding the most strenuous exertions, to raise the intelligence of the people above a certain level. Whatever may be the facilities of acquiring information, whatever may be the pro-

[1] When Tocqueville wrote, Jackson was in the White House, Webster, Clay, Calhoun and J. Q. Adams in the Congress.—H. S. C.

fusion of easy methods and of cheap science, the human mind can never be instructed and educated without devoting a considerable space of time to those objects.

The greater or the lesser possibility of subsisting without labour is therefore the necessary boundary of intellectual improvement. This boundary is more remote in some countries and more restricted in others ; but it must exist somewhere as long as the people is constrained to work in order to procure the means of physical subsistence, that is to say, as long as it retains its popular character. It is therefore quite as difficult to imagine a State in which all the citizens should be very well informed as a State in which they all should be wealthy ; these two difficulties may be looked upon as correlative. It may very readily be admitted that the mass of the citizens are sincerely disposed to promote the welfare of their country ; nay more, it even may be allowed that the lower classes are less apt to be swayed by considerations of personal interest than the higher orders : but it is always more or less impossible for them to discern the best means of attaining the end which they desire with sincerity. Long and patient observation, joined to a multitude of different notions, is required to form a just estimate of the character of a single individual ; and can it be supposed that the vulgar have the power of succeeding in an inquiry which misleads the penetration of genius itself ? The people has neither the time nor the means which are essential to the prosecution of an investigation of this kind : its conclusions are hastily formed from a superficial inspection of the more prominent features of a question. Hence it often assents to the clamour of a mountebank who knows the secret of stimulating its tastes, while its truest friends frequently fail in their exertions.

Moreover, the democracy is not only deficient in that soundness of judgment which is necessary to select men really deserving of its confidence, but it has neither the desire nor the inclination to find them out. It cannot be denied that democratic institutions have a very strong tendency to promote the feeling of envy in the human heart; not so much because they afford to every one the means of rising to the level of any of his fellow-citizens, as because those means perpetually disappoint the persons who employ them. Democratic institutions awaken and foster a passion for equality which they can never entirely satisfy. This complete equality eludes the grasp of the people at the very moment at which it thinks to hold it fast, and "flies," as Pascal says, "with eternal flight"; the people is excited in the pursuit of an advantage, which is more precious because it is not sufficiently remote to be unknown, or sufficiently near to be enjoyed. The lower orders are agitated by the chance of success, they are irritated by its uncertainty; and they pass from the enthusiasm of pursuit to the exhaustion of ill success, and lastly to the acrimony of disappointment. Whatever transcends their own limits appears to be an obstacle to their desires, and there is no kind of superiority, however legitimate it may be, which is not irksome in their sight. . . .

In the United States the people is not disposed to hate the superior classes of society; but it is not very favourably inclined toward them, and it carefully excludes them from the exercise of authority. It does not entertain any dread of distinguished talents, but it is rarely captivated by them; and it awards its approbation very sparingly to such as have risen without the popular support.

While the natural propensities of democracy induce the people to reject the most distinguished citizens as its rulers, these individuals are no less apt to retire from a political career in which it is almost impossible to retain their independence, or to advance without degrading themselves. This opinion has been very candidly set forth by Chancellor Kent, who says, in speaking with great eulogiums of that part of the Constitution which empowers the Executive to nominate the judges : " It is indeed probable that the men who are best fitted to discharge the duties of this high office would have too much reserve in their manners, and too much austerity in their principles, for them to be returned by the majority at an election where universal suffrage is adopted." Such were the opinions which were printed without contradiction in America in the year 1830.

I hold it to be sufficiently demonstrated that universal suffrage is by no means a guarantee of the wisdom of the popular choice ; and that, whatever its advantages may be, this is not one of them.

When a State is threatened by serious dangers, the people frequently succeeds in selecting the citizens who are the most able to save it. It has been observed that man rarely retains his customary level in presence of very critical circumstances ; he rises above or he sinks below his usual condition, and the same thing occurs in nations at large. Extreme perils sometimes quench the energy of a people instead of stimulating it ; they excite without directing its passions, and instead of clearing they confuse its powers of perception. The Jews deluged the smoking ruins of their temple with the carnage of the remnant of their host. But it is more common, both in the case of nations and in that of individuals, to find extraordinary virtues arising from the very imminence of the danger. Great characters are then thrown into relief, as edifices which are concealed by the gloom of night are illuminated by the glare of a conflagration. At those dangerous times genius no longer abstains from presenting itself in the arena ; and the people, alarmed by the perils of its situation, buries its envious passions in a short oblivion. Great names may then be drawn from the balloting-box. . . .

There are certain laws of a democratic nature which contribute to correct, in some measure, the dangerous tendencies of democracy. On entering the House of Representatives at Washington one is struck by the vulgar demeanour of that great assembly. The eye frequently does not discover a man of celebrity within its walls. Its members are almost all obscure individuals whose names present no associations to the mind : they are mostly village lawyers, men in trade, or even persons belonging to the lower classes of society. In a country in which education is very general, it is said that the representatives of the people do not always know how to write correctly.

At a few yards' distance from this spot is the door of the Senate, which contains within a small space a large proportion of the celebrated men of America. Scarcely an individual is to be perceived in it who does not recall the idea of an active and illustrious career : the Senate is composed of eloquent advocates, distinguished generals, wise magistrates, and statesmen of note, whose language would at all times do honour to the most remarkable parliamentary debates of Europe.

What, then, is the cause of this strange contrast, and why are the most able citizens to be found in one assembly rather than in the other ? Why is the former body remarkable for its vulgarity and its poverty of talent, while the latter seems to enjoy a monopoly of intelligence and of sound judgment ? Both of these assemblies emanate from the people ;

both of them are chosen by universal suffrage; and no voice has hitherto been heard to assert in America that the Senate is hostile to the interests of the people. From what cause, then, does so startling a difference arise? The only reason which appears to me adequately to account for it is, that the House of Representatives is elected by the populace directly, and that the Senate is elected by elected bodies.[1] The whole body of the citizens names the legislature of each State, and the Federal Constitution converts these legislatures into so many electoral bodies, which return the members of the Senate. The senators are elected by an indirect application of universal suffrage; for the legislatures which name them are not aristocratic or privileged bodies which exercise the electoral franchise in their own right; but they are chosen by the totality of the citizens; they are generally elected every year, and new members may constantly be chosen who will employ their electoral rights in conformity with the wishes of the public. But this transmission of the popular authority through an assembly of chosen men operates an important change in it, by refining its discretion and improving the forms which it adopts. Men who are chosen in this manner accurately represent the majority of the nation which governs them; but they represent the elevated thoughts which are current in the community, the propensities which prompt its nobler actions, rather than the petty passions which disturb or the vices which disgrace it.

The time already may be anticipated at which the American republics will be obliged to introduce the

[1] It may be observed that there was no perceptible decline in the quality of Senators or the prestige of the Senate with the inauguration of popular election in 1913. —H. S. C.

plan of election by an elected body more frequently into their system of representation, or they will incur no small risk of perishing miserably among the shoals of democracy. . . .

When elections recur at long intervals the State is exposed to violent agitation every time they take place. Parties exert themselves to the utmost in order to gain a prize which is so rarely within their reach ; and as the evil is almost irremediable for the candidates who fail, the consequences of their disappointed ambition may prove most disastrous : if, on the other hand, the legal struggle can be repeated within a short space of time, the defeated parties take patience. When elections occur frequently, their recurrence keeps society in a perpetual state of feverish excitement, and imparts a continual instability to public affairs.

Thus, on the one hand, the State is exposed to the perils of a revolution, on the other to perpetual mutability ; the former system threatens the very existence of the Government, the latter is an obstacle to all steady and consistent policy. The Americans have preferred the second of these evils to the first ; but they were led to this conclusion by their instinct much more than by their reason ; for a taste for variety is one of the characteristic passions of democracy. An extraordinary mutability has, by this means, been introduced into their legislation. Many of the Americans consider the instability of their laws as a necessary consequence of a system whose general results are beneficial. But no one in the United States affects to deny the fact of this instability, or to contend that it is not a great evil.

Hamilton, after having demonstrated the utility of a power which might prevent, or which might at least impede, the promulgation of bad laws, adds :

' It might perhaps be said that the power of preventing bad laws includes that of preventing good ones, and may be used to the one purpose as well as to the other. But this objection will have little weight with those who can properly estimate the mischiefs of that inconstancy and mutability in the laws which form the greatest blemish in the character and genius of our governments ' (*The Federalist*, No. 73). And again in No. 62 of the same work he observes : ' The facility and excess of law-making seem to be the diseases to which our governments are most liable. . . . The mischievous effects of the mutability in the public councils arising from a rapid succession of new members would fill a volume : every new election in the States is found to change one half of the representatives. From this change of men must proceed a change of opinions and of measures, which forfeits the respect and confidence of other nations, poisons the blessings of liberty itself, and diminishes the attachment and reverence of the people toward a political system which betrays so many marks of infirmity.' . . .

Public officers in the United States are commingled with the crowd of citizens ; they have neither palaces, nor guards, nor ceremonial costumes. This simple exterior of the persons in authority is connected not only with the peculiarities of the American character, but with the fundamental principles of that society. In the estimation of the democracy a government is not a benefit, but a necessary evil. A certain degree of power must be granted to public officers, for they would be of no use without it. But the ostensible semblance of authority is by no means indispensable to the conduct of affairs, and it is needlessly offensive to the susceptibility of the public. The public officers themselves are well aware that they only enjoy the superiority over their fellow-citizens which they derive from their authority upon condition of putting themselves on a level with the whole community by their manners. A public officer in the United States is uniformly civil, accessible to all the world, attentive to all requests, and obliging in his replies. I was pleased by these characteristics of a democratic government ; and I was struck by the manly independence of the citizens, who respect the office more than the officer, and who are less attached to the emblems of authority than to the man who bears them.

I am inclined to believe that the influence which costumes really exercise, in an age like that in which we live, has been a good deal exaggerated. I never perceived that a public officer in America was the less respected while he was in the discharge of his duties because his own merit was set off by no adventitious signs. On the other hand, it is very doubtful whether a peculiar dress contributes to the respect which public characters ought to have for their own position, at least when they are not otherwise inclined to respect it. When a magistrate (and in France such instances are not rare) indulges his trivial wit at the expense of the prisoner, or derides the predicament in which a culprit is placed, it would be well to deprive him of his robes of office, to see whether he would recall some portion of the natural dignity of mankind when he is reduced to the apparel of a private citizen.

A democracy may, however, allow a certain show of magisterial pomp, and clothe its officers in silks and gold, without seriously compromising its principles. Privileges of this kind are transitory ; they belong to the place, and are distinct from the individual : but if public officers are not uniformly remunerated by the State, the public charges must be intrusted to men of opulence and independence, who constitute the basis of an aristocracy ; and if the people still retains its right of election, that election can only be made from a certain class of citizens. When a democratic republic renders offices which had formerly been remunerated gratuitous, it may safely be believed that the State is advancing to monarchical institutions ; and when a monarchy begins to remunerate such officers as had hitherto been unpaid, it is a sure sign that it is approaching toward a despotic or a republican form of government. The substitution of paid for unpaid functionaries is of itself, in my opinion, sufficient to constitute a serious revolution.

I look upon the entire absence of gratuitous functionaries in America as one of the most prominent signs of the absolute dominion which democracy exercises in that country. All public services, of whatsoever nature they may be, are paid ; so that every one has not merely the right, but also the means of performing them. Although, in democratic States, all the citizens are qualified to occupy stations in the Government, all are not tempted to try for them. The number and the capacities of the candidates are more apt to restrict the choice of electors than the conditions of the candidateship.

In nations in which the principle of election extends to every place in the State no political career can, properly speaking, be said to exist. Men are promoted as if by chance to the rank which they enjoy, and they are by no means sure of retaining it. The consequence is that in tranquil times public functions offer but few lures to ambition. In the United States the persons who engage in the perplexities of political life are individuals of very moderate pretensions.

The pursuit of wealth generally diverts men of great talents and of great passions from the pursuit of power, and it very frequently happens that a man does not undertake to direct the fortune of the State until he has discovered his incompetence to conduct his own affairs. The vast number of very ordinary men who occupy public stations is quite as attributable to these causes as to the bad choice of the democracy. In the United States, I am not sure that the people would return the men of superior abilities who might solicit its support, but it is certain that men of this description do not come forward.

In two different kinds of government the magistrates exercise a considerable degree of arbitrary power ; namely, under the absolute government of a single individual, and under that of a democracy. This identical result proceeds from causes which are nearly analogous.

In despotic States the fortune of no citizen is secure ; and public officers are not more safe than private individuals. The sovereign, who has under his control the lives, the property, and sometimes the honour of the men whom he employs, does not scruple to allow them a great latitude of action, because he is convinced that they will not use it to his prejudice. In despotic States the sovereign is so attached to the exercise of his power that he dislikes the constraint even of his own regulations ; and he is well pleased that his agents should follow a somewhat fortuitous line of conduct, provided he be certain that their actions will never counteract his desires.

In democracies, as the majority has every year the right of depriving the officers whom it has appointed of their power, it has no reason to fear any abuse of their authority. As the people is always able to signify its wishes to those who conduct the Government, it prefers leaving them to make their own exertions to prescribing an invariable rule of conduct which would at once fetter their activity and the popular authority.

It may even be observed, on attentive consideration, that under the rule of a democracy the arbitrary power of the magistrate must be still greater than in despotic States. In the latter the sovereign has the power of punishing all the faults with which he becomes acquainted, but it would be vain for him to hope to become acquainted with all those which are committed. In the former the sovereign power is not only supreme, but it is universally present. The American functionaries are, in point of fact, much more independent in the sphere of action which the law traces out for them than any public officer in Europe. Very frequently the object which they are to accomplish is simply pointed out to them, and the choice of the means is left to their own discretion. . . .

Nowhere has so much been left by the law to the arbitrary determination of the magistrate as in democratic republics, because this arbitrary power is unattended by any alarming consequences. It even may be asserted that the freedom of the magistrate increases as the elective franchise is extended, and as the duration of the time of office is shortened. Hence arises the great difficulty which attends the conversion of a democratic republic into a monarchy. The magistrate ceases to be elective, but he retains the rights and the habits of an elected officer, which lead directly to despotism.

It is only in limited monarchies that the law, which prescribes the sphere in which public officers are to act, superintends all their measures. The cause of this may be easily detected. In limited monarchies the power is divided between the king and the people, both of whom are interested in the stability of the magistrate. The king does not venture to place the public officers under the control of the people, lest they should be tempted to betray his interests ; on the other hand, the people fears lest the magistrates should serve to oppress the liberties of the country, if they were entirely dependent upon the Crown ; they cannot, therefore, be said to depend on either the one or the other. The same cause which induces the king and the people to render public officers independent suggests the necessity of such securities as may prevent their independence from encroaching upon the authority of the former and the liberties of the latter. They consequently agree as to the necessity of restricting the functionary to a line of conduct laid down beforehand, and they are interested in confining him by certain regulations which he cannot evade.

The authority which public men possess in America is so brief, and they are so soon commingled with the ever-changing population of the country, that the acts of a community frequently leave fewer traces than the occurrences of a private family. The public administration is, so to speak, oral and traditionary. But little is committed to writing, and that little is wafted away forever, like the leaves of the Sibyl, by the smallest breeze. . . .

The instability of the administration has penetrated into the habits of the people : it even appears to suit the general taste, and no one cares for what occurred before his time. No methodical system is pursued ; no archives are formed ; and no documents are brought together when it would be very easy to do so. Where they exist, little store is set upon them ; and I have among my papers several original public documents which were given to me in answer to some of my inquiries. In America society seems to live from hand to mouth, like an army in the field. Nevertheless, the art of administration may undoubtedly be ranked as a science, and no sciences can be improved if the discoveries and observations of successive generations are not connected together in the order in which they occur. . . . But the persons who conduct the administration in America can seldom afford any instruction to each other ; and when they assume the direction of society, they simply possess those attainments which are most widely disseminated in the community, and no experience peculiar to themselves. Democracy, carried to its furthest limits, is therefore prejudicial to the art of government ; and for this reason it is better adapted to a people already versed in the conduct of an administration than to a nation which is uninitiated in public affairs.

This remark, indeed, is not exclusively applicable to the science of administration. Although a democratic government is founded upon a very simple and natural principle, it always presupposes the existence of a high degree of culture and enlightenment in society. At the first glance it may be imagined to belong to the earliest ages of the world ; but maturer observation will convince us that it could only come last in the succession of human history.

Before we can affirm whether a democratic form of government is economical or not, we must establish a suitable standard of comparison. The question would be one of easy solution if we were to attempt to draw a parallel between a democratic republic and an absolute monarchy. The public expenditure would be found to be more considerable under the former than under the latter ; such is the case with all free States compared to those which are not so. It is certain that despotism ruins individuals by preventing them from producing wealth, much more than by depriving them of the wealth they have produced ; it dries up the source of riches, while it usually respects acquired property. Freedom, on the contrary, engenders far more benefits than it destroys ; and the nations which are favoured by free institutions invariably find that their resources increase even more rapidly than their taxes.

My present object is to compare free nations to each other, and to point out the influence of democracy upon the finances of a State.

Communities, as well as organic bodies, are subject to certain fixed rules in their formation which they cannot evade. They are composed of certain elements which are common to them at all times and under all circumstances. The people may always be mentally divided into three distinct classes. The first of these classes consists of the wealthy ; the second, of those who are in easy circumstances ; and the third is composed of those who have little or no property, and who subsist more especially by the work which they perform for the two superior orders. The proportion of the individuals who are included in these three divisions may vary according to the condition of society, but the divisions themselves can never be obliterated.

It is evident that each of these classes will exercise an influence peculiar to its own propensities upon the administration of the finances of the State. If the first of the three exclusively possesses the legislative power, it is probable that it will not be sparing of the public funds, because the taxes which are levied on a large fortune only tend to diminish the sum of superfluous enjoyment, and are, in point of fact, but little felt. If the second class has the power of making the laws, it will certainly not be lavish of taxes, because nothing is so onerous as a large impost which is levied upon a small income. The government of the middle classes appears to me to be the most economical, though perhaps not the most enlightened, and certainly not the most generous, of free governments.

But let us now suppose that the legislative authority is vested in the lowest orders : there are two striking reasons which show that the tendency of the expenditure will be to increase, not to diminish. As the great majority of those who create the laws are possessed of no property upon which taxes can be imposed, all the money which is spent for the community appears to be spent for their advantage, at no cost of their own ; and those who are possessed of some little property readily find means of regulating the taxes so that they are burdensome to the wealthy and profitable to the poor, although the rich are unable to take the same advantage when they are in possession of the Government.

In countries in which the poor should be exclusively invested with the power of making the laws no great economy of public expenditure ought to be expected : that expenditure will always be considerable ; either because the taxes do not weigh upon those who levy them, or because they are levied in such a manner as not to weigh upon those classes. In other words, the government of the democracy is the only one under which the power which lays on taxes escapes the payment of them.

It may be objected (but the argument has no real weight) that the true interest of the people is indissolubly connected with that of the wealthier portion of the community, since it cannot but suffer by the severe measures to which it resorts. But is it not the true interest of kings to render their subjects happy, and the true interest of nobles to admit recruits into their order on suitable grounds? If remote advantages had power to prevail over the passions and the exigencies of the moment, no such thing as a tyrannical sovereign or an exclusive aristocracy could ever exist.

Again, it may be objected that the poor are never invested with the sole power of making the laws; but I reply, that wherever universal suffrage has been established the majority of the community unquestionably exercises the legislative authority; and if it be proved that the poor always constitute the majority, it may be added, with perfect truth, that in the countries in which they possess the elective franchise they possess the sole power of making laws. But it is certain that in all the nations of the world the greater number has always consisted of those persons who hold no property, or of those whose property is insufficient to exempt them from the necessity of working in order to procure an easy subsistence. Universal suffrage does therefore, in point of fact, invest the poor with the government of society.

The disastrous influence which popular authority may sometimes exercise upon the finances of a State was very clearly seen in some of the democratic republics of antiquity, in which the public treasure was exhausted in order to relieve indigent citizens, or to supply the games and theatrical amusements of the populace. It is true that the representative system was then very imperfectly known, and that, at the present time, the influence of popular passion is less felt in the conduct of public affairs; but it may be believed that the delegate will in the end conform to the principles of his constituents, and favour their propensities as much as their interests.

The extravagance of democracy is, however, less to be dreaded in proportion as the people acquires a share of property, because on the one hand the contributions of the rich are then less needed, and, on the other, it is more difficult to lay on taxes which do not affect the interests of the lower classes. On this account universal suffrage would be less dangerous in France than in England, because in the latter country the property on which taxes may be levied is vested in fewer hands. America, where the great majority of the citizens possess some fortune, is in a still more favourable position than France.

There are still further causes which may increase the sum of public expenditure in democratic countries. When the aristocracy governs, the individuals who conduct the affairs of State are exempted by their own station in society from every kind of privation ; they are contented with their position ; power and renown are the objects for which they strive ; and, as they are placed far above the obscurer throng of citizens, they do not always distinctly perceive how the well-being of the mass of the people ought to redound to their own honour. They are not indeed callous to the sufferings of the poor, but they cannot feel those miseries as acutely as if they were themselves partakers of them. Provided that the people appear to submit to its lot, the rulers are satisfied, and they demand nothing further from the Government. An aristocracy is more intent upon the means of maintaining its influence than upon the means of improving its condition.

When, on the contrary, the people is invested with the supreme authority, the perpetual sense of their own miseries impels the rulers of society to seek for perpetual ameliorations. A thousand different objects are subjected to improvement ; the most trivial details are sought out as susceptible of amendment ; and those changes which are accompanied with considerable expense are more especially advocated, since the object is to render the condition of the poor more tolerable, who cannot pay for themselves.

Moreover, all democratic communities are agitated by an ill-defined excitement and by a kind of feverish impatience, that engender a multitude of innovations, almost all of which are attended with expense.

In monarchies and aristocracies the natural taste which the rulers have for power and for renown is stimulated by the promptings of ambition, and they are frequently incited by these temptations to very costly undertakings. In democracies, where the rulers labour under privations, they can only be courted by such means as improve their well-being, and these improvements cannot take place without a sacrifice of money. When a people begins to reflect upon its situation, it discovers a multitude of wants to which it had not before been subject, and to satisfy these exigencies recourse must be had to the coffers of the State. Hence it arises that the public charges increase in proportion as civilization spreads, and that imposts are augmented as knowledge pervades the community.

The last cause which frequently renders a democratic government dearer than any other is, that a democracy does not always succeed in moderating its expenditure, because it does not understand the art of being economical. As the designs which it entertains are frequently changed, and the agents of those designs are still more frequently removed, its undertakings are often ill conducted or left unfinished : in the former case the State spends sums out of all proportion to the end which it proposes to accomplish ; in the second, the expense itself is unprofitable.

There is a powerful reason which usually induces democracies to economize upon the salaries of public officers. As the number of citizens who dispense the remuneration is extremely large in democratic countries, so the number of persons who can hope to be benefited by the receipt of it is comparatively small. In aristocratic countries, on the contrary, the individuals who fix high salaries have almost always a vague hope of profiting by them. These appointments may be looked upon as a capital which they create for their own use, or at least as a resource for their children.

It must be allowed, however, that a democratic State is most parsimonious toward its principal agents. In America the secondary officers are much better paid, and the dignitaries of the administration much worse, than they are elsewhere.

These opposite effects result from the same cause ; the people fixes the salaries of the public officers in both cases ; and the scale of remuneration is determined by the consideration of its own wants. It is held to be fair that the servants of the public should be placed in the same easy circumstances as the public itself ; but when the question turns upon the salaries of the great officers of State, this rule fails, and chance alone can guide the popular decision. The poor have no adequate conception of the wants which the higher classes of society may feel. The sum which is scanty to the rich appears enormous to the poor man whose wants do not extend beyond the necessaries of life ; and in his estimation the Governor of a State, with his two or three hundred [pounds] a year, is a very fortunate and enviable being. If you undertake to convince him that the representative of a great people ought to be able to maintain some show of splendour in the eyes of foreign nations, he will perhaps assent to your meaning ; but when he reflects on his own humble dwelling, and on the hard-earned produce of his wearisome toil, he remembers all that he could do with a salary which you say is insufficient, and he is startled or almost frightened at the sight of such uncommon wealth. Besides, the secondary public officer is almost on a level with the people, while the others are raised above it. The former may therefore excite his interest, but the latter begins to arouse his envy. This is very clearly seen in the United States, where the salaries seem to decrease as the authority of those who receive them augments.

Under the rule of an aristocracy it frequently happens, on the contrary, that while the high officers are receiving munificent salaries, the inferior ones have not more than enough to procure the necessaries of life. The reason of this fact is easily discoverable from causes very analogous to those to which I have just alluded. If a democracy is unable to conceive the pleasures of the rich or to witness them without envy, an aristocracy is slow to understand, or, to speak more correctly, is unacquainted with, the privations of the poor. The poor man is not (if we use the term aright) the fellow of the rich one ; but he is a being of another species. An aristocracy is therefore apt to care but little for the fate of its subordinate agents ; and their salaries are only raised when they refuse to perform their service for too scanty a remuneration.

It is the parsimonious conduct of democracy toward its principal officers that has countenanced a supposition of far more economical propensities than any which it really possesses. It is true that it scarcely allows the means of honourable subsistence to the individuals who conduct its affairs ; but enormous sums are lavished to meet the exigencies or to facilitate the enjoyments of the people. The money raised by taxation may be better employed, but it is not saved. In general, democracy gives largely to the community, and very sparingly to those who govern it. The reverse is the case on aristocratic countries, where the money of the State is expended to the profit of the persons who are at the head of affairs.

We are liable to frequent errors in the research of those facts which exercise a serious influence upon the fate of mankind, since nothing is more difficult than to appreciate their real value. One people is naturally inconsistent and enthusiastic ; another is sober and calculating ; and these characteristics originate in their physical constitution or in remote causes with which we are unacquainted.

There are nations which are fond of parade and the bustle of festivity, and which do not regret the costly gaieties of an hour. Others, on the contrary, are attached to more retiring pleasures, and seem almost ashamed of appearing to be pleased. In some countries the highest value is set upon the beauty of public edifices ; in others the productions of art are treated with indifference, and everything which is unproductive is looked down upon with contempt. In some renown, in others money, is the ruling passion.

Independently of the laws, all these causes concur to exercise a very powerful influence upon the conduct of the finances of the State. If the Americans never spend the money of the people in galas, it is not only because the imposition of taxes is under the control of the people, but because the people takes no delight in public rejoicings. If they repudiate all ornament from their architecture, and set no store on any but the more practical and homely advantages, it is not only because they live under democratic institutions, but because they are a commercial nation. The habits of private life are continued in public ; and we ought carefully to distinguish that economy which depends upon their institutions from that which is the natural result of their manners and customs. . . .

On casting my eyes over the different republics which form the confederation, I perceive that their Governments lack perseverance in their undertakings, and that they exercise no steady control over the men whom they employ. Whence I naturally infer that they must often spend the money of the people to no purpose, or consume more of it than is really necessary to their undertakings. Great efforts are made, in accordance with the democratic origin of society, to satisfy the exigencies of the lower orders, to open the career of power to their endeavours, and to diffuse knowledge and comfort among them. The poor are maintained, immense sums are annually devoted to public instruction, all services whatsoever are remunerated, and the most subordinate agents are liberally paid. If this kind of government appears to me to be useful and rational, I am nevertheless constrained to admit that it is expensive.

Wherever the poor direct public affairs and dispose of the national resources, it appears certain that, as they profit by the expenditure of the State, they are apt to augment that expenditure.

I conclude, therefore, . . . that the democratic government of the Americans is not a cheap government, as is sometimes asserted ; and I have no hesitation in predicting that, if the people of the United States is ever involved in serious difficulties, its taxation will speedily be increased to the rate of that which prevails in the greater part of the aristocracies and the monarchies of Europe. . . .

It is difficult to say what degree of exertion a democratic government may be capable of making at a crisis in the history of the nation. But no great democratic republic has hitherto existed in the world. To style the oligarchy which ruled over France in 1793 by that name would be to offer an insult to the republican form of government. The United States afford the first example of the kind.

The American Union has now subsisted for half a century, in the course of which time its existence has only once been attacked, namely, during the War of Independence. At the commencement of that long war, various occurrences took place which betokened an extraordinary zeal for the service of the country. But as the contest was prolonged, symptoms of private egotism began to show themselves. No money was poured into the public treasury ; few recruits could be raised to join the army ; the people wished to acquire independence, but was very ill disposed to undergo the privations by which alone it could be obtained. 'Tax laws,' says Hamilton in *The Federalist* (No. 12), ' have in vain been multiplied ; new methods to enforce the collection have in vain been tried ; the public expectation has been uniformly disappointed and the treasuries of the States have remained empty. The popular system of administration inherent in the nature of popular government, coinciding with the real scarcity of money incident to a languid and mutilated state of trade, has hitherto defeated every experiment for extensive collections, and has at length taught the different legislatures the folly of attempting them.'

The United States have not had any serious war to carry on since that period. In order, therefore, to appreciate the sacrifices which democratic nations may impose upon themselves, we must wait until the American people is obliged to put half its entire income at the disposal of the Government, as was done by the English ; or until it sends forth a twentieth part of its population to the field of battle, as was done by France. . . .

We have seen that the Federal Constitution intrusts the permanent direction of the external interests of the nation to the President and the Senate, which tends in some degree to detach the general foreign policy of the Union from the control of the people. It cannot therefore be asserted with truth that the external affairs of State are conducted by the democracy.

The policy of America owes its rise to Washington, and after him to Jefferson, who established those principles which it observes at the present day. . . .

Washington . . . succeeded in maintaining his country in a state of peace while all the other nations of the globe were at war ; and he laid it down as a fundamental doctrine, that the true interest of the Americans consisted in a perfect neutrality with regard to the internal dissensions of the European Powers.

Jefferson went still further, and introduced a maxim into the policy of the Union which affirms that ' the Americans ought never to solicit any privileges from foreign nations, in order not to be obliged to grant similar privileges themselves.'

These two principles, which were so plain and so just as to be adapted to the capacity of the populace, have greatly simplified the foreign policy of the United States. As the Union takes no part in the affairs of Europe, it has, properly speaking, no foreign interests to discuss, since it has at present no powerful neighbours on the American continent. The country is as much removed from the passions of the Old World by its position as by the line of policy which it has chosen, and it is neither called upon to repudiate nor to espouse the conflicting interests of Europe ; while the dissensions of the New World are still concealed within the bosom of the future.

The Union is free from all pre-existing obligations, and it is consequently enabled to profit by the experience of the old nations of Europe, without being obliged, as they are, to make the best of the past, and to adapt it to their present circumstances ; or to accept that immense inheritance which they derive from their forefathers — an inheritance of glory mingled with calamities, and of alliances conflicting with national antipathies. The foreign policy of the United States is reduced by its very nature to await the chances of the future history of the nation, and for the present it consists more in abstaining from interference than in exerting its activity.

It is therefore very difficult to ascertain at present what degree of sagacity the American democracy will display in the conduct of the foreign policy of the country ; and upon this point its adversaries, as well as its advocates, must suspend their judgment. As for myself, I have no hesitation in avowing my conviction that it is most especially in the conduct of foreign relations that democratic governments appear to me to be decidedly inferior to governments carried on upon different principles. Experience, instruction, and habit may almost always succeed in creating a species of practical discretion in democracies, and that science of the daily occurrences of life which is called good sense. Good sense may suffice to direct the ordinary course of society ; and among a people whose education has been provided for, the advantages of democratic liberty in the internal affairs of the country may more than compensate for the evils inherent in a democratic government. But such is not always the case in the mutual relations of foreign nations.

Foreign politics demand scarcely any of those qualities which a democracy possesses ; and they require, on the contrary, the perfect use of almost all those faculties in which it is deficient. Democracy is favourable to the increase of the internal resources of the State ; it tends to diffuse a moderate independence ; it promotes the growth of public spirit, and fortifies the respect which is entertained for law in all classes of society ; and these are advantages which only exercise an indirect influence over the relations which one people bears to another. But a democracy is unable to regulate the details of an important undertaking, to persevere in a design, and to work out its execution in the presence of serious obstacles. It cannot combine its measures with secrecy, and it will not await their consequences with patience. These are qualities which more especially belong to an individual or to an aristocracy ; and they are precisely the means by which an individual people attains to a predominant position.

If, on the contrary, we observe the natural defects of aristocracy, we shall find that their influence is comparatively innoxious in the direction of the external affairs of a State. The capital fault of which aristocratic bodies may be accused is that they are more apt to contrive their own advantage than that of the mass of the people. In foreign politics it is rare for the interest of the aristocracy to be in any way distinct from that of the people.

The propensity which democracies have to obey the impulse of passion rather than the suggestions of prudence, and to abandon a mature design for the gratification of a momentary caprice, was very clearly seen in America on the breaking out of the French

Revolution. It was then as evident to the simplest capacity as it is at the present time that the interest of the Americans forbade them to take any part in the contest which was about to deluge Europe with blood, but which could by no means injure the welfare of their own country. Nevertheless, the sympathies of the people declared themselves with so much violence in behalf of France that nothing but the inflexible character of Washington, and the immense popularity which he enjoyed, could have prevented the Americans from declaring war against England. And even then, the exertions which the austere reason of that great man made to repress the generous but imprudent passions of his fellow-citizens very nearly deprived him of the sole recompense which he had ever claimed — that of his country's love. The majority then reprobated the line of policy which he adopted, and which has since been unanimously approved by the nation. If the Constitution and the favour of the public had not intrusted the direction of the foreign affairs of the country to Washington, it is certain that the American nation would at that time have taken the very measures which it now condemns. . . .

Chapter XIII

THE REAL ADVANTAGES THAT AMERICAN SOCIETY
DERIVES FROM DEMOCRATIC GOVERNMENT

BEFORE I enter upon the subject of the present chapter I am induced to remind the reader of what I have more than once adverted to in the course of this book. The political institutions of the United States appear to me to be one of the forms of government which a democracy may adopt ; but I do not regard the American Constitution as the best, or as the only one, which a democratic people may establish. In showing the advantages which the Americans derive from the government of democracy, I am therefore very far from meaning, or from believing, that similar advantages can only be obtained from the same laws.

The defects and the weaknesses of a democratic government may be discovered very readily ; they are demonstrated by the most flagrant instances, while its beneficial influence is less perceptibly exercised. A single glance suffices to detect its evil consequences, but its good qualities can only be discerned by long observation. The laws of the American democracy are frequently defective or incomplete ; they sometimes attack vested rights, or give a sanction to others which are dangerous to the community ; but even if they were good, the frequent changes which they undergo would be an evil. How comes it, then, that the American republics prosper and maintain their position ?

In the consideration of laws a distinction must be carefully observed between the end at which they aim and the means by which they are directed to that end, between their absolute and their relative excellence. If it be the intention of the legislator to favour the interests of the minority at the expense of the majority, and if the measures he takes are so combined as to accomplish the object he has in view with the least possible expense of time and exertion, the law may be well drawn up, although its purpose be bad ; and the more efficacious it is, the greater is the mischief which it causes.

Democratic laws generally tend to promote the welfare of the greatest possible number ; for they emanate from the majority of the citizens, who are subject to error, but who cannot have an interest opposed to their own advantage. The laws of an aristocracy tend, on the contrary, to concentrate wealth and power in the hands of the minority, because an aristocracy, by its very nature, constitutes a minority. It therefore may be asserted, as a general proposition, that the purpose of a democracy in the conduct of its legislation is useful to a greater number of citizens than that of an aristocracy. This is, however, the sum total of its advantages.

Aristocracies are infinitely more expert in the science of legislation than democracies ever can be. They are possessed of a self-control which protects them from the errors of temporary excitement, and they form lasting designs which they mature with the assistance of favourable opportunities. Aristocratic government proceeds with the dexterity of art ; it understands how to make the collective force of all its laws converge at the same time to a given point. Such is not the case with democracies, whose laws are almost always ineffective or inopportune. The means of democracy are therefore more imperfect than those of aristocracy, and the measures which it unwittingly adopts are frequently opposed to its own cause ; but the object it has in view is more useful.

Let us now imagine a community so organized by

nature, or by its constitution, that it can support the transitory action of bad laws, and that it can await, without destruction, the general tendency of the legislation : we shall then be able to conceive that a democratic government, notwithstanding its defects, will be most fitted to conduce to the prosperity of this community. This is precisely what has occurred in the United States ; and I repeat, what I have before remarked, that the great advantage of the Americans consists in their being able to commit faults which they may afterward repair.

An analogous observation may be made respecting public officers. It is easy to perceive that the American democracy frequently errs in the choice of the individuals to whom it intrusts the power of the administration ; but it is more difficult to say why the State prospers under their rule. In the first place, it is to be remarked that if in a democratic State the governors have less honesty and less capacity than elsewhere, the governed, on the other hand, are more enlightened and more attentive to their interests. As the people in democracies is more incessantly vigilant in its affairs and more jealous of its rights, it prevents its representatives from abandoning that general line of conduct which its own interest prescribes. In the second place, it must be remembered that if the democratic magistrate is more apt to misuse his power, he possesses it for a shorter period of time. But there is yet another reason which is still more general and conclusive. It is no doubt of importance to the welfare of nations that they should be governed by men of talents and virtue : but it is perhaps still more important that the interests of those men should not differ from the interests of the community at large ; for, if such were the case, virtues of a high order might become useless, and talents might be turned to a bad account. I say that it is important that the interests of the persons in authority hould not conflict with or oppose the interests of the community at large ; but I do not insist upon their having the same interests as the whole population, because I am not aware that such a state of things ever existed in any country.

No political form has been discovered hitherto which is equally favourable to the prosperity and the development of all the classes into which society is divided. These classes continue to form, as it were, a certain number of distinct nations in the same nation ; and experience has shown that it is no less dangerous to place the fate of these classes exclusively in the hands of any one of them than it is to make one people the arbiter of the destiny of another. When the rich alone govern, the interest of the poor is always endangered ; and when the poor make the laws, that of the rich incurs very serious risks. The advantage of democracy does not consist, therefore, as has sometimes been asserted, in favouring the prosperity of all, but simply in contributing to the well-being of the greatest possible number.

The men who are intrusted with the direction of public affairs in the United States are frequently inferior, both in point of capacity and of morality, to those whom aristocratic institutions would raise to power. But their interest is identified and confounded with that of the majority of their fellow-citizens. They may frequently be faithless and frequently mistaken, but they will never systematically adopt a line of conduct opposed to the will of the majority ; and it is impossible that they should give a dangerous or an exclusive tendency to the government.

The maladministration of a democratic magistrate

is a mere isolated fact, which only occurs during the short period for which he is elected. Corruption and incapacity do not act as common interests, which may connect men permanently with one another. A corrupt or an incapable magistrate will not concert his measures with another magistrate, simply because that individual is as corrupt and as incapable as himself; and these two men will never unite their endeavours to promote the corruption and inaptitude of their remote posterity. The ambition and the manœuvres of the one will serve, on the contrary, to unmask the other. The vices of a magistrate, in democratic states, are usually peculiar to his own person.

But under aristocratic governments public men are swayed by the interest of their order, which, if it is sometimes confounded with the interests of the majority, is very frequently distinct from them. This interest is the common and lasting bond which unites them together; it induces them to coalesce, and to combine their efforts in order to attain an end which does not always insure the greatest happiness of the greatest number; and it serves not only to connect the persons in authority, but to unite them to a considerable portion of the community, since a numerous body of citizens belongs to the aristocracy, without being invested with official functions. The aristocratic magistrate is therefore constantly supported by a portion of the community, as well as by the Government of which he is a member.

The common purpose which connects the interest of the magistrates in aristocracies with that of a portion of their contemporaries identifies it with that of future generations; their influence belongs to the future as much as to the present. The aristocratic magistrate is urged at the same time toward the same point by the passions of the community, by his own, and I may almost add by those of his posterity. Is it, then, wonderful that he does not resist such repeated impulses? And, indeed, aristocracies are often carried away by the spirit of their order without being corrupted by it; and they unconsciously fashion society to their own ends, and prepare it for their own descendants.

The English aristocracy is perhaps the most liberal which ever existed, and no body of men has ever uninterruptedly furnished so many honourable and enlightened individuals to the government of a country. It cannot, however, escape observation that in the legislation of England the good of the poor has been sacrificed to the advantage of the rich, and the rights of the majority to the privileges of the few. The consequence is, that England, at the present day, combines the extremes of fortune in the bosom of her society, and her perils and calamities are almost equal to her power and her renown.

In the United States, where the public officers have no interests to promote connected with their caste, the general and constant influence of the Government is beneficial, although the individuals who conduct it are frequently unskilful and sometimes contemptible. There is, indeed, a secret tendency in democratic institutions to render the exertions of the citizens subservient to the prosperity of the community, notwithstanding their private vices and mistakes; while in aristocratic institutions there is a secret propensity which, notwithstanding the talents and the virtues of those who conduct the government, leads them to contribute to the evils which oppress their fellow-creatures. In aristocratic governments public men may frequently do injuries which they do not intend, and in democratic states they produce advantages which they never thought of. . . .

In the United States the inhabitants were thrown but as yesterday upon the soil which they now occupy, and they brought neither customs nor traditions with them there; they meet each other for the first time with no previous acquaintance; in short, the instinctive love of their country can scarcely exist in their minds; but every one takes as zealous an interest in the affairs of his township, his county, and of the whole State, as if they were his own, because every one, in his sphere, takes an active part in the government of society.

The lower orders in the United States are alive to the perception of the influence exercised by the general prosperity upon their own welfare; and simple as this observation is, it is one which is but too rarely made by the people. But in America the people regards this prosperity as the result of its own exertions; the citizen looks upon the fortune of the public as his private interest, and he co-operates in its success, not so much from a sense of pride or of duty, as from what I shall venture to term cupidity.

It is unnecessary to study the institutions and the history of the Americans in order to discover the truth of this remark, for their manners render it sufficiently evident. As the American participates in all that is done in his country, he thinks himself obliged to defend whatever may be censured; for it is not only his country which is attacked upon these occasions, but it is himself. The consequence is, that his national pride resorts to a thousand artifices, and to all the petty tricks of individual vanity.

Nothing is more embarrassing in the ordinary intercourse of life than this irritable patriotism of the Americans. A stranger may be very well inclined to praise many of the institutions of their country, but he begs permission to blame some of the peculiarities which he observes—a permission which is, however, inexorably refused. America is therefore a free country, in which, lest anybody should be hurt by your remarks, you are not allowed to speak freely of private individuals or of the State, of the citizens or of the authorities, of public or of private undertakings, or, in short, of anything at all, except it be of the climate and the soil ; and even then Americans will be found ready to defend either the one or the other, as if they had been contrived by the inhabitants of the country.

In our times option must be made between the patriotism of all and the government of a few ; for the force and activity which the first confers are irreconcilable with the guarantees of tranquillity which the second furnishes.

After the idea of virtue, I know no higher principle than that of right. . . . There are no great nations— it may almost be added that there would be no society —without the notion of rights ; for what is the condition of a mass of rational and intelligent beings who are only united together by the bond of force ?

I am persuaded that the only means which we possess at the present time of inculcating the notion of rights, and of rendering it, as it were, palpable to the senses, is to invest all the members of the community with the peaceful exercise of certain rights : this is very clearly seen in children, who are men without the strength and the experience of manhood. When a child begins to move in the midst of the objects which surround him, he is instinctively led to turn everything which he can lay his hands upon to his own purposes ; he has no notion of the property of others ; but as he gradually learns the value of things, and begins to perceive that he may in his turn be deprived of his possessions, he becomes more circumspect, and he observes those rights in others which he wishes to have respected in himself. The principle which the child derives from the possession of his toys is taught to the man by the objects which he may call his own. In America those complaints against property in general which are so frequent in Europe are never heard, because in America there are no paupers ; and as every one has property of his own to defend, every one recognizes the principle upon which he holds it.

The same thing occurs in the political world. In America the lowest classes have conceived a very high notion of political rights, because they exercise those rights ; and they refrain from attacking those of other people, in order to insure their own from attack. While in Europe the same classes sometimes recalcitrate even against the supreme power, the American submits without a murmur to the authority of the pettiest magistrate.

This truth is exemplified by the most trivial details of national peculiarities. In France very few pleasures are exclusively reserved for the higher classes ; the poor are admitted wherever the rich are received, and they consequently behave with propriety, and respect whatever contributes to the enjoyments in which they themselves participate. In England, where wealth has a monopoly of amusement as well as of power, complaints are made that whenever the poor happen to steal into the inclosures which are reserved for the pleasures of the rich, they commit acts of wanton mischief : can this be wondered at, since care has been taken that they should have nothing to lose ?

The government of democracy brings the notion of political rights to the level of the humblest citizens, just as the dissemination of wealth brings the notion of property within the reach of all the members of the community ; and I confess that, to my mind, this is one of its greatest advantages. I do not assert that it is easy to teach men to exercise political rights ; but I maintain that, when it is possible, the effects which result from it are highly important ; and I add that, if there ever was a time at which such an attempt ought to be made, that time is our own. It is clear that the influence of religious belief is shaken, and that the notion of divine rights is declining ; it is evident that public morality is vitiated, and the notion of moral rights is also disappearing : these are general symptoms of the substitution of argument for faith, and of calculation for the impulses of sentiment. If, in the midst of this general disruption, you do not succeed in connecting the notions of right with that of personal interest, which is the only immutable point in the human heart, what means will you have of governing the world except by fear ? When I am told that, since the laws are weak and the populace is wild, since passions are excited and the authority of virtue is paralysed, no measures must be taken to increase the rights of the democracy, I reply, that it is for these very reasons that some measures of the kind must be taken ; and I am persuaded that governments are still more interested in taking them than society at large, because governments are liable to be destroyed and society cannot perish.

I am not, however, inclined to exaggerate the example which America furnishes. In those States the people were invested with political rights at a time when they could scarcely be abused, for the citizens were few in number and simple in their manners. As they have increased, the Americans have not augmented the power of the democracy, but they have, if I may use the expression, extended its dominions.

It cannot be doubted that the moment at which

political rights are granted to a people that before has been without them is a very critical, though it be a necessary, one. A child may kill before he is aware of the value of life ; and he may deprive another person of his property before he is aware that his own may be taken away from him. The lower orders, when first they are invested with political rights, stand, in relation to those rights, in the same position as the child does to the whole of Nature, and the celebrated adage may then be applied to them, *Homo puer robustus*. This truth may even be perceived in America. The States in which the citizens have enjoyed their rights longest are those in which they make the best use of them.

It cannot be repeated too often that nothing is more fertile in prodigies than the art of being free ; but there is nothing more arduous than the apprenticeship of liberty. Such is not the case with despotic institutions : despotism often promises to make amends for a thousand previous ills ; it supports the right, it protects the oppressed, and it maintains public order. The nation is lulled by the temporary prosperity which accrues to it, until it is roused to a sense of its own misery. Liberty, on the contrary, is generally established in the midst of agitation, it is perfected by civil discord, and its benefits cannot be appreciated until it is already old.

It is not always feasible to consult the whole people, either directly or indirectly, in the formation of the law ; but it cannot be denied that, when such a measure is possible, the authority of the law is very much augmented. This popular origin, which impairs the excellence and the wisdom of legislation, contributes prodigiously to increase its power. There is an amazing strength in the expression of the determination of a whole people, and when it declares itself the imagination of those who are most inclined to contest it is overawed by its authority. The truth of this fact is very well known by parties, and they consequently strive to make out a majority whenever they can. If they have not the greater number of voters on their side, they assert that the true majority abstained from voting ; and if they are foiled even there, they have recourse to the body of those persons who had no votes to give.

In the United States, except slaves, servants, and paupers in the receipt of relief from the townships, there is no class of persons who do not exercise the elective franchise, and who do not indirectly contribute to make the laws. Those who design to attack the laws must consequently either modify the opinion of the nation or trample upon its decision.

A second reason, which is still more weighty, may be further adduced : in the United States every one is personally interested in enforcing the obedience of the whole community to the law ; for as the minority may shortly rally the majority to its principles, it is interested in professing that respect for the decrees of the legislator which it may soon have occasion to claim for its own. However irksome an enactment may be, the citizen of the United States complies with it, not only because it is the work of the majority, but because it originates in his own authority, and he regards it as a contract to which he is himself a party.

In the United States, then, that numerous and turbulent multitude does not exist which always looks upon the law as its natural enemy, and accordingly surveys it with fear and with distrust. It is impossible, on the other hand, not to perceive that all classes display the utmost reliance upon the legislation of their country, and that they are attached to it by a kind of parental affection.

I am wrong, however, in saying all classes; for as in America the European scale of authority is inverted, the wealthy are there placed in a position analogous to that of the poor in the Old World, and it is the opulent classes which frequently look upon the law with suspicion. I have already observed that the advantage of democracy is not, as has been sometimes asserted, that it protects the interests of the whole community, but simply that it protects those of the majority. In the United States, where the poor rule, the rich have always some reason to dread the abuses of their power. This natural anxiety of the rich may produce a sullen dissatisfaction, but society is not disturbed by it; for the same reason which induces the rich to withhold their confidence in the legislative authority makes them obey its mandates; their wealth, which prevents them from making the law, prevents them from withstanding it. Among civilized nations revolts are rarely excited, except by such persons as have nothing to lose by them; and if the laws of a democracy are not always worthy of respect, at least they always obtain it; for those who usually infringe the laws have no excuse for not complying with the enactments they have themselves made, and by which they are themselves benefited, while the citizens whose interests might be promoted by the infraction of them are induced, by their character and their stations, to submit to the decisions of the legislature, whatever they may be. Besides which, the people in America obeys the law not only because it emanates from the popular authority, but because that authority may modify it in any points which may prove vexatious; a law is observed because it is a self-imposed evil in the first place, and an evil of transient duration in the second.

On passing from a country in which free institutions

are established to one where they do not exist, the traveller is struck by the change; in the former all is bustle and activity, in the latter everything is calm and motionless. In the one, amelioration and progress are the general topics of inquiry; in the other, it seems as if the community only aspired to repose in the enjoyment of the advantages which it has acquired. Nevertheless, the country which exerts itself so strenuously to promote its welfare is generally more wealthy and more prosperous than that which appears to be so contented with its lot; and when we compare them together, we can scarcely conceive how so many new wants are daily felt in the former, while so few seem to occur in the latter.

If this remark is applicable to those free countries in which monarchical and aristocratic institutions subsist, it is still more striking with regard to democratic republics. In these States it is not only a portion of the people which is busied with the amelioration of its social condition, but the whole community is engaged in the task; and it is not the exigencies and the convenience of a single class for which a provision is to be made, but the exigencies and the convenience of all ranks of life.

It is not impossible to conceive the surpassing liberty which the Americans enjoy; some idea may likewise be formed of the extreme equality which subsists among them, but the political activity which pervades the United States must be seen in order to be understood. No sooner do you set foot upon American soil than you are stunned by a kind of tumult; a confused clamour is heard on every side; and a thousand simultaneous voices demand the immediate satisfaction of their social wants. Everything is in motion around you; here, the people of one quarter of a town are met to decide upon the building of a church; there, the election of a representative is going on; a little farther the delegates of a district are posting to the town in order to consult upon some local improvements; or in another place the labourers of a village quit their ploughs to deliberate upon the project of a road or a public school. Meetings are called for the sole purpose of declaring their disapprobation of the line of conduct pursued by the Government; while in other assemblies the citizens salute the authorities of the day as the fathers of their country. Societies are formed which regard drunkenness as the principal cause of the evils under which the State labours, and which solemnly bind themselves to give a constant example of temperance.

The great political agitation of the American legislative bodies, which is the only kind of excitement that attracts the attention of foreign countries, is a mere episode or a sort of continuation of that universal movement which originates in the lowest classes of the people and extends successively to all the ranks of society. It is impossible to spend more efforts in the pursuit of enjoyment.

The cares of political life take a most prominent place in the occupation of a citizen in the United States, and almost the only pleasure of which an American has any idea is to take a part in the Government, and to discuss the part he has taken. This feeling pervades the most trifling habits of life; even the women frequently attend public meetings and listen to political harangues as a recreation after their household labours. Debating clubs are to a certain extent a substitute for theatrical entertainments: an American cannot converse, but he can discuss; and when he attempts to talk he falls into a dissertation. He speaks to you as if he was addressing a meeting;

and if he should chance to warm in the course of the discussion, he will infallibly say, ' Gentlemen,' to the person with whom he is conversing.

In some countries the inhabitants display a certain repugnance to avail themselves of the political privileges with which the law invests them ; it would seem that they set too high a value upon their time to spend it on the interests of the community ; and they prefer to withdraw within the exact limits of a wholesome egotism, marked out by four sunk fences and a quickset hedge. But if an American were condemned to confine his activity to his own affairs, he would be robbed of one half of his existence ; he would feel an immense void in the life which he is accustomed to lead, and his wretchedness would be unbearable. I am persuaded that, if ever a despotic government is established in America, it will find it more difficult to surmount the habits which free institutions have engendered than to conquer the attachment of the citizens to freedom.

This ceaseless agitation which democratic government has introduced into the political world influences all social intercourse. I am not sure that upon the whole this is not the greatest advantage of democracy. And I am much less inclined to applaud it for what it does than for what it causes to be done.

It is incontestable that the people frequently conducts public business very badly ; but it is impossible that the lower orders should take a part in public business without extending the circle of their ideas, and without quitting the ordinary routine of their mental acquirements. The humblest individual who is called upon to co-operate in the government of society acquires a certain degree of self-respect ; and as he possesses authority, he can command the services of minds much more enlightened than his own. He is canvassed by a multitude of applicants, who seek to deceive him in a thousand different ways, but who instruct him by their deceit. He takes a part in political undertakings which did not originate in his own conception, but which give him a taste for undertakings of the kind. New ameliorations are daily pointed out in the property which he holds in common with others, and this gives him the desire of improving that property which is more peculiarly his own. He is perhaps neither happier nor better than those who came before him, but he is better informed and more active. I have no doubt that the democratic institutions of the United States, joined to the physical constitution of the country, are the cause (not the direct, as is so often asserted, but the indirect cause) of the prodigious commercial activity of the inhabitants. It is not engendered by the laws, but the people learns how to promote it by the experience derived from legislation.

When the opponents of democracy assert that a single individual performs the duties which he undertakes much better than the government of the community, it appears to me that they are perfectly right. The government of an individual, supposing an equality of instruction on either side, is more consistent, more persevering, and more accurate than that of a multitude, and it is much better qualified judiciously to discriminate the characters of the men it employs. If any deny what I advance, they have certainly never seen a democratic government, or have formed their opinion upon very partial evidence. It is true that even when local circumstances and the disposition of the people allow democratic institutions to subsist, they never display a regular and methodical system of government. Democratic liberty is far from accomplishing all the projects it undertakes, with the skill of an adroit despotism. It frequently abandons them before they have borne their fruits, or risks them when the consequences may prove dangerous; but in the end it produces more than any absolute government, and if it do fewer things well, it does a greater number of things. Under its sway the transactions of the public administration are not nearly so important as what is done by private exertion. Democracy does not confer the most skilful kind of government upon the people, but it produces that which the most skilful governments are frequently unable to awaken, namely, an all-pervading and restless activity, a superabundant force, and an energy which is inseparable from it, and which may, under favourable circumstances, beget the most amazing benefits. These are the true advantages of democracy.

In the present age, when the destinies of Christendom seem to be in suspense, some hasten to assail democracy as its foe while it is yet in its early growth; and others are ready with their vows of adoration for this new deity which is springing forth from chaos: but both parties are very imperfectly acquainted with the object of their hatred or of their desires; they strike in the dark, and distribute their blows by mere chance.

We must first understand what the purport of society and the aims of government are held to be. If it be your intention to confer a certain elevation upon the human mind, and to teach it to regard the things of this world with generous feelings, to inspire men with a scorn of mere temporal advantage, to give birth to living convictions, and to keep alive the spirit of honourable devotedness; if you hold it to be a good thing to refine the habits, to embellish the manners, to cultivate the arts of a nation, and to promote the love of poetry, of beauty, and of renown;

if you would constitute a people not unfitted to act with power upon all other nations, nor unprepared for those high enterprises which, whatever be the result of its efforts, will leave a name forever famous in time—if you believe such to be the principal object of society, you must avoid the government of democracy, which would be a very uncertain guide to the end you have in view.

But if you hold it to be expedient to divert the moral and intellectual activity of man to the production of comfort, and to the acquirement of the necessaries of life; if a clear understanding be more profitable to man than genius; if your object be not to stimulate the virtues of heroism, but to create habits of peace; if you had rather witness vices than crimes and are content to meet with fewer noble deeds, provided offences be diminished in the same proportion; if, instead of living in the midst of a brilliant state of society, you are contented to have prosperity around you; if, in short, you are of opinion that the principal object of a Government is not to confer the greatest possible share of power and of glory upon the body of the nation, but to insure the greatest degree of enjoyment and the least degree of misery to each of the individuals who compose it— if such be your desires, you can have no surer means of satisfying them than by equalizing the conditions of men, and establishing democratic institutions.

But if the time be passed at which such a choice was possible, and if some superhuman power impel us toward one or the other of these two governments without consulting our wishes, let us at least endeavour to make the best of that which is allotted to us; and let us so inquire into its good and its evil propensities as to be able to foster the former and repress the latter to the utmost.

Chapter XIV

UNLIMITED POWER OF THE MAJORITY IN THE UNITED STATES, AND ITS CONSEQUENCES

THE very essence of democratic government consists in the absolute sovereignty of the majority; for there is nothing in democratic States which is capable of resisting it. Most of the American Constitutions have sought to increase this natural strength of the majority by artificial means.

The legislature is, of all political institutions, the one which is most easily swayed by the wishes of the majority. The Americans determined that the members of the legislature should be elected by the people immediately, and for a very brief term, in order to subject them, not only to the general convictions, but even to the daily passions, of their constituents. The members of both Houses are taken from the same class in society, and are nominated in the same manner; so that the modifications of the legislative bodies are almost as rapid and quite as irresistible as those of a single assembly. It is to a legislature thus constituted that almost all the authority of the government has been intrusted.

But while the law increased the strength of those authorities which of themselves were strong, it enfeebled more and more those which were naturally weak. It deprived the representatives of the executive of all stability and independence, and by subjecting them completely to the caprices of the legislature, it robbed them of the slender influence which the nature of a democratic government might have allowed them to retain. In several States the judicial power was also submitted to the elective discretion of the majority, and in all of them its existence was made to depend on the pleasure of the legislative authority, since the representatives were empowered annually to regulate the stipend of the judges.

Custom, however, has done even more than law. A proceeding which will in the end set all the guarantees of representative government at naught is becoming more and more general in the United States; it frequently happens that the electors, who choose a delegate, point out a certain line of conduct to him, and impose upon him a certain number of positive obligations which he is pledged to fulfil. With the exception of the tumult, this comes to the same thing as if the majority of the populace held its deliberations in the market-place.

Several other circumstances concur in rendering the power of the majority in America not only preponderant, but irresistible. The moral authority of the majority is partly based upon the notion that there is more intelligence and more wisdom in a great number of men collected together than in a single individual, and that the number of legislators is more important than their quality. The theory of equality is, in fact, applied to the intellect of man: and human pride is thus assailed in its last retreat by a doctrine which the minority hesitate to admit, and in which they very slowly concur. Like all other powers, and perhaps more than all other powers, the authority of the many requires the sanction of time; at first it enforces obedience by constraint, but its laws are not respected until they have long been maintained.

The right of governing society, which the majority supposes itself to derive from its superior intelligence, was introduced into the United States by the first settlers, and this idea, which would be sufficient of itself to create a free nation, has now been amalgamated with the manners of the people and the minor incidents of social intercourse.

The French, under the old monarchy, held it for a maxim (which is still a fundamental principle of the English Constitution) that the King could do no wrong ; and if he did do wrong, the blame was imputed to his advisers. This notion was highly favourable to habits of obedience, and it enabled the subject to complain of the law without ceasing to love and honour the lawgiver. The Americans entertain the same opinion with respect to the majority.

The moral power of the majority is founded upon yet another principle, which is, that the interests of the many are to be preferred to those of the few. It readily will be perceived that the respect here professed for the rights of the majority must naturally increase or diminish according to the state of parties. When a nation is divided into several irreconcilable factions, the privilege of the majority is often overlooked, because it is intolerable to comply with its demands.

If there existed in America a class of citizens whom the legislating majority sought to deprive of exclusive privileges which they had possessed for ages, and to bring down from an elevated station to the level of the ranks of the multitude, it is probable that the minority would be less ready to comply with its laws. But as the United States were colonized by men holding equal rank among themselves, there is as yet no natural or permanent source of dissension between the interests of its different inhabitants.

There are certain communities in which the persons who constitute the minority can never hope to draw over the majority to their side, because they must then give up the very point which is at issue between them. Thus, an aristocracy can never become a majority while it retains its exclusive privileges, and it cannot cede its privileges without ceasing to be an aristocracy.

In the United States political questions cannot be taken up in so general and absolute a manner, and all parties are willing to recognize the rights of the majority, because they all hope to turn those rights to their own advantage at some future time. The majority therefore in that country exercises a prodigious actual authority, and a moral influence which is scarcely less preponderant ; no obstacles exist which can impede or so much as retard its progress, or which can induce it to heed the complaints of those whom it crushes upon its path. This state of things is fatal in itself and dangerous for the future.

I have already spoken of the natural defects of democratic institutions, and they all of them increase in the exact ratio of the power of the majority. To begin with the most evident : the mutability of the laws is an evil inherent in democratic government, because it is natural to democracies to raise men to power in very rapid succession. But this evil is more or less sensible in proportion to the authority and the means of action which the legislature possesses.

In America the authority exercised by the legislative bodies is supreme ; nothing prevents them from accomplishing their wishes with celerity, and with irresistible power, while they are supplied by new representatives every year. That is to say, the circumstances which contribute most powerfully to democratic instability, and which admit of the free application of caprice to every object in the State, are here in full operation. In conformity with this principle, America is, at the present day, the country in the world where laws last the shortest time.[1]

---

[1] But constitutions the longest ! The United States constitution is today the oldest written constitution in the world. Some State constitutions, too, have gone substantially unchanged for a century.—H. S. C.

Almost all the American constitutions have been amended within the course of thirty years : there is therefore not a single American State which has not modified the principles of its legislation in that lapse of time. As for the laws themselves, a single glance upon the archives of the different States of the Union suffices to convince one that in America the activity of the legislator never slackens. Not that the American democracy is naturally less stable than any other, but that it is allowed to follow its capricious propensities in the formation of the laws.

The omnipotence of the majority, and the rapid as well as absolute manner in which its decisions are executed in the United States [1] has not only the effect of rendering the law unstable, but it exercises the same influence upon the execution of the law and the conduct of the public administration. As the majority is the only power which it is important to court, all its projects are taken up with the greatest ardour, but no sooner is its attention distracted than all this ardour ceases ; while in the free States of Europe the administration is at once independent and secure, so that the projects of the legislature are put into execution, although its immediate attention may be directed to other objects.

In America certain ameliorations are undertaken with much more zeal and activity than elsewhere ; in Europe the same ends are promoted by much less social effort, more continuously applied.

Some years ago several pious individuals undertook to ameliorate the condition of the prisons. The public was excited by the statements which they put forward, and the regeneration of criminals became a very popular undertaking. New prisons were built, and for the first time the idea of reforming as well as

[1] Subject of course to judicial nullification.—H. S. C.

of punishing the delinquent formed a part of prison discipline. But this happy alteration, in which the public had taken so hearty an interest, and which the exertions of the citizens had irresistibly accelerated, could not be completed in a moment. While the new penitentiaries were being erected (and it was the pleasure of the majority that they should be terminated with all possible celerity), the old prisons existed, which still contained a great number of offenders. These jails became more unwholesome and more corrupt in proportion as the new establishments were beautified and improved, forming a contrast which may readily be understood. The majority was so eagerly employed in founding the new prisons that those which already existed were forgotten; and as the general attention was diverted to a novel object, the care which hitherto had been bestowed upon the others ceased. The salutary regulations of discipline were first relaxed, and afterward broken; so that in the immediate neighbourhood of a prison which bore witness to the mild and enlightened spirit of our time, dungeons might be met with which reminded the visitor of the barbarity of the Middle Ages.

I hold it to be an impious and an execrable maxim that, politically speaking, a people has a right to do whatsoever it pleases, and yet I have asserted that all authority originates in the will of the majority. Am I, then, in contradiction with myself?

A general law—which bears the name of Justice— has been made and sanctioned, not only by a majority of this or that people, but by a majority of mankind. The rights of every people are consequently confined within the limits of what is just. A nation may be considered in the light of a jury which is empowered to represent society at large, and to apply the great and general law of justice. Ought such a jury, which represents society, to have more power than the society in which the laws it applies originate?

When I refuse to obey an unjust law, I do not contest the right which the majority has of commanding, but I simply appeal from the sovereignty of the people to the sovereignty of mankind. It has been asserted that a people can never entirely outstep the boundaries of justice and of reason in those affairs which are more peculiarly its own, and that consequently full power may fearlessly be given to the majority by which it is represented. But this language is that of a slave.

A majority taken collectively may be regarded as a being whose opinions, and most frequently whose interests, are opposed to those of another being, which is styled a minority. If it be admitted that a man, possessing absolute power, may misuse that power by wronging his adversaries, why should a majority not be liable to the same reproach? Men are not apt to change their characters by agglomeration; nor does their patience in the presence of obstacles increase with the consciousness of their strength. And for these reasons I can never willingly invest any number of my fellow-creatures with that unlimited authority which I should refuse to any one of them.

I do not think that it is possible to combine several principles in the same government, so as at the same time to maintain freedom, and really to oppose them to one another. The form of government which is usually termed mixed has always appeared to me to be a mere chimera. Accurately speaking, there is no such thing as a mixed government (with the meaning usually given to that word), because in all communities some one principle of action may be discovered which preponderates over the others. . . .

I am of opinion that some one social power must always be made to predominate over the others ; but I think that liberty is endangered when this power is checked by no obstacles which may retard its course, and force it to moderate its own vehemence.

Unlimited power is in itself a bad and dangerous thing ; human beings are not competent to exercise it with discretion, and God alone can be omnipotent, because his wisdom and his justice are always equal to his power. But no power upon earth is so worthy of honour for itself, or of reverential obedience to the rights which it represents, that I would consent to admit its uncontrolled and all-predominant authority. When I see that the right and the means of absolute command are conferred on a people or upon a king, upon an aristocracy or a democracy, a monarchy or a republic, I recognize the germ of tyranny, and I journey onward to a land of more hopeful institutions.

In my opinion the main evil of the present democratic institutions of the United States does not arise, as is often asserted in Europe, from their weakness, but from their overpowering strength ; and I am not so much alarmed at the excessive liberty which reigns in that country as at the very inadequate securities which exist against tyranny.

When an individual or a party is wronged in the United States, to whom can he apply for redress ? If to public opinion, public opinion constitutes the majority ; if to the legislature, it represents the majority, and implicitly obeys its injunctions ; if to the executive power, it is appointed by the majority, and remains a passive tool in its hands ; the public troops consist of the majority under arms ; the jury is the majority invested with the right of hearing judicial cases ; and in certain States even the judges are elected by the majority.[1] However iniquitous or absurd the evil of which you complain may be, you must submit to it as well as you can.

If, on the other hand, a legislative power could be so constituted as to represent the majority without necessarily being the slave of its passions; an executive, so as to retain a certain degree of uncontrolled authority; and a judiciary, so as to remain independent of the two other powers; a government would be formed which would still be democratic without incurring any risk of tyrannical abuse.[2]

I do not say that tyrannical abuses frequently occur in America at the present day, but I maintain that no sure barrier is established against them, and that the causes which mitigate the government are to be found in the circumstances and the manners of the country more than in its laws.

A distinction must be drawn between tyranny and arbitrary power. Tyranny may be exercised by means of the law, and in that case it is not arbitrary; arbitrary power may be exercised for the good of the community at large, in which case it is not tyrannical. Tyranny usually employs arbitrary means, but, if necessary, it can rule without them.

In the United States the unbounded power of the majority, which is favourable to the legal despotism of the legislature, is likewise favourable to the arbitrary

---

[1] At the time Tocqueville wrote, judicial nullification of legislative acts was comparatively rare. Within the last half-century it has become increasingly common and elected judges appear as ready to exercise this power as do appointed judges or those with permanent tenure.—H. S. C.

[2] This would appear to be an accurate description of the national Government of the United States at the present time.—H. S. C.

authority of the magistrate. The majority has an entire control over the law when it is made and when it is executed ; and as it possesses an equal authority over those who are in power and the community at large, it considers public officers as its passive agents, and readily confides the task of serving its designs to their vigilance. The details of their office and the privileges which they are to enjoy are rarely defined beforehand ; but the majority treats them as a master does his servants when they are always at work in his sight, and he has the power of directing or reprimanding them at every instant.

In general the American functionaries are far more independent than the French civil officers within the sphere which is prescribed to them. Sometimes, even, they are allowed by the popular authority to exceed those bounds ; and as they are protected by the opinion, and backed by the co-operation, of the majority, they venture upon such manifestations of their power as astonish a European. By this means habits are formed in the heart of a free country which may some day prove fatal to its liberties.

It is in the examination of the display of public opinion in the United States that we clearly perceive how far the power of the majority surpasses all the powers with which we are acquainted in Europe. Intellectual principles exercise an influence which is so invisible, and often so inappreciable, that they baffle the toils of oppression. At the present time the most absolute monarchs in Europe are unable to prevent certain notions, which are opposed to their authority, from circulating in secret throughout their dominions, and even in their courts. Such is not the case in America ; as long as the majority is still undecided, discussion is carried on ; but as soon as its decision is irrevocably pronounced, a submissive silence is observed, and the friends, as well as the opponents, of the measure unite in assenting to its propriety. The reason of this is perfectly clear : no monarch is so absolute as to combine all the powers of society in his own hands, and to conquer all opposition with the energy of a majority which is invested with the right of making and of executing the laws.

The authority of a king is purely physical, and it controls the actions of the subject without subduing his private will ; but the majority possesses a power which is physical and moral at the same time ; it acts upon the will as well as upon the actions of men, and it represses not only all contest, but all controversy.

I know no country in which there is so little true independence of mind and freedom of discussion as in America. In any constitutional state in Europe every sort of religious and political theory may be advocated and propagated abroad ; for there is no country in Europe so subdued by any single authority as not to contain citizens who are ready to protect the man who raises his voice in the cause of truth from the consequences of his hardihood. If he is unfortunate enough to live under an absolute government, the people is upon his side ; if he inhabits a free country, he may find a shelter behind the authority of the throne, if he require one. The aristocratic part of society supports him in some countries, and the democracy in others. But in a nation where democratic institutions exist, organized like those of the United States, there is but one sole authority, one single element of strength and of success, with nothing beyond it.

In America, the majority raises very formidable barriers to the liberty of opinion : within these barriers an author may write whatever he pleases, but he will repent it if he ever step beyond them. Not that he is exposed to the terrors of an *auto-da-fé*, but he is tormented by the slights and persecutions of daily obloquy. His political career is closed for ever, since he has offended the only authority which is able to promote his success. Every sort of compensation, even that of celebrity, is refused to him. Before he published his opinions he imagined that he held them in common with many others ; but no sooner has he declared them openly than he is loudly censured by his overbearing opponents, while those who think like him, without having the courage to speak, abandon him in silence. He yields at length, oppressed by the daily efforts he has been making, and he subsides into silence, as if he was tormented by remorse for having spoken the truth.

Fetters and headsmen were the coarse instruments which tyranny formerly employed ; but the civilization of our age has refined the arts of despotism, which seemed, however, to have been sufficiently perfected before. The excesses of monarchical power had devised a variety of physical means of oppression : the democratic republics of the present day have rendered it as entirely an affair of the mind as that will which it is intended to coerce. Under the absolute sway of an individual despot the body was attacked in order to subdue the soul, and the soul escaped the blows which were directed against it and rose superior to the attempt ; but such is not the course adopted by tyranny in democratic republics ; there the body is left free, and the soul is enslaved. The sovereign can no longer say, " You shall think as I do on pain of death " ; but he says : " You are free to think differently from me, and to retain your life, your property, and all that you possess ; but if such be your determination, you are henceforth an alien among your people. You may retain your civil rights, but they will be useless to you, for you will never be chosen by your fellow-citizens if you solicit their suffrages, and they will affect to scorn you if you solicit their esteem. You will remain among men, but you will be deprived of the rights of mankind. Your fellow-creatures will shun you like an impure being, and those who are most persuaded of your innocence will abandon you too, lest they should be shunned in their turn. Go in peace! I have given you your life, but it is an existence incomparably worse than death."

Monarchical institutions have thrown an odium upon despotism; let us beware lest democratic republics should restore oppression, and should render it less odious and less degrading in the eyes of the many, by making it still more onerous to the few. . . .

The tendencies to which I have just alluded are as yet very slightly perceptible in political society, but they already begin to exercise an unfavourable influence upon the national character of the Americans. I am inclined to attribute the singular paucity of distinguished political characters to the ever-increasing activity of the despotism of the majority in the United States. When the American Revolution broke out they arose in great numbers, for public opinion then served, not to tyrannize over, but to direct the exertions of individuals. Those celebrated men took a full part in the general agitation of mind common at that period, and they attained a high degree of personal fame, which was reflected back upon the nation, but which was by no means borrowed from it. . . .

In free countries, where every one is more or less

called upon to give his opinion in the affairs of state ; in democratic republics, where public life is incessantly commingled with domestic affairs, where the sovereign authority is accessible on every side, and where its attention can almost always be attracted by vociferation, more persons are to be met with who speculate upon its foibles and live at the cost of its passions than in absolute monarchies. Not because men are naturally worse in these States than elsewhere, but the temptation is stronger, and of easier access at the same time. The result is a far more extensive debasement of the characters of citizens.

Democratic republics extend the practice of currying favour with the many, and they introduce it into a greater number of classes at once : this is one of the most serious reproaches that can be addressed to them. In democratic States organized on the principles of the American republics, this is more especially the case, where the authority of the majority is so absolute and so irresistible that a man must give up his rights as a citizen, and almost abjure his quality as a human being, if he intends to stray from the track which it lays down.

In that immense crowd which throngs the avenues to power in the United States I found very few men who displayed any of that manly candour and that masculine independence of opinion which frequently distinguished the Americans in former times, and which constitutes the leading feature in distinguished characters, wheresoever they may be found. It seems, at first sight, as if all the minds of the Americans were formed upon one model, so accurately do they correspond in their manner of judging. A stranger does, indeed, sometimes meet with Americans who dissent from these rigorous formularies ; with men who deplore the defects of the laws, the mutability and the ignorance of democracy; who even go so far as to observe the evil tendencies which impair the national character, and to point out such remedies as it might be possible to apply; but no one is there to hear these things besides yourself, and you, to whom these secret reflections are confided, are a stranger and a bird of passage. They are very ready to communicate truths which are useless to you, but they continue to hold a different language in public. . . .

Despotism debases the oppressed much more than the oppressor : in absolute monarchies the king has often great virtues, but the courtiers are invariably servile. It is true that the American courtiers do not say 'Sire,' or 'Your Majesty'—a distinction without a difference. They are for ever talking of the natural intelligence of the populace they serve ; they do not debate the question as to which of the virtues of their master is pre-eminently worthy of admiration, for they assure him that he possesses all the virtues under heaven without having acquired them, or without caring to acquire them ; they do not give him their daughters and their wives to be raised at his pleasure to the rank of his concubines, but, by sacrificing their opinions, they prostitute themselves. Moralists and philosophers in America are not obliged to conceal their opinions under the veil of allegory ; but, before they venture upon a harsh truth, they say : 'We are aware that the people which we are addressing is too superior to all the weaknesses of human nature to lose the command of its temper for an instant ; and we should not hold this language if we were not speaking to men whom their virtues and their intelligence render more worthy of freedom than all the rest of the world.' It would have been impossible for the sycophants of Louis XIV to flatter more dexterously. For my part, I am persuaded that in all governments, whatever their nature may be, servility will cower to force, and adulation will cling to power. The only means of preventing men from degrading themselves is to invest no one with that unlimited authority which is the surest method of debasing them.

Governments usually fall a sacrifice to impotence or to tyranny. In the former case their power escapes from them ; it is wrested from their grasp in the latter. Many observers, who have witnessed the anarchy of democratic States, have imagined that the government of those States was naturally weak and impotent. The truth is, that when once hostilities are begun between parties, the government loses its control over society. But I do not think that a democratic power is naturally without force or without resources : say, rather, that it is almost always by the abuse of its force and the misemployment of its resources that a democratic government fails. Anarchy is almost always produced by its tyranny or its mistakes, but not by its want of strength.

It is important not to confound stability with force, or the greatness of a thing with its duration. In democratic republics, the power which directs society is not stable ; for it often changes hands and assumes a new direction. But whichever way it turns, its force is almost irresistible. The governments of the American republics appear to me to be as much centralized as those of the absolute monarchies of Europe, and more energetic than they are. I dö not, therefore, imagine that they will perish from weakness.

If ever the free institutions of America are destroyed, that event may be attributed to the unlimited author-

H

ity of the majority, which may at some future time urge the minorities to desperation, and oblige them to have recourse to physical force. Anarchy will then be the result, but it will have been brought about by despotism. . .

Chapter XV

CAUSES WHICH MITIGATE THE TYRANNY OF THE MAJORITY IN THE UNITED STATES

I HAVE already pointed out the distinction which is to be made between a centralized government and a centralized administration. The former exists in America, but the latter is nearly unknown there. If the directing power of the American communities had both these instruments of government at its disposal, and united the habit of executing its own commands to the right of commanding ; if, after having established the general principles of government, it descended to the details of public business ; and if, having regulated the great interests of the country, it could penetrate into the privacy of individual interests, freedom would soon be banished from the New World.

But in the United States the majority, which so frequently displays the tastes and the propensities of a despot, is still destitute of the more perfect instruments of tyranny. In the American republics the activity of the central Government never as yet has been extended beyond a limited number of objects sufficiently prominent to call forth its attention. The secondary affairs of society never have been regulated by its authority, and nothing hitherto has betrayed its desire of interfering in them. The majority is become more and more absolute, but it has not increased the prerogatives of the central government ; those great prerogatives have been confined to a certain sphere ; and although the despotism of the majority may be galling upon one point, it cannot be said to extend to all. However the predominant party in the nation may be carried away by its passions, however ardent it may be in the pursuit of its projects, it cannot oblige all the citizens to comply with its desires in the same manner and at the same time throughout the country. When the central Government which represents that majority has issued a decree, it must intrust the execution of its will to agents, over whom it frequently has no control, and whom it cannot perpetually direct. The townships, municipal bodies, and counties may therefore be looked upon as concealed breakwaters, which check or part the tide of popular excitement. If an oppressive law were passed, the liberties of the people would still be protected by the means by which that law would be put in execution : the majority cannot descend to the details and (as I will venture to style them) the puerilities of administrative tyranny. Nor does the people entertain that full consciousness of its authority which would prompt it to interfere in these matters ; it knows the extent of its natural powers, but it is unacquainted with the increased resources which the art of government might furnish. . . .

In visiting the Americans and in studying their laws we perceive that the authority they have intrusted to members of the legal profession, and the influence which these individuals exercise in the Government, is the most powerful existing security against the excesses of democracy. . . .

Men who have more especially devoted themselves to legal pursuits derive from those occupations certain habits of order, a taste for formalities, and a kind of instinctive regard for the regular connection of ideas, which naturally render them very hostile to the revolutionary spirit and the unreflecting passions of the multitude.

The special information which lawyers derive from their studies insures them a separate station in society, and they constitute a sort of privileged body in the

scale of intelligence. This notion of their superiority
perpetually recurs to them in the practice of their
profession : they are the masters of a science which is
necessary, but which is not very generally known ;
they serve as arbiters between the citizens ; and the
habit of directing the blind passions of parties in
litigation to their purpose inspires them with a
certain contempt for the judgment of the multitude.
To this it may be added that they naturally constitute
a body, not by any previous understanding, or by an
agreement which directs them to a common end ; but
the analogy of their studies and the uniformity of their
proceedings connect their minds together, as much as
a common interest could combine their endeavours.

A portion of the tastes and of the habits of the
aristocracy may consequently be discovered in the
characters of men in the profession of the law. They
participate in the same instinctive love of order and of
formalities ; and they entertain the same repugnance
to the actions of the multitude, and the same secret
contempt of the government of the people. I do not
mean to say that the natural propensities of lawyers are sufficiently strong to sway them irresistibly ;
for they, like most other men, are governed by
their private interests and the advantages of the
moment. . . .

In a community in which lawyers are allowed to
occupy, without opposition, that high station which
naturally belongs to them, their general spirit will be
eminently conservative and anti-democratic. When
an aristocracy excludes the leaders of that profession
from its ranks, it excites enemies which are the more
formidable to its security as they are independent of
the nobility by their industrious pursuits ; and they
feel themselves to be its equal in point of intelligence,
although they enjoy less opulence and less power.

But whenever an aristocracy consents to impart some of its privileges to these same individuals, the two classes coalesce very readily, and assume, as it were, the consistency of a single order of family interests. . . .

Lawyers are attached to public order beyond every other consideration, and the best security of public order is authority. It must not be forgotten that, if they prize the free institutions of their country much, they nevertheless value the legality of those institutions far more : they are less afraid of tyranny than of arbitary power ; and provided that the legislature take upon itself to deprive men of their independence, they are not dissatisfied. . . .

The government of democracy is favourable to the political power of lawyers ; for when the wealthy, the noble, and the prince are excluded from the government, they are sure to occupy the highest stations, in their own right, as it were, since they are the only men of information and sagacity, beyond the sphere of the people, who can be the objects of the popular choice. If, then, they are led by their tastes to combine with the aristocracy and to support the Crown, they are naturally brought into contact with the people by their interests. They like the government of democracy, without participating in its propensities and without imitating its weaknesses ; whence they derive a twofold authority, from it and over it. The people in democratic States does not mistrust the members of the legal profession, because it is well known that they are interested in serving the popular cause ; and it listens to them without irritation, because it does not attribute to them any sinister designs. The object of lawyers is not, indeed, to overthrow the institutions of democracy, but they constantly endeavour to give it an impulse which diverts it from its real tendency, by means which are foreign to its nature. Lawyers belong to the people by birth and interest, to the aristocracy by habit and by taste, and they may be looked upon as the natural bond and connecting link of the two great classes of society.

The profession of the law is the only aristocratic element which can be amalgamated without violence with the natural elements of democracy, and which can be advantageously and permanently combined with them. I am not unacquainted with the defects which are inherent in the character of that body of men ; but without this admixture of lawyer-like sobriety with the democratic principle, I question whether democratic institutions could long be maintained, and I cannot believe that a republic could subsist at the present time if the influence of lawyers in public business did not increase in proportion to the power of the people.

This aristocratic character, which I hold to be common to the legal profession, is much more distinctly marked in the United States and in England than in any other country. This proceeds not only from the legal studies of the English and American lawyers, but from the nature of the legislation, and the position which those persons occupy in the two countries. The English and the Americans have retained the law of precedents ; that is to say, they continue to found their legal opinions and the decisions of their courts upon the opinions and the decisions of their forefathers. In the mind of an English or American lawyer a taste and a reverence for what is old is almost always united to a love of regular and lawful proceedings.

This predisposition has another effect upon the character of the legal profession and upon the general course of society. The English and American lawyers investigate what has been done ; the French advocate inquires what should have been done ; the former produce precedents, the latter reasons. A French observer is surprised to hear how often an English or an American lawyer quotes the opinions of others, and how little he alludes to his own ; while the reverse occurs in France. There the most trifling litigation is never conducted without the introduction of an entire system of ideas peculiar to the counsel employed ; and the fundamental principles of law are discussed in order to obtain a perch of land by the decision of the court. This abnegation of his own opinion, and this implicit deference to the opinion of his forefathers, which are common to the English and American lawyers, this subjection of thought which he is obliged to profess, necessarily give him more timid habits and more sluggish inclinations in England and America than in France.

The French Codes are often difficult of comprehension, but they can be read by every one ; nothing, on the other hand, can be more impenetrable to the uninitiated than a legislation founded upon precedents. The indispensable want of legal assistance which is felt in England and in the United States, and the high opinion which is generally entertained of the ability of the legal profession, tend to separate it more and more from the people, and to place it in a distinct class. The French lawyer is simply a man extensively acquainted with the statutes of his country ; but the English or American lawyer resembles the hierophants of Egypt, for, like them, he is the sole interpreter of an occult science.

The station which lawyers occupy in England and America exercises no less an influence upon their habits and their opinions. The English aristocracy, which has taken care to attract to its sphere whatever is at all analogous to itself, has conferred a high degree of importance and of authority upon the members of the legal profession. In English society lawyers do not occupy the first rank, but they are contented with the station assigned to them ; they constitute, as it were, the younger branch of the English aristocracy, and they are attached to their elder brothers, although they do not enjoy all their privileges. The English lawyers consequently mingle the taste and the ideas of the aristocratic circles in which they move with the aristocratic interests of their profession. . . .

In America there are no nobles or men of letters, and the people is apt to mistrust the wealthy ; lawyers consequently form the highest political class, and the most cultivated circle of society. They have, therefore, nothing to gain by innovation, which adds a conservative interest to their natural taste for public order. If I were asked where I place the American aristocracy, I should reply without hesitation that it is not composed of the rich, who are united together by no common tie, but that it occupies the judicial bench and the bar.

The more we reflect upon all that occurs in the United States the more shall we be persuaded that the lawyers as a body form the most powerful, if not the only, counterpoise to the democratic element. In that country we perceive how eminently the legal profession is qualified by its powers, and even by its defects, to neutralize the vices which are inherent in popular government. When the American people is intoxicated by passion, or carried away by the impetuosity of its ideas, it is checked and stopped by the almost invisible influence of its legal counsellors, who secretly oppose their aristocratic propensities to its democratic instincts, their superstitious attachment to what is antique to its love of novelty, their narrow views to its immense designs, and their habitual procrastination to its ardent impatience.

The courts of justice are the most visible organs by which the legal profession is enabled to control the democracy. The judge is a lawyer, who, independently of the taste for regularity and order which he has contracted in the study of legislation, derives an additional love of stability from his own inalienable functions. His legal attainments have already raised him to a distinguished rank among his fellow-citizens ; his political power completes the distinction of his station, and gives him the inclinations natural to privileged classes.

Armed with the power of declaring the laws to be unconstitutional, the American magistrate perpetually interferes in political affairs. He cannot force the people to make laws, but at least he can oblige it not to disobey its own enactments, or to act inconsistently with its own principles. I am aware that a secret tendency to diminish the judicial power exists in the United States, and by most of the constitutions of the several States the Government can, upon the demand of the two houses of the legislature, remove the judges from their station. By some other constitutions the members of the tribunals are elected, and they are even subjected to frequent re-elections. I venture to predict that these innovations will sooner or later be attended with fatal consequences, and that it will be found out at some future period that the attack which is made upon the judicial power has affected the democratic republic itself.

It must not, however, be supposed that the legal spirit of which I have been speaking has been confined, in the United States, to the courts of justice ; it extends far beyond them. As the lawyers constitute the only enlightened class which the people does not mistrust, they are naturally called upon to occupy most of the public stations. They fill the legislative assemblies, and they conduct the administration ; they consequently exercise a powerful influence upon the formation of the law, and upon its execution. The lawyers are, however, obliged to yield to the current of public opinion, which is too strong for them to resist it, but it is easy to find indications of what their conduct would be if they were free to act as they chose. The Americans, who have made such copious innovations in their political legislation, have introduced very sparing alterations in their civil laws, and that with great difficulty, although those laws are frequently repugnant to their social condition. The reason of this is, that in matters of civil law the majority is obliged to defer to the authority of the legal profession, and that the American lawyers are disinclined to innovate when they are left to their own choice. . . .

The influence of the legal habits which are common in America extends beyond the limits I have just pointed out. Scarcely any question arises in the United States which does not become, sooner or later, a subject of judicial debate ; hence all parties are obliged to borrow the ideas, and even the language, usual in judicial proceedings in their daily controversies. As most public men are, or have been, legal practitioners, they introduce the customs and technicalities of their profession into the affairs of the country. The jury extends this habitude to all classes. The language of the law thus becomes, in some measure, a vulgar tongue ; the spirit of the law, which is produced in the schools and courts of justice, gradually penetrates beyond their walls into the bosom of society, where it descends to the lowest classes, so that the whole people contracts the habits and the tastes of the magistrate. The lawyers of the United States form a party which is but little feared and scarcely perceived, which has no badge peculiar to itself, which adapts itself with great flexibility to the exigencies of the time, and accommodates itself to all the movements of the social body ; but this party extends over the whole community, and it penetrates into all classes of society ; it acts upon the country imperceptibly, but it finally fashions it to suit its purposes.

Since I have been led by my subject to recur to the administration of justice in the United States, I will not pass over this point without adverting to the institution of the jury. Trial by jury may be considered in two separate points of view, as a judicial and as a political institution. . . .

My present object is to consider the jury as a political institution, and any other course would divert me from my subject. Of trial by jury, considered as a judicial institution, I shall here say but very few words. When the English adopted trial by jury they were a semi-barbarous people ; they are become, in course of time, one of the most enlightened nations of the earth ; and their attachment to this institution seems to have increased with their increasing cultivation. They soon spread beyond their insular boundaries to every corner of the habitable globe ; some have formed colonies, others independent states ; the mother-country has maintained its monarchical constitution ; many of its offspring have founded powerful republics ; but wherever the English have been they have boasted of the privilege of trial by jury. They have established it, or hastened to re-establish it, in all their settlements. A judicial institution which obtains the suffrages of a great people for so long a series of ages, which is zealously renewed at every epoch of civilization, in all the climates of the earth and under every form of human government, cannot be contrary to the spirit of justice.

I turn, however, from this part of the subject. To look upon the jury as a mere judicial institution is to confine our attention to a very narrow view of it ; for however great its influence may be upon the decisions of the law courts, that influence is very subordinate to the powerful effects which it produces on the destinies of the community at large. The jury is above all a political institution, and it must be regarded in this light in order to be duly appreciated.

By the jury I mean a certain number of citizens chosen indiscriminately, and invested with a temporary right of judging. Trial by jury, as applied to the repression of crime, appears to me to introduce an eminently republican element into the Government upon the following grounds :

The institution of the jury may be aristocratic or democratic, according to the class of society from which the jurors are selected ; but it always preserves its republican character, inasmuch as it places the real direction of society in the hands of the governed, or of a portion of the governed, instead of leaving it under the authority of the Government. Force is never more than a transient element of success ; and after force comes the notion of right. A government which should only be able to crush its enemies upon a field of battle would very soon be destroyed. The true sanction of political laws is to be found in penal legislation, and if that sanction be wanting the law will sooner or later lose its cogency. He who punishes infractions of the law is therefore the real master of society. Now the institution of the jury raises the people itself, or at least a class of citizens, to the bench of judicial authority. The institution of the jury consequently invests the people, or that class of citizens, with the direction of society.

In England the jury is returned from the aristocratic portion of the nation ; the aristocracy makes the laws, applies the laws, and punishes all infractions of the laws ; everything is established upon a consistent footing, and England may with truth be said to constitute an aristocratic republic. In the United States the same system is applied to the whole people. Every American citizen is qualified to be an elector, a juror, and is eligible to office. The system of the jury, as it is understood in America, appears to me to be as direct and as extreme a consequence of the sovereignty of the people as universal suffrage. These institutions are two instruments of equal power, which contribute to the supremacy of the majority. All the sovereigns who have chosen to govern by their own authority, and to direct society instead of obeying its directions, have destroyed or enfeebled the institution of the jury. The monarchs of the House of Tudor sent to prison jurors who refused to convict, and Napoleon caused them to be returned by his agents.

However clear most of these truths may seem to be, they do not command universal assent. . . . If the question arises as to the proper qualification of jurors, it is confined to a discussion of the intelligence and knowledge of the citizens who may be returned, as if the jury was merely a judicial institution. This appears to me to be the least part of the subject. The jury is pre-eminently a political institution ; it must be regarded as one form of the sovereignty of the people ; when that sovereignty is repudiated, it must be rejected, or it must be adapted to the laws by which that sovereignty is established. The jury is that portion of the nation to which the execution of the laws is intrusted, as the Houses of Parliament constitute that part of the nation which makes the laws ; and in order that society may be governed with consistency and uniformity, the list of citizens qualified to serve on juries must increase and diminish with the list of electors. This I hold to be the point of view most worthy of the attention of the legislator, and all that remains is merely accessory.

I am so entirely convinced that the jury is preeminently a political institution that I still consider it in this light when it is applied in civil causes. Laws are always unstable unless they are founded upon the manners of a nation ; manners are the only durable and resisting power in a people. When the jury is reserved for criminal offences, the people only witnesses its occasional action in certain particular cases ; the ordinary course of life goes on without its interference, and it is considered as an instrument, but not as the only instrument, of obtaining justice. This is true a fortiori when the jury is applied only to certain criminal causes.

When, on the contrary, the influence of the jury is extended to civil causes, its application is constantly palpable ; it affects all the interests of the community ; every one co-operates in its work : it thus penetrates into all the usages of life, it fashions the human mind to its peculiar forms, and is gradually associated with the idea of justice itself.

The institution of the jury, if confined to criminal causes, is always in danger, but when once it is introduced into civil proceedings it defies the aggressions of time and of man. If it had been as easy to remove the jury from the manners as from the laws of England, it would have perished under Henry VIII and Elizabeth, and the civil jury did in reality, at that period, save the liberties of the country. In whatever manner the jury be applied, it cannot fail to exercise a powerful influence upon the national character ; but this influence is prodigiously increased when it is introduced into civil causes. The jury, and more especially the jury in civil cases, serves to communicate the spirit of the judges to the minds of all the citizens ; and this spirit, with the habits which attend it, is the soundest preparation for free institutions. It imbues all classes with a respect for the thing judged, and with the notion of right. If these two elements be removed, the love of independence is reduced to a mere destructive passion. It teaches men to practise equity, every man learns to judge his neighbour as he would himself be judged ; and this is especially true of the jury in civil causes, for, while the number of persons who have reason to apprehend a criminal prosecution is small, every one is liable to have a civil action brought against him. The jury teaches every man not to recoil before the responsibility of his own actions, and impresses him with that manly confidence without which political virtue cannot exist. It invests each citizen with a kind of magistracy, it makes them all feel the duties which they are bound to discharge toward society, and the part which they take in the Government. By obliging men to turn their attention to affairs which are not exclusively their own, it rubs off that individual egotism which is the rust of society.

The jury contributes most powerfully to form the judgment and to increase the natural intelligence of a people, and this is, in my opinion, its greatest advantage. It may be regarded as a gratuitous public school ever open, in which every juror learns to exercise his rights, enters into daily communication with the most learned and enlightened members of the upper classes, and becomes practically acquainted with the laws of his country, which are brought within the reach of his capacity by the efforts of the bar, the advice of the judge, and even by the passions of the parties. I think that the practical intelligence and political good sense of the Americans are mainly attributable to the long use which they have made of the jury in civil causes. I do not know whether the jury is useful to those who are in litigation; but I am certain it is highly beneficial to those who decide the litigation; and I look upon it as one of the most efficacious means for the education of the people which society can employ. . . .

In England and in America the judges exercise an influence upon criminal trials which the French judges have never possessed. The reason for this difference may easily be discovered: the English and American magistrates establish their authority in civil causes, and only transfer it afterward to tribunals of another kind, where that authority was not acquired. In some cases (and they are frequently the most important ones) the American judges have the right of deciding causes alone. Upon these occasions they are accidentally placed in the position which the French judges habitually occupy, but they are invested with far more power than the latter; they are still surrounded by the reminiscence of the jury, and their judgment has almost as much authority as the voice of the community at large, represented by that institution. Their influence extends beyond the limits of the courts; in the recreations of private life as well as in the turmoil of public business, abroad and in the legislative assemblies, the American judge is constantly surrounded by men who are accustomed to regard his intelligence as superior to their own, and after having exercised his power in the decision of causes, he continues to influence the habits of thought and the characters of the individuals who took a part in his judgment.

The jury, then, which seems to restrict the rights of magistracy, does in reality consolidate its power, and in no country are the judges so powerful as there, where the people partakes their privileges. It is more especially by means of the jury in civil causes that the American magistrates imbue all classes of society with the spirit of their profession. Thus the jury, which is the most energetic means of making the people rule, is also the most efficacious means of teaching it to rule well.

Chapter XVI

PRINCIPAL CAUSES WHICH TEND TO MAINTAIN THE
DEMOCRATIC REPUBLIC IN THE UNITED STATES

A DEMOCRATIC republic subsists in the United States, and the principal object of this book has been to account for the fact of its existence. Several of the causes which contribute to maintain the institutions of America have been involuntarily passed by or only hinted at as I was borne along by my subject. Others I have been unable to discuss, and those on which I have dwelt most are, as it were, buried in the details of the former parts of this work. I think, therefore, that before I proceed to speak of the future, I cannot do better than collect within a small compass the reasons which best explain the present. In this retrospective chapter I shall be succinct, for I shall take care to remind the reader very summarily of what he already knows ; and I shall only select the most prominent of those facts which I have not yet pointed out.

All the causes which contribute to the maintenance of the democratic republic in the United States are reducible to three heads :

I. The peculiar and accidental situation in which Providence has placed the Americans.

II. The laws.

III. The manners and customs of the people.

A thousand circumstances, independent of the will of man, concur to facilitate the maintenance of a democratic republic in the United States. Some of these peculiarities are known, the others may easily be pointed out ; but I shall confine myself to the most prominent among them.

The Americans have no neighbours, and consequently they have no great wars, or financial crises, or inroads, or conquest to dread; they require neither great taxes, nor great armies, nor great generals; and they have nothing to fear from a scourge which is more formidable to republics than all these evils combined, namely, military glory. It is impossible to deny the inconceivable influence which military glory exercises upon the spirit of a nation. General Jackson, whom the Americans have twice elected to be the head of their Government, is a man of a violent temper and mediocre talents; no one circumstance in the whole course of his career ever proved that he is qualified to govern a free people, and indeed the majority of the enlightened classes of the Union has always been opposed to him. But he was raised to the presidency, and has been maintained in that lofty station, solely by the recollection of a victory which he gained twenty years ago under the walls of New Orleans, a victory which was, however, a very ordinary achievement, and which could only be remembered in a country where battles are rare. Now the people which is thus carried away by the illusions of glory is unquestionably the most cold and calculating, the most unmilitary . . . and the most prosaic of all the peoples of the earth.

America has no great capital city, whose influence is directly or indirectly felt over the whole extent of the country, which I hold to be one of the first causes of the maintenance of republican institutions in the United States. In cities men cannot be prevented from concerting together, and from awakening a mutual excitement which prompts sudden and passionate resolutions. Cities may be looked upon as large assemblies, of which all the inhabitants are members; their populace exercises a prodigious influence upon the magistrates, and frequently executes its own wishes without their intervention.

To subject the provinces to the metropolis is therefore not only to place the destiny of the empire in the hands of a portion of the community, which may be reprobated as unjust, but to place it in the hands of a populace acting under its own impulses, which must be avoided as dangerous. The preponderance of capital cities is therefore a serious blow upon the representative system, and it exposes modern republics to the same defect as the republics of antiquity, which all perished from not having been acquainted with that form of government.

It would be easy for me to adduce a great number of secondary causes which have contributed to establish, and which concur to maintain, the democratic republic of the United States. But I discern two principal circumstances among these favourable elements, which I hasten to point out. I have already observed that the origin of the American settlements may be looked upon as the first and most efficacious cause to which the present prosperity of the United States may be attributed. The Americans had the chances of birth in their favour, and their forefathers imported that equality of conditions into the country whence the democratic republic has very naturally taken its rise. Nor was this all they did ; for besides this republican condition of society, the early settlers bequeathed to their descendants those customs, manners, and opinions which contribute most to the success of a republican form of government. When I reflect upon the consequences of this primary circumstance, methinks I see the destiny of America embodied in the first Puritan who landed on those shores, just as the human race was represented by the first man.

The chief circumstance which has favoured the establishment and the maintenance of a democratic

republic in the United States is the nature of the
territory which the Americans inhabit. Their
ancestors gave them the love of equality and of
freedom, but God himself gave them the means of
remaining equal and free, by placing them upon a
boundless continent, which is open to their exertions.
General prosperity is favourable to the stability of all
governments, but more particularly of a democratic
constitution, which depends upon the dispositions of
the majority, and more particularly of that portion of
the community which is most exposed to feel the
pressure of want. When the people rules, it must be
rendered happy, or it will overturn the State, and
misery is apt to stimulate it to those excesses to which
ambition rouses kings. The physical causes, independent of the laws, which contribute to promote
general prosperity, are more numerous in America
than they have ever been in any other country in the
world, at any other period of history. In the United
States not only is legislation democratic, but Nature
herself favours the cause of the people.

In what part of human tradition can be found anything at all similar to that which is occurring under
our eyes in North America? The celebrated communities of antiquity were all founded in the midst of
hostile nations, which they were obliged to subjugate
before they could flourish in their place. Even the
moderns have found, in some parts of South America,
vast regions inhabited by a people of inferior civilization, but which occupied and cultivated the soil. To
found their new State it was necessary to extirpate or
to subdue a numerous population, until civilization
has been made to blush for their success. But North
America was only inhabited by wandering tribes,
who took no thought of the natural riches of the soil,
and that vast country was still, properly speaking,

an empty continent, a desert land awaiting its inhabitants.

Everything is extraordinary in America, the social condition of the inhabitants, as well as the laws ; but the soil upon which these institutions are founded is more extraordinary than all the rest. When man was first placed upon the earth by the Creator, the earth was inexhaustible in its youth, but man was weak and ignorant ; and when he had learned to explore the treasures which it contained, hosts of his fellow-creatures covered its surface, and he was obliged to earn an asylum for repose and for freedom by the sword. At that same period North America was discovered, as if it had been kept in reserve by the Deity, and had just risen from beneath the waters of the deluge.

That continent still presents, as it did in the primeval time, rivers which rise from never-failing sources, green and moist solitudes, and fields which the ploughshare of the husbandman has never turned. In this state it is offered to man, not in the barbarous and isolated condition of the early ages, but to a being who is already in possession of the most potent secrets of the natural world, who is united to his fellow-men, and instructed by the experience of fifty centuries. At this very time thirteen millions of civilized Europeans are peaceably spreading over those fertile plains, with whose resources and whose extent they are not yet themselves accurately acquainted. Three or four thousand soldiers drive the wandering races of the aborigines before them ; these are followed by the pioneers, who pierce the woods, scare off the beasts of prey, explore the courses of the inland streams, and make ready the triumphal procession of civilization across the waste.

The favourable influence of the temporal prosperity of America upon the institutions of that country has been so often described by others, and adverted to by myself, that I shall not enlarge upon it beyond the addition of a few facts. An erroneous notion is generally entertained that the deserts of America are peopled by European emigrants, who annually disembark upon the coasts of the New World, while the American population increases and multiplies upon the soil which its forefathers tilled. The European settler, however, usually arrives in the United States without friends, and sometimes without resources ; in order to subsist he is obliged to work for hire, and he rarely proceeds beyond that belt of industrious population which adjoins the ocean. The desert cannot be explored without capital or credit ; and the body must be accustomed to the rigours of a new climate before it can be exposed to the chances of forest life. It is the Americans themselves who daily quit the spots which gave them birth to acquire extensive domains in a remote country. Thus the European leaves his cottage for the transatlantic shores ; and the American, who is born on that very coast, plunges in his turn into the wilds of central America. This double emigration is incessant ; it begins in the remotest parts of Europe, it crosses the Atlantic Ocean, and it advances over the solitudes of the New World. Millions of men are marching at once toward the same horizon ; their language, their religion, their manners differ, their object is the same. The gifts of fortune are promised in the West, and to the West they bend their course.

No event can be compared with this continuous removal of the human race, except perhaps those irruptions which preceded the fall of the Roman Empire. Then, as well as now, generations of men were impelled forward in the same direction to meet and struggle on the same spot ; but the designs of

Providence were not the same; then, every new-comer was the harbinger of destruction and of death; now, every adventurer brings with him the elements of prosperity and of life. The future still conceals from us the ulterior consequences of this emigration of the Americans toward the West; but we can readily apprehend its more immediate results. As a portion of the inhabitants annually leave the States in which they were born, the population of these States increases very slowly, although they have long been established: thus in Connecticut, which contains only fifty-nine inhabitants to the square mile, the population has not been increased by more than one quarter in forty years, while that of England has been augmented by one third in the lapse of the same period. The European emigrant always lands, therefore, in a country which is but half full, and where hands are in request; he becomes a workman in easy circumstances; his son goes to seek his fortune in unpeopled regions, and he becomes a rich land-owner. The former amasses the capital which the latter invests, and the stranger as well as the native is unacquainted with want.

The laws of the United States are extremely favourable to the division of property; but a cause which is more powerful than the laws prevents property from being divided to excess. This is very perceptible in the States which are beginning to be thickly peopled; Massachusetts is the most populous part of the Union, but it contains only eighty inhabitants to the square mile, which is much less than in France, where one hundred and sixty-two are reckoned to the same extent of country. But in Massachusetts estates are very rarely divided; the eldest son takes the land, and the others go to seek their fortune in the desert. The law has abolished the rights of primogeniture, but circumstances have concurred to re-establish it under a form of which none can complain, and by which no just rights are impaired.

A single fact will suffice to show the prodigious number of individuals who leave New England, in this manner, to settle themselves in the wilds. We were assured in 1830 that thirty-six of the members of Congress were born in the little State of Connecticut. The population of Connecticut, which constitutes only one forty-third part of that of the United States, thus furnished one eighth of the whole body of representatives. The State of Connecticut, however, only sends five delegates to Congress; and the thirty-one others sit for the new Western States. If these thirty-one individuals had remained in Connecticut, it is probable that instead of becoming rich land-owners they would have remained humble labourers, that they would have lived in obscurity without being able to rise into public life, and that, far from becoming useful members of the legislature, they might have been unruly citizens.

These reflections do not escape the observation of the Americans any more than of ourselves. 'It cannot be doubted,' says Chancellor Kent in his *Treatise on American Law*, 'that the division of landed estates must produce great evils when it is carried to such excess as that each parcel of land is insufficient to support a family; but these disadvantages never have been felt in the United States, and many generations must elapse before they can be felt. The extent of our inhabited territory, the abundance of adjacent land, and the continual stream of emigration flowing from the shores of the Atlantic toward the interior of the country, suffice as yet, and will long suffice, to prevent the parcelling out of estates.'

It is difficult to describe the rapacity with which the American rushes forward to secure the immense booty which fortune proffers to him. In the pursuit he fearlessly braves the arrow of the Indian and the distempers of the forest; he is unimpressed by the silence of the woods; the approach of beasts of prey does not disturb him; for he is goaded onward by a passion more intense than the love of life. Before him lies a boundless continent, and he urges onward as if time pressed, and he was afraid of finding no room for his exertions. I have spoken of the emigration from the older States, but how shall I describe that which takes place from the more recent ones? Fifty years have scarcely elapsed since that of Ohio was founded; the greater part of its inhabitants were not born within its confines; its capital has only been built thirty years, and its territory is still covered by an immense extent of uncultivated fields; nevertheless, the population of Ohio is already proceeding westward, and most of the settlers who descend to the fertile savannas of Illinois are citizens of Ohio. These men left their first country to improve their condition; they quit their resting-place to ameliorate it still more; fortune awaits them everywhere, but happiness they cannot attain. The desire of prosperity is become an ardent and restless passion in their minds which grows by what it gains. They early broke the ties which bound them to their natal earth, and they have contracted no fresh ones on their way. Emigration was at first necessary to them as a means of subsistence; and it soon becomes a sort of game of chance, which they pursue for the emotions it excites as much as for the gain it procures.

Sometimes the progress of man is so rapid that the desert reappears behind him. The woods stoop to give him a passage, and spring up again when he has passed. It is not uncommon in crossing the new States of the West to meet with deserted dwellings in the midst of the wilds; the traveller frequently discovers the vestiges of a log-house in the most solitary retreats, which bear witness to the power, and no less to the inconstancy, of man. In these abandoned fields, and over these ruins of a day, the primeval forest soon scatters a fresh vegetation, the beasts resume the haunts which were once their own, and Nature covers the traces of man's path with branches and with flowers, which obliterate his evanescent track.

I remember that, in crossing one of the woodland districts which still cover the State of New York, I reached the shores of a lake embosomed in forests coeval with the world. A small island, covered with woods whose thick foliage concealed its banks, rose from the centre of the waters. Upon the shores of the lake no object attested the presence of man, except a column of smoke which might be seen on the horizon rising from the tops of the trees to the clouds, and seeming to hang from heaven rather than to be mounting to the sky. An Indian shallop was hauled up on the sand, which tempted me to visit the islet that had first attracted my attention, and in a few minutes I set foot upon its banks. The whole island formed one of those delicious solitudes of the New World which almost lead civilized man to regret the haunts of the savage. A luxuriant vegetation bore witness to the incomparable fruitfulness of the soil. The deep silence which is common to the wilds of North America was only broken by the hoarse cooing of the wood-pigeon, and the tapping of the woodpecker upon the bark of trees. I was far from supposing that this spot had ever been inhabited, so completely did Nature seem to be left to her own caprices; but when

I reached the centre of the isle I thought that I discovered some traces of man. I then proceeded to examine the surrounding objects with care, and I soon perceived that a European had undoubtedly been led to seek a refuge in this retreat. Yet what changes had taken place in the scene of his labours ! The logs which he had hastily hewn to build himself a shed had sprouted afresh ; the very props were intertwined with living verdure, and his cabin was transformed into a bower. In the midst of these shrubs a few stones were to be seen, blackened with fire and sprinkled with thin ashes ; the hearth no doubt had been here, and the chimney in falling had covered it with rubbish. I stood for some time in silent admiration of the exuberance of Nature and the littleness of man : and when I was obliged to leave that enchanting solitude, I exclaimed with melancholy, " Are ruins, then, already here ? "

In Europe we are wont to look upon a restless disposition, an unbounded desire of riches, and an excessive love of independence, as propensities very formidable to society. Yet these are the very elements which insure a long and peaceful duration to the republics of America. Without these unquiet passions the population would collect in certain spots, and would soon be subject to wants like those of the Old World, which it is difficult to satisfy ; for such is the present good fortune of the New World, that the vices of its inhabitants are scarcely less favourable to society than their virtues. These circumstances exercise a great influence on the estimation in which human actions are held in the two hemispheres. The Americans frequently term what we should call cupidity a laudable industry ; and they blame as faint-heartedness what we consider to be the virtue of moderate desires. . . .

At the present time America presents a field for human effort far more extensive than any sum of labour which can be applied to work it. In America too much knowledge cannot be diffused; for all knowledge, while it may serve him who possesses it, turns also to the advantage of those who are without it. New wants are not to be feared, since they can be satisfied without difficulty; the growth of human passions need not be dreaded, since all passions may find an easy and a legitimate object; nor can men be put in possession of too much freedom, since they are scarcely ever tempted to misuse their liberties.

The American republics of the present day are like companies of adventurers formed to explore in common the waste lands of the New World, and busied in a flourishing trade. The passions which agitate the Americans most deeply are not their political but their commercial passions; or, to speak more correctly, they introduce the habits they contract in business into their political life. They love order, without which affairs do not prosper; and they set an especial value upon a regular conduct, which is the foundation of a solid business; they prefer the good sense which amasses large fortunes to that enterprising spirit which frequently dissipates them; general ideas alarm their minds, which are accustomed to positive calculations, and they hold practice in more honour than theory.

It is in America that one learns to understand the influence which physical prosperity exercises over political actions, and even over opinions which ought to acknowledge no sway but that of reason; and it is more especially among strangers that this truth is perceptible. Most of the European emigrants to the New World carry with them that wild love of independence and of change which our calamities are so apt to engender. I sometimes met with Europeans in the United States who had been obliged to leave their own country on account of their political opinions. They all astonished me by the language they held, but one of them surprised me more than all the rest. As I was crossing one of the most remote districts of Pennsylvania I was benighted, and obliged to beg for hospitality at the gate of a wealthy planter, who was a Frenchman by birth. He bade me sit down beside his fire, and we began to talk with that freedom which befits persons who meet in the backwoods, two thousand leagues from their native country. I was aware that my host had been a great leveller and an ardent demagogue forty years ago, and that his name was not unknown to fame. I was therefore not a little surprised to hear him discuss the rights of property as an economist or a land-owner might have done : he spoke of the necessary grada-tions which fortune establishes among men, of obedience to established laws, of the influence of good morals in commonwealths, and of the support which religious opinions give to order and to freedom ; he even went so far as to quote an evangelical authority in corroboration of one of his political tenets. . . .

The influence of prosperity acts still more freely upon the American than upon strangers. The American has always seen the connection of public order and public prosperity, intimately united as they are, go on before his eyes ; he does not conceive that one can subsist without the other ; he has therefore nothing to forget ; nor has he, like so many Euro-peans, to unlearn the lessons of his early education.

The principal aim of this book has been to make known the laws of the United States ; if this purpose has been accomplished, the reader is already enabled to judge for himself which are the laws that really tend to maintain the democratic republic, and which endanger its existence. . . . It is not my intention to retrace the path I have already pursued, and a very few lines will suffice to recapitulate what I have previously explained.

Three circumstances seem to me to contribute most powerfully to the maintenance of the democratic republic in the United States.

The first is that Federal form of Government which the Americans have adopted, and which enables the Union to combine the power of a great empire with the security of a small State.

The second consists in those municipal institutions which limit the despotism of the majority, and at the same time impart a taste for freedom and a knowledge of the art of being free to the people.

The third is to be met with in the constitution of the judicial power. I have shown in what manner the courts of justice serve to repress the excesses of democracy, and how they check and direct the impulses of the majority without stopping its activity.

Chapter XVII

THE INFLUENCE OF MANNERS AND RELIGION UPON DEMOCRATIC INSTITUTIONS IN THE UNITED STATES

I HAVE previously remarked that the manners of the people may be considered as one of the general causes to which the maintenance of a democratic republic in the United States is attributable. I here used the word manners with the meaning which the ancients attached to the word *mores*; for I apply it not only to manners in their proper sense of what constitutes the character of social intercourse, but I extend it to the various notions and opinions current among men, and to the mass of those ideas which constitute their character of mind. I comprise, therefore, under this term the whole moral and intellectual condition of a people. My intention is not to draw a picture of American manners, but simply to point out such features of them as are favourable to the maintenance of political institutions.

Every religion is to be found in juxtaposition to a political opinion which is connected with it by affinity. If the human mind be left to follow its own bent, it will regulate the temporal and spiritual institutions of society upon one uniform principle; and man will endeavour, if I may use the expression, to harmonize the state in which he lives upon earth with the state which he believes to await him in heaven. The greatest part of British America was peopled by men who, after having shaken off the authority of the Pope, acknowledged no other religious supremacy; they brought with them into the New World a form of Christianity which I cannot better describe than by styling it a democratic and republican religion. This sect contributed powerfully to the establishment of a democracy and a republic, and

 I

from the earliest settlement of the emigrants politics and religion contracted an alliance which never has been dissolved.

About fifty years ago Ireland began to pour a Catholic population into the United States ; on the other hand, the Catholics of America made proselytes, and at the present moment more than a million of Christians professing the truths of the Church of Rome are to be met with in the Union.[1] The Catholics are faithful to the observances of their religion ; they are fervent and zealous in the support and belief of their doctrines. Nevertheless, they constitute the most republican and the most democratic class of citizens which exists in the United States ; and although this fact may surprise the observer at first, the causes by which it is occasioned may easily be discovered upon reflection.

I think that the Catholic religion has erroneously been looked upon as the natural enemy of democracy. Among the various sects of Christians, Catholicism seems to me, on the contrary, to be one of those which are most favourable to the equality of conditions. In the Catholic Church, the religious community is composed of only two elements, the priest and the people. The priest alone rises above the rank of his flock, and all below him are equal.

On doctrinal points the Catholic faith places all human capacities upon the same level ; it subjects the wise and ignorant, the man of genius and the vulgar crowd, to the details of the same creed ; it imposes the same observances upon the rich and the needy, it inflicts the same austerities upon the strong and the weak, it listens to no compromise with mortal man, but, reducing all the human race to the same

[1] The Roman Catholic population of the United States in 1943 was 22,945,247.—H. s. c.

standard, it confounds all the distinctions of society at the foot of the same altar, even as they are confounded in the sight of God. If Catholicism predisposes the faithful to obedience, it certainly does not prepare them for inequality ; but the contrary may be said of Protestantism, which generally tends to make men independent, more than to render them equal.

Catholicism is like an absolute monarchy ; if the sovereign be removed, all the other classes of society are more equal than they are in republics. It has not infrequently occurred that the Catholic priest has left the service of the altar to mix with the governing powers of society, and to take his place among the civil gradations of men. This religious influence has sometimes been used to secure the interests of that political state of things to which he belonged. At other times Catholics have taken the side of aristocracy from a spirit of religion.

But no sooner is the priesthood entirely separated from the Government, as is the case in the United States, than it is found that no class of men are more naturally disposed than the Catholics to transfuse the doctrine of the equality of conditions into the political world. If, then, the Catholic citizens of the United States are not forcibly led by the nature of their tenets to adopt democratic and republican principles, at least they are not necessarily opposed to them ; and their social position, as well as their limited number, obliges them to adopt these opinions. Most of the Catholics are poor, and they have no chance of taking a part in the Government unless it be open to all the citizens. They constitute a minority, and all rights must be respected in order to insure to them the free exercise of their own privileges. These two causes induce them, unconsciously, to adopt political doctrines which they would perhaps support with less zeal if they were rich and preponderant.

The Catholic clergy of the United States has never attempted to oppose this political tendency, but it seeks rather to justify its results. The priests in America have divided the intellectual world into two parts : in the one they place the doctrines of revealed religion, which command their assent ; in the other they leave those truths which they believe to have been freely left open to the researches of political inquiry. Thus the Catholics of the United States are at the same time the most faithful believers and the most zealous citizens.

It may be asserted that in the United States no religious doctrine displays the slightest hostility to democratic and republican institutions. The clergy of all the different sects hold the same language, their opinions are consonant to the laws, and the human intellect flows onward in one sole current. . . .

The sects which exist in the United States are innumerable. They all differ in respect to the worship which is due from man to his Creator, but they all agree in respect to the duties which are due from man to man. Each sect adores the Deity in its own peculiar manner, but all the sects preach the same moral law in the name of God. If it be of the highest importance to man, as an individual, that his religion should be true, the case of society is not the same. Society has no future life to hope for or to fear ; and provided the citizens profess a religion, the peculiar tenets of that religion are of very little importance to its interests. Moreover, almost all the sects of the United States are comprised within the great unity of Christianity, and Christian morality is everywhere the same.

It may be believed without unfairness that a certain

number of Americans pursue a peculiar form of worship, from habit more than from conviction. In the United States the sovereign authority is religious, and consequently hypocrisy must be common ; but there is no country in the whole world in which the Christian religion retains a greater influence over the souls of men than in America ; and there can be no greater proof of its utility, and of its conformity to human nature, than that its influence is most powerfully felt over the most enlightened and free nation of the earth.

I have remarked that the members of the American clergy in general, without even excepting those who do not admit religious liberty, are all in favour of civil freedom ; but they do not support any particular political system. They keep aloof from parties and from public affairs. In the United States religion exercises but little influence upon the laws and upon the details of public opinion, but it directs the manners of the community, and by regulating domestic life it regulates the State.

I do not question that the great austerity of manners which is observable in the United States arises, in the first instance, from religious faith. Religion is often unable to restrain man from the numberless temptations of fortune ; nor can it check that passion for gain which every incident of his life contributes to arouse, but its influence over the mind of woman is supreme, and women are the protectors of morals. There is certainly no country in the world where the tie of marriage is so much respected as in America, or where conjugal happiness is more highly or worthily appreciated. In Europe almost all the disturbances of society arise from the irregularities of domestic life. To despise the natural bonds and legitimate pleasures of home, is to contract a taste for excesses, a restlessness of heart, and the evil of fluctuating desires. Agitated by the tumultuous passions which frequently disturb his dwelling, the European is galled by the obedience which the legislative powers of the State exact. But when the American retires from the turmoil of public life to the bosom of his family, he finds in it the image of order and of peace. There his pleasures are simple and natural, his joys are innocent and calm; and as he finds that an orderly life is the surest path to happiness, he accustoms himself without difficulty to moderate his opinions as well as his tastes. While the European endeavours to forget his domestic troubles by agitating society, the American derives from his own home that love of order which he afterward carries with him into public affairs.

In the United States the influence of religion is not confined to the manners, but it extends to the intelligence of the people. Among the Anglo-Americans, there are some who profess the doctrines of Christianity from a sincere belief in them, and others who do the same because they are afraid to be suspected of unbelief. Christianity, therefore, reigns without any obstacle, by universal consent; the consequence is, as I have before observed, that every principle of the moral world is fixed and determinate, although the political world is abandoned to the debates and the experiments of men. Thus the human mind is never left to wander across a boundless field; and, whatever may be its pretensions, it is checked from time to time by barriers which it cannot surmount. Before it can perpetrate innovation, certain primal and immutable principles are laid down, and the boldest conceptions of human device are subjected to certain forms which retard and stop their completion.

The imagination of the Americans, even in its greatest flights, is circumspect and undecided; its impulses are checked, and its works unfinished. These habits of restraint recur in political society, and are singularly favourable both to the tranquillity of the people and to the durability of the institutions it has established. Nature and circumstances concurred to make the inhabitants of the United States bold men, as is sufficiently attested by the enterprising spirit with which they seek for fortune. If the mind of the Americans were free from all trammels, they would very shortly become the most daring innovators and the most implacable disputants in the world. But the revolutionists of America are obliged to profess an ostensible respect for Christian morality and equity, which does not easily permit them to violate the laws that oppose their designs ; nor would they find it easy to surmount the scruples of their partisans, even if they were able to get over their own. Hitherto no one in the United States has dared to advance the maxim that everything is permissible with a view to the interests of society ; an impious adage which seems to have been invented in an age of freedom to shelter all the tyrants of future ages. Thus while the law permits the Americans to do what they please, religion prevents them from conceiving, and forbids them to commit, what is rash or unjust.

Religion in America takes no direct part in the government of society, but nevertheless it must be regarded as the foremost of the political institutions of that country ; for if it does not impart a taste for freedom, it facilitates the use of free institutions. Indeed, it is in this same point of view that the inhabitants of the United States themselves look upon religious belief. I do not know whether all the Americans have a sincere faith in their religion, for who can search the human heart ? but I am certain that they hold it to be indispensable to the maintenance of republican institutions. This opinion is not peculiar to a class of citizen or to a party, but it belongs to the whole nation, and to every rank of society.

In the United States, if a political character attacks a sect, this may not prevent even the partisans of that very sect from supporting him ; but if he attacks all the sects together, every one abandons him, and he remains alone.

While I was in America, a witness, who happened to be called at the assizes of the county of Westchester (State of New York), declared that he did not believe in the existence of God, or in the immortality of the soul. The judge refused to admit his evidence, on the ground that the witness had destroyed beforehand all the confidence of the court in what he was about to say. The newspapers related the fact without any further comment.

The Americans combine the notions of Christianity and of liberty so intimately in their minds that it is impossible to make them conceive the one without the other, and with them this conviction does not spring from that barren traditionary faith which seems to vegetate in the soul rather than to live.

I have known of societies formed by the Americans to send out ministers of the Gospel into the new Western States to found schools and churches there, lest religion should be suffered to die away in those remote settlements, and the rising States be less fitted to enjoy free institutions than the people from which they emanated. I met with wealthy New Englanders who abandoned the country in which they were born in order to lay the foundations of Christianity and of freedom on the banks of the Missouri, or in the prairies of Illinois. Thus religious zeal is perpetually stimulated in the United States by the duties of patriotism. These men do not act from an exclusive consideration of the promises of a future life ; eternity is only one motive of their devotion to the cause ; and if you converse with these missionaries of Christian civilization, you will be surprised to find how much value they set upon the goods of this world, and that you meet with a politician where you expected to find a priest. They will tell you that ' all the American republics are collectively involved with each other ; if the republics of the West were to fall into anarchy, or to be mastered by a despot, the republican institutions which now flourish upon the shores of the Atlantic Ocean would be in great peril. It is therefore our interest that the new States should be religious, in order to maintain our liberties.'

Such are the opinions of the Americans, and if any hold that the religious spirit which I admire is the very thing most amiss in America, . . . I can only reply that those who hold this language have never been in America, and that they have never seen a religious or a free nation. When they return from their expedition, we shall hear what they have to say. . . .

The philosophers of the eighteenth century explained the gradual decay of religious faith in a very simple manner. Religious zeal, said they, must necessarily fail, the more generally liberty is established and knowledge diffused. Unfortunately, facts are by no means in accordance with their theory. There are certain populations in Europe whose unbelief is only equalled by their ignorance and their debasement, while in America one of the freest and most enlightened nations in the world fulfils all the outward duties of religion with fervour.

Upon my arrival in the United States, the religious aspect of the country was the first thing that struck my attention ; and the longer I stayed there the more did I perceive the great political consequences resulting from this state of things, to which I was unaccustomed. In France I had almost always seen the spirit of religion and the spirit of freedom pursuing courses diametrically opposed to each other ; but in America I found that they were intimately united, and that they reigned in common over the same country. My desire to discover the causes of this phenomenon increased from day to day. In order to satisfy it I questioned the members of all the different sects ; and I more especially sought the society of the clergy, who are the depositaries of the different persuasions, and who are more especially interested in their duration. As a member of the Roman Catholic Church I was more particularly brought into contact with several of its priests, with whom I became intimately acquainted. To each of these men I expressed my astonishment and I explained my doubts ; I found that they differed upon matters of detail alone ; and that they mainly attributed the peaceful dominion of religion in their country to the separation of Church and State. I do not hesitate to affirm that during my stay in America I did not meet with a single individual, of the clergy or of the laity, who was not of the same opinion upon this point.

This led me to examine more attentively than I had hitherto done, the station which the American clergy occupy in political society. I learned with surprise that they filled no public appointments ; not one of them is to be met with in the administration, and they are not even represented in the legislative assemblies. In several States the law excludes them from political life, public opinion in all. And when I came to inquire into the prevailing spirit of the clergy, I found that most of its members seemed to retire of their own accord from the exercise of power, and that they made it the pride of their profession to abstain from politics. . . .

I perceived that these ministers of the Gospel eschewed all parties with the anxiety attendant upon personal interest. These facts convinced me that what I had been told was true ; and it then became my object to investigate their causes, and to inquire how it happened that the real authority of religion was increased by a state of things which diminished its apparent force : these causes did not long escape my researches. . . .

As long as a religion is sustained by those feelings, propensities, and passions which are found to occur under the same forms, at all the different periods of history, it may defy the efforts of time ; or at least it can only be destroyed by another religion. But when religion clings to the interests of the world, it becomes almost as fragile a thing as the powers of earth. It is the only one of them all which can hope for immortality ; but if it be connected with their ephemeral authority, it shares their fortunes, and may fall with those transient passions which supported them for a day. The alliance which religion contracts with political powers must needs be onerous to itself ; since it does not require their assistance to live, and by giving them its assistance it may be exposed to decay. . . .

In proportion as a nation assumes a democratic condition of society, and as communities display democratic propensities, it becomes more and more dangerous to connect religion with political institutions ; for the time is coming when authority will be bandied from hand to hand, when political theories will succeed each other, and when men, laws, and constitutions will disappear, or be modified from day to day, and this, not for a season only, but unceasingly.

Agitation and mutability are inherent in the nature of democratic republics, just as stagnation and inertness are the law of absolute monarchies.

If the Americans, who change the head of the Government once in four years, who elect new legislators every two years, and renew the provincial officers every twelvemonth ; if the Americans, who have abandoned the political world to the attempts of innovators, had not placed religion beyond their reach, where could it abide in the ebb and flow of human opinions ? where would that respect which belongs to it be paid, amid the struggles of faction ? and what would become of its immortality, in the midst of perpetual decay ? The American clergy were the first to perceive this truth, and to act in conformity with it. They saw that they must renounce their religious influence if they were to strive for political power ; and they chose to give up the support of the State rather than to share its vicissitudes.

In America, religion is perhaps less powerful than it has been at certain periods in the history of certain peoples ; but its influence is more lasting. It restricts itself to its own resources, but of those none can deprive it : its circle is limited to certain principles, but those principles are entirely its own, and under its undisputed control. . . .

I have but little to add to what I have already said concerning the influence which the instruction and the habits of the Americans exercise upon the maintenance of their political institutions.

America has hitherto produced very few writers of distinction ; it possesses no great historians, and not a single eminent poet.[1] The inhabitants of that

[1] It must be remembered that Tocqueville was writing on the eve of the great literary renaissance in America.— H. S. C.

country look upon what are properly styled literary pursuits with a kind of disapprobation ; and there are towns of very second-rate importance in Europe in which more literary works are annually published than in the twenty-four States of the Union put together. The spirit of the Americans is averse to general ideas ; and it does not seek theoretical discoveries. Neither politics nor manufactures direct them to these occupations ; and although new laws are perpetually enacted in the United States, no great writers have hitherto inquired into the general principles of their legislation. The Americans have lawyers and commentators, but no jurists[1] ; and they furnish examples rather than lessons to the world. The same observation applies to the mechanical arts. In America, the inventions of Europe are adopted with sagacity ; they are perfected, and adapted with admirable skill to the wants of the country. Manufactures exist, but the science of manufacture is not cultivated ; and they have good workmen, but very few inventors. Fulton was obliged to proffer his services to foreign nations for a long time before he was able to devote them to his own country.

The observer who is desirous of forming an opinion on the state of instruction among the Anglo-Americans must consider the same object from two different points of view. If he only singles out the learned, he will be astonished to find how rare they are ; but if he counts the ignorant, the American people will appear to be the most enlightened community in the world. The whole population, as I observed in another place, is situated between these two extremes. In New England, every citizen receives the elementary

---

[1] In the light of Tocqueville's acquaintance with the work of Marshall and Story this is an astonishing generalization.—H. S. C.

notions of human knowledge; he is, moreover, taught the doctrines and the evidences of his religion, the history of his country, and the leading features of its Constitution. In the States of Connecticut and Massachusetts, it is extremely rare to find a man imperfectly acquainted with all these things, and a person wholly ignorant of them is a sort of phenomenon.

When I compare the Greek and Roman Republics with these American States, the manuscript libraries of the former, and their rude population, with the innumerable journals and the enlightened people of the latter; when I remember all the attempts that are made to judge the modern republics by the assistance of those of antiquity, and to infer what will happen in our time from what took place two thousand years ago, I am tempted to burn my books, in order to apply none but novel ideas to so novel a condition of society.

What I have said of New England must not, however, be applied indistinctly to the whole Union; as we advance toward the West or the South, the instruction of the people diminishes. In the States which are adjacent to the Gulf of Mexico, a certain number of individuals may be found, as in our own countries, who are devoid of the rudiments of instruction. But there is not a single district in the United States sunk in complete ignorance; and for a very simple reason: the peoples of Europe started from the darkness of a barbarous condition, to advance toward the light of civilization; their progress has been unequal; some of them have improved apace, while others have loitered in their course, and some have stopped, and are still sleeping upon the way.

Such has not been the case in the United States.

The Anglo-Americans settled in a state of civilization, upon that territory which their descendants occupy ; they had not to begin to learn, and it was sufficient for them not to forget.   Now the children of these same Americans are the persons who, year by year, transport their dwellings into the wilds ; and with their dwellings their acquired information and their esteem for knowledge.   Education has taught them the utility of instruction, and has enabled them to transmit that instruction to their posterity.   In the United States society has no infancy, but it is born into man's estate.

The Americans never use the word " peasant," because they have no idea of the peculiar class which that term denotes ;   the ignorance of more remote ages, the simplicity of rural life, and the rusticity of the villager have not been preserved among them ; and they are alike unacquainted with the virtues, the vices, the coarse habits, and the simple graces of an early stage of civilization.   At the extreme borders of the confederate States, upon the confines of society and of the wilderness, a population of bold adventurers have taken up their abode, who pierce the solitudes of the American woods, and seek a country there, in order to escape that poverty which awaited them in their native provinces.   As soon as the pioneer arrives upon the spot which is to serve him for a retreat, he fells a few trees and builds a log-house.   Nothing can offer a more miserable aspect than these isolated dwellings.   The traveller who approaches one of them toward nightfall, sees the flicker of the hearth-flame through the chinks in the walls ; and at night, if the wind rises, he hears the roof of boughs shake to and fro in the midst of the great forest trees.   Who would not suppose that this poor hut is the asylum of rudeness and ignorance ?

Yet no sort of comparison can be drawn between the pioneer and the dwelling which shelters him. Everything about him is primitive and unformed, but he is himself the result of the labour and the experience of eighteen centuries. He wears the dress and he speaks the language of cities ; he is acquainted with the past, curious of the future, and ready for argument upon the present ; he is, in short, a highly civilized being, who consents, for a time, to inhabit the backwoods, and who penetrates into the wilds of the New World with the Bible, an axe, and a file of newspapers.

It is difficult to imagine the incredible rapidity with which public opinion circulates in the midst of these deserts. I do not think that so much intellectual intercourse takes place in the most enlightened and populous districts of France. It cannot be doubted that, in the United States, the instruction of the people powerfully contributes to the support of a democratic republic ; and such must always be the case, I believe, where instruction which awakens the understanding is not separated from moral education which amends the heart. But I by no means exaggerate this benefit, and I am still further from thinking, as so many people do think in Europe, that men can be made citizens instantaneously by teaching them to read and write. True information is mainly derived from experience ; and if the Americans had not been gradually accustomed to govern themselves, their book-learning would not assist them much at the present day.

I have lived a great deal with the people in the United States, and I cannot express how much I admire their experience and their good sense. An American should never be allowed to speak of Europe ; for he will then probably display a vast deal of presumption and very foolish pride. He will take up with those crude and vague notions which are so useful to the ignorant all over the world. But if you question him respecting his own country, the cloud which dimmed his intelligence will immediately disperse ; his language will become as clear and as precise as his thoughts. He will inform you what his rights are, and by what means he exercises them ; he will be able to point out the customs which obtain in the political world. You will find that he is well acquainted with the rules of the administration, and that he is familiar with the mechanism of the laws. The citizen of the United States does not acquire his practical science and his positive notions from books ; the instruction he has acquired may have prepared him for receiving those ideas, but it did not furnish them. The American learns to know the laws by participating in the act of legislation ; and he takes a lesson in the forms of government from governing. The great work of society is ever going on beneath his eyes, and, as it were, under his hands.

In the United States politics are the end and aim of education ; in Europe its principal object is to fit men for private life. The interference of the citizens in public affairs is too rare an occurrence for it to be anticipated beforehand. Upon casting a glance over society in the two hemispheres, these differences are indicated even by its external aspect.

In Europe we frequently introduce the ideas and the habits of private life into public affairs ; and as we pass at once from the domestic circle to the government of the State, we frequently may be heard to discuss the great interests of society in the same manner in which we converse with our friends. The Americans, on the other hand, transfuse the habits of public life into their manners in private ; and in their country the jury is introduced into the games of schoolboys, and parliamentary forms are observed in the order of a feast.

I have remarked that the maintenance of democratic institutions in the United States is attributable to the circumstances, the laws, and the manners of that country. Most Europeans are only acquainted with the first of these three causes, and they are apt to give it a preponderating importance which it does not really possess.

It is true that the Anglo-Americans settled in the New World in a state of social equality ; the low-born and the noble were not to be found among them ; and professional prejudices were always as entirely unknown as the prejudices of birth. Thus, as the condition of society was democratic, the empire of democracy was established without difficulty. But this circumstance is by no means peculiar to the United States ; almost all the transatlantic colonies were founded by men equal among themselves, or who became so by inhabiting them. In no one part of the New World have Europeans been able to create an aristocracy. Nevertheless, democratic institutions prosper nowhere but in the United States.

The American Union has no enemies to contend with ; it stands in the wilds like an island in the ocean. But the Spaniards of South America were no less isolated by nature ; yet their position has not relieved them from the charge of standing armies. They make war upon each other when they have no foreign enemies to oppose ; and the Anglo-American democracy is the only one which has hitherto been able to maintain itself in peace.

The territory of the Union presents a boundless field to human activity, and inexhaustible materials for industry and labour. The passion of wealth takes the place of ambition, and the warmth of faction is mitigated by a sense of prosperity. But in what portion of the globe shall we meet with more fertile plains, with mightier rivers, or with more unexplored and inexhaustible riches than in South America ?

Nevertheless, South America has been unable to maintain democratic institutions. If the welfare of nations depended on their being placed in a remote position, with an unbounded space of habitable territory before them, the Spaniards of South America would have no reason to complain of their fate. And although they might enjoy less prosperity than the inhabitants of the United States, their lot might still be such as to excite the envy of some nations in Europe. There are, however, no nations upon the face of the earth more miserable than those of South America.

Thus, not only are physical causes inadequate to produce results analogous to those which occur in North America, but they are unable to raise the population of South America above the level of European States, where they act in a contrary direction. Physical causes do not, therefore, affect the destiny of nations so much as has been supposed.

I have met with men in New England who were on the point of leaving a country, where they might have remained in easy circumstances, to go to seek their fortune in the wilds. Not far from that district I found a French population in Canada, which was closely crowded on a narrow territory, although the same wilds were at hand ; and while the emigrant from the United States purchased an extensive estate with the earnings of a short term of labour, the Canadian paid as much for land as he would have done in France. Nature offers the solitudes of the New World to Europeans ; but they are not always acquainted with the means of turning her gifts to account. Other peoples of America have the same physical conditions of prosperity as the Anglo-Americans, but without their laws and their manners ; and these peoples are wretched. The laws and manners of the Anglo-Americans are therefore that efficient cause of their greatness which is the object of my inquiry.

I am far from supposing that the American laws are pre-eminently good in themselves ; I do not hold them to be applicable to all democratic peoples ; and several of them seem to me to be dangerous, even in the United States. Nevertheless, it cannot be denied that the American legislation, taken collectively, is extremely well adapted to the genius of the people and the nature of the country which it is intended to govern. The American laws are therefore good, and to them must be attributed a large portion of the success which attends the government of democracy in America : but I do not believe them to be the principal cause of that success ; and if they seem to me to have more influence upon the social happiness of the Americans than the nature of the country, on the other hand there is reason to believe that their effect is still inferior to that produced by the manners of the people.

The Federal laws undoubtedly constitute the most important part of the legislation of the United States. Mexico, which is not less fortunately situated than the Anglo-American Union, has adopted the same laws, but is unable to accustom itself to the government of democracy. Some other cause is therefore at work, independently of those physical circumstances and peculiar laws which enable the democracy to rule in the United States.

Another still more striking proof may be adduced. Almost all the inhabitants of the territory of the

Union are the descendants of a common stock;[1] they speak the same language, they worship God in the same manner, they are affected by the same physical causes, and they obey the same laws. Whence, then, do their characteristic differences arise? Why, in the Eastern States of the Union, does the republican Government display vigour and regularity, and proceed with mature deliberation? Whence does it derive the wisdom and the durability which mark its acts, while in the Western States, on the contrary, society seems to be ruled by the powers of chance? There, public business is conducted with an irregularity and a passionate and feverish excitement, which does not announce a long or sure duration.

I am no longer comparing the Anglo-American States to foreign nations; but I am contrasting them with each other, and endeavouring to discover why they are so unlike. The arguments which are derived from the nature of the country and the difference of legislation are here all set aside. Recourse must be had to some other cause; and what other cause can there be except the manners of the people?

It is in the Eastern States that the Anglo-Americans have been longest accustomed to the government of democracy, and that they have adopted the habits and conceived the notions most favourable to its maintenance. Democracy has gradually penetrated into their customs, their opinions, and the forms of social intercourse; it is to be found in all the details of daily life as equally as in the laws. In the Eastern States the instruction and practical education of the people have been most perfected, and religion has been most thoroughly amalgamated with liberty. Now these

[1] Tocqueville wrote before the beginning of large-scale migration from Ireland and Germany.—H. S. C.

habits, opinions, customs, and convictions are precisely the constituent elements of that which I have denominated manners.

In the Western States, on the contrary, a portion of the same advantages is still wanting. Many of the Americans of the West were born in the woods, and they mix the ideas and the customs of savage life with the civilization of their parents. Their passions are more intense; their religious morality less authoritative; and their convictions less secure. The inhabitants exercise no sort of control over their fellow-citizens, for they are scarcely acquainted with each other. The nations of the West display, to a certain extent, the inexperience and the rude habits of a people in its infancy; for although they are composed of old elements, their assemblage is of recent date.

The manners of the Americans of the United States are, then, the real cause which renders that people the only one of the American nations that is able to support a democratic Government; and it is the influence of manners which produces the different degrees of order and of prosperity that may be distinguished in the several Anglo-American democracies. Thus the effect which the geographical position of a country may have upon the duration of democratic institutions is exaggerated in Europe. Too much importance is attributed to legislation, too little to manners. These three great causes serve, no doubt, to regulate and direct the American democracy; but if they were to be classed in their proper order, I should say that the physical circumstances are less efficient than the laws, and the laws very subordinate to the manners of the people. I am convinced that the most advantageous situation and the best possible laws cannot maintain a constitution in spite of the manners of a country ; while the latter may turn the most unfavourable positions and the worst laws to some advantage. The importance of manners is a common truth to which study and experience incessantly direct our attention. It may be regarded as a central point in the range of human observation, and the common termination of all inquiry. So seriously do I insist upon this head, that if I have hitherto failed in making the reader feel the important influence which I attribute to the practical experience, the habits, the opinions, in short, to the manners of the Americans, upon the maintenance of their institutions, I have failed in the principal object of my work.

I have asserted that the success of democratic institutions in the United States is more intimately connected with the laws themselves, and the manners of the people, than with the nature of the country. But does it follow that the same causes would of themselves produce the same results if they were put into operation elsewhere ; and if the country is no adequate substitute for laws and manners, can laws and manners in their turn prove a substitute for the country ? It will readily be understood that the necessary elements of a reply to this question are wanting : other peoples are to be found in the New World besides the Anglo-Americans, and as these people are affected by the same physical circumstances as the latter, they may fairly be compared together. But there are no nations out of America which have adopted the same laws and manners, being destitute of the physical advantages peculiar to the Anglo-Americans. No standard of comparison therefore exists, and we can only hazard an opinion upon this subject.

It appears to me, in the first place, that a careful

distinction must be made between the institutions of the United States and democratic institutions in general. When I reflect upon the state of Europe, its mighty nations, its populous cities, its formidable armies, and the complex nature of its politics, I cannot suppose that even the Anglo-Americans, if they were transported to our hemisphere, with their ideas, their religion, and their manners, could exist without considerably altering their laws. But a democratic nation may be imagined, organized differently from the American poeple. It is not impossible to conceive a government really established upon the will of the majority ; but in which the majority, repressing its natural propensity to equality, should consent, with a view to the order and the stability of the State, to invest a family or an individual with all the prerogatives of the executive. A democratic society might exist, in which the forces of the nation would be more centralized than they are in the United States ; the people would exercise a less direct and less irresistible influence upon public affairs, and yet every citizen invested with certain rights would participate, within his sphere, in the conduct of the government. The observations I made among the Anglo-Americans induce me to believe that democratic institutions of this kind, prudently introduced into society, so as gradually to mix with the habits and to be interfused with the opinions of the people, might subsist in other countries besides America. If the laws of the United States were the only imaginable democratic laws, or the most perfect which it is possible to conceive, I should admit that the success of those institutions affords no proof of the success of democratic institutions in general, in a country less favoured by natural circumstances. But as the laws of America appear to me to be defective in several respects, and as I can readily imagine others of the same general nature, the peculiar advantages of that country do not prove that democratic institutions cannot succeed in a nation less favoured by circumstances, if ruled by better laws.

If human nature were different in America from what it is elsewhere ; or if the social condition of the Americans engendered habits and opinions among them different from those which originate in the same social condition in the Old World, the American democracies would afford no means of predicting what may occur in other democracies. If the Americans displayed the same propensities as all other democratic nations, and if their legislators had relied upon the nature of the country and the favour of circumstances to restrain those propensities within due limits, the prosperity of the United States would be exclusively attributable to physical causes, and it would afford no encouragement to a people inclined to imitate their example, without sharing their natural advantages. But neither of these suppositions is borne out by facts.

In America the same passions are to be met with as in Europe ; some originating in human nature, others in the democratic condition of society. Thus in the United States I found that restlessness of heart which is natural to men, when all ranks are nearly equal and the chances of elevation are the same to all. I found the democratic feeling of envy expressed under a thousand different forms. I remarked that the people frequently displayed, in the conduct of affairs, a consummate mixture of ignorance and presumption ; and I inferred that in America men are liable to the same failings and the same absurdities as among ourselves. But upon examining the state of society more attentively, I speedily discovered that the Americans had made great and successful efforts to counteract these imperfections of human nature, and to correct the natural defects of democracy. Their divers municipal laws appeared to me to be a means of restraining the ambition of the citizens within a narrow sphere, and of turning those same passions which might have worked havoc in the State, to the good of the township or the parish. The American legislators have succeeded to a certain extent in opposing the notion of rights to the feelings of envy ; the permanence of the religious world to the continual shifting of politics ; the experience of the people to its theoretical ignorance ; and its practical knowledge of business to the impatience of its desires.

The Americans, then, have not relied upon the nature of their country to counterpoise those dangers which originate in their Constitution and in their political laws. To evils which are common to all democratic peoples they have applied remedies which none but themselves had ever thought of before ; and although they were the first to make the experiment, they have succeeded in it.

The manners and laws of the Americans are not the only ones which may suit a democratic people ; but the Americans have shown that it would be wrong to despair of regulating democracy by the aid of manners and of laws. If other nations should borrow this general and pregnant idea from the Americans, without, however, intending to imitate them in the peculiar application which they have made of it ; if they should attempt to fit themselves for that social condition, which it seems to be the will of Providence to impose upon the generations of this age, and so to escape from the despotism or the anarchy which threatens them ; what reason is there to suppose that their efforts would not be crowned with success? The organization and the establishment of democracy in Christendom is the great political problem of the time. The Americans, unquestionably, have not resolved this problem, but they furnish useful data to those who undertake the task.

It may readily be discovered with what intention I undertook the foregoing inquiries. The question here discussed is interesting not only to the United States, but to the whole world ; it concerns, not a nation, but all mankind. If those nations whose social condition is democratic could only remain free as long as they are inhabitants of the wilds, we could not but despair of the future destiny of the human race ; for democracy is rapidly acquiring a more extended sway, and the wilds are gradually peopled with men. If it were true that laws and manners are insufficient to maintain democratic institutions, what refuge would remain open to the nations, except the despotism of a single individual? I am aware that there are many worthy persons at the present time who are not alarmed at this latter alternative, and who are not so tired of liberty as to be glad of repose, far from those storms by which it is attended. But these individuals are ill acquainted with the haven toward which they are bound. They are so deluded by their recollections as to judge the tendency of absolute power by what it was formerly, and not by what it might become at the present time.

If absolute power were re-established among the democratic nations of Europe, I am persuaded that it would assume a new form, and appear under features unknown to our forefathers. There was a time in Europe when the laws and the consent of the people had invested princes with almost unlimited authority ; but they scarcely ever availed themselves of it. I do not speak of the prerogatives of the nobility, of the authority of supreme courts of justice, of corporations and their chartered rights, or of provincial privileges, which served to break the blows of the sovereign authority, and to maintain a spirit of resistance in the nation. Independently of these political institutions—which, however opposed they might be to personal liberty, served to keep alive the love of freedom in the mind of the public, and which may be esteemed to have been useful in this respect —the manners and opinions of the nation confined the royal authority within barriers which were not less powerful, although they were less conspicuous. Religion, the affections of the people, the benevolence of the prince, the sense of honour, family pride, provincial prejudices, custom, and public opinion limited the power of kings, and restrained their authority within an invisible circle. The constitution of nations was despotic at that time, but their manners were free. Princes had the right, but they had neither the means nor the desire, of doing whatever they pleased.

But what now remains of those barriers which formerly arrested the aggression of tyranny? Since religion has lost its empire over the souls of men, the most prominent boundary which divided good from evil is overthrown; the very elements of the moral world are indeterminate; the princes and the peoples of the earth are guided by chance, and none can define the natural limits of despotism and the bound of licence. Long revolutions have for ever destroyed the respect which surrounded the rulers of the State; and since they have been relieved from the burden of public esteem, princes may henceforward surrender themselves without fear to the seductions of arbitrary power.

When kings find that the hearts of their subjects are turned toward them, they are clement, because they are conscious of their strength, and they are chary of the affection of their people, because the affection of their people is the bulwark of the throne. A mutual interchange of good-will then takes place between the prince and the people, which resembles the gracious intercourse of domestic society. The subjects may murmur at the sovereign's decree, but they are grieved to displease him; and the sovereign chastises his subjects with the light hand of parental affection.

But when once the spell of royalty is broken in the tumult of revolution; when successive monarchs have crossed the throne, so as alternately to display to the people the weakness of their right and the harshness of their power, the sovereign is no longer regarded by any as the Father of the State, and he is feared by all as its master. If he be weak, he is despised; if he be strong, he is detested. He is himself full of animosity and alarm; he finds that he is as a stranger in his own country, and he treats his subjects like conquered enemies. . . .

While the nobles enjoyed their power, and indeed long after that power was lost, the honour of aristocracy conferred an extraordinary degree of force upon their personal opposition. They afforded instances of men who, notwithstanding their weakness, still entertained a high opinion of their personal value, and dared to cope single-handed with the efforts of the public authority. But at the present day, when all ranks are more and more confounded, when the individual disappears in the throng, and is easily lost in the midst of a common obscurity, when the honour of monarchy has almost lost its empire without being succeeded by public virtue, and when nothing can enable man to rise above himself, who shall say at what point the exigencies of power and the servility of weakness will stop ? . . .

The annals of France furnish nothing analogous to the condition in which that country might then be thrown. But it may more aptly be assimilated to the times of old, and to those hideous eras of Roman oppression, when the manners of the people were corrupted, their traditions obliterated, their habits destroyed, their opinions shaken, and freedom, expelled from the laws, could find no refuge in the land ; when nothing protected the citizens, and the citizens no longer protected themselves ; when human nature was the sport of man, and princes wearied out the clemency of Heaven before they exhausted the patience of their subjects. Those who hope to revive the monarchy of Henry IV or of Louis XIV appear to me to be afflicted with mental blindness ; and when I consider the present condition of several European nations—a condition to which all the others tend— I am led to believe that they will soon be left with no other alternative than democratic liberty, or the tyranny of the Cæsars.

And, indeed, it is deserving of consideration, whether men are to be entirely emancipated or entirely enslaved ; whether their rights are to be made equal, or wholly taken away from them. If the rulers of society were reduced either gradually to raise the crowd to their own level, or to sink the citizens below that of humanity, would not the doubts of many be resolved, the consciences of many be healed, and the community prepared to make great sacrifices with little difficulty ? In that case, the gradual growth of democratic manners and institutions should be regarded, not as the best, but as the only means of preserving freedom ; and without liking the government of democracy, it might be adopted as the most applicable and the fairest remedy for the present ills of society.

It is difficult to associate a people in the work of government ; but it is still more difficult to supply it with experience, and to inspire it with the feelings which it requires in order to govern well. I grant that the caprices of democracy are perpetual ; its instruments are rude ; its laws imperfect. But if it were true that soon no just medium would exist between the empire of democracy and the dominion of a single arm, should we not rather incline toward the former than submit voluntarily to the latter ? And if complete equality be our fate, is it not better to be levelled by free institutions than by despotic power ?

Those who, after having read this book, should imagine that my intention in writing it has been to propose the laws and manners of the Anglo-Americans for the imitation of all democratic peoples, would commit a very great mistake ; they must have paid more attention to the form than to the substance of my ideas. My aim has been to show, by the example of America, that laws, and especially manners, may exist which will allow a democratic people to remain free. But I am very far from thinking that we ought to follow the example of the American democracy, and copy the means which it has employed to attain its ends ; for I am well aware of the influence which the nature of a country and its political precedents exercise upon a constitution ; and I should regard it as a great misfortune for mankind if liberty were to exist over all the world under the same forms.

But I am of opinion that if we do not succeed in gradually introducing democratic institutions into France, and if we despair of imparting to the citizens those ideas and sentiments which first prepare them

for freedom, and afterward allow them to enjoy it,
there will be no independence at all, either for the
middle classes or the nobility, for the poor or for the
rich, but an equal tyranny over all ; and I foresee
that if the peaceable empire of the majority be not
founded among us in time, we shall sooner or later
arrive at the unlimited authority of a single despot.

Chapter XVIII

THE CHANCES OF THE DURATION OF THE UNION

THE maintenance of the existing institutions of the several States depends in some measure upon the maintenance of the Union itself. It is therefore important in the first instance to inquire into the probable fate of the Union. . . .

Among the various reasons which tend to render the existing Union useful to the Americans, two principal causes are peculiarly evident to the observer. Although the Americans are, as it were, alone upon their continent, their commerce makes them the neighbours of all the nations with which they trade. Notwithstanding their apparent isolation, the Americans require a certain degree of strength, which they cannot retain otherwise than by remaining united to each other. If the States were to split, they would not only diminish the strength which they are now able to display toward foreign nations, but they would soon create foreign powers upon their own territory. A system of inland custom-houses would then be established ; the valleys would be divided by imaginary boundary lines ; the courses of the rivers would be confined by territorial distinctions ; and a multitude of hindrances would prevent the Americans from exploring the whole of that vast continent which Providence has allotted to them for a dominion. At present they have no invasion to fear, and consequently no standing armies to maintain, no taxes to levy. If the Union were dissolved, all these burdensome measures might ere long be required. The Americans are then very powerfully interested in the maintenance of their Union. On the other hand, it is almost impossible to discover any sort of material interest which might at present tempt a portion of the

Union to separate from the other States.

When we cast our eyes upon the map of the United States, we perceive the chain of the Alleghany Mountains, running from the north-east to the south-west, and crossing nearly one thousand miles of country ; and we are led to imagine that the design of Providence was to raise between the valley of the Mississippi and the coasts of the Atlantic Ocean one of those natural barriers which break the mutual intercourse of men, and form the necessary limits of different States. But the average height of the Alleghanies does not exceed twenty-five hundred feet ; their greatest elevation is not above four thousand feet ; their rounded summits, and the spacious valleys which they conceal within their passes, are of easy access from several sides. Besides which, the principal rivers which fall into the Atlantic Ocean—the Hudson, the Susquehanna, and the Potomac—take their rise beyond the Alleghanies, in an open district, which borders upon the valley of the Mississippi. These streams quit this tract of country, make their way through the barrier which would seem to torn them westward, and as they wind through the mountains they open an easy and natural passage to man. No natural barrier exists in the regions which are now inhabited by the Anglo-Americans ; the Alleghanies are so far from serving as a boundary to separate nations that they do not even serve as a frontier to the States. New York, Pennsylvania, and Virginia comprise them within their borders, and extend as much to the west as to the east of the line. . . . The vast extent of territory occupied by the Anglo-American republics has given rise to doubts as to the maintenance of their Union. Here a distinction must be made ; contrary interests sometimes arise in the different provinces of a vast empire, which often terminate in open dissensions ; and the extent of the country is then most prejudicial to the power of the State. But if the inhabitants of these vast regions are not divided by contrary interests, the extent of the territory may be favourable to their prosperity ; for the unity of the Government promotes the interchange of the different productions of the soil, and increases their value by facilitating their consumption.

It is indeed easy to discover different interests in the different parts of the Union, but I am unacquainted with any which are hostile to each other. The Southern States are almost exclusively agricultural. The Northern States are more peculiarly commercial and manufacturing. The States of the West are at the same time agricultural and manufacturing. In the South, the crops consist of tobacco, of rice, of cotton, and of sugar ; in the North and the West, of wheat and maize. These are different sources of wealth ; but union is the means by which these sources are opened to all, and rendered equally advantageous to the several districts.

The North, which ships the produce of the Anglo-Americans to all parts of the world, and brings back the produce of the globe to the Union, is evidently interested in maintaining the confederation in its present condition, in order that the number of American producers and consumers may remain as large as possible. The North is the most natural agent of communication between the South and the West of the Union on the one hand, and the rest of the world upon the other ; the North is therefore interested in the union and prosperity of the South and the West, in order that they may continue to furnish raw materials for its manufactures, and cargoes for its shipping.

The South and the West, on their side, are still

more directly interested in the preservation of the Union, and the prosperity of the North. The produce of the South is, for the most part, exported beyond seas; the South and the West consequently stand in need of the commercial resources of the North. They are likewise interested in the maintenance of a powerful fleet by the Union, to protect them efficaciously. The South and the West have no vessels, but they cannot refuse a willing subsidy to defray the expenses of the navy; for if the fleets of Europe were to blockade the ports of the South and the delta of the Mississippi, what would become of the rice of the Carolinas, the tobacco of Virginia, and the sugar and cotton which grow in the valley of the Mississippi? Every portion of the Federal budget therefore contributes to the maintenance of material interests which are common to all the confederate States.

Independently of this commercial utility, the South and the West of the Union derive great political advantages from their connection with the North. The South contains an enormous slave population; a population which is already alarming, and still more formidable for the future. The States of the West lie in the remoter parts of a single valley; and all the rivers which intersect their territory rise in the Rocky Mountains or in the Alleghanies, and fall into the Mississippi, which bears them onward to the Gulf of Mexico. The Western States are consequently entirely cut off, by their position, from the traditions of Europe and the civilization of the Old World. The inhabitants of the South, then, are induced to support the Union in order to avail themselves of its protection against the blacks; and the inhabitants of the West in order not to be excluded from a free communication with the rest of the globe, and shut up in the wilds of central America. The North cannot but desire the maintenance of the Union, in order to remain, as it now is, the connecting link between that vast body and the other parts of the world.

The temporal interests of all the several parts of the Union are, then, intimately connected; and the same assertion holds true respecting those opinions and sentiments which may be termed the immaterial interests of men.

The inhabitants of the United States talk a great deal of their attachment to their country; but I confess that I do not rely upon that calculating patriotism which is founded upon interest, and which a change in the interests at stake may obliterate. Nor do I attach much importance to the language of the Americans, when they manifest, in their daily conversation, the intention of maintaining the Federal system adopted by their forefathers. A government retains its sway over a great number of citizens, far less by the voluntary and rational consent of the multitude, than by that instinctive, and to a certain extent involuntary agreement, which results from similarity of feelings and resemblances of opinion. I will never admit that men constitute a social body, simply because they obey the same head and the same laws. Society can only exist when a great number of men consider a great number of things in the same point of view; when they hold the same opinions upon many subjects, and when the same occurrences suggest the same thoughts and impressions to their minds.

The observer who examines the present condition of the United States upon this principle, will readily discover that, although the citizens are divided into twenty-four distinct sovereignties, they nevertheless constitute a single people; and he may perhaps be led to think that the state of the Anglo-American

Union is more truly a state of society than that of certain nations of Europe which live under the same legislation and the same prince.

Although the Anglo-Americans have several religious sects, they all regard religion in the same manner. They are not always agreed upon the measures which are most conducive to good government, and they vary upon some of the forms of government which it is expedient to adopt; but they are unanimous upon the general principles which ought to rule human society. From Maine to the Floridas, and from the Missouri to the Atlantic Ocean, the people is held to be the legitimate source of all power. The same notions are entertained respecting liberty and equality, the liberty of the press, the right of association, the jury, and the responsibility of the agents of Government.

If we turn from their political and religious opinions to the moral and philosophical principles which regulate the daily actions of life and govern their conduct, we shall still find the same uniformity. The Anglo-Americans acknowledge the absolute moral authority of the reason of the community, as they acknowledge the political authority of the mass of citizens; and they hold that public opinion is the surest arbiter of what is lawful or forbidden, true or false. The majority of them believe that a man will be led to do what is just and good by following his own interest rightly understood. They hold that every man is born in possession of the right of self-government, and that no one has the right of constraining his fellow-creatures to be happy. They have all a lively faith in the perfectibility of man; they are of opinion that the effects of the diffusion of knowledge must necessarily be advantageous, and the consequences of ignorance fatal; they all consider society as a body in a state of improvement, humanity as a changing scene, in which nothing is, or ought to be, permanent; and they admit that what appears to them to be good to-day may be superseded by something better to-morrow. I do not give all these opinions as true, but I quote them as characteristic of the Americans.

The Anglo-Americans are not only united together by these common opinions, but they are separated from all other nations by a common feeling of pride. For the last fifty years no pains have been spared to convince the inhabitants of the United States that they constitute the only religious, enlightened, and free people. They perceive that, for the present, their own democratic institutions succeed, while those of other countries fail; hence they conceive an overweening opinion of their superiority, and they are not very remote from believing themselves to belong to a distinct race of mankind.

The dangers which threaten the American Union do not originate in the diversity of interests or of opinions, but in the various characters and passions of the Americans. The men who inhabit the vast territory of the United States are almost all the issue of a common stock; but the effects of the climate, and more especially of slavery, have gradually introduced very striking differences between the British settler of the Southern States and the British settler of the North. In Europe it is generally believed that slavery has rendered the interests of one part of the Union contrary to those of another part; but I by no means remarked this to be the case: slavery has not created interests in the South contrary to those of the North, but it has modified the character and changed the habits of the natives of the South. . . .

The States which gave their assent to the Federal

Contract in 1790 were thirteen in number ; the Union now consists of twenty-four members. The population, which amounted to nearly four millions in 1790, had more than trebled in the space of forty years ; and in 1830 it amounted to nearly thirteen millions. Changes of such magnitude cannot take place without some danger. . . .

Since the first settlement of the British colonies, the number of inhabitants has about doubled every twenty-two years. I perceive no causes which are likely to check this progressive increase of the Anglo-American population for the next hundred years ; and before that space of time has elapsed, I believe that the territories and dependencies of the United States will be covered by more than a hundred millions of inhabitants, and divided into forty States. I admit that these hundred millions of men have no hostile interests. I suppose, on the contrary, that they are all equally interested in the maintenance of the Union ; but I am still of opinion that where there are a hundred millions of men, and forty distinct nations, unequally strong, the continuance of the Federal Government can only be a fortunate accident.

Whatever faith I may have in the perfectibility of man, until human nature is altered, and men wholly transformed, I shall refuse to believe in the duration of a government which is called upon to hold together forty different peoples, disseminated over a territory equal to one half of Europe in extent ; to avoid all rivalry, ambition, and struggles between them, and to direct their independent activity to the accomplishment of the same designs.

But the greatest peril to which the Union is exposed by its increase arises from the continual changes which take place in the position of its internal strength. The distance from Lake Superior to the

Gulf of Mexico extends from the forty-seventh to the thirtieth degree of latitude, a distance of more than twelve hundred miles as the bird flies. The frontier of the United States winds along the whole of this immense line, sometimes falling within its limits, but more frequently extending far beyond it, into the waste. It has been calculated that the whites advance every year a mean distance of seventeen miles along the whole of this vast boundary. Obstacles, such as an unproductive district, a lake or an Indian nation unexpectedly encountered, are sometimes met with. The advancing column then halts for a while; its two extremities fall back upon themselves, and as soon as they are reunited they proceed onward. This gradual and continuous progress of the European race toward the Rocky Mountains has the solemnity of a providential event; it is like a deluge of men rising unabatedly, and daily driven onward by the hand of God.

Within this first line of conquering settlers towns are built, and vast States founded. In 1790 there were only a few thousand pioneers sprinkled along the valleys of the Mississippi; and at the present day these valleys contain as many inhabitants as were to be found in the whole Union in 1790. Their population amounts to nearly four millions. The city of Washington was founded in 1800, in the very centre of the Union [1]; but such are the changes which have taken place that it now stands at one of the extremities; and the delegates of the most remote Western States are already obliged to perform a journey as long as that from Vienna to Paris.

All the States are borne onward at the same time in the path of fortune, but of course they do not all

[1] Not quite. By 1800 Kentucky and Tennessee had been admitted to the Union.—H. S. C.

increase and prosper in the same proportion. To the North of the Union the detached branches of the Alleghany chain, which extend as far as the Atlantic Ocean, form spacious roads and ports, which are constantly accessible to vessels of the greatest burden. But from the Potomac to the mouth of the Mississippi the coast is sandy and flat. In this part of the Union the mouths of almost all the rivers are obstructed ; and the few harbours which exist among these lagoons afford much shallower water to vessels, and much fewer commercial advantages than those of the North.

This first natural cause of inferiority is united to another cause proceeding from the laws. We have already seen that slavery, which is abolished in the North, still exists in the South ; and I have pointed out its fatal consequences upon the prosperity of the planter himself.

The North is therefore superior to the South both in commerce and manufacture ; the natural consequence of which is the more rapid increase of population and of wealth within its borders. The States situated upon the shores of the Atlantic Ocean are already half peopled. Most of the land is held by an owner ; and these districts cannot, therefore, receive so many emigrants as the Western States, where a boundless field is still open to their exertions. The valley of the Mississippi is far more fertile than the coast of the Atlantic Ocean. This reason, added to all the others, contributes to drive the Europeans westward—a fact which may be rigorously demonstrated by figures. It is found that the sum total of the population of all the United States has about trebled in the course of forty years. But in the recent States adjacent to the Mississippi the population has increased thirty-one fold within the same space of time.

The relative position of the central Federal power

is continually displaced. Forty years ago the majority of the citizens of the Union was established upon the coast of the Atlantic, in the environs of the spot upon which Washington now stands ; but the great body of the people is now advancing inland and to the North, so that in twenty years the majority will unquestionably be on the western side of the Alleghanies. If the Union goes on to subsist, the basin of the Mississippi is evidently marked out, by its fertility and its extent, as the future centre of the Federal Government. In thirty or forty years that tract of country will have assumed the rank which naturally belongs to it. . . . In a few years the States which founded the Union will lose the direction of its policy, and the population of the valleys of the Mississippi will preponderate in the Federal assemblies.

This constant gravitation of the Federal power and influence toward the North-west is shown every ten years, when a general census of the population is made, and the number of delegates which each State sends to Congress is settled afresh. In 1790 Virginia had nineteen representatives in Congress. This number continued to increase until the year 1813, when it reached to twenty-three ; from that time it began to decrease, and in 1833 Virginia elected only twenty-one representatives. During the same period the State of New York progressed in the contrary direction : in 1790 it had ten representatives in Congress ; in 1813, twenty-seven ; in 1823, thirty-four ; and in 1833, forty. The State of Ohio had only one representative in 1803, and in 1833 it had already nineteen.

It is difficult to imagine a durable union of a people which is rich and strong with one which is poor and weak, even if it were proved that the strength and wealth of the one are not the causes of the weakness and poverty of the other. But union is still more difficult to maintain at a time at which one party is losing strength, and the other is gaining it. This rapid and disproportionate increase of certain States threatens the independence of the others. New York might perhaps succeed, with its two millions of inhabitants and its forty representatives, in dictating to the other States in Congress. But even if the more powerful States make no attempt to bear down the lesser ones, the danger still exists; for there is almost as much in the possibility of the act as in the act itself. The weak generally mistrust the justice and the reason of the strong. The States which increase less rapidly than the others look upon those which are more favoured by fortune with envy and suspicion. Hence arise the deep-seated uneasiness and ill-defined agitation which are observable in the South, and which form so striking a contrast to the confidence and prosperity which are common to other parts of the Union. I am inclined to think that the hostile measures taken by the Southern provinces upon a recent occasion are attributable to no other cause. The inhabitants of the Southern States are, of all the Americans, those who are most interested in the maintenance of the Union; they would assuredly suffer most from being left to themselves; and yet they are the only citizens who threaten to break the tie of confederation. But it is easy to perceive that the South, which has given four Presidents—Washington, Jefferson, Madison, and Monroe—to the Union, which perceives that it is losing its Federal influence, and that the number of its representatives in Congress is diminishing from year to year, while those of the Northern and Western States are increasing; the South, which is peopled with ardent and irascible beings, is becoming more and more irritated and alarmed. The citizens reflect upon their present position and remember their past influence, with the melancholy uneasiness of men who suspect oppression : if they discover a law of the Union which is not unequivocally favourable to their interests, they protest against it as an abuse of force ; and if their ardent remonstrances are not listened to, they threaten to quit an association which loads them with burdens while it deprives them of their due profits. . . .

If the changes which I have described were gradual, so that each generation at least might have time to disappear with the order of things under which it had lived, the danger would be less ; but the progress of society in America is precipitate, and almost revolutionary. The same citizen may have lived to see his State take the lead in the Union, and afterward become powerless in the Federal assemblies ; and an Anglo-American republic has been known to grow as rapidly as a man passing from birth and infancy to maturity in the course of thirty years. It must not be imagined, however, that the States which lose their preponderance also lose their population or their riches : no stop is put to their prosperity, and they even go on to increase more rapidly than any kingdom in Europe. But they believe themselves to be impoverished because their wealth does not augment as rapidly as that of their neighbours ; and they think that their power is lost, because they suddenly come into collision with a power greater than their own : thus they are more hurt in their feelings and their passions than in their interests. But this is amply sufficient to endanger the maintenance of the Union. If kings and peoples had only had their true interests in view ever since the beginning of the world, the name of war would scarcely be known among mankind.

Thus the prosperity of the United States is the source of the most serious dangers that threaten them, since it tends to create in some of the confederate States that over-excitement which accompanies a rapid increase of fortune ; and to awaken in others those feelings of envy, mistrust, and regret which usually attend upon the loss of it. The Americans contemplate this extraordinary and hasty progress with exultation ; but they would be wiser to consider it with sorrow and alarm. The Americans of the United States must inevitably become one of the greatest nations in the world ; their offset will cover almost the whole of North America ; the continent which they inhabit is their dominion, and it cannot escape them. What urges them to take possession of it so soon ? Riches, power, and renown cannot fail to be theirs at some future time, but they rush upon their fortune as if but a moment remained for them to make it their own. . . .

What is understood by a republican government in the United States is the slow and quiet action of society upon itself. It is a regular state of things really founded upon the enlightened will of the people. It is a conciliatory government under which resolutions are allowed time to ripen ; and in which they are deliberately discussed, and executed with mature judgment. The republicans in the United States set a high value upon morality, respect religious belief, and acknowledge the existence of rights. They profess to think that a people ought to be moral, religious, and temperate, in proportion as it is free. What is called the republic in the United States is the tranquil rule of the majority, which, after having had time to examine itself, and to give proof of its existence, is the common source of all the powers of the State. But the power of the majority is not of itself unlimited. In the moral world humanity, justice, and reason enjoy an undisputed supremacy ; in the political world vested rights are treated with no less deference. The majority recognizes these two barriers ; and if it now and then oversteps them, it is because, like individuals, it has passions, and, like them, it is prone to do what is wrong, while it discerns what is right.

But the demagogues of Europe have made strange discoveries. A republic is not, according to them, the rule of the majority, as has hitherto been thought, but the rule of those who are strenuous partisans of the majority. It is not the people who preponderates in this kind of government, but those who are best versed in the good qualities of the people. A happy distinction, which allows men to act in the name of nations without consulting them, and to claim their gratitude while their rights are spurned. A republican government, moreover, is the only one which claims the right of doing whatever it chooses, and despising what men have hitherto respected, from the highest moral obligations to the vulgar rules of common sense. It had been supposed, until our time, that despotism was odious, under whatever form it appeared. But it is a discovery of modern days that there are such things as legitimate tyranny and holy injustice, provided they are exercised in the name of the people.

The ideas which the Americans have adopted respecting the republican form of government, render it easy for them to live under it, and endure its duration. If, in their country, this form often be practically bad, it is at least theoretically good ; and, in the end, the people always acts in conformity to it.

It was impossible at the foundation of the States, and it would still be difficult, to establish a centre, administration in America. The inhabitants are dispersed over too great a space, and separated by too many natural obstacles, for one man to undertake to direct the details of their existence. America is therefore pre-eminently the country of provincial and municipal government. To this cause, which was plainly felt by all the Europeans of the New World, the Anglo-Americans added several others peculiar to themselves.

At the time of the settlement of the North American colonies, municipal liberty had already penetrated into the laws as well as the manners of the English; and the emigrants adopted it, not only as a necessary thing, but as a benefit which they knew how to appreciate. We have already seen the manner in which the colonies were founded : every province, and almost every district, was peopled separately by men who were strangers to each other, or who associated with very different purposes. The English settlers in the United States, therefore, early perceived that they were divided into a great number of small and distinct communities which belonged to no common centre ; and that it was needful for each of these little communities to take care of its own affairs, since there did not appear to be any central authority which was naturally bound and easily enabled to provide for them. Thus, the nature of the country, the manner in which the British colonies were founded, the habits of the first emigrants, in short, everything, united to promote, in an extraordinary degree, municipal and provincial liberties.

In the United States, therefore, the mass of the institutions of the country is essentially republican ; and in order permanently to destroy the laws which form the basis of the republic, it would be necessary to abolish all the laws at once. At the present day it would be even more difficult for a party to succeed in founding a monarchy in the United States than for a set of men to proclaim that France should henceforward be a republic. Royalty would not find a system of legislation prepared for it beforehand ; and a monarchy would then exist, really surrounded by republican institutions. The monarchical principle would likewise have great difficulty in penetrating into the manners of the Americans.

In the United States, the sovereignty of the people is not an isolated doctrine bearing no relation to the prevailing manners and ideas of the people : it may, on the contrary, be regarded as the last link of a chain of opinions which binds the whole Anglo-American world. That Providence has given to every human being the degree of reason necessary to direct himself in the affairs which interest him exclusively ; such is the grand maxim upon which civil and political society rests in the United States. The father of a family applies it to his children ; the master to his servants ; the township to its officers ; the province to its townships ; the State to the provinces ; the Union to the State ; and when extended to the nation, it becomes the doctrine of the sovereignty of the people.

Thus, in the United States, the fundamental principle of the republic is the same which governs the greater part of human actions ; republican notions insinuate themselves into all the ideas, opinions, and habits of the Americans, while they are formally recognized by the legislation : and before this legislation can be altered the whole community must undergo very serious changes. In the United States, even the religion of most of the citizens is republican, since it submits the truths of the other world to private judgment : as in politics the care of its temporal interests is abandoned to the good sense of the people. Thus every man is allowed freely to take that road which he thinks will lead him to heaven ; just as the law permits every citizen to have the right of choosing his government.

It is evident that nothing but a long series of events, all having the same tendency, can substitute for this combination of laws, opinions, and manners a mass of opposite opinions, manners, and laws.

If republican principles are to perish in America, they can only yield after a laborious social process, often interrupted, and as often resumed ; they will have many apparent revivals, and will not become totally extinct until an entirely new people shall have succeeded to that which now exists. Now, it must be admitted that there is no sympton or presage of the approach of such a revolution. There is nothing more striking to a person newly arrived in the United States than the kind of tumultuous agitation in which he finds political society. The laws are incessantly changing, and at first sight it seems impossible that a people so variable in its desires should avoid adopting, within a short space of time, a completely new form of government. Such apprehensions are, however, premature ; the instability which affects political institutions is of two kinds, which ought not to be confounded : the first, which modifies secondary laws, is not incompatible with a very settled state of society ; the other shakes the very foundations of the Constitution, and attacks the fundamental principles of legislation ; this species of instability is always followed by troubles and revolutions, and the nation which suffers under it is in a state of violent transition.

Experience shows that these two kinds of legislative instability have no necessary connection ; for they have been found united or separate, according to times and circumstances. The first is common in the United States, but not the second : the Americans often change their laws, but the foundation of the Constitution is respected.

In our days the republican principle rules in America, as the monarchical principle did in France under Louis XIV. The French of that period were not only friends of the monarchy, but they thought it impossible to put anything in its place ; they received it as we receive the rays of the sun and the return of the seasons. Among them the royal power had neither advocates nor opponents. In like manner does the republican Government exist in America, without contention or opposition ; without proofs and arguments, by a tacit agreement, a sort of *concensus universalis*. It is, however, my opinion, that by changing their administrative forms as often as they do, the inhabitants of the United States compromise the future stability of their Government.

It may be apprehended that men, perpetually thwarted in their designs by the mutability of the legislation, will learn to look upon republican institutions as an inconvenient form of society ; the evil resulting from the instability of the secondary enactments might then raise a doubt as to the nature of the fundamental principles of the Constitution, and indirectly bring about a revolution ; but this epoch is still very remote.

It may, however, be foreseen even now that when the Americans lose their republican institutions they will speedily arrive at a despotic Government, without a long interval of limited monarchy. Montesquieu remarked that nothing is more absolute than the authority of a prince who immediately succeeds a republic, since the powers which had fearlessly been intrusted to an elected magistrate are then transferred to an hereditary sovereign. This is true in general, but it is more peculiarly applicable to a democratic republic. In the United States, the magistrates are not elected by a particular class of citizens, but by the majority of the nation; they are the immediate representatives of the passions of the multitude; and as they are wholly dependent upon its pleasure, they excite neither hatred nor fear : hence, as I have already shown, very little care has been taken to limit their influence, and they are left in possession of a vast deal of arbitrary power. This state of things has engendered habits which would outlive itself; the American magistrate would retain his power, but he would cease to be responsible for the exercise of it ; and it is impossible to say what bounds could then be set to tyranny.

Some of our European politicians expect to see an aristocracy arise in America, and they already predict the exact period at which it will be able to assume the reins of government. I have previously observed, and I repeat my assertion, that the present tendency of American society appears to me to become more and more democratic. Nevertheless, I do not assert that the Americans will not, at some future time, restrict the circle of political rights in their country, or confiscate those rights to the advantage of a single individual ; but I cannot imagine that they will ever bestow the exclusive exercise of them upon a privileged class of citizens, or, in other words, that they will ever found an aristocracy. . . .

I do not think a single people can be quoted, since human society began to exist, which has, by its own free will and by its own exertions, created an aristocracy within its own bosom. All the aristocracies of the Middle Ages were founded by military conquest ; the conqueror was the noble, the vanquished became the serf. Inequality was then imposed by force; and after it had been introduced into the manners of the country it maintained its own authority, and was sanctioned by the legislation. Communities have existed which were aristocratic from their earliest origin, owing to circumstances anterior to that event, and which became more democratic in each succeeding age. Such was the destiny of the Romans, and of the barbarians after them. But a people, having taken its rise in civilization and democracy, which should gradually establish an inequality of conditions, until it arrived at inviolable privileges and exclusive castes, would be a novelty in the world; and nothing intimates that America is likely to furnish so singular an example.

Chapter XIX

FUTURE PROSPECTS OF THE UNITED STATES

I HAVE now nearly reached the close of my inquiry; hitherto, in speaking of the future destiny of the United States, I have endeavoured to divide my subject into distinct portions, in order to study each of them with more attention. My present object is to embrace the whole from one single point; the remarks I shall make will be less detailed, but they will be more sure. I shall perceive each object less distinctly, but I shall descry the principal facts with more certainty. A traveller who has just left the walls of an immense city climbs the neighbouring hill; as he goes farther off he loses sight of the men whom he has so recently quitted; their dwellings are confused in a dense mass; he can no longer distinguish the public squares, and he can scarcely trace out the great thoroughfares; but his eye has less difficulty in following the boundaries of the city, and for the first time he sees the shape of the vast whole. Such is the future destiny of the British race in North America to my eye; the details of the stupendous picture are overhung with shade, but I conceive a clear idea of the entire subject.

The territory now occupied or possessed by the United States of America forms about one-twentieth part of the habitable earth. But extensive as these confines are, it must not be supposed that the Anglo-American race will always remain within them; indeed, it has already far overstepped them. . . .

The lands of the New World belong to the first occupant, and they are the natural reward of the swiftest pioneer. Even the countries which are already peopled will have some difficulty in securing themselves from this invasion. I have already alluded to what is taking place in the province of Texas. The inhabitants of the United States are perpetually migrating to Texas, where they purchase land ; and although they conform to the laws of the country, they are gradually founding the empire of their own language and their own manners. The province of Texas is still part of the Mexican dominions, but it will soon contain no Mexicans ; the same thing has occurred whenever the Anglo-Americans have come into contact with populations of a different origin.

It cannot be denied that the British race has acquired an amazing preponderance over all the other European races in the New World ; and that it is very superior to them in civilization, in industry, and in power. As long as it is only surrounded by desert or thinly peopled countries, as long as it encounters no dense populations upon its route, through which it cannot work its way, it will assuredly continue to spread. The lines marked out by treaties will not stop it ; but it will everywhere transgress these imaginary barriers.

The geographical position of the British race in the New World is peculiarly favourable to its rapid increase. Above its northern frontiers the icy regions of the Pole extend ; and a few degrees below its southern confines lies the burning climate of the Equator. The Anglo-Americans are, therefore, placed in the most temperate and habitable zone of the continent. . . .

It must not, then, be imagined that the impulse of the British race in the New World can be arrested. The dismemberment of the Union, and the hostilities which might ensue, the abolition of republican institutions, and the tyrannical government which might succeed it, may retard this impulse, but they cannot prevent it from ultimately fulfilling the destinies to which that race is reserved. No power upon earth can close upon the emigrants that fertile wilderness which offers resources to all industry, and a refuge from all want. Future events, of whatever nature they may be, will not deprive the Americans of their climate or of their inland seas, of their great rivers or of their exuberant soil. Nor will bad laws, revolutions, and anarchy be able to obliterate that love of prosperity and that spirit of enterprise which seem to be the distinctive characteristics of their race, or to extinguish that knowledge which guides them on their way.

Thus, in the midst of the uncertain future, one event at least is sure. At a period which may be said to be near (for we are speaking of the life of a nation), the Anglo-Americans will alone cover the immense space contained between the Polar regions and the Tropics, extending from the coasts of the Atlantic to the shores of the Pacific Ocean. The territory which will probably be occupied by the Anglo-Americans at some future time may be computed to equal three quarters of Europe in extent. The climate of the Union is, upon the whole, preferable to that of Europe, and its natural advantages are not less great; it is therefore evident that its population will at some future time be proportionate to our own. Europe, divided as it is between so many different nations, and torn as it has been by incessant wars and the barbarous manners of the Middle Ages, has notwithstanding attained a population of four hundred and ten inhabitants to the square league. What cause can prevent the United States from having as numerous a population in time?

Many ages must elapse before the divers offsets of the British race in America cease to present the same homogeneous characteristics : and the time cannot be foreseen at which a permanent inequality of conditions will be established in the New World. Whatever differences may arise, from peace or from war, from freedom or oppression, from prosperity or want, between the destinies of the different descendants of the great Anglo-American family, they will at least preserve an analogous social condition, and they will hold in common the customs and the opinions to which that social condition has given birth.

In the Middle Ages, the tie of religion was sufficiently powerful to imbue all the different populations of Europe with the same civilization. The British of the New World have a thousand other reciprocal ties ; and they live at a time when the tendency to equality is general among mankind. The Middle Ages were a period when everything was broken up ; when each people, each province, each city, and each family had a strong tendency to maintain its distinct individuality. At the present time an opposite tendency seems to prevail, and the nations seem to be advancing to unity. Our means of intellectual intercourse unite the most remote parts of the earth ; and it is impossible for men to remain strangers to each other, or to be ignorant of the events which are taking place in any corner of the globe. The consequence is that there is less difference, at the present day, between the Europeans and their descendants in the New World than there was between certain towns in the thirteenth century which were only separated by a river. If this tendency to assimilation brings foreign nations closer to each other, it must *a fortiori* prevent the descendants of the same people from becoming aliens to each other.

The time will therefore come when one hundred and fifty millions of men will be living in North

America, equal in condition, the progeny of one race, owing their origin to the same cause, and preserving the same civilization, the same language, the same religion, the same habits, the same manners, and imbued with the same opinions, propagated under the same forms. The rest is uncertain, but this is certain ; and it is a fact new to the world—a fact fraught with such portentous consequences as to baffle the efforts even of the imagination.

There are, at the present time, two great nations in the world which seem to tend toward the same end, although they started from different points : I allude to the Russians and the Americans. Both of them have grown up unnoticed ; and while the attention of mankind was directed elsewhere, they have suddenly assumed a most prominent place among the nations ; and the world learned their existence and their greatness at almost the same time.

All other nations seem to have nearly reached their natural limits, and only to be charged with the maintenance of their power ; but these are still in the act of growth ; all the others are stopped, or continue to advance with extreme difficulty ; these are proceeding with ease and with celerity along a path to which the human eye can assign no term. The American struggles against the natural obstacles which oppose him ; the adversaries of the Russian are men ; the former combats the wilderness and savage life ; the latter, civilization with all its weapons and its arts : the conquests of the one are therefore gained by the ploughshare ; those of the other by the sword. The Anglo-American relies upon personal interest to accomplish his ends, and gives free scope to the unguided exertions and common sense of the citizens ; the Russian centres all the authority of society in a single arm : the principal instrument of the former is freedom ; of the latter servitude. Their starting-point is different, and their courses are not the same ; yet each of them seems to be marked out by the will of Heaven to sway the destinies of half the globe.

END OF PART ONE

PART TWO

THE AUTHOR'S PREFACE TO THE SECOND PART

THE Americans live in a democratic state of society, which has naturally suggested to them certain laws and a certain political character. This same state of society has, moreover, engendered amongst them a multitude of feelings and opinions which were unknown amongst the elder aristocratic communities of Europe : it has destroyed or modified all the relations which before existed, and established others of a novel kind. The aspect of civil society has been no less affected by these changes than that of the political world. The former subject has been treated of in the work on the Democracy of America, which I published five years ago ; to examine the latter is the object of the present book ; but these two parts complete each other, and form one and the same work.

I must at once warn the reader against an error which would be extremely prejudicial to me. When he finds that I attribute so many different consequences to the principle of equality, he may thence infer that I consider that principle to be the sole cause of all that takes place in the present age : but this would be to impute to me a very narrow view. A multitude of opinions, feelings, and propensities are now in existence, which owe their origin to circumstances unconnected with or even contrary to the principle of equality. Thus if I were to select the United States as an example, I could easily prove that the nature of the country, the origin of its inhabitants, the religion of its founders, their acquired knowledge, and their former habits, have exercised, and still exercise, independently of democracy, a vast influence upon the thoughts and feelings of that people. Different causes, but no less distinct from the circumstances of the equality of conditions, might be traced in Europe, and would explain a great proportion of the occurrences taking place amongst us.

I acknowledge the existence of all these different causes, and their power, but my subject does not lead me to treat of them. I have not undertaken to unfold the reason of all our inclinations and all our notions : my only object is to show in what respects the principle of equality has modified both the former and the latter.

Some readers may perhaps be astonished that—firmly persuaded as I am that the democratic revolution which we are witnessing is an irresistible fact against which it would be neither desirable nor wise to struggle—I should often have had occasion in this book to address language of such severity to those democratic communities which this revolution has brought into being. My answer is simply, that it is because I am not an adversary of democracy, that I have sought to speak of democracy in all sincerity.

Men will not accept truth at the hands of their enemies, and truth is seldom offered to them by their friends : for this reason I have spoken it. I was persuaded that many would take upon themselves to announce the new blessings which the principle of equality promises to mankind, but that few would dare to point out from afar the dangers with which it threatens them. To those perils therefore I have turned my chief attention, and believing that I have discovered them clearly, I have not had the cowardice to leave them untold.

I trust that my readers will find in this Second Part the impartiality which seems to have been remarked in the former work. Placed as I am in the midst of the conflicting opinions between which we are divided, I have endeavoured to suppress within me for a time the favourable sympathies or the adverse emotions with which each of them inspires me. If those who read this book can find a single sentence intended to flatter any of the great parties which have agitated my country, or any of those petty factions which now harass and weaken it, let such readers raise their voices to accuse me.

The subject I have sought to embrace is immense, for it includes the greater part of the feelings and opinions to which the new state of society has given birth. Such a subject is doubtless above my strength, and in treating it I have not succeeded in satisfying myself. But, if I have not been able to reach the goal which I had in view, my readers will at least do me the justice to acknowledge that I have conceived and followed up my undertaking in a spirit not unworthy of success.

A. DE T.

March 1840

Chapter XX

THE INFLUENCES OF DEMOCRACY UPON PHILOSOPHY

I THINK that in no country in the civilized world is less attention paid to philosophy than in the United States. The Americans have no philosophical school of their own; and they care but little for all the schools into which Europe is divided, the very names of which are scarcely known to them.[1] Nevertheless it is easy to perceive that almost all the inhabitants of the United States conduct their understanding in the same manner, and govern it by the same rules—that is to say, that without ever having taken the trouble to define the rules of a philosophical method, they are in possession of one, common to the whole people. To evade the bondage of system and habit, of family-maxims, class-opinions, and, in some degree, of national prejudices; to accept tradition only as a means of information, and existing facts only as a lesson used in doing otherwise and doing better; to seek the reason of things for one's self, and in one's self alone; to tend to results without being bound to means, and to aim at the substance through the form—such are the principal characteristics of what I shall call the philosophical method of the Americans. But if I go further, and if I seek among these characteristics that which predominates over and includes almost all the rest, I discover that in most of the operations of the mind each American appeals to the individual exercise of his own understanding alone. America is therefore one of the countries in the world where philosophy is least studied, and where the

---

[1] At the time Tocqueville wrote, American interest in German Idealism was lively and Transcendentalism, a characteristically American form of Idealism, was widely accepted.—H. S. C.

295

precepts of Descartes are best applied. Nor is this surprising. The Americans do not read the works of Descartes, because their social condition deters them from speculative studies ; but they follow his maxims because this very social condition naturally disposes their understanding to adopt them. In the midst of the continual movement which agitates a democratic community the tie which unites one generation to another is relaxed or broken ; every man readily loses the trace of the ideas of his forefathers or takes no care about them. Nor can men living in this state of society derive their belief from the opinions of the class to which they belong ; for, so to speak, there are no longer any classes, or those which still exist are composed of such mobile elements that their body can never exercise a real control over its members. As to the influence which the intelligence of one man has on that of another, it must necessarily be very limited in a country where the citizens, placed on the footing of a general similitude, are all closely seen by each other ; and where, as no signs of incontestable greatness or superiority are perceived in any one of them, they are constantly brought back to their own reason as the most obvious and proximate source of truth. It is not only confidence in this or that man which is then destroyed, but the taste for trusting the *ipse dixit* of any man whatsoever. Every one shuts himself up in his own breast, and affects from that point to judge the world.

The practice which obtains among the Americans of fixing the standard of their judgment in themselves alone, leads them to other habits of mind. As they perceive that they succeed in resolving without assistance all the little difficulties which their practical life presents, they readily conclude that everything in the world may be explained, and that nothing in it transcends the limits of the understanding. Thus they fall to denying what they cannot comprehend ; which leaves them but little faith for whatever is extraordinary, and an almost insurmountable distaste for whatever is supernatural. As it is on their own testimony that they are accustomed to rely, they like to discern the object which engages their attention with extreme clearness ; they therefore strip off as much as possible all that covers it, they rid themselves of whatever separates them from it, they remove whatever conceals it from sight, in order to view it more closely and in the broad light of day. This disposition of the mind soon leads them to contemn forms, which they regard as useless and inconvenient veils placed between them and the truth. . . .

When the ranks of society are unequal, and men unlike each other in condition, there are some individuals invested with all the power of superior intelligence, learning, and enlightenment, while the multitude is sunk in ignorance and prejudice. Men living at these aristocratic periods are therefore naturally induced to shape their opinions by the superior standard of a person or a class of persons, while they are averse to recognize the infallibility of the mass of the people.

The contrary takes place in ages of equality. The nearer the citizens are drawn to the common level of an equal and similar condition, the less prone does each man become to place implicit faith in a certain man or a certain class of men. But his readiness to believe the multitude increases, and opinion is more than ever mistress of the world. Not only is common opinion the only guide which private judgment retains among a democratic people, but among such a people it possesses a power infinitely beyond what it has elsewhere. At periods of equality men have no faith in one another, by reason of their common resemblance ; but this very resemblance gives them almost unbounded confidence in the judgment of the public ; for it would not seem probable, as they are all endowed with equal means of judging, but that the greater truth should go with the greater number.

When the inhabitant of a democratic country compares himself individually with all those about him, he feels with pride that he is the equal of any one of them ; but when he comes to survey the totality of his fellows, and to place himself in contrast to so huge a body, he is instantly overwhelmed by the sense of his own insignificance and weakness. The same equality which renders him independent of each of his fellow-citizens taken severally exposes him alone and unprotected to the influence of the greater number. The public has therefore among a democratic people a singular power, of which aristocratic nations could never so much as conceive an idea ; for it does not persuade to certain opinions, but it enforces them, and infuses them into the faculties by a sort of enormous pressure of the minds of all upon the reason of each.

In the United States the majority undertakes to supply a multitude of ready-made opinions for the use of individuals, who are thus relieved from the necessity of forming opinions of their own. Everybody there adopts great numbers of theories, on philosophy, morals, and politics, without inquiry, upon public trust ; and if we look to it very narrowly, it will be perceived that religion herself holds her sway there, much less as a doctrine of revelation than as a commonly received opinion. The fact that the political laws of the Americans are such that the majority rules the community with sovereign sway, materially increases the power which that majority naturally exercises over the mind. For nothing is more customary in man than to recognize superior wisdom in the person of his oppressor. This political omnipotence of the majority in the United States doubtless augments the influence which public opinion would obtain without it over the mind of each member of the community; but the foundations of that influence do not rest upon it. They must be sought for in the principle of equality itself, not in the more or less popular institutions which men living under that condition may give themselves. The intellectual dominion of the greater number would probably be less absolute among a democratic people governed by a king than in the sphere of a pure democracy, but it will always be extremely absolute; and by whatever political laws men are governed in the ages of equality, it may be foreseen that faith in public opinion will become a species of religion there, and the majority its ministering prophet.

Thus intellectual authority will be different, but it will not be diminished; and far from thinking that it will disappear, I augur that it may readily acquire too much preponderance, and confine the action of private judgment within narrower limits than are suited either to the greatness or the happiness of the human race. In the principle of equality I very clearly discern two tendencies; the one leading the mind of every man to untried thoughts, the other inclined to prohibit him from thinking at all. And I perceive how, under the dominion of certain laws, democracy would extinguish that liberty of the mind to which a democratic social condition is favourable; so that, after having broken all the bondage once imposed on it by ranks or by men, the human mind would be closely fettered to the general will of the greatest number.

If the absolute power of the majority were to be

substituted by democratic nations for all the different powers which checked or retarded overmuch the energy of individual minds, the evil would only have changed its symptoms. Men would not have found the means of independent life ; they would simply have invented (no easy task) a new dress for servitude. There is—and I cannot repeat it too often—there is in this matter for profound reflection for those who look on freedom as a holy thing, and who hate not only the despot, but despotism. . . .

General ideas are no proof of the strength, but rather of the insufficiency, of the human intellect ; for there are in Nature no beings exactly alike, no things precisely identical, nor any rules indiscriminately and alike applicable to several objects at once. The chief merit of general ideas is, that they enable the human mind to pass a rapid judgment on a great many objects at once ; but, on the other hand, the notions they convey are never otherwise than incomplete, and they always cause the mind to lose as much in accuracy as it gains in comprehensiveness. As social bodies advance in civilization, they acquire the knowledge of new facts, and they daily lay hold almost unconsciously of some particular truths. The more truths of this kind a man apprehends, the more general ideas is he naturally led to conceive. A multitude of particular facts cannot be seen separately, without at last discovering the common tie which connects them. Several individuals lead to the perception of the species ; several species to that of the genus. Hence the habit and the taste for general ideas will always be greatest among a people of ancient cultivation and extensive knowledge. . . .

The state of civilization is insufficient by itself to explain what suggests to the human mind the love of general ideas, or diverts it from them. When the conditions of men are very unequal, and inequality itself is the permanent state of society, individual men gradually become so dissimilar that each class assumes the aspect of a distinct race : only one of these classes is ever in view at the same instant ; and losing sight of that general tie which binds them all within the vast bosom of mankind, the observation invariably rests not on man, but on certain men. Those who live in this aristocratic state of society never, therefore, conceive very general ideas respecting themselves, and that is enough to imbue them with an habitual distrust of such ideas, and an instinctive aversion to them.

He, on the contrary, who inhabits a democratic country sees around him, on every hand, men differing but little from each other ; he cannot turn his mind to any one portion of mankind without expanding and dilating his thought till it embraces the whole. All the truths which are applicable to himself appear to him equally and similarly applicable to each of his fellow-citizens and fellow-men. Having contracted the habit of generalizing his ideas in the study which engages him most, and interests him more than others, he transfers the same habit to all his pursuits ; and thus it is that the craving to discover general laws in everything, to include a great number of objects under the same formula, and to explain a mass of facts by a single cause, becomes an ardent, and sometimes an undiscerning, passion in the human mind. . . .

In the ages of equality all men are independent of each other, isolated and weak. The movements of the multitude are not permanently guided by the will of any individuals ; at such times humanity seems always to advance of itself. In order, therefore, to explain what is passing in the world, man is driven to seek for some great causes, which, acting in the same manner on all our fellow-creatures, thus impel them all involuntarily to pursue the same track. This again naturally leads the human mind to conceive general ideas, and superinduces a taste for them.

I have already shown in what way the equality of conditions leads every man to investigate truths for himself. It readily may be perceived that a method of this kind must insensibly beget a tendency to general ideas in the human mind. When I repudiate the traditions of rank, profession, and birth ; when I escape from the authority of example, to seek out, by the single effort of my reason, the path to be followed, I am inclined to derive the motives of my opinions from human nature itself ; which leads me necessarily, and almost unconsciously, to adopt a great number of very general notions. . . .

Men living in democratic countries eagerly lay hold of general ideas because they have but little leisure, and because these ideas spare them the trouble of studying particulars. This is true ; but it is only to be understood to apply to those matters which are not the necessary and habitual subjects of their thoughts. Mercantile men will take up very eagerly, and without any very close scrutiny, all the general ideas on philosophy, politics, science, or the arts which may be presented to them ; but for such as relate to commerce, they will not receive them without inquiry, or adopt them without reserve. The same thing applies to statesmen with regard to general ideas in politics. If, then, there be a subject upon which a democratic people is peculiarly liable to abandon itself, blindly and extravagantly, to general ideas, the best corrective that can be used will be to make that subject a part of the daily practical occupation of that people. The people will then be compelled to enter upon its details, and the details will teach them the weak points of the theory. This remedy may frequently be a painful one, but its effect is certain.

Thus it happens that the democratic institutions which compel every citizen to take a practical part in the government moderate that excessive taste for general theories in politics which the principle of equality suggests.

Chapter XXI

THE INFLUENCES OF DEMOCRACY UPON RELIGION

. . . It must be acknowledged that equality, which brings great benefits into the world, nevertheless suggests to men (as will be shown hereafter) some very dangerous propensities. It tends to isolate them from each other, to concentrate every man's attention upon himself; and it lays open the soul to an inordinate love of material gratification. The greatest advantage of religion is to inspire diametrically contrary principles. There is no religion which does not place the object of man's desires above and beyond the treasures of earth, and which does not naturally raise his soul to regions far above those of the senses. Nor is there any which does not impose on man some sort of duties to his kind, and thus draws him at times from the contemplation of himself. This occurs in religions the most false and dangerous. Religious nations are therefore naturally strong on the very point on which democratic nations are weak; which shows of what importance it is for men to preserve their religion as their conditions become more equal.

I have neither the right nor the intention of examining the supernatural means which God employs to infuse religious belief into the heart of man. I am at this moment considering religions in a purely human point of view: my object is to inquire by what means they may most easily retain their sway in the democratic ages upon which we are entering. It has been shown that, at times of general cultivation and equality, the human mind does not consent to adopt dogmatical opinions without reluctance, and feels their necessity acutely in spiritual matters only. This proves, in the first place, that at such times religions ought, more cautiously than at any other, to confine themselves within their own precincts; for in seeking to extend their power beyond religious matters, they incur a risk of not being believed at all. The circle within which they seek to bound the human intellect ought therefore to be carefully traced, and beyond its verge the mind should be left in entire freedom to its own guidance. . . .

I find that in order for religions to maintain their authority, humanly speaking, in democratic ages, they must not only confine themselves strictly within the circle of spiritual matters: their power also depends very much on the nature of the belief they inculcate, on the external forms they assume, and on the obligations they impose. The preceding observation, that equality leads men to very general and very extensive notions, is principally to be understood as applied to the question of religion. Men living in a similar and equal condition in the world readily conceive the idea of the one God, governing every man by the same laws, and granting to every man future happiness on the same conditions. The idea of the unity of mankind constantly leads them back to the idea of the unity of the Creator; while, on the contrary, in a state of society where men are broken up into very unequal ranks, they are apt to devise as many deities as there are nations, castes, classes, or families, and to trace a thousand private roads to Heaven. . . .

Another truth is no less clear—that religions ought to assume fewer external observances in democratic periods than at any others. In speaking of philosophical method among the Americans, I have shown that nothing is more repugnant to the human mind in an age of equality than the idea of subjection to forms. Men living at such times are impatient of figures; to their eyes symbols appear to be the puerile artifice which is used to conceal or to set off truths, which should more naturally be bared to the light of open day : they are unmoved by ceremonial observances, and they are predisposed to attach a secondary importance to the details of public worship. Those whose care it is to regulate the external forms of religion in a democratic age should pay a close attention to these natural propensities of the human mind, in order not unnecessarily to run counter to them. I firmly believe in the necessity of forms, which fix the human mind in the contemplation of abstract truths, and stimulate its ardour in the pursuit of them, while they invigorate its powers of retaining them steadfastly. Nor do I suppose that it is possible to maintain a religion without external observances ; but, on the other hand, I am persuaded that, in the ages upon which we are entering, it would be peculiarly dangerous to multiply them beyond measure ; and that they ought rather to be limited to as much as is absolutely necessary to perpetuate the doctrine itself, which is the substance of religions of which the ritual is only the form. A religion which should become more minute, more peremptory, and more surcharged with small observances at a time in which men are becoming more equal, would soon find itself reduced to a band of fanatical zealots in the midst of an infidel people. . . .

We shall have occasion to see that, of all the passions which originate in, or are fostered by, equality, there is one which it renders peculiarly intense, and which it infuses at the same time into the heart of every man : I mean the love of well-being. The taste for well-being is the prominent and indelible feature of democratic ages. It may be believed that a religion which should undertake to destroy so deep-seated a passion would meet its own destruction thence in the end ; and if it attempted to wean men entirely from the contemplation of the good things of this world, in order to devote their faculties exclusively to the thought of another, it may be foreseen that the soul would at length escape from its grasp, to plunge into the exclusive enjoyment of present and material pleasures. The chief concern of religions is to purify, to regulate, and to restrain the excessive and exclusive taste for well-being which men feel at periods of equality ; but they would err in attempting to control it completely or to eradicate it. They will not succeed in curing men of the love of riches : but they may still persuade men to enrich themselves by none but honest means.

This brings me to a final consideration, which comprises, as it were, all the others. The more the conditions of men are equalized and assimilated to each other, the more important is it for religions, while they carefully abstain from the daily turmoil of secular affairs, not needlessly to run counter to the ideas which generally prevail, and the permanent interests which exist in the mass of the people. For as public opinion grows to be more and more evidently the first and most irresistible of existing powers, the religious principle has no external support strong enough to enable it long to resist its attacks. . . .

I have shown elsewhere how the American clergy stand aloof from secular affairs. This is the most obvious, but it is not the only, example of their self-restraint. In America religion is a distinct sphere, in which the priest is sovereign, but out of which he takes care never to go. Within its limits he is the master of the mind ; beyond them, he leaves men to themselves, and surrenders them to the independence and instability which belong to their nature and their age. I have seen no country in which Christianity is clothed with fewer forms, figures, and observances than in the United States ; or where it presents more distinct, more simple, or more general notions to the mind. Although the Christians of America are divided into a multitude of sects, they all look upon their religion in the same light. This applies to Roman Catholicism as well as to the other forms of belief. There are no Romish priests who show less taste for the minute individual observances, for extraordinary or peculiar means of salvation, or who cling more to the spirit, and less to the letter of the law, than the Roman Catholic priests of the United States. Nowhere is that doctrine of the Church, which prohibits the worship reserved to God alone from being offered to the Saints, more clearly inculcated or more generally followed. Yet the Roman Catholics of America are very submissive and very sincere.

Another remark is applicable to the clergy of every communion. The American ministers of the Gospel do not attempt to draw or to fix all the thoughts of man upon the life to come ; they are willing to surrender a portion of his heart to the cares of the present ; seeming to consider the goods of this world as important, although as secondary, objects. If they take no part themselves in productive labour, they are at least interested in its progression, and ready to applaud its results ; and while they never cease to point to the other world as the great object of the hopes and fears of the believer, they do not forbid him honestly to court prosperity in this. Far from attempting to show that these things are distinct and contrary to one another, they study rather to find out on what point they are most nearly and closely connected.

All the American clergy know and respect the intellectual supremacy exercised by the majority ; they never sustain any but necessary conflicts with it.

They take no share in the altercations of parties, but they readily adopt the general opinions of their country and their age ; and they allow themselves to be borne away without opposition in the current of feeling and opinion by which everything around them is carried along. They endeavour to amend their contemporaries, but they do not quit fellowship with them. Public opinion is therefore never hostile to them ; it rather supports and protects them ; and their belief owes its authority at the same time to the strength which is its own, and to that which they borrow from the opinions of the majority.

Thus it is that, by respecting all democratic tendencies not absolutely contrary to herself, and by making use of several of them for her own purposes, Religion sustains an advantageous struggle with that spirit of individual independence which is her most dangerous antagonist. . . .

Equality suggests to the human mind several ideas which would not have originated from any other source, and it modifies almost all those previously entertained. I take as an example the idea of human perfectibility, because it is one of the principal notions that the intellect can conceive, and because it constitutes of itself a great philosophical theory, which is every instant to be traced by its consequences in the practice of human affairs. Although man has many points of resemblance with the brute creation, one characteristic is peculiar to himself—he improves : they are incapable of improvement. Mankind could not fail to discover this difference from its earliest period. The idea of perfectibility is therefore as old as the world ; equality did not give birth to it, although it has imparted to it a novel character.

When the citizens of a community are classed according to their rank, their profession, or their

birth, and when all men are constrained to follow the
career which happens to open before them, every one
thinks that the utmost limits of human power are to
be discerned in proximity to himself, and none seeks
any longer to resist the inevitable law of his destiny.
Not, indeed, that an aristocratic people absolutely
contests man's faculty of self-improvement, but they
do not hold it to be indefinite ; amelioration they
conceive, but not change : they imagine that the
future condition of society may be better, but not
essentially different ; and while they admit that mankind has made vast strides in improvement, and may
still have some to make, they assign to it beforehand
certain impassable limits. Thus they do not presume
that they have arrived at the supreme good or at
absolute truth (what people or what man was ever
wild enough to imagine it ?), but they cherish a
persuasion that they have pretty nearly reached that
degree of greatness and knowledge which our imperfect nature admits of ; and as nothing moves about
them they are willing to fancy that everything is in its
fit place. Then it is that the legislator affects to lay
down eternal laws ; that kings and nations will raise
none but imperishable monuments ; and that the
present generation undertakes to spare generations to
come the care of regulating their destinies.

In proportion as castes disappear and the classes of
society approximate—as manners, customs, and laws
vary, from the tumultuous intercourse of men—as
new facts arise—as new truths are brought to light—
as ancient opinions are dissipated, and others take
their place—the image of an ideal perfection, for ever
on the wing, presents itself to the human mind.
Continual changes are then every instant occurring
under the observation of every man : the position of
some is rendered worse ; and he learns but too well

that no people and no individual, how enlightened soever they may be, can lay claim to infallibility—the condition of others is improved ; whence he infers that man is endowed with an indefinite faculty of improvement. His reverses teach him that none may hope to have discovered absolute good—his success stimulates him to the never-ending pursuit of it. Thus, for ever seeking—for ever falling, to rise again—often disappointed, but not discouraged—he tends unceasingly toward that unmeasured greatness so indistinctly visible at the end of the long track which humanity has yet to tread. It can scarcely be believed how many facts naturally flow from the philosophical theory of the indefinite perfectibility of man, or how strong an influence it exercises even on men who, living entirely for the purposes of action and not of thought, seem to conform their actions to it, without knowing anything about it. I accost an American sailor, and I inquire why the ships of his country are built so as to last but for a short time ; he answers without hesitation that the art of navigation is every day making such rapid progress that the finest vessel would become almost useless if it lasted beyond a certain number of years. In these words, which fall accidentally and on a particular subject from a man of rude attainments, I recognize the general and systematic idea upon which a great people directs all its concerns.

Aristocratic nations are naturally too apt to narrow the scope of human perfectibility ; democratic nations to expand it beyond compass.

Chapter XXII

THE INFLUENCES OF DEMOCRACY UPON SCIENCE
AND THE ARTS

It must be acknowledged that among few of the civilized nations of our time have the higher sciences made less progress than in the United States; and in few have great artists, fine poets, or celebrated writers been more rare. Many Europeans, struck by this fact, have looked upon it as a natural and inevitable result of equality; and they have supposed that if a democratic state of society and democratic institutions were ever to prevail over the whole earth, the human mind would gradually find its beacon-lights grow dim, and men would relapse into a period of darkness. To reason thus is, I think, to confound several ideas which it is important to divide and to examine separately: it is to mingle, unintentionally, what is democratic with what is only American.

The religion professed by the first emigrants, and bequeathed by them to their descendants, simple in its form of worship, austere and almost harsh in its principles, and hostile to external symbols and to ceremonial pomp, is naturally unfavourable to the fine arts, and only yields a reluctant sufferance to the pleasures of literature. The Americans are a very old and a very enlightened people, who have fallen upon a new and unbounded country, where they may extend themselves at pleasure, and which they may fertilize without difficulty. This state of things is without a parallel in the history of the world. In America, then, every one finds facilities, unknown elsewhere, for making or increasing his fortune. The spirit of gain is always on the stretch, and the human mind, constantly diverted from the pleasures of imagination and the labours of the intellect, is there swayed by no impulse but the pursuit of wealth. Not only are manufacturing and commercial classes to be found in the United States, as they are in all other countries ; but, what never occurred elsewhere, the whole community is simultaneously engaged in productive industry and commerce. I am convinced that if the Americans had been alone in the world, with the freedom and the knowledge acquired by their forefathers, and the passions which are their own, they would not have been slow to discover that progress cannot long be made in the application of the sciences without cultivating the theory of them ; that all the arts are perfected by one another ; and, however absorbed they might have been by the pursuit of the principal object of their desires, they would speedily have admitted that it is necessary to turn aside from it occasionally in order the better to attain it in the end.

The taste for the pleasures of the mind is, moreover, so natural to the heart of civilized man that among the polite nations, which are least disposed to give themselves up to these pursuits, a certain number of citizens are always to be found who take part in them. This intellectual craving, when once felt, would very soon have been satisfied. But at the very time when the Americans were naturally inclined to require nothing of science but its special applications to the useful arts and the means of rendering life comfortable, learned and literary Europe was engaged in exploring the common sources of truth, and in improving at the same time all that can minister to the pleasures or satisfy the wants of man. At the head of the enlightened nations of the Old World the inhabitants of the United States more particularly distinguished one, to which they were closely united by a common origin and by kindred habits. Among this people they found distinguished men of science, artists of skill, writers of eminence, and they were enabled to enjoy the treasures of the intellect without requiring to labour in amassing them. I cannot consent to separate America from Europe, in spite of the ocean which intervenes. I consider the people of the United States as that portion of the English people which is commissioned to explore the wilds of the New World ; while the rest of the nation, enjoying more leisure and less harassed by the drudgery of life, may devote its energies to thought, and enlarge in all directions the empire of the mind.

The position of the Americans is therefore quite exceptional, and it may be believed that no democratic people will ever be placed in a similar one. Their strictly Puritanical origin—their exclusively commercial habits—even the country they inhabit, which seems to divert their minds from the pursuit of science, literature, and the arts—the proximity of Europe, which allows them to neglect these pursuits without relapsing into barbarism—a thousand special causes, of which I have only been able to point out the most important—have singularly concurred to fix the mind of the American upon purely practical objects. His passions, his wants, his education, and everything about him seem to unite in drawing the native of the United States earthward : his religion alone bids him turn, from time to time, a transient and distracted glance to heaven. Let us cease then to view all democratic nations under the mask of the American people, and let us attempt to survey them at length with their own proper features. . . .

When men living in a democratic state of society are enlightened, they readily discover that they are confined and fixed within no limits which constrain them to take up with their present fortune. They all, therefore, conceive the idea of increasing it ; if they are free, they all attempt it, but all do not succeed in the same manner. The legislature, it is true, no longer grants privileges, but they are bestowed by Nature. As natural inequality is very great, fortunes become unequal as soon as every man exerts all his faculties to get rich. The law of descent prevents the establishment of wealthy families ; but it does not prevent the existence of wealthy individuals. It constantly brings back the members of the community to a common level, from which they as constantly escape : and the inequality of fortunes augments in proportion as knowledge is diffused and liberty increased. . . .

Free and democratic communities, then, will always contain a considerable number of people enjoying opulence or competency. The wealthy will not be linked so closely to each other as the members of the former aristocratic class of society : their propensities will be different, and they will scarcely ever enjoy leisure as secure or as complete : but they will be far more numerous than those who belonged to that class of society ever could be. These persons will not be strictly confined to the cares of practical life, and they will still be able, though in different degrees, to indulge in the pursuits and pleasures of the intellect. In those pleasures they will indulge ; for if it be true that the human mind leans on one side to the narrow, the practical, and the useful, it naturally rises on the other to the infinite, the spiritual, and the beautiful. Physical wants confine it to the earth ; but, as soon as the tie is loosened, it will unbend itself again.

Not only will the number of those who can take an interest in the productions of the mind be enlarged, but the taste for intellectual enjoyment will descend, step by step,. even to those who, in aristocratic societies, seem to have neither time nor ability to indulge in them. When hereditary wealth, the privileges of rank, and the prerogatives of birth have ceased to be, and when every man derives his strength from himself alone, it becomes evident that the chief cause of disparity between the fortunes of men is the mind. Whatever tends to invigorate, to extend, or to adorn the mind, instantly rises to great value. The utility of knowledge becomes singularly conspicuous even to the eyes of the multitude : those who have no taste for its charms set store upon its results, and make some efforts to acquire it. . . .

As soon as the multitude begins to take an interest in the labours of the mind, it finds out that to excel in some of them is a powerful method of acquiring fame, power, or wealth. The restless ambition which equality begets instantly takes this direction as it does all others. The number of those who cultivate science, letters, and the arts becomes immense. The intellectual world starts into prodigious activity : every one endeavours to open for himself a path there, and to draw the eyes of the public after him. Something analogous occurs to what happens in society in the United States, politically considered. What is done is often imperfect, but the attempts are innumerable ; and, although the results of individual effort are commonly very small, the total amount is always very large.

It is therefore not true to assert that men living in democratic ages are naturally indifferent to science, literature, and the arts : only it must be acknowledged that they cultivate them after their own fashion, and bring to the task their own peculiar qualifications and deficiencies.

If a democratic state of society and democratic institutions do not stop the career of the human mind, they incontestably guide it in one direction in preference to another. Their effects, thus circumscribed, are still exceedingly great ; and I trust I may be pardoned if I pause for a moment to survey them. We had occasion, in speaking of the philosophical method of the American people, to make several remarks, which must here be turned to account.

Equality begets in man the desire of judging of everything for himself : it gives him, in all things, a taste for the tangible and the real, a contempt for tradition and for forms. These general tendencies are principally discernible in the peculiar subject of this chapter. Those who cultivate the sciences among a democratic people are always afraid of losing their way in visionary speculation. They mistrust systems ; they adhere closely to facts and the study of facts with their own senses. As they do not easily defer to the mere name of any fellow-man, they are never inclined to rest upon any man's authority ; but, on the contrary, they are unremitting in their efforts to point out the weaker points of their neighbours' opinions. Scientific precedents have very little weight with them ; they are never long detained by the subtilty of the schools, nor ready to accept big words for sterling coin ; they penetrate, as far as they can, into the principal parts of the subject which engages them, and they expound them in the vernacular tongue. Scientific pursuits then follow a freer and a safer course, but a less lofty one.

The mind may, as it appears to me, divide science into three parts. The first comprises the most theoretical principles, and those more abstract notions whose application is either unknown or very remote. The second is composed of those general truths which still belong to pure theory, but lead nevertheless by a straight and short road to practical results. Methods of application and means of execution make up the third. Each of these different portions of science may be separately cultivated, although reason and experience show that none of them can prosper long, if it be absolutely cut off from the other two.

In America the purely practical part of science is admirably understood, and careful attention is paid to the theoretical portion which is immediately requisite to application. On this head the Americans always display a clear, free, original, and inventive power of mind. But scarcely any one in the United States devotes himself to the essentially theoretical and abstract portion of human knowledge. In this respect the Americans carry to excess a tendency which is, I think, discernible, though in a less degree, among all democratic nations. . . .

The greater part of the men who constitute these nations are extremely eager in the pursuit of actual and physical gratification. As they are always dissatisfied with the position which they occupy, and are always free to leave it, they think of nothing but the means of changing their fortune, or of increasing it. To minds thus predisposed, every new method which leads by a shorter road to wealth, every machine which spares labour, every instrument which diminishes the cost of production, every discovery which facilitates pleasures or augments them, seems to be the grandest effort of the human intellect. It is chiefly from these motives that a democratic people addicts itself to scientific pursuits—that it understands, and that it respects them. In aristocratic ages, science is more particularly called upon to furnish gratification to the mind ; in democracies, to the body. You may be sure that the more a nation is democratic, enlightened, and free, the greater will be the number of these interested promoters of scientific genius, and the more will discoveries immediately applicable to productive industry confer gain, fame, and even power on their authors. For in democracies the working class takes a part in public affairs ; and public honours, as well as pecuniary remuneration, may be awarded to those who deserve them. In a community thus organized it easily may be conceived that the human mind may be led insensibly to the neglect of theory ; and that it is urged, on the contrary, with unparalleled vehemence to the applications of science, or at least to that portion of theoretical science which is necessary to those who make such applications. In vain will some innate propensity raise the mind toward the loftier spheres of the intellect ; interest draws it down to the middle zone. There it may develop all its energy and restless activity, there it may engender all its wonders. These very Americans, who have not discovered one of the general laws of mechanics, have introduced into navigation an engine which changes the aspect of the world. . . .

I believe in the high calling of scientific minds. If the democratic principle does not, on the one hand, induce men to cultivate science for its own sake, on the other it enormously increases the number of those who do cultivate it. Nor is it credible that, from among so great a multitude no speculative genius should from time to time arise, inflamed by the love of truth alone. Such a one, we may be sure, would dive into the deepest mysteries of Nature, whatever be the spirit of his country or his age. He requires no assistance in his course—enough that he be not checked in it.

All that I meant to say is this : permanent inequality of conditions leads men to confine themselves to the arrogant and sterile research of abstract truths ;

while the social condition and the institutions of democracy prepare them to seek the immediate and useful practical results of the sciences. This tendency is natural and inevitable : it is curious to be acquainted with it, and it may be necessary to point it out. If those who are called upon to guide the nations of our time clearly discerned from afar off these new tendencies, which will soon be irresistible, they would understand that, possessing education and freedom, men living in democratic ages cannot fail to improve the industrial part of science ; and that henceforward all the efforts of the constituted authorities ought to be directed to support the highest branches of learning, and to foster the nobler passion for science itself. In the present age the human mind must be coerced into theoretical studies ; it runs of its own accord to practical applications ; and, instead of perpetually referring it to the minute examination of secondary effects, it is well to divert it from them sometimes, in order to raise it up to the contemplation of primary causes. . . .

It would be to waste the time of my readers and my own if I strove to demonstrate how the general mediocrity of fortunes, the absence of superfluous wealth, the universal desire of comfort, and the constant efforts by which every one attempts to procure it, make the taste for the useful predominate over the love of the beautiful in the heart of man. Democratic nations, among which all these things exist, will therefore cultivate the arts which serve to render life easy, in preference to those whose object is to adorn it. They will habitually prefer the useful to the beautiful, and they will require that the beautiful should be useful. But I propose to go further ; and after having pointed out this first feature, to sketch several others.

It commonly happens that in the ages of privilege the practice of almost all the arts becomes a privilege; and that every profession is a separate walk, upon which it is not allowable for every one to enter. Even when productive industry is free, the fixed character which belongs to aristocratic nations gradually segregates all the persons who practise the same art, till they form a distinct class, always composed of the same families, whose members are all known to each other, and among whom a public opinion of their own and a species of corporate pride soon spring up. In a class or guild of this kind, each artisan has not only his fortune to make, but his reputation to preserve. He is not exclusively swayed by his own interest, or even by that of his customer, but by that of the body to which he belongs; and the interest of that body is, that each artisan should produce the best possible workmanship. In aristocratic ages, the object of the arts is therefore to manufacture as well as possible— not with the greatest despatch, or at the lowest rate.

When, on the contrary, every profession is open to all—when a multitude of persons are constantly embracing and abandoning it—and when its several members are strangers to each other, indifferent, and from their numbers hardly seen among themselves; the social tie is destroyed, and each workman, standing alone, endeavours simply to gain the greatest possible quantity of money at the least possible cost. The will of the customer is then his only limit. But at the same time a corresponding revolution takes place in the customer also. In countries in which riches as well as power are concentrated, and retained in the hands of the few, the use of the greater part of this world's goods belongs to a small number of individuals, who are always the same. Necessity, public opinion, or moderate desires exclude all others from the enjoyment of them. As this aristocratic class remains fixed at the pinnacle of greatness on which it stands, without diminution or increase, it is always acted upon by the same wants and affected by them in the same manner. The men of whom it is composed naturally derive from their superior and hereditary position a taste for what is extremely well made and lasting. This affects the general way of thinking of the nation in relation to the arts. It often occurs, among such a people, that even the peasant will rather go without the objects he covets than procure them in a state of imperfection. In aristocracies, then, the handicraftsmen work for only a limited number of very fastidious customers : the profit they hope to make depends principally on the perfection of their workmanship.

Such is no longer the case when, all privileges being abolished, ranks are intermingled, and men are for ever rising or sinking upon the ladder of society. Among a democratic people a number of citizens always exist whose patrimony is divided and decreasing. They have contracted, under more prosperous circumstances, certain wants, which remain after the means of satisfying such wants are gone ; and they are anxiously looking out for some surreptitious method of providing for them. On the other hand, there are always in democracies a large number of men whose fortune is upon the increase, but whose desires grow much faster than their fortunes : and who gloat upon the gifts of wealth in anticipation, long before they have means to command them. Such men are eager to find some short cut to these gratifications, already almost within their reach. From the combination of these two causes the result is, that in democracies there is always a multitude of individuals whose wants are above their means, and who are very willing to take up with imperfect satisfaction rather than abandon the object of their desires.

The artisan readily understands these passions, for he himself partakes in them : in an aristocracy he would seek to sell his workmanship at a high price to the few ; he now conceives that the more expeditious way of getting rich is to sell them at a low price to all. But there are only two ways of lowering the price of commodities. The first is to discover some better, shorter, and more ingenious method of producing them : the second is to manufacture a larger quantity of goods, nearly similar, but of less value. Among a democratic population, all the intellectual faculties of the workman are directed to these two objects : he strives to invent methods which may enable him not only to work better, but quicker and cheaper ; or, if he cannot succeed in that, to diminish the intrinsic qualities of the thing he makes, without rendering it wholly unfit for the use for which it is intended. When none but the wealthy had watches, they were almost all very good ones : few are now made which are worth much, but everybody has one in his pocket. Thus the democratic principle not only tends to direct the human mind to the useful arts, but it induces the artisan to produce with greater rapidity a quantity of imperfect commodities, and the consumer to content himself with these commodities. . . .

The handicraftsmen of democratic ages endeavour not only to bring their useful productions within the reach of the whole community, but they strive to give to all their commodities attractive qualities which they do not in reality possess. In the confusion of all ranks every one hopes to appear what he is not, and makes great exertions to succeed in this object. This sentiment, indeed, which is but too natural to the heart of man, does not originate in the democratic principle ; but that principle applies it to material objects. To mimic virtue is of every age ; but the hypocrisy of luxury belongs more particularly to the ages of democracy.

To satisfy these new cravings of human vanity the arts have recourse to every species of imposture : and these devices sometimes go so far as to defeat their own purpose. Imitation diamonds are now made which easily may be mistaken for real ones ; as soon as the art of fabricating false diamonds shall have reached so high a degree of perfection that they cannot be distinguished from real ones, it is probable that both one and the other will be abandoned, and become mere pebbles again.

This leads me to speak of those arts which are called the fine arts, by way of distinction. I do not believe that it is a necessary effect of a democratic social condition and of democratic institutions to diminish the number of men who cultivate the fine arts ; but these causes exert a very powerful influence on the manner in which these arts are cultivated. Many of those who had already contracted a taste for the fine arts are impoverished : on the other hand, many of those who are not yet rich begin to conceive that taste, at least by imitation ; and the number of consumers increases, but opulent and fastidious consumers become more scarce. Something analogous to what I have already pointed out in the useful arts then takes place in the fine arts ; the productions of artists are more numerous, but the merit of each production is diminished. No longer able to soar to what is great, they cultivate what is pretty and elegant ; and appearance is more attended to than reality. In aristocracies a few great pictures are produced ; in democratic countries, a vast number of insignificant ones. In the former, statues are raised of bronze; in the latter, they are modelled in plaster.

When I arrived for the first time at New York, by that part of the Atlantic Ocean which is called the Sound, I was surprised to perceive along the shore, at some distance from the city, a considerable number of little palaces of white marble, several of which were built after the models of ancient architecture. When I went the next day to inspect more closely the building which had particularly attracted my notice, I found that its walls were of white-washed brick, and its columns of painted wood. All the edifices which I had admired the night before were of the same kind.

The social condition and the institutions of democracy impart, moreover, certain peculiar tendencies to all the imitative arts, which it is easy to point out. They frequently withdraw them from the delineation of the soul to fix them exclusively on that of the body: and they substitute the representation of motion and sensation for that of sentiment and thought: in a word, they put the Real in the place of the Ideal. I doubt whether Raphael studied the minutest intricacies of the mechanism of the human body as thoroughly as the draughtsmen of our own time. He did not attach the same importance to rigorous accuracy on this point as they do, because he aspired to surpass Nature. He sought to make of man something which should be superior to man, and to embellish beauty's self. . . . The painters of the Middle Ages generally sought far above themselves, and away from their own time, for mighty subjects, which left to their imagination an unbounded range. Our painters frequently employ their talents in the exact imitation of the details of private life, which they have always before their eyes; and they are for ever copying trivial objects, the originals of which are only too abundant in Nature.

I have just observed that in democratic ages monuments of the arts tend to become more numerous and less important. I now hasten to point out the exception to this rule. In a democratic community individuals are very powerless ; but the State which represents them all, and contains them all in its grasp, is very powerful. Nowhere do citizens appear so insignificant as in a democratic nation ; nowhere does the nation itself appear greater, or does the mind more easily take in a wide general survey of it. In democratic communities the imagination is compressed when men consider themselves ; it expands indefinitely when they think of the State. Hence it is that the same men who live on a small scale in narrow dwellings frequently aspire to gigantic splendour in the erection of their public monuments.

The Americans traced out the circuit of an immense city on the site which they intended to make their capital, but which, up to the present time, is hardly more densely peopled than Pontoise, though, according to them, it will one day contain a million inhabitants. They have already rooted up trees for ten miles round, lest they should interfere with the future citizens of this imaginary metropolis. They have erected a magnificent palace for Congress in the centre of the city, and have given it the pompous name of the Capitol. The several States of the Union are every day planning and erecting for themselves prodigious undertakings, which would astonish the engineers of the great European nations. Thus democracy not only leads men to a vast number of inconsiderable productions ; it also leads them to raise some monuments on the largest scale : but between these two extremes there is a blank. A few scattered remains of enormous buildings can therefore teach us nothing of the social condition and the institutions of the people by whom they were raised. I may add, though the remark leads me to step out of my subject, that they do not make us better acquainted with its greatness, its civilization, and its real prosperity. Whensoever a power of any kind shall be able to make a whole people co-operate in a single undertaking, that power, with a little knowledge and a great deal of time, will succeed in obtaining something enormous from the co-operation of efforts so multiplied. But this does not lead to the conclusion that the people was very happy, very enlightened, or even very strong. . . .

Chapter XXIII

**THE INFLUENCES OF DEMOCRACY UPON LANGUAGE
AND LITERATURE**

ALTHOUGH America is perhaps in our days the civilized country in which literature is least attended to, a large number of persons are nevertheless to be found there who take an interest in the productions of the mind, and who make them, if not the study of their lives, at least the charm of their leisure hours. But England supplies these readers with the larger portion of the books which they require. Almost all important English books are republished in the United States. The literary genius of Great Britain still darts its rays into the recesses of the forests of the New World. There is hardly a pioneer's hut which does not contain a few odd volumes of Shakespeare. I remember that I read the feudal play of *Henry V* for the first time in a log-house.

Not only do the Americans constantly draw upon the treasures of English literature, but it may be said with truth that they find the literature of England growing on their own soil. The larger part of that small number of men in the United States who are engaged in the composition of literary works are English in substance, and still more so in form. Thus they transport into the midst of democracy the ideas and literary fashions which are current among the aristocratic nation they have taken for their model. They paint with colours borrowed from foreign manners ; and as they hardly ever represent the country they were born in as it really is, they are seldom popular there. The citizens of the United States are themselves so convinced that it is not for them that books are published, that before they can make up their minds upon the merit of one of their authors they generally wait till his fame has been ratified in England, just as in pictures the author of an original is held to be entitled to judge of the merit of a copy. The inhabitants of the United States have then at present, properly speaking, no literature.[1] The only authors whom I acknowledge as American are the journalists. They, indeed, are not great writers, but they speak the language of their countrymen, and make themselves heard by them. Other authors are aliens; they are to the Americans what the imitators of the Greeks and Romans were to us at the revival of learning—an object of curiosity, not of general sympathy. They amuse the mind, but they do not act upon the manners of the people.

I have already said that this state of things is very far from originating in democracy alone, and that the causes of it must be sought for in several peculiar circumstances independent of the democratic principle. If the Americans, retaining the same laws and social condition, had had a different origin, and had been transported into another country, I do not question that they would have had a literature. Even as they now are, I am convinced that they will ultimately have one; but its character will be different from that which marks the American literary productions of our time, and that character will be peculiarly its own. Nor is it impossible to trace this character beforehand. . . .

Let us transport ourselves into the midst of a democracy, not unprepared by ancient traditions and present culture to partake in the pleasures of the mind. Ranks are there intermingled and confounded;

[1] By the late 1830s Irving, Cooper and Simms had already done much of their best work, Poe had published three slender volumes of poetry, and Emerson had printed his lectures on Nature and the American Scholar.—H. S. C.

knowledge and power are both infinitely subdivided, and, if I may use the expression, scattered on every side. Here, then, is a motley multitude, whose intellectual wants are to be supplied. These new votaries of the pleasures of the mind have not all received the same education : they do not possess the same degree of culture as their fathers, nor any resemblance to them—nay, they perpetually differ from themselves, for they live in a state of incessant change of place, feelings, and fortunes. The mind of each member of the community is therefore unattached to that of his fellow-citizens by tradition or by common habits ; and they never have had the power, the inclination, nor the time to concert together. It is, however, from the bosom of this heterogeneous and agitated mass that authors spring ; and from the same source their profits and their fame are distributed. I can understand without difficulty that, under these circumstances, I must expect to meet in the literature of such a people with but few of those strict conventional rules which are admitted by readers and by writers in aristocratic ages. If it should happen that the men of some one period were agreed upon any such rules, that would prove nothing for the following period ; for among democratic nations each new generation is a new people. Among such nations, then, literature will not easily be subjected to strict rules, and it is impossible that any such rules should ever be permanent.

In democracies it is by no means the case that all the men who cultivate literature have received a literary education ; and most of those who have some tinge of *belles-lettres* are either engaged in politics, or in a profession which only allows them to taste occasionally and by stealth the pleasures of the mind. These pleasures, therefore, do not constitute the principal charm of their lives ; but they are considered as a transient and necessary recreation amid the serious labours of life. Such men can never acquire a sufficiently intimate knowledge of the art of literature to appreciate its more delicate beauties ; and the minor shades of expression must escape them. As the time they can devote to letters is very short, they seek to make the best use of the whole of it. They prefer books which may be easily procured, quickly read, and which require no learned research to be understood. They ask for beauties, self-proffered and easily enjoyed ; above all, they must have what is unexpected and new. Accustomed to the struggle, the crosses, and the monotony of practical life, they require rapid emotions, startling passages—truths or errors brilliant enough to rouse them up, and to plunge them at once, as if by violence, into the midst of a subject.

Why should I say more ? or who does not understand what is about to follow, before I have expressed it ? Taken as a whole, literature in democratic ages can never present, as it does in the periods of aristocracy, an aspect of order, regularity, science, and art ; its form will, on the contrary, ordinarily be slighted, sometimes despised. Style will frequently be fantastic, incorrect, overburdened, and loose— almost always vehement and bold. Authors will aim at rapidity of execution, more than at perfection of detail. Small productions will be more common than bulky books ; there will be more wit than erudition, more imagination than profundity ; and literary performances will bear marks of an untutored and rude vigour of thought—frequently of great variety and singular fecundity. The object of authors will be to astonish rather than to please, and to stir the passions more than to charm the taste. Here and there, indeed, writers will doubtless occur who will choose a different track, and who will, if they are gifted with superior abilities, succeed in finding readers, in spite of their defects or their better qualities ; but these exceptions will be rare, and even the authors who shall so depart from the received practice in the main subject of their works, will always relapse into it in some lesser details. . . .

Democracy not only infuses a taste for letters among the trading classes, but introduces a trading spirit into literature. In aristocracies, readers are fastidious and few in number ; in democracies, they are far more numerous and far less difficult to please. The consequence is, that among aristocratic nations no one can hope to succeed without immense exertions, and that these exertions may bestow a great deal of fame, but never can earn much money ; while among democratic nations, a writer may flatter himself that he will obtain at a cheap rate a meagre reputation and a large fortune. For this purpose he need not be admired ; it is enough that he is liked. The ever-increasing crowd of readers, and their continual craving for something new, insure the sale of books which nobody much esteems.

In democratic periods the public frequently treat authors as kings do their courtiers ; they enrich, and they despise them. What more is needed by the venal souls which are born in courts, or which are worthy to live there ? Democratic literature is always infested with a tribe of writers who look upon letters as a mere trade : and for some few great authors who adorn it you may reckon thousands of idea-mongers. . . .

A very superficial survey of the literary remains of the ancients will suffice to convince us that if those writers were sometimes deficient in variety, or fertility in their subjects, or in boldness, vivacity, or power of generalization in their thoughts, they always displayed exquisite care and skill in their details. Nothing in their works seems to be done hastily or at random : every line is written for the eye of the connoisseur, and is shaped after some conception of ideal beauty. No literature places those fine qualities, in which the writers of democracies are naturally deficient, in bolder relief than that of the ancients ; no literature, therefore, ought to be more studied in democratic ages. This study is better suited than any other to combat the literary defects inherent in those ages : as for their more praiseworthy literary qualities, they will spring up of their own accord, without its being necessary to learn to acquire them.

It is important that this point should be clearly understood. A particular study may be useful to the literature of a people, without being appropriate to its social and political wants. If men were to persist in teaching nothing but the literature of the dead languages in a community where every one is habitually led to make vehement exertions to augment or to maintain his fortune, the result would be a very polished, but a very dangerous, race of citizens. For as their social and political condition would give them every day a sense of wants which their education would never teach them to supply, they would perturb the State, in the name of the Greeks and Romans, instead of enriching it by their productive industry.

It is evident that in democratic communities the interest of individuals, as well as the security of the commonwealth, demands that the education of the greater number should be scientific, commercial, and industrial, rather than literary. Greek and Latin should not be taught in all schools ; but it is important that those who by their natural disposition or their fortune are destined to cultivate letters or prepared to relish them, should find schools where a complete knowledge of ancient literature may be acquired, and where the true scholar may be formed. A few excellent universities would do more toward the attainment of this object than a vast number of bad grammar-schools, where superfluous matters, badly learned, stand in the way of sound instruction in necessary studies. . . .

If the reader has rightly understood what I have already said on the subject of literature in general, he will have no difficulty in comprehending that species of influence which a democratic social condition and democratic institutions may exercise over language itself, which is the chief instrument of thought.

American authors may truly be said to live more in England than in their own country ; since they constantly study the English writers, and take them every day for their models. But such is not the case with the bulk of the population, which is more immediately subjected to the peculiar causes acting upon the United States. It is not then to the written but to the spoken language that attention must be paid if we would detect the modifications which the idiom of an aristocratic people may undergo when it becomes the language of a democracy.

Englishmen of education, and more competent judges than I can be myself of the nicer shades of expression, have frequently assured me that the language of the educated classes in the United States is notably different from that of the educated classes in Great Britain. They complain not only that the Americans have brought into use a number of new words—the difference and the distance between the two countries might suffice to explain that much—but that these new words are more especially taken from the jargon of parties, the mechanical arts, or the language of trade. They assert, in addition to this, that old English words are often used by the Americans in new acceptations ; and lastly, that the inhabitants of the United States frequently intermingle their phraseology in the strangest manner, and sometimes place words together which are always kept apart in the language of the mother-country.[1] . . .

In aristocracies, language must naturally partake of that state of repose in which everything remains. Few new words are coined, because few new things are made ; and even if new things were made, they would be designated by known words, whose meaning has been determined by tradition. If it happens that the human mind bestirs itself at length, or is roused by light breaking in from without, the novel expressions which are introduced are characterized by a degree of learning, intelligence, and philosophy which shows that they do not originate in a democracy. After the fall of Constantinople had turned the tide of science and literature toward the west, the French language was almost immediately invaded by a multitude of new words, which had all Greek or Latin roots. An erudite neologism then sprang up in France which was confined to the educated classes, and which produced no sensible effect, or at least a very gradual one, upon the people. All the nations of Europe successively exhibited the same change. Milton alone introduced more than six hundred words into the English language, almost all derived from the Latin, the Greek, or the Hebrew. The constant agitation which prevails in a democratic community tends unceasingly, on the contrary, to change the character

[1] See H. L. Mencken, *The American Language* (4th ed.), p. 12 ff., for the history of British complaints about the Americanization of English.—H. S. C.

of the language, as it does the aspect of affairs. In the midst of this general stir and competition of minds a great number of new ideas are formed, old ideas are lost, or reappear, or are subdivided into an infinite variety of minor shades. The consequence is, that many words must fall into desuetude, and others must be brought into use.

Democratic nations love change for its own sake; and this is seen in their language as much as in their politics. Even when they do not need to change words, they sometimes feel a wish to transform them. The genius of a democratic people is not only shown by the great number of words they bring into use, but also by the nature of the ideas these new words represent. Among such a people the majority lays down the law in language as well as in everything else; its prevailing spirit is as manifest in that as in other respects. But the majority is more engaged in business than in study—in political and commercial interests than in philosophical speculation or literary pursuits. Most of the words coined or adopted for its use will therefore bear the mark of these habits; they will mainly serve to express the wants of business, the passions of party, or the details of the public administration. In these departments the language will constantly spread, while on the other hand it will gradually lose ground in metaphysics and theology. . . .

In the absence of knowledge of the dead languages, democratic nations are apt to borrow words from living tongues; for their mutual intercourse becomes perpetual, and the inhabitants of different countries imitate each other the more readily as they grow more like each other every day.

But it is principally upon their own languages that democratic nations attempt to perpetuate innovations. From time to time they resume forgotten expressions in their vocabulary, which they restore to use ; or they borrow from some particular class of the community a term peculiar to it, which they introduce with a figurative meaning into the language of daily life.   Many expressions which originally belonged to the technical language of a profession or a party are thus drawn into general circulation.

The most common expedient employed by democratic nations to make an innovation in language consists in giving some unwonted meaning to an expression already in use.   This method is very simple, prompt, and convenient ; no learning is required to use it aright, and ignorance itself rather facilitates the practice ; but that practice is most dangerous to the language. When a democratic people doubles the meaning of a word in this way, they sometimes render the signification which it retains as ambiguous as that which it acquires.   An author begins by a slight deflection of a known expression from its primitive meaning, and he adapts it, thus modified, as well as he can to his subject. A second writer twists the sense of the expression in another way ; a third takes possession of it for another purpose ; and as there is no common appeal to the sentence of a permanent tribunal which may definitely settle the signification of the word, it remains in an ambiguous condition. The consequence is that writers hardly ever appear to dwell upon a single thought, but they always seem to point their aim at a knot of ideas, leaving the reader to judge which of them has been hit. This is a deplorable consequence of democracy.[1] . . .

[1] It is remarkable that Tocqueville is guilty of precisely this failing in his use of the word ' democracy ', which he nowhere defines and to which he gives throughout his volumes a variety of meanings —H. S. C.

The principle of equality necessarily introduces several other changes into language. In aristocratic ages, when each nation tends to stand aloof from all others and likes to have distinct characteristics of its own, it often happens that several peoples which have a common origin become nevertheless estranged from each other, so that, without ceasing to understand the same language, they no longer all speak it in the same manner. In these ages each nation is divided into a certain number of classes, which see but little of each other, and do not intermingle. Each of these classes contracts, and invariably retains, habits of mind peculiar to itself, and adopts by choice certain words and certain terms, which afterward pass from generation to generation, like their estates. The same idiom then comprises a language of the poor and a language of the rich—a language of the citizen and a language of the nobility—a learned language and a vulgar one. The deeper the divisions, and the more impassable the barriers of society become, the more must this be the case. . . . When, on the contrary, men, being no longer restrained by ranks, meet on terms of constant intercourse—when castes are destroyed, and the classes of society are recruited and intermixed with each other, all the words of a language are mingled. Those which are unsuitable to the greater number perish; the remainder form a common store, whence every one chooses pretty nearly at random. Almost all the different dialects which divided the idioms of European nations are manifestly declining; there is no patois in the New World, and it is disappearing every day from the old countries.

The influence of this revolution in social conditions is as much felt in style as it is in phraseology. Not only does every one use the same words, but a habit springs up of using them without discrimination. The rules which style had set up are almost abolished : the line ceases to be drawn between expressions which seem by their very nature vulgar, and others which appear to be refined. Persons springing from different ranks of society carry the terms and expressions they are accustomed to use with them, into whatever circumstances they may pass ; thus the origin of words is lost like the origin of individuals, and there is as much confusion in language as there is in society. . . .

I shall not quit this topic without touching on a feature of democratic languages which is perhaps more characteristic of them than any other. It has already been shown that democratic nations have a taste, and sometimes a passion, for general ideas, and that this arises from their peculiar merits and defects. This liking for general ideas is displayed in democratic languages by the continual use of generic terms or abstract expressions, and by the manner in which they are employed. This is the great merit and the great imperfection of these languages. Democratic nations are passionately addicted to generic terms or abstract expressions, because these modes of speech enlarge thought, and assist the operations of the mind by enabling it to include several objects in a small compass. . . .

These abstract terms which abound in democratic languages, and which are used on every occasion without attaching them to any particular fact, enlarge and obscure the thoughts they are intended to convey ; they render the mode of speech more succinct, and the idea contained in it less clear. But with regard to language, democratic nations prefer obscurity to labour. I know not, indeed, whether this loose style has not some secret charm for those who speak and write among these nations. As the men who live there are frequently left to the efforts of their individual powers of mind, they are almost always a prey to doubt ; and as their situation in life is for ever changing, they are never held fast to any of their opinions by the certain tenure of their fortunes. Men living in democratic countries are, then, apt to entertain unsettled ideas, and they require loose expressions to convey them. As they never know whether the idea they express to-day will be appropriate to the new position they may occupy to-morrow, they naturally acquire a liking for abstract terms. An abstract term is like a box with a false bottom : you may put in it what ideas you please, and take them out again without being observed. . . .

I now proceed to inquire whether, among the actions, the sentiments, and the opinions of democratic nations, there are any which lead to a conception of ideal beauty, and which may for this reason be considered as natural sources of poetry. It must, in the first place, be acknowledged that the taste for ideal beauty, and the pleasure derived from the expression of it, are never so intense or so diffused among a democratic as among an aristocratic people. In aristocratic nations it sometimes happens that the body goes on to act as it were spontaneously, while the higher faculties are bound and burdened by repose. Among these nations the people will very often display poetic tastes, and sometimes allow their fancy to range beyond and above what surrounds them. But in democracies the love of physical gratification, the notion of bettering one's condition, the excitement of competition, the charm of anticipated success, are so many spurs to urge men onward in the active professions they have embraced, without allowing them to deviate for an instant from the track. The main stress of the faculties is to this point. The imagination is not extinct ; but its chief function is to devise what may be useful, and to represent what is real.

The principle of equality not only diverts men from the description of ideal beauty—it also diminishes the number of objects to be described. Aristocracy, by maintaining society in a fixed position, is favourable to the solidity and duration of positive religions, as well as to the stability of political institutions. It not only keeps the human mind within a certain sphere of belief, but it predisposes the mind to adopt one faith rather than another. An aristocratic people will always be prone to place intermediate powers between God and man. In this respect it may be said that the aristocratic element is favourable to poetry. When the universe is peopled with supernatural creatures, not palpable to the senses but discovered by the mind, the imagination ranges freely, and poets, finding a thousand subjects to delineate, also find a countless audience to take an interest in their productions. In democratic ages it sometimes happens, on the contrary, that men are as much afloat in matters of belief as they are in their laws. Scepticism, then, draws the imagination of poets back to earth, and confines them to the real and visible world. Even when the principle of equality does not disturb religious belief, it tends to simplify it, and to divert attention from secondary agents, to fix it principally on the Supreme Power. Aristocracy naturally leads the human mind to the contemplation of the past, and fixes it there. Democracy, on the contrary, gives men a sort of instinctive distaste for what is ancient. In this respect aristocracy is far more favourable to poetry ; for things commonly grow larger and more obscure as they are more remote ; and for this twofold reason they are better suited to the delineation of the ideal.

After having deprived poetry of the past, the principle of equality robs it in part of the present. . . . In democratic communities, where men are all insignificant and very much alike, each man instantly sees all his fellows when he surveys himself. The poets of democratic ages can never, therefore, take any man in particular as the subject of a piece ; for an object of slender importance, which is distinctly seen on all sides, will never lend itself to an ideal conception. Thus the principle of equality, in proportion as it has established itself in the world, has dried up most of the old springs of poetry. Let us now attempt to show what new ones it may disclose.

When scepticism had depopulated heaven, and the progress of equality had reduced each individual to smaller and better known proportions, the poets, not yet aware of what they could substitute for the great themes which were departing together with the aristocracy, turned their eyes to inanimate Nature. As they lost sight of gods and heroes, they set themselves to describe streams and mountains. Thence originated, in the last century, that kind of poetry which has been called, by way of distinction, the descriptive. Some have thought that this sort of delineation, embellished with all the physical and inanimate objects which cover the earth, was the kind of poetry peculiar to democratic ages ; but I believe this to be an error, and that it only belongs to a period of transition.

I am persuaded that in the end democracy diverts the imagination from all that is external to man, and fixes it on man alone. Democratic nations may amuse themselves for a while with considering the productions of Nature ; but they are only excited in reality by a survey of themselves. Here, and here alone, the true sources of poetry among such nations are to be found ; and it may be believed that the poets who shall neglect to draw their inspirations hence, will lose all sway over the minds which they would enchant, and will be left in the end with none but unimpassioned spectators of their transports. I have shown how the ideas of progression and of the indefinite perfectibility of the human race belong to democratic ages. Democratic nations care but little for what has been, but they are haunted by visions of what will be ; in this direction their unbounded imagination grows and dilates beyond all measure. Here, then, is the wildest range open to the genius of poets, which allows them to remove their perform-ances to a sufficient distance from the eye. Demo-cracy shuts the past against the poet, but opens the future before him. As all the citizens who compose a democratic community are nearly equal and alike, the poet cannot dwell upon any one of them ; but the nation itself invites the exercise of his powers. The general similitude of individuals, which renders any one of them taken separately an improper subject of poetry, allows poets to include them all in the same imagery, and to take a general survey of the people itself. Democratic nations have a clearer perception than any others of their own aspect ; and an aspect so imposing is admirably fitted to the delineation of the ideal.

I readily admit that the Americans have no poets ; I cannot allow that they have no poetic ideas. In Europe people talk a great deal of the wilds of America, but the Americans themselves never think about them : they are insensible to the wonders of inanimate Nature, and they may be said not to perceive the mighty forests which surround them till they fall beneath the hatchet. Their eyes are fixed upon another sight : the American people views its own march across these wilds — drying swamps, turning the course of rivers, peopling solitudes, and subduing Nature. This magnificent image of themselves does not meet the gaze of the Americans at intervals only ; it may be said to haunt every one of them in his least as well as in his most important actions, and to be always flitting before his mind. Nothing conceivable is so petty, so insipid, so crowded with paltry interests, in one word so antipoetic, as the life of a man in the United States. But among the thoughts which it suggests there is always one which is full of poetry, and that is the hidden nerve which gives vigour to the frame.

In aristocratic ages each people, as well as each individual, is prone to stand separate and aloof from all others. In democratic ages, the extreme fluctuations of men and the impatience of their desires keep them perpetually on the move ; so that the inhabitants of different countries intermingle, see, listen to, and borrow from each other's stores. It is then not only the members of the same community who grow more alike ; communities are themselves assimilated to one another, and the whole assemblage presents to the eye of the spectator one vast democracy, each citizen of which is a people. This displays the aspect of mankind for the first time in the broadest light. All that belongs to the existence of the human race taken as a whole, to its vicissitudes and to its future, becomes an abundant mine of poetry. The poets who lived in aristocratic ages have been eminently successful in their delineations of certain incidents in the life of a people or a man ; but none of them ever ventured to include within his performances the destinies of mankind—a task which poets writing in democratic ages may attempt. At that same time at which every man, raising his eyes above his country, begins at length to discern mankind at large, the Divinity is more and more manifest to the human mind in full and entire majesty. If in democratic ages faith in positive religions be often shaken, and the belief in intermediate agents, by whatever name they are called, be overcast ; on the other hand men are disposed to conceive a far broader idea of Providence itself, and its interference in human affairs assumes a new and more imposing appearance to their eyes. Looking at the human race as one great whole, they easily conceive that its destinies are regulated by the same design ; and in the actions of every individual they are led to acknowledge a trace of that universal and eternal plan on which God rules our race. This consideration may be taken as another prolific source of poetry which is opened in democratic ages. Democratic poets will always appear trivial and frigid if they seek to invest gods, demons, or angels with corporeal forms, and if they attempt to draw them down from heaven to dispute the supremacy of earth. But if they strive to connect the great events they commemorate with the general providential designs which govern the universe, and, without showing the finger of the Supreme Governor, reveal the thoughts of the Supreme Mind, their works will be admired and understood, for the imagination of their contemporaries takes the direction of its own accord.

It may be foreseen in like manner that poets living in democratic ages will prefer the delineation of passions and ideas to that of persons and achievements. The language, the dress, and the daily actions of men in democracies are repugnant to ideal conceptions. These things are not poetical in themselves ; and if it were otherwise, they would cease to be so, because they are too familiar to all those to whom the poet would speak of them. This forces the poet constantly to search below the external surface which is palpable to the senses, in order to read the inner soul: and nothing lends itself more to the delineation of the Ideal than the scrutiny of the hidden depths in the immaterial nature of man. . . .

Among a democratic people poetry will not be fed with legendary lays or the memorials of old traditions. The poet will not attempt to people the universe with supernatural beings in whom his readers and his own fancy have ceased to believe ; nor will he present virtues and vices in the mask of frigid personification, which are better received under their own features. All these resources fail him ; but Man remains, and the poet needs no more. The destinies of mankind— man himself, taken aloof from his age and his country, and standing in the presence of Nature and of God, with his passions, his doubts, his rare prosperities, and inconceivable wretchedness—will become the chief if not the sole theme of poetry among these nations. Experience may confirm this assertion, if we consider the productions of the greatest poets who have appeared since the world has been turned to democracy. The authors of our age who have so admirably delineated the features of Faust, Childe Harold, Réné, and Jocelyn, did not seek to record the actions of an individual, but to enlarge and to throw light on some of the obscurer recesses of the human heart. Such are the poems of democracy. The principle of equality does not then destroy all the subjects of poetry : it renders them less numerous, but more vast.

I have frequently remarked that the Americans, who generally treat of business in clear, plain language, devoid of all ornament, and so extremely

simple as to be often coarse, are apt to become
inflated as soon as they attempt a more poetical
diction. They then vent their pomposity from one
end of a harangue to the other ; and to hear them
lavish imagery on every occasion, one might fancy
that they never spoke of anything with simplicity.
The English are more rarely given to a similar failing.
The cause of this may be pointed out without much
difficulty. In democratic communities each citizen
is habitually engaged in the contemplation of a very
puny object, namely, himself. If he ever raises his
looks higher, he then perceives nothing but the
immense form of society at large, or the still more
imposing aspect of mankind. His ideas are all either
extremely minute and clear, or extremely general and
vague : what lies between is an open void. When
he has been drawn out of his own sphere, therefore,
he always expects that some amazing object will be
offered to his attention ; and it is on these terms alone
that he consents to tear himself for an instant from
the petty complicated cares which form the charm
and the excitement of his life. This appears to me
sufficiently to explain why men in democracies, whose
concerns are in general so paltry, call upon their poets
for conceptions so vast and descriptions so unlimited.

The authors, on their part, do not fail to obey a
propensity of which they themselves partake ; they
perpetually inflate their imaginations, and expanding
them beyond all bounds, they not infrequently
abandon the great in order to reach the gigantic. By
these means they hope to attract the observation of
the multitude, and to fix it easily upon themselves :
nor are their hopes disappointed ; for as the multitude
seeks for nothing in poetry but subjects of very vast
dimensions, it has neither the time to measure with
accuracy the proportions of all the subjects set before

it, nor a taste sufficiently correct to perceive at once in what respect they are out of proportion. The author and the public at once vitiate one another. . . .

When the revolution which subverts the social and political state of an aristocratic people begins to penetrate into literature, it generally first manifests itself in the drama, and it always remains conspicuous there. The spectator of a dramatic piece is, to a certain extent, taken by surprise by the impression it conveys. He has no time to refer to his memory, or to consult those more able to judge than himself. It does not occur to him to resist the new literary tendencies which begin to be felt by him ; he yields to them before he knows what they are. Authors are very prompt in discovering which way the taste of the public is thus secretly inclined. They shape their productions accordingly ; and the literature of the stage, after having served to indicate the approaching literary revolution, speedily completes its accomplishment. If you would judge beforehand of the literature of a people which is lapsing into democracy, study its dramatic productions. . . .

If it be difficult for an aristocracy to prevent the people from getting the upper hand in the theatre, it will readily be understood that the people will be supreme there when democratic principles have crept into the laws and manners—when ranks are intermixed—when minds, as well as fortunes, are brought more nearly together—and when the upper class has lost, with its hereditary wealth, its power, its precedents, and its leisure. The tastes and propensities natural to democratic nations, in respect to literature, will therefore first be discernible in the drama, and it may be foreseen that they will break out there with vehemence. In written productions, the literary canons of aristocracy will be gently, gradually, and, so to speak, legally modified ; at the theatre they will be riotously overthrown.

The drama brings out most of the good qualities, and almost all the defects, inherent in democratic literature. Democratic peoples hold erudition very cheap, and care but little for what occurred at Rome and Athens ; they want to hear something which concerns themselves, and the delineation of the present age is what they demand. . . .

When the democratic classes rule the stage, they introduce as much licence in the manner of treating subjects as in the choice of them. As the love of the drama is, of all literary tastes, that which is most natural to democratic nations, the number of authors and of spectators, as well as of theatrical representations, is constantly increasing among these communities. A multitude composed of elements so different, and scattered in so many different places, cannot acknowledge the same rules or submit to the same laws. No concurrence is possible among judges so numerous, who know not when they may meet again ; and therefore each pronounces his own sentence on the piece. If the effect of democracy is generally to question the authority of all literary rules and conventions, on the stage it abolishes them altogether, and puts in their place nothing but the whim of each author and of each public.

The drama also displays in an especial manner the truth of what I have said before in speaking more generally of style and art in democratic literature. . . . In democracies, dramatic pieces are listened to, but not read. Most of those who frequent the amusements of the stage do not go there to seek the pleasures of the mind, but the keen emotions of the heart. They do not expect to hear a fine literary work, but to see a play ; and provided the author writes the language of his country correctly enough to be understood, and that his characters excite curiosity and awaken sympathy, the audience are satisfied. They ask no more of fiction, and immediately return to real life. Accuracy of style is therefore less required, because the attentive observance of its rules is less perceptible on the stage. As for the probability of the plot, it is incompatible with perpetual novelty, surprise, and rapidity of invention. It is therefore neglected, and the public excuses the neglect. You may be sure that if you succeed in bringing your audience into the presence of something that affects them, they will not care by what road you brought them there ; and they will never reproach you for having excited their emotions in spite of dramatic rules.

The Americans very broadly display all the different propensities which I have here described when they go to the theatres ; but it must be acknowledged that as yet a very small number of them go to theatres at all. Although play-goers and plays have prodigiously increased in the United States in the last forty years, the population indulges in this kind of amusement with the greatest reserve. This is attributable to peculiar causes, which the reader is already acquainted with, and of which a few words will suffice to remind him. The Puritans who founded the American republics were not only enemies to amusements, but they professed an especial abhorrence for the stage. They considered it as an abominable pastime ; and as long as their principles prevailed with undivided sway, scenic performances were wholly unknown among them. These opinions of the first fathers of the colony have left very deep marks on the minds of their descendants. The extreme regularity of habits and the great strictness of manners which are observable in the United States have as yet opposed additional obstacles to the growth of dramatic art. There are no dramatic subjects in a country which has witnessed no great political catastrophes, and in which love invariably leads by a straight and easy road to matrimony. People who spend every day in the week in making money, and the Sunday in going to church, have nothing to invite the Muse of Comedy. . . .

Historians who write in aristocratic ages are wont to refer all occurrences to the particular will or temper of certain individuals ; and they are apt to attribute the most important revolutions to very slight accidents. They trace out the smallest causes with sagacity, and frequently leave the greatest unperceived. Historians who live in democratic ages exhibit precisely opposite characteristics. Most of them attribute hardly any influence to the individual over the destiny of the race, nor to citizens over the fate of a people ; but, on the other hand, they assign great general causes to all petty incidents. These contrary tendencies explain each other.

When the historian of aristocratic ages surveys the theatre of the world, he at once perceives a very small number of prominent actors, who manage the whole piece. These great personages, who occupy the front of the stage, arrest the observation, and fix it on themselves ; and while the historian is bent on penetrating the secret motives which make them speak and act, the rest escape his memory. The importance of the things which some men are seen to do, gives him an exaggerated estimate of the influence which one man may possess ; and naturally leads him to think that, in order to explain the impulses of the multitude, it is necessary to refer them to the particular influence of some one individual.

When, on the contrary, all the citizens are independent of one another, and each of them is individually weak, no one is seen to exert a great, or still less a lasting power, over the community. At first sight, individuals appear to be absolutely devoid of any influence over it ; and society would seem to advance alone by the free and voluntary concurrence of all the men who compose it. This naturally prompts the mind to search for that general reason which operates upon so many men's faculties at the same time, and turns them simultaneously in the same direction. . . .

M. de Lafayette says somewhere in his *Memoirs* that the exaggerated system of general causes affords surprising consolations to second-rate statesmen. I will add that its effects are not less consolatory to second-rate historians; it can always furnish a few mighty reasons to extricate them from the most difficult part of their work, and it indulges the indolence or incapacity of their minds, while it confers upon them the honours of deep thinking.

For myself, I am of opinion that at all times one great portion of the events of this world are attributable to general facts, and another to special influences. These two kinds of cause are always in operation : their proportion only varies. General facts serve to explain more things in democratic than in aristocratic ages, and fewer things are then assignable to special influences. At periods of aristocracy the reverse takes place : special influences are stronger, general causes weaker—unless, indeed, we consider as a general cause the fact itself of the inequality of conditions, which allows some individuals to baffle the natural tendencies of all the rest. The historians who seek to describe what occurs in democratic societies are right, therefore, in assigning much to general causes, and in devoting their chief attention to discover them ; but they are wrong in wholly denying the special influence of individuals, because they cannot easily trace or follow it.

The historians who live in democratic ages are not only prone to assign a great cause to every incident, but they are also given to connect incidents together, so as to deduce a system from them. In aristocratic ages, as the attention of historians is constantly drawn to individuals, the connection of events escapes them ; or rather, they do not believe in any such connection. To them the clue of history seems every instant crossed and broken by the step of man. In democratic ages, on the contrary, as the historian sees much more of actions than of actors, he may easily establish some kind of sequence and methodical order among the former. Ancient literature, which is so rich in fine historical compositions, does not contain a single great historical system, while the poorest of modern literatures abound with them. It would appear that the ancient historians did not make sufficient use of those general theories which our historical writers are ever ready to carry to excess.

Those who write in democratic ages have another more dangerous tendency. When the traces of individual action upon nations are lost, it often happens that the world goes on to move, though the moving agent is no longer discoverable. As it becomes extremely difficult to discern and to analyse the reasons which, acting separately on the volition of each member of the community, concur in the end to produce movement in the old mass, men are led to believe that this movement is involuntary, and that societies unconsciously obey some superior force ruling over them. But even when the general fact which governs the private volition of all individuals is supposed to be discovered upon the earth, the principle of human free will is not secure. A cause sufficiently extensive to affect millions of men at once, and sufficiently strong to bend them all together in the same direction, may well seem irresistible : having seen that mankind do yield to it, the mind is close upon the inference that mankind cannot resist it.

Historians who live in democratic ages, then, not only deny that the few have any power of acting upon the destiny of a people, but they deprive the people themselves of the power of modifying their own condition, and they subject them either to an inflexible Providence, or to some blind necessity. According to them, each nation is indissolubly bound by its position, its origin, its precedents, and its character, to a certain lot which no efforts can ever change. They involve generation in generation, and thus, going back from age to age, and from necessity to necessity, up to the origin of the world, they forge a close and enormous chain, which girds and binds the human race. To their minds it is not enough to show what events have occurred : they would fain show that events could not have occurred otherwise. They take a nation arrived at a certain stage of its history, and they affirm that it could not but follow the track which brought it thither. It is easier to make such an assertion than to show by what means the nation might have adopted a better course.

In reading the historians of aristocratic ages, and especially those of antiquity, it would seem that, to be master of his lot, and to govern his fellow-creatures, man requires only to be master of himself. In perusing the historical volumes which our age has produced, it would seem that man is utterly powerless over himself and over all around him. The historians of antiquity taught how to command : those of our time teach only how to obey ; in their writings the author often appears great, but humanity is always diminutive. If this doctrine of necessity, which is so attractive to those who write history in democratic ages, passes from authors to their readers, till it infects the whole mass of the community and gets possession of the public mind, it will soon paralyse the activity of modern society, and reduce Christians to the level of the Turks. . . . Our contemporaries are but too prone to doubt of the human free will, because each of them feels himself confined on every side by his own weakness ; but they are still willing to acknowledge the strength and independence of men united in society. Let not this principle be lost sight of ; for the great object in our time is to raise the faculties of men, not to complete their prostration.

Among aristocratic nations all the members of the community are connected with and dependent upon each other ; the graduated scale of different ranks acts as a tie, which keeps every one in his proper place and the whole body in subordination. Something of the same kind always occurs in the political assemblies of these nations. Parties naturally range themselves under certain leaders, whom they obey by a sort of instinct, which is only the result of habits contracted elsewhere. They carry the manners of general society into the lesser assemblage.

In democratic countries it often happens that a great number of citizens are tending to the same point ; but each one only moves thither, or at least flatters himself that he moves, of his own accord. Accustomed to regulate his doings by personal impulse alone, he does not willingly submit to dictation from without. This taste and habit of independence accompany him into the councils of the nation. If he consents to connect himself with other men in the prosecution of the same purpose, at least he chooses to remain free to contribute to the common success after his own fashion. Hence it is that in democratic countries parties are so impatient of control, and are never manageable except in moments of great public danger. Even then the authority of leaders, which under such circumstances may be able to make men act or speak, hardly ever reaches the extent of making them keep silence.

Among aristocratic nations the members of political assemblies are at the same time members of the aristocracy. Each of them enjoys high established rank in his own right, and the position which he occupies in the assembly is often less important in his eyes than that which he fills in the country. This consoles him for playing no part in the discussion of public affairs, and restrains him from too eagerly attempting to play an insignificant one.

In America, it generally happens that a representative only becomes somebody from his position in the assembly. He is therefore perpetually haunted by a craving to acquire importance there, and he feels a petulant desire to be constantly obtruding his opinions upon the House. His own vanity is not the only stimulant which urges him on in this course, but that of his constituents, and the continual necessity of propitiating them. Among aristocratic nations, a member of the legislature is rarely in strict dependence upon his constituents : he is frequently to them a sort of unavoidable representative ; sometimes they are themselves strictly dependent upon him ; and if at length they reject him, he may easily get elected elsewhere, or, retiring from public life, he may still enjoy the pleasures of splendid idleness. In a democratic country like the United States a representative has hardly ever a lasting hold on the minds of his constituents. However small an electoral body may be, the fluctuations of democracy are constantly changing its aspect ; it must, therefore, be courted unceasingly. He is never sure of his supporters, and, if they forsake him, he is left without a resource ; for his natural position is not sufficiently elevated for him to be easily known to those not close to him ; and, with the complete state of independence prevailing among the people, he cannot hope that his friends or the Government will send him down to be returned by an electoral body unacquainted with him. The seeds of his fortune are therefore sown in his own neighbourhood ; from that nook of earth he must start to raise himself to the command of a people and to influence the destinies of the world. Thus it is natural that in democratic countries the members of political assemblies think more of their constituents than of their party, while in aristocracies they think more of their party than of their constituents.

But what ought to be said to gratify constituents is not always what ought to be said in order to serve the party to which representatives profess to belong. The general interest of a party frequently demands that members belonging to it should not speak on great questions which they understand imperfectly ; that they should speak but little on those minor questions which impede the great ones ; lastly, and for the most part, that they should not speak at all. To keep silence is the most useful service that an indifferent spokesman can render to the commonwealth. Constituents, however, do not think so. The population of a district sends a representative to take a part in the government of a country, because they entertain a very lofty notion of his merits. As men appear greater in proportion to the littleness of the objects by which they are surrounded, it may be assumed that the opinion entertained of the delegate will be so much the higher as talents are more rare among his constituents. It will therefore frequently happen that the less constituents have to expect from their representative, the more they will anticipate from him ; and, however incompetent he may be, they will not fail to call upon him for signal exertions, corresponding to the rank they have conferred upon him.

Independently of his position as a legislator of the State, electors also regard their representative as the natural patron of the constituency in the legislature ; they almost consider him as the proxy of each of his supporters, and they flatter themselves that he will not be less zealous in defence of their private interests than of those of the country. Thus electors are well assured beforehand that the representative of their choice will be an orator ; that he will speak often if he can, and that in case he is forced to refrain, he will strive at any rate to compress into his less frequent orations an inquiry into all the great questions of state, combined with a statement of all the petty grievances they have themselves to complain of ; so that, though he be not able to come forward frequently, he should on each occasion prove what he is capable of doing ; and that, instead of perpetually lavishing his powers, he should occasionally condense them in a small compass, so as to furnish a sort of complete and brilliant epitome of his constituents and of himself. On these terms they will vote for him at the next election. These conditions drive worthy men of humble abilities to despair, who, knowing their own powers, would never voluntarily have come forward. But thus urged on, the representative begins to speak, to the great alarm of his friends ; and rushing imprudently into the midst of the most celebrated orators, he perplexes the debate and wearies the House.

All laws which tend to make the representative more dependent on the elector, not only affect the conduct of the legislators, as I have remarked elsewhere, but also their language. They exercise a simultaneous influence on affairs themselves, and on the manner in which affairs are discussed.

There is hardly a member of Congress who can make up his mind to go home without having dispatched at least one speech to his constituents ; nor who will endure any interruption until he has introduced into his harangue whatever useful suggestions may be made touching the four-and-twenty States of which the Union is composed, and especially the district which he represents. He therefore presents to the mind of his auditors a succession of great general truths (which he himself only comprehends, and expresses, confusedly), and of petty minutiæ, which he is but too able to discover and to point out. The consequence is that the debates of that great assembly are frequently vague and perplexed, and that they seem rather to drag their slow length along than to advance toward a distinct object. Some such state of things will, I believe, always arise in the public assemblies of democracies.

Propitious circumstances and good laws might succeed in drawing to the legislature of a democratic people men very superior to those who are returned by the Americans to Congress ; but nothing will ever prevent the men of slender abilities who sit there from obtruding themselves with complacency, and in all ways, upon the public. The evil does not appear to me to be susceptible of entire cure, because it not only originates in the tactics of that assembly, but in its constitution and in that of the country. The inhabitants of the United States seem themselves to consider the matter in this light ; and they show their long experience of parliamentary life not by abstaining from making bad speeches, but by courageously submitting to hear them made. They are resigned to it, as to an evil which they know to be inevitable.

We have shown the petty side of political debates in democratic assemblies—let us now exhibit the more imposing one. The proceedings within the Parliament of England for the last one hundred and fifty years have never occasioned any great sensation out of that country ; the opinions and feelings expressed by the speakers have never awakened much sympathy, even among the nations placed nearest to the great arena of British liberty ; whereas Europe was excited by the very first debates which took place in the small colonial assemblies of America at the time of the Revolution. This was attributable not only to particular and fortuitous circumstances, but to general and lasting causes. I can conceive nothing more admirable or more powerful than a great orator debating on great questions of state in a democratic assembly. As no particular class is ever represented there by men commissioned to defend its own interests, it is always to the whole nation, and in the name of the whole nation, that the orator speaks. This expands his thoughts, and heightens his power of language. As precedents have there but little weight —as there are no longer any privileges attached to certain property, nor any rights inherent in certain bodies or in certain individuals, the mind must have recourse to general truths derived from human nature to resolve the particular question under discussion. Hence the political debates of a democratic people, however small it may be, have a degree of breadth which frequently renders them attractive to mankind.

All men are interested by them, because they treat of man, who is everywhere the same. Among the greatest aristocratic nations, on the contrary, the most general questions are almost always argued on some special grounds derived from the practice of a particular time, or the rights of a particular class; which interest that class alone, or at most the people among whom that class happens to exist. It is owing to this, as much as to the greatness of the French people, and the favourable disposition of the nations who listen to them, that the great effect which the French political debates sometimes produce in the world must be attributed. The orators of France frequently speak to mankind, even when they are addressing their countrymen only.

Chapter XXIV

INDIVIDUALISM IN DEMOCRATIC COUNTRIES

THE first and most intense passion that is engendered by the equality of conditions is, I need hardly say, the love of that same equality. My readers will therefore not be surprised that I speak of it before all others. Everybody has remarked that in our time, and especially in France, this passion for equality is every day gaining ground in the human heart. It has been said a hundred times that our contemporaries are far more ardently and tenaciously attached to equality than to freedom ; but as I do not find that the causes of the fact have been sufficiently analysed, I shall endeavour to point them out.

It is possible to imagine an extreme point at which freedom and equality would meet and be confounded together. Let us suppose that all the members of the community take a part in the government, and that each one of them has an equal right to take a part in it. As none is different from his fellows, none can exercise a tyrannical power : men will be perfectly free, because they will all be entirely equal ; and they will all be perfectly equal, because they will be entirely free. To this ideal state democratic nations tend. Such is the completest form that equality can assume upon earth ; but there are a thousand others which, without being equally perfect, are not less cherished by those nations.

The principle of equality may be established in civil society without prevailing in the political world. Equal rights may exist of indulging in the same pleasures, of entering the same professions, of frequenting the same places—in a word, of living in the same manner and seeking wealth by the same means, although all men do not take an equal share in the government. A kind of equality may even be established in the political world, though there should be no political freedom there. A man may be the equal of all his countrymen save one, who is the master of all without distinction, and who selects equally from among them all the agents of his power. Several other combinations might be easily imagined, by which very great equality would be united to institutions more or less free, or even to institutions wholly without freedom. Although men cannot become absolutely equal unless they be entirely free, and consequently equality, pushed to its farthest extent, may be confounded with freedom, yet there is good reason for distinguishing the one from the other. The taste which men have for liberty, and that which they feel for equality, are, in fact, two different things ; and I am not afraid to add that, among democratic nations, they are two unequal things.

Upon close inspection, it will be seen that there is in every age some peculiar and preponderating fact with which all others are connected ; this fact almost always gives birth to some pregnant idea or some ruling passion, that attracts to itself, and bears away in its course, all the feelings and opinions of the time : it is like a great stream, toward which each of the surrounding rivulets seems to flow. Freedom has appeared in the world at different times and under various forms ; it has not been exclusively bound to any social condition, and it is not confined to democracies. Freedom cannot, therefore, form the distinguishing characteristic of democratic ages. The peculiar and preponderating fact which marks those ages as its own is the equality of conditions ; the ruling passion of men in those periods is the love of this equality. Ask not what singular charm the men of democratic ages find in being equal, or what special reasons they may have for clinging so tenaciously to equality rather than to the other advantages which society holds out to them : equality is the distinguishing characteristic of the age they live in ; that, of itself, is enough to explain that they prefer it to all the rest.

But independently of this reason there are several others, that will at all times habitually lead men to prefer equality to freedom. If a people could ever succeed in destroying, or even in diminishing, the equality which prevails in its own body, this could only be accomplished by long and laborious efforts. Its social condition must be modified, its laws abolished, its opinions superseded, its habits changed, its manners corrupted. But political liberty is more easily lost ; to neglect to hold it fast is to allow it to escape. Men therefore not only cling to equality because it is dear to them ; they also adhere to it because they think it will last for ever.

That political freedom may compromise in its excesses the tranquillity, the property, the lives of individuals, is obvious to the narrowest and most unthinking minds. But, on the contrary, none but attentive and clear-sighted men perceive the perils with which equality threatens us, and they commonly avoid pointing them out. They know that the calamities they apprehend are remote, and flatter themselves that they will only fall upon future generations, for which the present generation takes but little thought. The evils which freedom sometimes brings with it are immediate ; they are apparent to all, and all are more or less affected by them. The evils which extreme equality may produce are slowly disclosed ; they creep gradually into the social frame ; they are only seen at intervals, and at the moment at which they become most violent habit already causes them to be no longer felt. The advantages which freedom brings are only shown by length of time; and it is always easy to mistake the cause in which they originate. The advantages of equality are instantaneous, and they may be traced constantly from their source. Political liberty bestows exalted pleasures, from time to time, upon a certain number of citizens. Equality every day confers a number of small enjoyments on every man. The charms of equality are felt every instant, and are within the reach of all; the noblest hearts are not insensible to them, and the most vulgar souls exult in them. The passion which equality engenders must therefore be at once strong and general. Men cannot enjoy political liberty unpurchased by some sacrifices, and they never obtain it without great exertions. But the pleasures of equality are self-proffered: each of the petty incidents of life seems to occasion them, and in order to taste them nothing is required but to live.

Democratic nations are at all times fond of equality, but there are certain epochs at which the passion they entertain for it swells to the height of fury. This occurs at the moment when the old social system, long menaced, completes its own destruction after a last intestine struggle, and when the barriers of rank are at length thrown down. At such times men pounce upon equality as their booty, and they cling to it as to some precious treasure which they fear to lose. The passion for equality penetrates on every side into men's hearts, expands there, and fills them entirely. Tell them not that by this blind surrender of themselves to an exclusive passion they risk their dearest interests: they are deaf. Show them not freedom escaping from their grasp, while they are looking another way: they are blind—or rather, they can discern but one sole object to be desired in the universe. . . .

I think that democratic communities have a natural taste for freedom : left to themselves, they will seek it, cherish it, and view any privation of it with regret. But for equality, their passion is ardent, insatiable, incessant, invincible : they call for equality in freedom ; and if they cannot obtain that, they still call for equality in slavery. They will endure poverty, servitude, barbarism — but they will not endure aristocracy. This is true at all times, and especially true in our own. All men and all powers seeking to cope with this irresistible passion will be overthrown and destroyed by it. In our age, freedom cannot be established without it, and despotism itself cannot reign without its support.

I have shown how it is that in ages of equality every man seeks for his opinions within himself : I am now about to show how it is that, in the same ages, all his feelings are turned toward himself alone. Individualism is a novel expression, to which a novel idea has given birth. Our fathers were only acquainted with egotism. Egotism is a passionate and exaggerated love of self, which leads a man to connect everything with his own person, and to prefer himself to everything in the world. Individualism is a mature and calm feeling, which disposes each member of the community to sever himself from the mass of his fellow-creatures ; and to draw apart with his family and his friends ; so that, after he has thus formed a little circle of his own, he willingly leaves society at large to itself. Egotism originates in blind instinct : individualism proceeds from erroneous judgment more than from depraved feelings ; it originates as much in the deficiencies of the mind as in the perversity of the heart. Egotism blights the germ of all virtue ; individualism, at first, only saps the virtues of public life ; but, in the long run, it attacks and destroys all others, and is at length absorbed in downright egotism. Egotism is a vice as old as the world, which does not belong to one form of society more than to another : individualism is of democratic origin, and it threatens to spread in the same ratio as the equality of conditions.

Among aristocratic nations, as families remain for centuries in the same condition, often on the same spot, all generations become, as it were, contemporaneous. A man almost always knows his forefathers and respects them : he thinks he already sees his remote descendants, and he loves them. He willingly imposes duties on himself toward the former and the latter ; and he will frequently sacrifice his personal gratifications to those who went before and to those who will come after him. Aristocratic institutions have, moreover, the effect of closely binding every man to several of his fellow-citizens. As the classes of an aristocratic people are strongly marked and permanent, each of them is regarded by its own members as a sort of lesser country, more tangible and more cherished than the country at large. As in aristocratic communities all the citizens occupy fixed positions, one above the other, the result is that each of them always sees a man above himself whose patronage is necessary to him, and below himself another man whose co-operation he may claim. Men living in aristocratic ages are therefore almost always closely attached to something placed out of their own sphere, and they are often disposed to forget themselves. It is true that in those ages the notion of human fellowship is faint, and that men seldom think of sacrificing themselves for mankind ; but they often sacrifice themselves for other men. In democratic ages, on the contrary, when the duties of each individual to the race are much more clear, devoted service to any one man becomes more rare ; the bond of human affection is extended, but it is relaxed.

Among democratic nations new families are constantly springing up, others are constantly falling away, and all that remain change their condition ; the woof of time is every instant broken, and the track of generations effaced. Those who went before are soon forgotten ; of those who will come after no one has any idea : the interest of man is confined to those in close propinquity to himself. As each class approximates to other classes, and intermingles with them, its members become indifferent and as strangers to one another. Aristocracy had made a chain of all the members of the community, from the peasant to the king : democracy breaks that chain, and severs every link of it. As social conditions become more equal, the number of persons increases who, although they are neither rich enough nor powerful enough to exercise any great influence over their fellow-creatures, have nevertheless acquired or retained sufficient education and fortune to satisfy their own wants. They owe nothing to any man, they expect nothing from any man ; they acquire the habit of always considering themselves as standing alone, and they are apt to imagine that their whole destiny is in their own hands. Thus not only does democracy make every man forget his ancestors, but it hides his descendants, and separates his contemporaries from him ; it throws him back for ever upon himself alone, and threatens in the end to confine him entirely within the solitude of his own heart.

The period when the construction of democratic society upon the ruins of an aristocracy has just been completed, is especially that at which this separation of men from one another, and the egotism resulting from it, most forcibly strike the observation. Democratic communities not only contain a large number of independent citizens, but they are filled constantly with men who, having entered but yesterday upon their independent condition, are intoxicated with their new power. They entertain a presumptuous confidence in their strength, and as they do not suppose that they can henceforward ever have occasion to claim the assistance of their fellow-creatures, they do not scruple to show that they care for nobody but themselves.

An aristocracy seldom yields without a protracted struggle, in the course of which implacable animosities are kindled between the different classes of society. These passions survive the victory, and traces of them may be observed in the midst of the democratic confusion which ensues. Those members of the community who were at the top of the late gradations of rank cannot immediately forget their former greatness ; they will long regard themselves as aliens in the midst of the newly composed society. They look upon all those whom this state of society has made their equals as oppressors, whose destiny can excite no sympathy ; they have lost sight of their former equals, and feel no longer bound by a common interest to their fate : each of them, standing aloof, thinks that he is reduced to care for himself alone. Those, on the contrary, who were formerly at the foot of the social scale, and who have been brought up to the common level by a sudden revolution, cannot enjoy their newly acquired independence without secret uneasiness ; and if they meet with some of their former superiors on the same footing as themselves, they stand aloof from them with an expression of triumph and of fear. It is, then, commonly at the outset of democratic society that citizens are most disposed to live apart. Democracy leads men not to draw near to their fellow-creatures ; but democratic revolutions lead them to shun each other, and perpetuate in a state of equality the animosities which the state of inequality engendered. The great advantage of the Americans is that they have arrived at a state of democracy without having to endure a democratic revolution ; and that they are born equal, instead of becoming so.

Despotism, which is of a very timorous nature, is never more secure of continuance than when it can keep men asunder ; and all its influence is commonly exerted for that purpose. No vice of the human heart is so acceptable to it as egotism : a despot easily forgives his subjects for not loving him, provided they do not love each other. He does not ask them to assist him in governing the state ; it is enough that they do not aspire to govern it themselves. He stigmatizes as turbulent and unruly spirits those who would combine their exertions to promote the prosperity of the community, and, perverting the natural meaning of words, he applauds as good citizens those who have no sympathy for any but themselves. Thus the vices that despotism engenders are precisely those that equality fosters. These two things mutually and perniciously complete and assist each other. Equality places men side by side, unconnected by any common tie ; despotism raises barriers to keep them asunder ; the former predisposes them not to consider their fellow-creatures, the latter makes general indifference a sort of public virtue.

Despotism, then, which is at all times dangerous, is more particularly to be feared in democratic ages. It is easy to see that in those same ages men stand most in need of freedom. When the members of a community are forced to attend to public affairs, they are necessarily drawn from the circle of their own interests, and snatched at times from self-observation. As soon as a man begins to treat of public affairs in public, he begins to perceive that he is not so independent of his fellow-men as he had at first imagined, and that, in order to obtain their support, he must often lend them his co-operation.

When the public is supreme, there is no man who does not feel the value of public good-will, or who does not endeavour to court it by drawing to himself the esteem and affection of those among whom he is to live. Many of the passions which congeal and keep asunder human hearts are then obliged to retire and hide below the surface. Pride must be dissembled; disdain dares not break out; egotism fears its own self. Under a free government, as most public offices are elective, the men whose elevated minds or aspiring hopes are too closely circumscribed in private life, constantly feel that they cannot do without the population which surrounds them. Men learn at such times to think of their fellow-men from ambitious motives; and they frequently find it, in a manner, their interest to forget themselves.

I may here be met by an objection derived from electioneering intrigues, the meannesses of candidates, and the calumnies of their opponents. These are opportunities for animosity which occur the oftener the more frequent elections become. Such evils are doubtless great, but they are transient; whereas the benefits which attend them remain. The desire of being elected may lead some men for a time to violent hostility; but this same desire leads all men in the long run mutually to support each other; and if it happens that an election accidentally severs two friends, the electoral system brings a multitude of citizens permanently together, who would always have remained unknown to each other. Freedom engenders private animosities, but despotism gives birth to general indifference.

The Americans have combated by free institutions the tendency of equality to keep men asunder, and they have subdued it. The legislators of America did not suppose that a general representation of the whole nation would suffice to ward off a disorder at once so natural to the frame of democratic society, and so fatal : they also thought that it would be well to infuse political life into each portion of the territory, in order to multiply to an infinite extent opportunities of acting in concert for all the members of the community, and to make them constantly feel their mutual dependence on each other. The plan was a wise one. The general affairs of a country only engage the attention of leading politicians, who assemble from time to time in the same places ; and as they often lose sight of each other afterward, no lasting ties are established between them. But if the object be to have the local affairs of a district conducted by the men who reside there, the same persons are always in contact, and they are, in a manner, forced to be acquainted, and to adapt themselves to one another.

It is difficult to draw a man out of his own circle to interest him in the destiny of the State, because he does not clearly understand what influence the destiny of the State can have upon his own lot. But if it be proposed to make a road across the end of his estate, he will see at a glance that there is a connection between this small public affair and his greatest private affairs ; and he will discover, without its being shown to him, the close tie which unites private to general interest. Thus, far more may be done by intrusting to the citizens the administration of minor affairs than by surrendering to them the control of important ones, toward interesting them in the public welfare, and convincing them that they constantly stand in need one of the other in order to provide for it. A brilliant achievement may win for you the favour of a people at one stroke ; but to earn the love and respect of the population which surrounds you, a long succession of little services rendered and of obscure good deeds—a constant habit of kindness, and an established reputation for disinterestedness—will be required. Local freedom, then, which leads a great number of citizens to value the affection of their neighbours and of their kindred, perpetually brings men together, and forces them to help one another, in spite of the propensities which sever them.

In the United States the more opulent citizens take great care not to stand aloof from the people ; on the contrary, they constantly keep on easy terms with the lower classes : they listen to them, they speak to them every day. They know that the rich in democracies always stand in need of the poor ; and that in democratic ages you attach a poor man to you more by your manner than by benefits conferred. The magnitude of such benefits, which sets off the difference of conditions, causes a secret irritation to those who reap advantage from them ; but the charm of simplicity of manners is almost irresistible : their affability carries men away, and even their want of polish is not always displeasing. This truth does not take root at once in the minds of the rich. They generally resist it as long as the democratic revolution lasts, and they do not acknowledge it immediately after that revolution is accomplished. They are very ready to do good to the people, but they still choose to keep them at arm's length ; they think that is sufficient, but they are mistaken. They might spend fortunes thus without warming the hearts of the population around them—that population does not ask them for the sacrifice of their money, but of their pride.

It would seem as if every imagination in the United States were upon the stretch to invent means of increasing the wealth and satisfying the wants of the public. The best-informed inhabitants of each district constantly use their information to discover new truths which may augment the general prosperity ; and if they have made any such discoveries, they eagerly surrender them to the mass of the people.

When the vices and weaknesses, frequently exhibited by those who govern in America, are closely examined, the prosperity of the people occasions—but improperly occasions—surprise. Elected magistrates do not make the American democracy flourish ; it flourishes because the magistrates are elective.

It would be unjust to suppose that the patriotism and the zeal that every American displays for the welfare of his fellow-citizens are wholly insincere. Although private interest directs the greater part of human actions in the United States as well as elsewhere, it does not regulate them all. I must say that I have often seen Americans make great and real sacrifices to the public welfare ; and I have remarked a hundred instances in which they hardly ever failed to lend faithful support to each other. The free institutions which the inhabitants of the United States possess, and the political rights of which they make so much use, remind every citizen, and in a thousand ways, that he lives in society. They every instant impress upon his mind the notion that it is the duty, as well as the interest of men, to make themselves useful to their fellow-creatures ; and as he sees no particular ground of animosity to them, since he is never either their master or their slave, his heart readily leans to the side of kindness. Men attend to the interests of the public, first by necessity, afterward by choice : what was intentional becomes an instinct ; and by dint of working for the good of one's fellow-citizens, the habit and the taste for serving them is at length acquired.

Many people in France consider equality of conditions as one evil, and political freedom as a second. When they are obliged to yield to the former, they strive at least to escape from the latter. But I contend that in order to combat the evils which equality may produce, there is only one effectual remedy—namely, political freedom.

Chapter XXV

PUBLIC ASSOCIATIONS

I DO not propose to speak of those political associations —by the aid of which men endeavour to defend themselves against the despotic influence of a majority—or against the aggressions of regal power. That subject I have already treated. If each citizen did not learn, in proportion as he individually becomes more feeble, and consequently more incapable of preserving his freedom single-handed, to combine with his fellow-citizens for the purpose of defending it, it is clear that tyranny would unavoidably increase together with equality.

Only those associations that are formed in civil life, without reference to political objects, are here adverted to. The political associations that exist in the United States are only a single feature in the midst of the immense assemblage of associations in that country. Americans of all ages, all conditions, and all dispositions, constantly form associations. They have not only commercial and manufacturing companies, in which all take part, but associations of a thousand other kinds—religious, moral, serious, futile, extensive or restricted, enormous or diminutive. The Americans make associations to give entertainments, to found establishments for education, to build inns, to construct churches, to diffuse books, to send missionaries to the antipodes ; and in this manner they found hospitals, prisons, and schools. If it be proposed to advance some truth, or to foster some feeling by the encouragement of a great example, they form a society. Wherever, at the head of some new undertaking, you see the Government in France, or a man of rank in England, in the United States you will be sure to find an association.

I met with several kinds of associations in America, of which I confess I had no previous notion; and I have often admired the extreme skill with which the inhabitants of the United States succeed in proposing a common object to the exertions of a great many men, and in getting them voluntarily to pursue it. I have since travelled over England, whence the Americans have taken some of their laws and many of their customs; and it seemed to me that the principle of association was by no means so constantly or so adroitly used in that country. The English often perform great things singly; whereas the Americans form associations for the smallest undertakings. It is evident that the former people consider association as a powerful means of action, but the latter seem to regard it as the only means they have of acting.

Thus the most democratic country on the face of the earth is that in which men have in our time carried to the highest perfection the art of pursuing in common the object of their common desires, and have applied this new science to the greatest number of purposes. Is this the result of accident? or is there in reality any necessary connection between the principle of association and that of equality? Aristocratic communities always contain, among a multitude of persons who by themselves are powerless, a small number of powerful and wealthy citizens, each of whom can achieve great undertakings single-handed. In aristocratic societies men do not need to combine in order to act, because they are strongly held together. Every wealthy and powerful citizen constitutes the head of a permanent and compulsory association, composed of all those who are dependent upon him, or whom he makes subservient to the execution of his designs. Among democratic nations, on the contrary, all the citizens are independent and feeble ; they can do hardly anything by themselves, and none of them can oblige his fellow-men to lend him their assistance. They all, therefore, fall into a state of incapacity, if they do not learn voluntarily to help each other. If men living in democratic countries had no right and no inclination to associate for political purposes, their independence would be in great jeopardy ; but they might long preserve their wealth and their cultivation : whereas if they never acquired the habit of forming associations in ordinary life, civilization itself would be endangered. A people among whom individuals should lose the power of achieving great things single-handed, without acquiring the means of producing them by united exertions, would soon relapse into barbarism.

Unhappily, the same social condition that renders associations so necessary to democratic nations renders their formation more difficult among those nations than among all others. When several members of an aristocracy agree to combine, they easily succeed in doing so ; as each of them brings great strength to the partnership, the number of its members may be very limited ; and when the members of an association are limited in number, they may easily become mutually acquainted, understand each other, and establish fixed regulations. The same opportunities do not occur among democratic nations, where the associated members must always be very numerous for their association to have any power.

I am aware that many of my countrymen are not in the least embarrassed by this difficulty. They contend that the more enfeebled and incompetent the citizens become, the more able and active the Government ought to be rendered, in order that society at large may execute what individuals can no longer accomplish. They believe this answers the whole difficulty, but I think they are mistaken. A government might perform the part of some of the largest American companies ; and several States, members of the Union, have already attempted it ; but what political power could ever carry on the vast multitude of lesser undertakings that the American citizens perform every day, with the assistance of the principle of association ? It is easy to foresee that the time is drawing near when man will be less and less able to produce, of himself alone, the commonest necessaries of life. The task of the governing power will therefore perpetually increase, and its very efforts will extend it every day. The more it stands in the place of associations, the more will individuals, losing the notion of combining together, require its assistance : these are causes and effects that unceasingly engender each other. . . .

Feelings and opinions are recruited, the heart is enlarged, and the human mind is developed by no other means than by the reciprocal influence of men upon each other. I have shown that these influences are almost null in democratic countries : they must therefore be artificially created, and this can only be accomplished by associations.

When the members of an aristocratic community adopt a new opinion, or conceive a new sentiment, they give it a station, as it were, beside themselves, upon the lofty platform where they stand ; and opinions or sentiments so conspicuous to the eyes of the multitude are easily introduced into the minds or hearts of all around. In democratic countries the governing power alone is naturally in a condition to act in this manner ; but it is easy to see that its action is always inadequate, and often dangerous. A government can no more be competent to keep alive and to renew the circulation of opinions and feelings among a great people than to manage all the speculations of productive industry. No sooner does a government attempt to go beyond its political sphere and to enter upon this new track, than it exercises, even unintentionally, an insupportable tyranny; for a government can only dictate strict rules, the opinions which it favours are rigidly enforced, and it is never easy to discriminate between its advice and its commands. Worse still will be the case if the government really believes itself interested in preventing all circulation of ideas; it will then stand motionless, and oppressed by the heaviness of voluntary torpor. Governments, therefore, should not be the only active powers: associations ought, in democratic nations, to stand in lieu of those powerful private individuals whom the equality of conditions has swept away.

As soon as several of the inhabitants of the United States have taken up an opinion or a feeling that they wish to promote in the world, they look out for mutual assistance; and as soon as they have found each other out, they combine. From that moment they are no longer isolated men, but a power seen from afar, whose actions serve for an example, and whose language is listened to. The first time I heard in the United States that a hundred thousand men had bound themselves publicly to abstain from spirituous liquors, it appeared to me more like a joke than a serious engagement; and I did not at once perceive why these temperate citizens could not content themselves with drinking water by their own firesides. I at last understood that three hundred thousand Americans, alarmed by the progress of drunkenness around them, had made up their minds to patronize temperance. They acted just in the same way as a man of high rank who should dress very plainly, in order to inspire the humbler orders with a contempt of luxury. It is probable that if these hundred thousand men had lived in France, each of them would singly have memorialized the government to watch the public-houses all over the kingdom.

Nothing, in my opinion, is more deserving of our attention than the intellectual and moral associations of America. The political and industrial associations of that country strike us forcibly; but the others elude our observation, or if we discover them, we understand them imperfectly, because we have hardly ever seen anything of the kind. It must, however, be acknowledged that they are as necessary to the American people as the former, and perhaps more so. In democratic countries the science of association is the mother of science; the progress of all the rest depends upon the progress it has made. Among the laws that rule human societies there is one that seems to be more precise and clear than all others. If men are to remain civilized, or to become so, the art of associating together must grow and improve in the same ratio in which the equality of conditions is increased.

When men are no longer united among themselves by firm and lasting ties, it is impossible to obtain the co-operation of any great number of them, unless you can persuade every man whose concurrence you require that his private interest obliges him voluntarily to unite his exertions to the exertions of all the rest. This can only be habitually and conveniently effected by means of a newspaper; nothing but a newspaper can drop the same thought into a thousand minds at the same moment. A newspaper is an adviser who does not require to be sought, but who comes of his own accord, and talks to you briefly every day of the common weal, without distracting you from your private affairs.

Newspapers, therefore, become more necessary in proportion as men become more equal, and individualism more to be feared. To suppose that they only serve to protect freedom would be to diminish their importance : they maintain civilization. I shall not deny that in democratic countries newspapers frequently lead the citizens to launch together in very ill-digested schemes ; but if there were no newspapers there would be no common activity. The evil which they produce is therefore much less than that which they cure.

The effect of a newspaper is not only to suggest the same purpose to a great number of persons, but also to furnish means for executing in common the designs that they may have singly conceived. The principal citizens who inhabit an aristocratic country discern each other from afar ; and if they wish to unite their forces, they move toward each other, drawing a multitude of men after them. It frequently happens, on the contrary, in democratic countries, that a great number of men who wish or who want to combine cannot accomplish it, because as they are very insignificant and lost amid the crowd, they cannot see, and know not where to find, one another. A newspaper then takes up the notion or the feeling that had occurred simultaneously, but singly, to each of them. All are then immediately guided toward this beacon ; and these wandering minds, which had long sought each other in darkness, at length meet and unite.

The newspaper brought them together, and the newspaper is still necessary to keep them united. In order that an association among a democratic people should have any power, it must be a numerous body. The persons of whom it is composed are therefore scattered over a wide extent, and each of them is detained in the place of his domicile by the narrowness of his income, or by the small unremitting exertions by which he earns it. Means then must be found to converse every day without seeing each other, and to take steps in common without having met. Thus hardly any democratic association can do without newspapers. There is consequently a necessary connection between public associations and newspapers : newspapers make associations, and associations make newspapers ; and if it has been correctly advanced that associations will increase in number as the conditions of men become more equal, it is not less certain that the number of newspapers increases in proportion to that of associations. Thus it is in America that we find at the same time the greatest number of associations, and the greatest number of newspapers.

This connection between the number of newspapers and that of associations leads us to the discovery of a further connection between the state of the periodical press and the form of the administration in a country ; and shows that the number of newspapers must diminish or increase among a democratic people, in proportion as its administration is more or less centralized. For among democratic nations the exercise of local powers cannot be intrusted to the principal members of the community as in aristocracies. Those powers must either be abolished, or placed in the hands of very large numbers of men, who then, in fact, constitute an association permanently established by law for the purpose of administering the affairs of a certain extent of territory ; and they require a journal, to bring to them every day, in the midst of their own minor concerns, some intelligence of the state of their public weal. The more numerous local powers are, the greater is the number of men in whom they are vested by law ; and as this want is hourly felt, the more profusely do newspapers abound.

The extraordinary subdivision of administrative power has much more to do with the enormous number of American newspapers than the great political freedom of the country and the absolute liberty of the press. If all the inhabitants of the Union had the suffrage—but a suffrage which should only extend to the choice of their legislators in Congress—they would require but few newspapers, because they would only have to act together on a few very important but very rare occasions. But within the pale of the great association of the nation, lesser associations have been established by law in every country, every city, and, indeed, in every village, for the purposes of local administration. The laws of the country thus compel every American to co-operate every day of his life with some of his fellow-citizens for a common purpose, and each one of them requires a newspaper to inform him what all the others are doing.

I am of opinion that a democratic people, without any national representative assemblies, but with a great number of small local powers, would have in the end more newspapers than another people governed by a centralized administration and an elective legislation. What best explains to me the enormous circulation of the daily press in the United States, is that among the Americans I find the utmost national freedom combined with local freedom of every kind. There is a prevailing opinion in France and England that the circulation of newspapers would be indefinitely increased by removing the taxes which have been laid upon the press. This is a very exaggerated estimate of the effects of such a reform.

Newspapers increase in numbers, not according to their cheapness, but according to the more or less frequent want that a great number of men may feel for intercommunication and combination.

In like manner I should attribute the increasing influence of the daily press to causes more general than those by which it is commonly explained. A newspaper can only subsist on the condition of publishing sentiments or principles common to a large number of men. A newspaper, therefore, always represents an association that is composed of its habitual readers. This association may be more or less defined, more or less restricted, more or less numerous ; but the fact that the newspaper keeps alive, is a proof that at least the germ of such an association exists in the minds of its readers.

This leads me to a last reflection, with which I shall conclude this topic. The more equal the conditions of men become, and the less strong men individually are, the more easily do they give way to the current of the multitude, and the more difficult is it for them to adhere by themselves to an opinion that the multitude discard. A newspaper represents an association ; it may be said to address each of its readers in the name of all the others, and to exert its influence over them in proportion to their individual weakness. The power of the newspaper press must therefore increase as the social conditions of men become more equal.

There is only one country on the face of the earth where the citizens enjoy unlimited freedom of association for political purposes. This same country is the only one in the world where the continual exercise of the right of association has been introduced into civil life, and where all the advantages that civilization can confer are procured by means of it. In all the countries where political associations are prohibited, civil associations are rare. It is hardly probable that this is the result of accident ; but the inference should rather be that there is a natural, and perhaps a necessary, connection between these two kinds of associations. Certain men happen to have a common interest in some concern—either a commercial undertaking is to be managed, or some speculation in manufactures to be tried ; they meet, they combine, and thus by degrees they become familiar with the principle of association. The greater is the multiplicity of small affairs, the more do men, even without knowing it, acquire facility in prosecuting great undertakings in common. Civil associations, therefore, facilitate political association : but, on the other hand, political association singularly strengthens and improves associations for civil purposes. In civil life every man may, strictly speaking, fancy that he can provide for his own wants ; in politics, he can fancy no such thing. When a people, then, have any knowledge of public life, the notion of association, and the wish to coalesce, present themselves every day to the minds of the whole community : whatever natural repugnance may restrain men from acting in concert, they will always be ready to combine for the sake of a party. Thus political life makes the love and practice of association more general ; it imparts a desire of union, and teaches the means of combination to numbers of men who would have always lived apart.

Politics not only give birth to numerous associations, but to associations of great extent. In civil life it seldom happens that any one interest draws a very large number of men to act in concert ; much skill is required to bring such an interest into existence : but in politics opportunities present themselves every day. Now it is solely in great associations that the general value of the principle of association is displayed. Citizens who are individually powerless do not very clearly anticipate the strength which they may acquire by uniting together ; it must be shown to them in order to be understood. Hence it is often easier to collect a multitude for a public purpose than a few persons ; a thousand citizens do not see what interest they have in combining together—ten thousand will be perfectly aware of it. In politics men combine for great undertakings ; and the use they make of the principle of association in important affairs practically teaches them that it is their interest to help each other in those of less moment. A political association draws a number of individuals at the same time out of their own circle ; however they may be naturally kept asunder by age, mind, and fortune, it places them nearer together and brings them into contact. Once met, they can always meet again.

Men can embark in few civil partnerships without risking a portion of their possessions ; this is the case with all manufacturing and trading companies. When men are as yet but little versed in the art of association, and are unacquainted with its principal rules, they are afraid, when first they combine in this manner, of buying their experience dear. They therefore prefer depriving themselves of a powerful instrument of success to running the risks which attend the use of it. They are, however, less reluctant to join political associations, which appear to them to be without danger, because they adventure no money in them. But they cannot belong to these associations for any length of time without finding out how order is maintained among a large number of men, and by what contrivance they are made to advance, harmoniously and methodically, to the same object. Thus they learn to surrender their own will to that of all the rest, and to make their own exertions subordinate to the common impulse—things which it is not less necessary to know in civil than in political associations. Political associations may therefore be considered as large free schools, where all the members of the community go to learn the general theory of association.

But even if political association did not directly contribute to the progress of civil association, to destroy the former would be to impair the latter. When citizens can only meet in public for certain purposes, they regard such meetings as a strange proceeding of rare occurence, and they rarely think at all about it. When they are allowed to meet freely for all purposes, they ultimately look upon public association as the universal, or in a manner the sole means, which men can employ to accomplish the different purposes they may have in view. Every new want instantly revives the notion. The art of association then becomes, as I have said before, the mother of action, studied and applied by all.

When some kinds of associations are prohibited and others allowed, it is difficult to distinguish the former from the latter beforehand. In this state of doubt men abstain from them altogether, and a sort of public opinion passes current, that tends to cause any association whatsoever to be regarded as a bold and almost an illicit enterprise.

It is therefore chimerical to suppose that the spirit of association, when it is repressed on some one point, will nevertheless display the same vigour on all others ; and that if men be allowed to prosecute certain undertakings in common, that is quite enough for them eagerly to set about them. When the members of a community are allowed and accustomed to combine for all purposes, they will combine as readily for the lesser as for the more important ones ; but if they are only allowed to combine for small affairs, they will be neither inclined nor able to effect it. It is in vain that you will leave them entirely free to prosecute their business on joint-stock account : they will hardly care to avail themselves of the rights you have granted to them ; and, after having exhausted your strength in vain efforts to put down prohibited associations, you will be surprised that you cannot persuade men to form the associations you encourage.

I do not say that there can be no civil associations in a country where political association is prohibited ; for men can never live in society without embarking in some common undertakings : but I maintain that in such a country civil associations will always be few in number, feebly planned, unskilfully managed, that they will never form any vast designs, or that they will fail in the execution of them.

This naturally leads me to think that freedom of association in political matters is not so dangerous to public tranquillity as is supposed ; and that possibly, after having agitated society for some time, it may strengthen the State in the end. In democratic countries political associations are, so to speak, the only powerful persons who aspire to rule the State. Accordingly, the governments of our time look upon associations of this kind just as sovereigns in the Middle Ages regarded the great vassals of the crown : they entertain a sort of instinctive abhorrence of them, and they combat them on all occasions. They bear, on the contrary, a natural good-will to civil associations, because they readily discover that, instead of directing the minds of the community to public affairs, these institutions serve to divert them from such reflections ; and that, by engaging them more and more in the pursuit of objects that cannot be

O

attained without public tranquillity, they deter them from revolutions. But these governments do not attend to the fact that political associations tend amazingly to multiply and facilitate those of a civil character, and that in avoiding a dangerous evil they deprive themselves of an efficacious remedy.

When you see the Americans freely and constantly forming associations for the purpose of promoting some political principle, of raising one man to the head of affairs, or of wresting power from another, you have some difficulty in understanding that men so independent do not constantly fall into the abuse of freedom. If, on the other hand, you survey the infinite number of trading companies which are in operation in the United States, and perceive that the Americans are on every side unceasingly engaged in the execution of important and difficult plans, which the slightest revolution would throw into confusion, you will readily comprehend why people so well employed are by no means tempted to perturb the State, nor to destroy that public tranquillity by which they all profit.

Is it enough to observe these things separately, or should we not discover the hidden tie which connects them? In their political associations, the Americans of all conditions, minds, and ages, daily acquire a general taste for association, and grow accustomed to the use of it. There they meet together in large numbers, they converse, they listen to each other, and they are mutually stimulated to all sorts of undertakings. They afterward transfer to civil life the notions they have thus acquired, and make them subservient to a thousand purposes. Thus it is by the enjoyment of a dangerous freedom that the Americans learn the art of rendering the dangers of freedom less formidable.

If a certain moment in the existence of a nation be

selected, it is easy to prove that political associations perturb the State, and paralyse productive industry ; but take the whole life of a people, and it may perhaps be easy to demonstrate that freedom of association in political matters is favourable to the prosperity and even to the tranquillity of the community.

I said in the former part of this work : " The unrestrained liberty of political association cannot be entirely assimilated to the liberty of the press. The one is at the same time less necessary and more dangerous than the other. A nation may confine it within certain limits without ceasing to be mistress of itself ; and it may sometimes be obliged to do so in order to maintain its own authority." And further on I added : " It cannot be denied that the unrestrained liberty of association for political purposes is the last degree of liberty which a people is fit for. If it does not throw them into anarchy, it perpetually brings them, as it were, to the verge of it." Thus I do not think that a nation is always at liberty to invest its citizens with an absolute right of association for political purposes ; and I doubt whether, in any country or in any age, it be wise to set no limits to freedom of association. A certain nation, it is said, could not maintain tranquillity in the community, cause the laws to be respected, or establish a lasting government, if the right of association were not confined within narrow limits. These blessings are doubtless invaluable, and I can imagine that, to acquire or to preserve them, a nation may impose upon itself severe temporary restrictions : but still it is well that the nation should know at what price these blessings are purchased. I can understand that it may be advisable to cut off a man's arm in order to save his life ; but it would be ridiculous to assert that he will be as dexterous as he was before he lost it.

Chapter XXVI

THE PRINCIPLE OF INTEREST RIGHTLY UNDERSTOOD

I HAVE already shown, in several parts of this work, by what means the inhabitants of the United States almost always manage to combine their own advantage with that of their fellow-citizens: my present purpose is to point out the general rule which enables them to do so. In the United States hardly anybody talks of the beauty of virtue; but they maintain that virtue is useful, and prove it every day. The American moralists do not profess that men ought to sacrifice themselves for their fellow-creatures because it is noble to make such sacrifices; but they boldly aver that such sacrifices are as necessary to him who imposes them upon himself as to him for whose sake they are made. They have found out that in their country and their age man is brought home to himself by an irresistible force; and losing all hope of stopping that force, they turn all their thoughts to the direction of it. They therefore do not deny that every man may follow his own interest; but they endeavour to prove that it is the interest of every man to be virtuous. I shall not here enter into the reasons they allege, which would divert me from my subject: suffice it to say that they have convinced their fellow-countrymen.

Montaigne said long ago, "Were I not to follow the straight road for its straightness, I should follow it for having found by experience that in the end it is commonly the happiest and most useful track." The doctrine of interest rightly understood is not then new, but among the Americans of our time it finds universal acceptance: it has become popular there; you may trace it at the bottom of all their actions, you will remark it in all they say. It is as often to be met with on the lips of the poor man as of the rich. In Europe the principle of interest is much grosser than it is in America, but at the same time it is less common, and especially it is less avowed ; among us men still constantly feign great abnegation which they no longer feel. The Americans, on the contrary, are fond of explaining almost all the actions of their lives by the principle of interest rightly understood ; they show with complacency how an enlightened regard for themselves constantly prompts them to assist each other, and inclines them willingly to sacrifice a portion of their time and property to the welfare of the State. In this respect I think they frequently fail to do themselves justice ; for in the United States, as well as elsewhere, people are sometimes seen to give way to those disinterested and spontaneous impulses which are natural to man ; but the Americans seldom allow that they yield to emotions of this kind ; they are more anxious to do honour to their philosophy than to themselves.

I might here pause, without attempting to pass a judgment on what I have described. The extreme difficulty of the subject would be my excuse, but I shall not avail myself of it ; and I had rather that my readers, clearly perceiving my object, should refuse to follow me than that I should leave them in suspense. The principle of interest rightly understood is not a lofty one, but it is clear and sure. It does not aim at mighty objects, but it attains without excessive exertion all those at which it aims. As it lies within the reach of all capacities, every one can without difficulty apprehend and retain it. By its admirable conformity to human weaknesses, it easily obtains great dominion ; nor is that dominion precarious, since the principle checks one personal interest by another, and uses, to direct the passions, the very same instrument which excites them. The principle of interest rightly understood produces no great acts of self-sacrifice, but it suggests daily small acts of self-denial. By itself it cannot suffice to make a man virtuous, but it disciplines a number of citizens in habits of regularity, temperance, moderation, foresight, self-command; and, if it does not lead men straight to virtue by the will, it gradually draws them in that direction by their habits. If the principle of interest rightly understood were to sway the whole moral world, extraordinary virtues would doubtless be more rare; but I think that gross depravity would then also be less common. The principle of interest rightly understood perhaps prevents some men from rising far above the level of mankind; but a great number of other men, who were falling far below it, are caught and restrained by it. Observe some few individuals, they are lowered by it; survey mankind, it is raised. I am not afraid to say that the principle of interest rightly understood appears to me the best suited of all philosophical theories to the wants of the men of our time, and that I regard it as their chief remaining security against themselves. Toward it, therefore, the minds of the moralists of our age should turn; even should they judge it to be incomplete, it must nevertheless be adopted as necessary.

I do not think upon the whole that there is more egotism among us than in America; the only difference is, that there it is enlightened—here it is not. Every American will sacrifice a portion of his private interests to preserve the rest; we would fain preserve the whole, and oftentimes the whole is lost. Everybody I see about me seems bent on teaching his contemporaries, by precept and example, that what is useful is never wrong. Will nobody undertake to make them understand how what is right may be useful ? No power upon earth can prevent the increasing equality of conditions from inclining the human mind to seek out what is useful, or from leading every member of the community to be wrapped up in himself. It must therefore be expected that personal interest will become more than ever the principal, if not the sole, spring of men's actions ; but it remains to be seen how each man will understand his personal interest. If the members of a community, as they become more equal, become more ignorant and coarse, it is difficult to foresee to what pitch of stupid excesses their egotism may lead them ; and no one can foretell into what disgrace and wretchedness they would plunge themselves, lest they should have to sacrifice something of their own well-being to the prosperity of their fellow-creatures. I do not think that the system of interest, as it is professed in America, is, in all its parts, self-evident ; but it contains a great number of truths so evident that men, if they are but educated, cannot fail to see them. Educate, then, at any rate ; for the age of implicit self-sacrifice and instinctive virtues is already flitting far away from us, and the time is fast approaching when freedom, public peace, and social order itself will not be able to exist without education.

If the principle of interest rightly understood had nothing but the present world in view, it would be very insufficient ; for there are many sacrifices which can only find their recompense in another ; and whatever ingenuity may be put forth to demonstrate the utility of virtue, it will never be an easy task to make that man live aright who has no thoughts of dying. It is therefore necessary to ascertain whether the principle of interest rightly understood is easily compatible with religious belief. The philosophers who inculcate this system of morals tell men that to be happy in this life they must watch their own passions and steadily control their excess; that lasting happiness can only be secured by renouncing a thousand transient gratifications; and that a man must perpetually triumph over himself in order to secure his own advantage. The founders of almost all religions have held the same language. The track they point out to man is the same, only that the goal is more remote; instead of placing in this world the reward of the sacrifices they impose, they transport it to another. Nevertheless I cannot believe that all those who practise virtue from religious motives are only actuated by the hope of a recompense. I have known zealous Christians who constantly forgot themselves, to work with greater ardour for the happiness of their fellow-men; and I have heard them declare that all they did was only to earn the blessings of a future state. I cannot but think that they deceive themselves: I respect them too much to believe them. . . .

The Americans do not affect a brutal indifference to a future state; they affect no puerile pride in despising perils which they hope to escape from. They therefore profess their religion without shame and without weakness; but there generally is, even in their zeal, something so indescribably tranquil, methodical, and deliberate that it would seem as if the head, far more than the heart, brought them to the foot of the altar. The Americans not only follow their religion from interest, but they often place in this world the interest which makes them follow it. In the Middle Ages the clergy spoke of nothing but a future state; they hardly cared to prove that a sincere Christian may be a happy man here below. But the American preachers are constantly referring to the earth; and it is only with great difficulty that they can divert their attention from it. To touch their congregations, they always show them how favourable religious opinions are to freedom and public tranquillity ; and it is often difficult to ascertain from their discourses whether the principal object of religion is to procure eternal felicity in the other world or prosperity in this.

In America the passion for physical well-being is not always exclusive, but it is general; and if all do not feel it in the same manner, yet it is felt by all. Carefully to satisfy all, even the least wants of the body, and to provide the little conveniences of life, is uppermost in every mind. Something of an analogous character is more and more apparent in Europe. Among the causes that produce these similar consequences in both hemispheres, several are so connected with my subject as to deserve notice.

When riches are hereditarily fixed in families, there are a great number of men who enjoy the comforts of life without feeling an exclusive taste for those comforts. The heart of man is not so much caught by the undisturbed possession of anything valuable as by the desire, as yet imperfectly satisfied, of possessing it, and by the incessant dread of losing it. In aristocratic communities, the wealthy, never having experienced a condition different from their own, entertain no fear of changing it; the existence of such conditions hardly occurs to them. The comforts of life are not to them the end of life, but simply a way of living; they regard them as existence itself—enjoyed, but scarcely thought of. As the natural and instinctive taste which all men feel for being well off is thus satisfied without trouble and without apprehension, their faculties are turned elsewhere, and cling to more arduous and more lofty undertakings, which excite and engross their minds. Hence it is that, in the midst of physical gratifications, the members of an aristocracy often display a haughty contempt of these very enjoyments, and exhibit singular powers of endurance under the privation of them. All the revolutions which have ever shaken or destroyed aristocracies, have shown how easily men accustomed to superfluous luxuries can do without the necessaries of life; whereas men who have toiled to acquire a competency can hardly live after they have lost it.

If I turn my observation from the upper to the lower classes, I find analogous effects produced by opposite causes. Among a nation where aristocracy predominates in society, and keeps it stationary, the people in the end get as much accustomed to poverty as the rich to their opulence. The latter bestow no anxiety on their physical comforts, because they enjoy them without an effort ; the former do not think of things which they despair of obtaining, and which they hardly know enough of to desire them. In communities of this kind, the imagination of the poor is driven to seek another world ; the miseries of real life inclose it around, but it escapes from their control, and flies to seek its pleasures far beyond. When, on the contrary, the distinctions of ranks are confounded together and privileges are destroyed— when hereditary property is subdivided, and education and freedom widely diffused, the desire of acquiring the comforts of the world haunts the imagination of the poor, and the dread of losing them that of the rich. Many scanty fortunes spring up ; those who possess them have a sufficient share of physical gratifications to conceive a taste for these pleasures— not enough to satisfy it. They never procure them without exertion, and they never indulge in them without apprehension. They are, therefore, always straining to pursue or to retain gratifications so delightful, so imperfect, so fugitive.

If I were to inquire what passion is most natural to

men who are stimulated and circumscribed by the obscurity of their birth or the mediocrity of their fortune, I could discover none more peculiarly appropriate to their condition than this love of physical prosperity. The passion for physical comforts is essentially a passion of the middle classes : with those classes it grows and spreads, with them it preponderates. From them it mounts into the higher orders of society, and descends into the mass of the people. I never met in America with any citizen so poor as not to cast a glance of hope and envy on the enjoyments of the rich, or whose imagination did not possess itself by anticipation of those good things which fate still obstinately withheld from him. On the other hand, I never perceived among the wealthier inhabitants of the United States that proud contempt of physical gratifications which is sometimes to be met with even in the most opulent and dissolute aristocracies. Most of these wealthy persons were once poor : they have felt the sting of want ; they were long a prey to adverse fortunes ; and now that the victory is won, the passions which accompanied the contest have survived it : their minds are, as it were, intoxicated by the small enjoyments which they have pursued for forty years. Not but that in the United States, as elsewhere, there are a certain number of wealthy persons who, having come into their property by inheritance, possess, without exertion, an opulence they have not earned. But even these men are not less devotedly attached to the pleasures of material life. The love of well-being is now become the predominant taste of the nation ; the great current of man's passions runs in that channel, and sweeps everything along in its course.

It may be supposed, from what has just been said, that the love of physical gratifications must constantly urge the Americans to irregularities in morals, disturb the peace of families, and threaten the security of society at large. Such is not the case : the passion for physical gratifications produces in democracies effects very different from those that it occasions in aristocratic nations. It sometimes happens that, wearied with public affairs and sated with opulence, amid the ruin of religious belief and the decline of the State, the heart of an aristocracy may by degrees be seduced to the pursuit of sensual enjoyments only. At other times the power of the monarch or the weakness of the people, without stripping the nobility of their fortunes, compels them to stand aloof from the administration of affairs, and while the road to mighty enterprise is closed, abandons them to the inquietude of their own desires ; they then fall back heavily upon themselves, and seek in the pleasures of the body oblivion of their former greatness. When the members of an aristocratic body are thus exclusively devoted to the pursuit of physical gratifications, they commonly concentrate in that direction all the energy which they derive from their long experience of power. Such men are not satisfied with the pursuit of comfort ; they require sumptuous depravity and splendid corruption. The worship they pay the senses is a gorgeous one ; and they seem to vie with each other in the art of degrading their own natures. The stronger, the more famous, and the more free an aristocracy has been, the more depraved will it then become ; and however brilliant may have been the lustre of its virtues, I dare predict that they will always be surpassed by the splendour of its vices.

The taste for physical gratifications leads a democratic people into no such excesses. The love of well-being is there displayed as a tenacious, exclusive, universal passion ; but its range is confined. To

build enormous palaces, to conquer or to mimic
Nature, to ransack the world in order to gratify the
passions of a man, is not thought of: but to add a
few roods of land to your field, to plant an orchard,
to enlarge a dwelling, to be always making life more
comfortable and convenient, to avoid trouble, and to
satisfy the smallest wants without effort and almost
without cost. These are small objects, but the soul
clings to them; it dwells upon them closely and day
by day, till they at last shut out the rest of the world,
and sometimes intervene between itself and Heaven.

This, it may be said, can only be applicable to
those members of the community who are in humble
circumstances; wealthier individuals will display
tastes akin to those which belonged to them in aristocratic ages. I contest the proposition: in point of
physical gratifications, the most opulent members of
a democracy will not display tastes very different
from those of the people; whether it be that, springing from the people, they really share those tastes, or
that they esteem it a duty to submit to them. In
democratic society the sensuality of the public has
taken a moderate and tranquil course, to which all
are bound to conform: it is as difficult to depart from
the common rule by one's vices as by one's virtues.
Rich men who live amid democratic nations are
therefore more intent on providing for their smallest
wants than for their extraordinary enjoyments; they
gratify a number of petty desires, without indulging
in any great irregularities of passion: thus they are
more apt to become enervated than debauched.

The especial taste that the men of democratic ages
entertain for physical enjoyments is not naturally
opposed to the principles of public order; nay, it
often stands in need of order that it may be gratified.
Nor is it adverse to regularity of morals, for good

morals contribute to public tranquillity and are favourable to industry. It may even be frequently combined with a species of religious morality : men wish to be as well off as they can in this world, without foregoing their chance of another. Some physical gratifications cannot be indulged in without crime ; from such they strictly abstain. The enjoyment of others is sanctioned by religion and morality ; to these the heart, the imagination, and life itself are unreservedly given up ; till, in snatching at these lesser gifts, men lose sight of those more precious possessions which constitute the glory and the greatness of mankind. The reproach I address to the principle of equality is not that it leads men away in the pursuit of forbidden enjoyments, but that it absorbs them wholly in quest of those which are allowed. By these means, a kind of virtuous materialism may ultimately be established in the world, which would not corrupt, but enervate the soul, and noiselessly unbend its springs of action.

Although the desire of acquiring the good things of this world is the prevailing passion of the American people, certain momentary outbreaks occur, when their souls seem suddenly to burst the bonds of matter by which they are restrained, and to soar impetuously toward Heaven. In all the States of the Union, but especially in the half-peopled country of the Far West, wandering preachers may be met with who hawk about the word of God from place to place. Whole families—old men, women, and children—cross rough passes and untrodden wilds, coming from a great distance to join a camp-meeting, where they totally forget for several days and nights, in listening to these discourses, the cares of business and even the most urgent wants of the body. Here and there, in the midst of American society, you meet with men, full of a fanatical and almost wild enthusiasm, which hardly exists in Europe. From time to time strange sects arise, that endeavour to strike out extraordinary paths to eternal happiness. Religious insanity is very common in the United States.

Nor ought these facts to surprise us. It was not man who implanted in himself the taste for what is infinite and the love of what is immortal : these lofty instincts are not the offspring of his capricious will ; their steadfast foundation is fixed in human nature, and they exist in spite of his efforts. He may cross and distort them—destroy them he cannot. The soul has wants that must be satisfied ; and whatever pains be taken to divert it from itself, it soon grows weary, restless, and disquieted amid the enjoyments of sense. If ever the faculties of the great majority of mankind were exclusively bent upon the pursuit of material objects, it might be anticipated that an amazing reaction would take place in the souls of some men. They would drift at large in the world of spirits, for fear of remaining shackled by the close bondage of the body.

It is not then wonderful if, in the midst of a community whose thoughts tend earthward, a small number of individuals are to be found who turn their looks to Heaven. I should be surprised if mysticism did not soon make some advance among a people solely engaged in promoting its own worldly welfare. It is said that the deserts of the Thebaid were peopled by the persecutions of the Emperors and the massacres of the Circus ; I should rather say that it was by the luxuries of Rome and the Epicurean philosophy of Greece. If their social condition, their present circumstances, and their laws did not confine the minds of the Americans so closely to the pursuit of worldly welfare, it is probable that they would display more reserve and more experience whenever their attention is turned to things immaterial, and that they would check themselves without difficulty. But they feel imprisoned within bounds which they will apparently never be allowed to pass. As soon as they have passed these bounds, their minds know not where to fix themselves, and they often rush unrestrained beyond the range of common sense.

In certain remote corners of the Old World you may still sometimes stumble upon a small district which seems to have been forgotten amid the general tumult, and to have remained stationary while everything around it was in motion. The inhabitants are for the most part extremely ignorant and poor; they take no part in the business of the country, and they are frequently oppressed by the government; yet their countenances are generally placid, and their spirits light. In America I saw the freest and most enlightened men placed in the happiest circumstances that the world affords: it seemed to me as if a cloud habitually hung upon their brow, and I thought them serious and almost sad even in their pleasures. The chief reason of this contrast is that the former do not think of the ills they endure—the latter are for ever brooding over advantages they do not possess. It is strange to see with what feverish ardour the Americans pursue their own welfare; and to watch the vague dread that constantly torments them lest they should not have chosen the shortest path which may lead to it. A native of the United States clings to this world's goods as if he were certain never to die; and he is so hasty in grasping at all within his reach that one would suppose he was constantly afraid of not living long enough to enjoy them. He clutches everything, he holds nothing fast, but soon loosens his grasp to pursue fresh gratifications.

In the United States a man builds a house to spend his latter years in it, and he sells it before the roof is on : he plants a garden, and lets it just as the trees are coming into bearing : he brings a field into tillage, and leaves other men to gather the crops : he embraces a profession, and gives it up : he settles in a place, which he soon afterward leaves, to carry his changeable longings elsewhere. If his private affairs leave him any leisure, he instantly plunges into the vortex of politics ; and if at the end of a year of unremitting labour he finds he has a few days' vacation, his eager curiosity whirls him over the vast extent of the United States, and he will travel fifteen hundred miles in a few days to shake off his happiness. Death at length overtakes him, but it is before he is weary of his bootless chase of that complete felicity which is for ever on the wing.

At first sight there is something surprising in this strange unrest of so many happy men, restless in the midst of abundance. The spectacle itself is, however, as old as the world ; the novelty is to see a whole people furnish an exemplification of it. Their taste for physical gratifications must be regarded as the original source of that secret inquietude that the actions of the Americans betray, and of that inconstancy of which they afford fresh examples every day. He who has set his heart exclusively upon the pursuit of worldly welfare is always in a hurry, for he has but a limited time at his disposal to reach it, to grasp it, and to enjoy it. The recollection of the brevity of life is a constant spur to him. Beside the good things which he possesses, he every instant fancies a thousand others which death will prevent him from trying if he does not try them soon. This thought fills him with anxiety, fear, and regret, and keeps his mind in ceaseless trepidation, which leads him perpetually to change his plans and his abode. If in addition to the taste for physical well-being a social condition be superadded, in which the laws and customs make no condition permanent, here is a great additional stimulant to this restlessness of temper. Men will then be seen continually to change their track, for fear of missing the shortest cut to happiness. It may readily be conceived that if men, passionately bent upon physical gratifications, desire eagerly, they are also easily discouraged : as their ultimate object is to enjoy, the means to reach that object must be prompt and easy, or the trouble of acquiring the gratification would be greater than the gratification itself. Their prevailing frame of mind, then, is at once ardent and relaxed, violent and enervated. Death is often less dreaded than perseverance in continuous efforts to one end.

The equality of conditions leads by a still straighter road to several of the effects which I have here described. When all the privileges of birth and fortune are abolished, when all professions are accessible to all, and a man's own energies may place him at the top of any one of them, an easy and unbounded career seems open to his ambition, and he will readily persuade himself that he is born to no vulgar destinies. But this is an erroneous notion, which is corrected by daily experience. The same equality which allows every citizen to conceive these lofty hopes renders all the citizens less able to realize them : it circumscribes their powers on every side, while it gives freer scope to their desires. Not only are they themselves powerless, but they are met at every step by immense obstacles, which they did not at first perceive. They have swept away the privileges of some of their fellow-creatures which stood in their way, but they have opened the door to universal competition : the barrier has changed its shape rather than its position. When men are nearly alike, and all follow the same track, it is very difficult for any one individual to walk quickly and cleave a way through the dense throng which surrounds and presses him. This constant strife between the propensities springing from the equality of conditions and the means it supplies to satisfy them harasses and wearies the mind.

It is possible to conceive men arrived at a degree of freedom which should completely content them ; they would then enjoy their independence without anxiety and without impatience. But men will never establish any equality with which they can be contented. Whatever efforts a people may make, they will never succeed in reducing all the conditions of society to a perfect level ; and even if they unhappily attained that absolute and complete depression, the inequality of minds would still remain, which, coming directly from the hand of God, will for ever escape the laws of man. However democratic, then, the social state and the political constitution of a people may be, it is certain that every member of the community will always find out several points about him that command his own position ; and we may foresee that his looks will be doggedly fixed in that direction. When inequality of conditions is the common law of society, the most marked inequalities do not strike the eye : when everything is nearly on the same level, the slightest are marked enough to hurt it. Hence the desire of equality always becomes more insatiable in proportion as equality is more complete.

Among democratic nations men easily attain a certain equality of conditions : they can never attain the equality they desire. It perpetually retires from before them, yet without hiding itself from their sight, and in retiring draws them on. At every moment they think they are about to grasp it ; it escapes at every moment from their hold. They are near enough to see its charms, but too far off to enjoy them ; and before they have fully tasted its delights they die. To these causes must be attributed that strange melancholy that oftentimes will haunt the inhabitants of democratic countries in the midst of their abundance, and that disgust at life that sometimes seizes upon them in the midst of calm and easy circumstances. Complaints are made in France that the number of suicides increases ; in America suicide is rare, but insanity is said to be more common than anywhere else. These are all different symptoms of the same disease. The Americans do not put an end to their lives, however disquieted they may be, because their religion forbids it ; and among them materialism may be said hardly to exist, notwithstanding the general passion for physical gratification. The will resists—reason frequently gives way.

In democratic ages enjoyments are more intense than in the ages of aristocracy, and especially the number of those who partake in them is larger : but, on the other hand, it must be admitted that man's hopes and his desires are oftener blasted, the soul is more stricken and perturbed, and care itself more keen.

When a democratic state turns to absolute monarchy, the activity that was before directed to public and to private affairs is all at once centred upon the latter : the immediate consequence is, for some time, great physical prosperity ; but this impulse soon slackens, and the amount of productive industry is checked. I know not if a single trading of manufacturing people can be cited, from the Tyrians down to the Florentines and the English, who were not a free people also. There is therefore a close bond

and necessary relation between these two elements—
freedom and productive industry. This proposition
is generally true of all nations, but especially of democratic nations. I have already shown that men who
live in ages of equality continually require to form
associations in order to procure the things they covet;
and, on the other hand, I have shown how great
political freedom improves and diffuses the art of
association. Freedom, in these ages, is therefore
especially favourable to the production of wealth;
nor is it difficult to perceive that despotism is especially
adverse to the same result. The nature of despotic
power in democratic ages is not to be fierce or cruel,
but minute and meddling. Despotism of this kind,
though it does not trample on humanity, is directly
opposed to the genius of commerce and the pursuits
of industry.

Thus the men of democratic ages require to be
free in order more readily to procure those physical
enjoyments for which they are always longing. It
sometimes happens, however, that the excessive taste
they conceive for these same enjoyments abandons
them to the first master who appears. The passion
for worldly welfare then defeats itself, and, without
perceiving it, throws the object of their desires to a
greater distance.

There is, indeed, a most dangerous passage in the
history of a democratic people. When the taste for
physical gratifications among such a people has grown
more rapidly than their education and their experience of free institutions, the time will come when men
are carried away, and lose all self-restraint, at the
sight of the new possessions they are about to lay hold
upon. In their intense and exclusive anxiety to make
a fortune, they lose sight of the close connection that
exists between the private fortune of each of them

and the prosperity of all. It is not necessary to do violence to such a people in order to strip them of the rights they enjoy ; they themselves willingly loosen their hold. The discharge of political duties appears to them to be a troublesome annoyance, that diverts them from their occupations and business. If they be required to elect representatives, to support the Government by personal service, to meet on public business, they have no time—they cannot waste their precious time in useless engagements : such idle amusements are unsuited to serious men who are engaged with the more important interests of life. These people think they are following the principle of self-interest, but the idea they entertain of that principle is a very rude one ; and the better to look after what they call their business, they neglect their chief business, which is to remain their own masters.

As the citizens who work do not care to attend to public business, and as the class which might devote its leisure to these duties has ceased to exist, the place of the Government is, as it were, unfilled. If at that critical moment some able and ambitious man grasps the supreme power, he will find the road to every kind of usurpation open before him. If he does but attend for some time to the material prosperity of the country, no more will be demanded of him. Above all, he must insure public tranquillity : men who are possessed by the passion of physical gratification generally find out that the turmoil of freedom disturbs their welfare before they discover how freedom itself serves to promote it. If the slightest rumour of public commotion intrudes into the petty pleasures of private life, they are aroused and alarmed by it. The fear of anarchy perpetually haunts them, and they are always ready to fling away their freedom at the first disturbance.

I readily admit that public tranquillity is a great good ; but at the same time I cannot forget that all nations have been enslaved by being kept in good order. Certainly it is not to be inferred that nations ought to despise public tranquillity ; but that state ought not to content them. A nation that asks nothing of its government but the maintenance of order is already a slave at heart—the slave of its own well-being, awaiting but the hand that will bind it. By such a nation the despotism of faction is not less to be dreaded than the despotism of an individual. When the bulk of the community is engrossed by private concerns, the smallest parties need not despair of getting the upper hand in public affairs. At such times it is not rare to see upon the great stage of the world, as we see at our theatres, a multitude represented by a few players, who alone speak in the name of an absent or inattentive crowd : they alone are in action while all are stationary ; they regulate everything by their own caprice ; they change the laws, and tyrannize at will over the manners of the country ; and then men wonder to see into how small a number of weak and worthless hands a great people may fall.

Hitherto the Americans have fortunately escaped all the perils that I have just pointed out ; and in this respect they are really deserving of admiration. Perhaps there is no country in the world where fewer idle men are to be met with than in America, or where all who work are more eager to promote their own welfare. But if the passion of the Americans for physical gratifications is vehement, at least it is not indiscriminating ; and reason, though unable to restrain it, still directs its course. An American attends to his private concerns as if he were alone in the world, and the next minute he gives himself up to the common weal as if he had forgotten them. At one time he seems animated by the most selfish cupidity, at another by the most lively patriotism. The human heart cannot be thus divided. The inhabitants of the United States alternately display so strong and so similar a passion for their own welfare and for their freedom that it may be supposed that these passions are united and mingled in some part of their character. And indeed the Americans believe their freedom to be the best instrument and surest safeguard of their welfare : they are attached to the one by the other. They by no means think that they are not called upon to take a part in the public weal ; they believe, on the contrary, that their chief business is to secure for themselves a government which will allow them to acquire the things they covet, and which will not debar them from the peaceful enjoyment of those possessions which they have acquired.

In the United States, on the seventh day of every week, the trading and working life of the nation seems suspended ; all noises cease ; a deep tranquillity, say rather the solemn calm of meditation, succeeds the turmoil of the week, and the soul resumes possession and contemplation of itself. Upon this day the marts of traffic are deserted ; every member of the community, accompanied by his children, goes to church, where he listens to strange language which would seem unsuited to his ear. He is told of the countless evils caused by pride and covetousness : he is reminded of the necessity of checking his desires, of the finer pleasures that belong to virtue alone, and of the true happiness that attends it. On his return home, he does not turn to the ledgers of his calling, but he opens the book of Holy Scripture ; there he meets with sublime or affecting descriptions of the greatness and goodness of the Creator, of the infinite magnificence of the handiwork of God, of the lofty destinies of man, of his duties, and of his immortal privileges. Thus it is that the American at times steals an hour from himself; and laying aside for a while the petty passions which agitate his life, and the ephemeral interests which engross it, he strays at once into an ideal world, where all is great, eternal, and pure.

I have endeavoured to point out in another part of this work the causes to which the maintenance of the political institutions of the Americans is attributable; and religion appeared to be one of the most prominent among them. I am now treating of the Americans in an individual capacity, and I again observe that religion is not less useful to each citizen than to the whole State. The Americans show, by their practice, that they feel the high necessity of imparting morality to democratic communities by means of religion. What they think of themselves in this respect is a truth of which every democratic nation ought to be thoroughly persuaded.

I do not doubt that the social and political constitutions of a people predispose them to adopt a certain belief and certain tastes, which afterward flourish without difficulty among them; while the same causes may divert a people from certain opinions and propensities, without any voluntary effort, and, as it were, without any distinct consciousness, on their part. The whole art of the legislator is correctly to discern beforehand these natural inclinations of communities of men, in order to know whether they should be assisted, or whether it may not be necessary to check them. For the duties incumbent on the legislator differ at different times; the goal toward which the human race ought ever to be tending is alone stationary; the means of reaching it are perpetually to be varied.

If I had been born in an aristocratic age, in the midst of a nation where the hereditary wealth of some, and the irremediable penury of others, should equally divert men from the idea of bettering their condition, and hold the soul as it were in a state of torpor fixed on the contemplation of another world, I should then wish that it were possible for me to rouse that people to a sense of their wants; I should seek to discover more rapid and more easy means for satisfying the fresh desires which I might have awakened; and, directing the most strenuous efforts of the human mind to physical pursuits, I should endeavour to stimulate it to promote the well-being of man. If it happened that some men were immoderately incited to the pursuit of riches, and displayed an excessive liking for physical gratifications, I should not be alarmed; these peculiar symptoms would soon be absorbed in the general aspect of the people.

The attention of the legislators of democracies is called to other cares. Give democratic nations education and freedom, and leave them alone. They will soon learn to draw from this world all the benefits that it can afford; they will improve each of the useful arts, and will day by day render life more comfortable, more convenient, and more easy. Their social condition naturally urges them in this direction; I do not fear that they will slacken their course.

But while man takes delight in this honest and lawful pursuit of his well-being, it is to be apprehended that he may in the end lose the use of his sublimest faculties; and that while he is busied in improving all around him, he may at length degrade himself. Here, and here only, does the peril lie. It should therefore be the unceasing object of the legis-

lators of democracies, and of all the virtuous and
enlightened men who live there, to raise the souls of
their fellow-citizens, and keep them lifted up toward
Heaven. It is necessary that all who feel an interest
in the future destinies of democratic society should
unite, and that all should make joint and continual
efforts to diffuse the love of the infinite, a sense of
greatness, and a love of pleasures not of earth. If
among the opinions of a democratic people any of
those pernicious theories exist that tend to inculcate
that all perishes with the body, let men by whom such
theories are professed be marked as the natural foes
of such a people. . . .

If it be easy to see that it is more particularly
important in democratic ages that spiritual opinions
should prevail, it is not easy to say by what means
those who govern democratic nations may make them
predominate. I am no believer in the prosperity, any
more than in the durability, of official philosophies ;
and as to state religions, I have always held that
if they be sometimes of momentary service to the
interests of political power, they always, sooner or
later, become fatal to the church. Nor do I think
with those who assert, that to raise religion in the
eyes of the people, and to make them do honour to
her spiritual doctrines, it is desirable indirectly to give
her ministers a political influence which the laws deny
them. I am so much alive to the almost inevitable
dangers which beset religious belief whenever the
clergy take part in public affairs, and I am so convinced that Christianity must be maintained at any
cost in the bosom of modern democracies, that I
would rather shut up the priesthood within the
sanctuary than allow them to step beyond it.

What means, then, remain in the hands of constituted authorities to bring men back to spiritual

opinions, or to hold them fast to the religion by which those opinions are suggested? My answer will do me harm in the eyes of politicians. I believe that the sole effectual means which governments can employ in order to have the doctrine of the immortality of the soul duly respected, is ever to act as if they believed in it themselves; and I think that it is only by scrupulous conformity to religious morality in great affairs that they can hope to teach the community at large to know, to love, and to observe it in the lesser concerns of life. . . .

In those countries in which unhappily irreligion and democracy coexist, the most important duty of philosophers and of those in power is to be always striving to place the objects of human actions far beyond man's immediate range. Circumscribed by the character of his country and his age, the moralist must learn to vindicate his principles in that position. He must constantly endeavour to show his contemporaries that, even in the midst of the perpetual commotion around them, it is easier than they think to conceive and to execute protracted undertakings. He must teach them that, although the aspect of mankind may have changed, the methods by which men may provide for their prosperity in this world are still the same; and that among democratic nations, as well as elsewhere, it is only by resisting a thousand petty selfish passions of the hour that the general and unquenchable passion for happiness can be satisfied.

The task of those in power is not less clearly marked out. At all times it is important that those who govern nations should act with a view to the future: but this is even more necessary in democratic and sceptical ages than in any others. By acting thus, the leading men of democracies not only make public affairs prosperous, but they also teach private individuals, by their example, the art of managing private concerns. Above all, they must strive as much as possible to banish chance from the sphere of politics. The sudden and undeserved promotion of a courtier produces only a transient impression in an aristocratic country, because the aggregate institutions and opinions of the nation habitually compel men to advance slowly in tracks which they cannot get out of. But nothing is more pernicious than similar instances of favour exhibited to the eyes of a democratic people : they give the last impulse to the public mind in a direction where everything hurries it onward. At times of scepticism and equality more especially, the favour of the people or of the prince, which chance may confer or chance withhold, ought never to stand in lieu of attainments or services. It is desirable that every advancement should there appear to be the result of some effort ; so that no greatness should be of too easy acquirement, and that ambition should be obliged to fix its gaze long upon an object before it is gratified. Governments must apply themselves to restore to men that love of the future with which religion and the state of society no longer inspire them ; and, without saying so, they must practically teach the community day by day that wealth, fame, and power are the rewards of labour— that great success stands at the utmost range of long desires, and that nothing lasting is obtained but what is obtained by toil. When men have accustomed themselves to foresee from afar what is likely to befall them in the world and to feed upon hopes, they can hardly confine their minds within the precise circumference of life, and they are ready to break the boundary and cast their looks beyond. I do not doubt that by training the members of a community to think of their future condition in this world they would be gradually and unconsciously brought nearer to religious convictions. Thus the means which allow men up to a certain point to go without religion, are perhaps, after all, the only means we still possess for bringing mankind back by a long and roundabout path to a state of faith.

Chapter XXVIII

OCCUPATIONS AND BUSINESS CALLINGS

AMONG a democratic people, where there is no hereditary wealth, every man works to earn a living, or has worked, or is born of parents who have worked. The notion of labour is therefore presented to the mind on every side as the necessary, natural, and honest condition of human existence. Not only is labour not dishonourable among such a people, but it is held in honour : the prejudice is not against it, but in its favour. In the United States a wealthy man thinks that he owes it to public opinion to devote his leisure to some kind of industrial or commercial pursuit, or to public business. He would think himself in bad repute if he employed his life solely in living. It is for the purpose of escaping this obligation to work that so many rich Americans come to Europe, where they find some scattered remains of aristocratic society, among which idleness is still held in honour.

Equality of conditions not only ennobles the notion of labour in men's estimation, but it raises the notion of labour as a source of profit. In aristocracies it is not exactly labour that is despised, but labour with a view to profit. Labour is honorific in itself, when it is undertaken at the sole bidding of ambition or of virtue. Yet in aristocratic society it constantly happens that he who works for honour is not insensible to the attractions of profit. But these two desires only intermingle in the innermost depths of his soul : he carefully hides from every eye the point at which they join ; he would fain conceal it from himself. In aristocratic countries there are few public officers who do not affect to serve their country without interested motives. Their salary is an incident of which they think but little, and of which they always affect not to think at all. Thus the notion of profit is kept distinct from that of labour; however they may be united in point of fact, they are not thought of together.

In democratic communities these two notions are, on the contrary, always palpably united. As the desire of well-being is universal—as fortunes are slender or fluctuating—as every one wants either to increase his own resources, or provide fresh ones for his progeny, men clearly see that it is profit which, if not wholly at least partially, leads them to work. Even those who are principally actuated by the love of fame are necessarily made familiar with the thought that they are not exclusively actuated by that motive; and they discover that the desire of getting a living is mingled in their minds with the desire of making life illustrious.

As soon as, on the one hand, labour is held by the whole community to be an honourable necessity of man's condition, and, on the other, as soon as labour is always ostensibly performed, wholly or in part, for the purpose of earning remuneration, the immense interval which separated different callings in aristocratic societies disappears. If all are not alike, all at least have one feature in common. No profession exists in which men do not work for money; and the remuneration which is common to them all gives them all an air of resemblance. This serves to explain the opinions which the Americans entertain with respect to different callings. In America no one is degraded because he works, for every one about him works also; nor is any one humiliated by the notion of receiving pay, for the President of the United States also works for pay. He is paid for commanding, other men for obeying orders. In the United States professions are more or less laborious, more or less

profitable ; but they are never either high or low :
every honest calling is honourable.

Agriculture is, perhaps, of all the useful arts that
which improves most slowly among democratic
nations. Frequently, indeed, it would seem to be
stationary, because other arts are making rapid
strides toward perfection. On the other hand, almost
all the tastes and habits which the equality of condition engenders naturally lead men to commercial
and industrial occupations.

Suppose an active, enlightened, and free man,
enjoying a competency, but full of desires : he is too
poor to live in idleness ; he is rich enough to feel himself protected from the immediate fear of want, and
he thinks how he can better his condition. This man
has conceived a taste for physical gratifications, which
thousands of his fellow-men indulge in around him ;
he has himself begun to enjoy these pleasures, and he
is eager to increase his means of satisfying these tastes
more completely. But life is slipping away, time is
urgent—to what is he to turn ? The cultivation of
the ground promises an almost certain result to his
exertions, but a slow one ; men are not enriched by
it without patience and toil. Agriculture is therefore only suited to those who have already large
superfluous wealth, or to those whose penury bids
them only seek a bare subsistence. The choice of
such a man as we have supposed is soon made ; he
sells his plot of ground, leaves his dwelling, and
embarks in some hazardous but lucrative calling.
Democratic communities abound in men of this kind ;
and in proportion as the equality of conditions
becomes greater, their multitude increases. Thus
democracy not only swells the number of working-
men, but it leads men to prefer one kind of labour to
another ; and while it diverts them from agriculture,

it encourages their taste for commerce and manufactures.

This spirit may be observed even among the richest members of the community. In democratic countries, however opulent a man is supposed to be, he is almost always discontented with his fortune, because he finds that he is less rich than his father was, and he fears that his sons will be less rich than himself. Most rich men in democracies are therefore constantly haunted by the desire of obtaining wealth, and they naturally turn their attention to trade and manufactures, which appear to offer the readiest and most powerful means of success. In this respect they share the instincts of the poor, without feeling the same necessities ; say rather, they feel the most imperious of all necessities, that of not sinking in the world.

In aristocracies the rich are at the same time those who govern. The attention which they unceasingly devote to important public affairs diverts them from the lesser cares which trade and manufactures demand. If the will of an individual happens nevertheless to turn his attention to business, the will of the body to which he belongs will immediately debar him from pursuing it ; for however men may declaim against the rule of numbers, they cannot wholly escape their sway ; and even among those aristocratic bodies which most obstinately refuse to acknowledge the rights of the majority of the nation, a private majority is formed which governs the rest.

In democratic countries, where money does not lead those who possess it to political power, but often removes them from it, the rich do not know how to spend their leisure. They are driven into active life by the inquietude and the greatness of their desires, by the extent of their resources, and by the taste for what is extraordinary, which is almost always felt by those who rise, by whatsoever means, above the crowd. Trade is the only road open to them. In democracies nothing is greater or more brilliant than commerce : it attracts the attention of the public, and fills the imagination of the multitude ; all energetic passions are directed toward it. Neither their own prejudices, nor those of anybody else, can prevent the rich from devoting themselves to it. The wealthy members of democracies never form a body which has manners and regulations of its own ; the opinions peculiar to their class do not restrain them, and the common opinions of their country urge them on. Moreover, as all the large fortunes which are to be met with in a democratic community are of commercial growth, many generations must succeed each other before their possessors can have entirely laid aside their habits of business.

Circumscribed within the narrow space which politics leave them, rich men in democracies eagerly embark in commercial enterprise : there they can extend and employ their natural advantages ; and indeed it is even by the boldness and the magnitude of their industrial speculations that we may measure the slight esteem in which productive industry would have been held by them if they had been born amid an aristocracy.

A similar observation is likewise applicable to all men living in democracies, whether they be poor or rich. Those who live in the midst of democratic fluctuations have always before their eyes the phantom of chance ; and they end by liking all undertakings in which chance plays a part. They are, therefore, all led to engage in commerce, not only for the sake of the profit it holds out to them, but for the love of the constant excitement occasioned by that pursuit.

The United States of America have only been

emancipated for half a century from the state of
colonial dependence in which they stood to Great
Britain ; the number of large fortunes there is small,
and capital is still scarce. Yet no people in the world
has made such rapid progress in trade and manufactures as the Americans : they constitute at the
present day the second maritime nation in the world ;
and although their manufactures have to struggle
with almost insurmountable natural impediments,
they are not prevented from making great and daily
advances. In the United States the greatest undertakings and speculations are executed without difficulty, because the whole population is engaged in
productive industry, and because the poorest as well
as the most opulent members of the commonwealth
are ready to combine their efforts for these purposes.
The consequence is, that a stranger is constantly
amazed by the immense public works executed by a
nation which contains, so to speak, no rich men. The
Americans arrived but as yesterday on the territory
which they inhabit, and they have already changed
the whole order of Nature for their own advantage.
They have joined the Hudson to the Mississippi, and
made the Atlantic Ocean communicate with the Gulf
of Mexico, across a continent of more than five
hundred leagues in extent which separates the two
seas. The longest railroads which have been con-
structed up to the present time are in America. But
what most astonishes me in the United States is not so
much the marvellous grandeur of some undertakings,
as the innumerable multitude of small ones. Almost
all the farmers of the United States combine some
trade with agriculture ; most of them make agriculture itself a trade. It seldom happens that an
American farmer settles for good upon the land which
he occupies : especially in the districts of the far

West he brings land into tillage in order to sell it again, and not to farm it : he builds a farmhouse on the speculation that, as the state of the country will soon be changed by the increase of population, a good price will be gotten for it. Every year a swarm of the inhabitants of the North arrive in the Southern States, and settle in the parts where the cotton-plant and the sugar-cane grow. These men cultivate the soil in order to make it produce in a few years enough to enrich them ; and they already look forward to the time when they may return home to enjoy the competency thus acquired. Thus the Americans carry their business-like qualities into agriculture ; and their trading passions are displayed in that as in their other pursuits.

The Americans make immense progress in productive industry, because they all devote themselves to it at once ; and for this same reason they are exposed to very unexpected and formidable embarrassments. As they are all engaged in commerce, their commercial affairs are affected by such various and complex causes that it is impossible to foresee what difficulties may arise. As they are all more or less engaged in productive industry, at the least shock given to business all private fortunes are put in jeopardy at the same time, and the State is shaken. I believe that the return of these commercial panics is an endemic disease of the democratic nations of our age. It may be rendered less dangerous, but it cannot be cured ; because it does not originate in accidental circumstances, but in the temperament of these nations.

I have shown that democracy is favourable to the growth of manufactures, and that it increases without limit the numbers of the manufacturing classes : we shall now see by what side-road manufacturers may possibly in their turn bring men back to aristocracy. It is acknowledged that when a workman is engaged every day upon the same detail, the whole commodity is produced with greater ease, promptitude, and economy. It is likewise acknowledged that the cost of the production of manufactured goods is diminished by the extent of the establishment in which they are made, and by the amount of capital employed or of credit. These truths had long been imperfectly discerned, but in our time they have been demonstrated. They have been already applied to many very important kinds of manufactures, and the humblest will gradually be governed by them. I know of nothing in politics which deserves to fix the attention of the legislator more closely than these two new axioms of the science of manufactures.

When a workman is unceasingly and exclusively engaged in the fabrication of one thing, he ultimately does his work with singular dexterity ; but at the same time he loses the general faculty of applying his mind to the direction of the work. He every day becomes more adroit and less industrious ; so that it may be said of him that in proportion as the workman improves the man is degraded. What can be expected of a man who has spent twenty years of his life in making heads for pins ? and to what can that mighty human intelligence, which has so often stirred the world, be applied in him, except it be to investigate the best method of making pins' heads ? When a workman has spent a considerable portion of his existence in this manner, his thoughts are for ever set upon the object of his daily toil ; his body has contracted certain fixed habits, which it can never shake off : in a word, he no longer belongs to himself, but to the calling which he has chosen. It is in vain that laws and manners have been at the pains to level all barriers around such a man, and to open to him on every side a thousand different paths to fortune; a theory of manufactures more powerful than manners and laws binds him to a craft, and frequently to a spot, which he cannot leave: it assigns to him a certain place in society beyond which he cannot go: in the midst of universal movement it has rendered him stationary.

In proportion as the principle of the division of labour is more extensively applied, the workman becomes more weak, more narrow-minded, and more dependent. The art advances, the artisan recedes. On the other hand, in proportion as it becomes more manifest that the productions of manufactures are by so much the cheaper and better as the manufacture is larger and the amount of capital employed more considerable, wealthy and educated men come forward to embark in manufactures which were heretofore abandoned to poor or ignorant handicraftsmen. The magnitude of the efforts required, and the importance of the results to be obtained, attract them. Thus at the very time at which the science of manufactures lowers the class of workmen, it raises the class of masters.

Whereas the workman concentrates his faculties more and more upon the study of a single detail, the master surveys a more extensive whole, and the mind of the latter is enlarged in proportion as that of the former is narrowed. In a short time the one will require nothing but physical strength without intelligence; the other stands in need of science, and almost of genius, to insure success. This man resembles more and more the administrator of a vast empire—that man, a brute. The master and the workman have then here no similarity, and their differences increase every day. They are only connected as the two rings at the extremities of a long chain. Each of them fills the station which is made for him, and out of which he does not get : the one is continually, closely, and necessarily dependent upon the other, and seems as much born to obey as that other is to command. What is this but aristocracy ?

As the conditions of men constituting the nation become more and more equal, the demand for manufactured commodities becomes more general and more extensive ; and the cheapness which places these objects within the reach of slender fortunes becomes a great element of success. Hence there are every day more men of great opulence and education who devote their wealth and knowledge to manufactures ; and who seek, by opening large establishments, and by a strict division of labour, to meet the fresh demands which are made on all sides. Thus, in proportion as the mass of the nation turns to democracy, that particular class which is engaged in manufactures becomes more aristocratic. Men grow more alike in the one—more unlike in the other ; and inequality increases in the less numerous class in the same ratio in which it decreases in the community. Hence it would appear, on searching to the bottom, that aristocracy should naturally spring out of the bosom of democracy.

But this kind of aristocracy by no means resembles those kinds that preceded it. It will be observed at once that, as it applies exclusively to manufactures and to some manufacturing calling, it is a monstrous exception in the general aspect of society. The small aristocratic societies which are formed by some manufacturers in the midst of the immense democracy of our age, contain, like the great aristocratic societies of former ages, some men who are very opulent, and a multitude who are wretchedly poor. The poor have few means of escaping from their condition and becoming rich; but the rich are constantly becoming poor, or they give up business when they have realized a fortune. Thus the elements of which the class of the poor is composed are fixed; but the elements of which the class of the rich is composed are not so. To say the truth, though there are rich men, the class of rich men does not exist; for these rich individuals have no feelings or purposes in common, no mutual traditions or mutual hopes; there are therefore members, but no body.

Not only are the rich not compactly united among themselves, but there is no real bond between them and the poor. Their relative position is not a permanent one; they are constantly drawn together or separated by their interests. The workman is generally dependent on the master, but not on any particular master; these two men meet in the factory, but know not each other elsewhere; and while they come into contact on one point, they stand very wide apart on all others. The manufacturer asks nothing of the workman but his labour; the workman expects nothing from him but his wages. The one contracts no obligation to protect, nor the other to defend; and they are not permanently connected either by habit or by duty. The aristocracy created by business rarely settles in the midst of the manufacturing population which it directs: the object is not to govern that population, but to use it. An aristocracy thus constituted can have no great hold upon those whom it employs; and even if it succeed in retaining them at one moment, they escape the next: it knows not how to will, and it cannot act. The territorial aristocracy of former ages was either bound by law, or thought itself bound by usage, to come to the relief of its serving-men, and to succour their distresses.

But the manufacturing aristocracy of our age first impoverishes and debases the men who serve it, and then abandons them to be supported by the charity of the public. This is a natural consequence of what has been said before. Between the workmen and the master there are frequent relations, but no real partnership.

I am of opinion, upon the whole, that the manufacturing aristocracy which is growing up under our eyes is one of the harshest which ever existed in the world; but at the same time it is one of the most confined and least dangerous. Nevertheless, the friends of democracy should keep their eyes anxiously fixed in this direction; for if ever a permanent inequality of conditions and aristocracy again penetrate into the world, it may be predicted that this is the channel by which they will enter.

Chapter XXIX

INFLUENCE OF DEMOCRACY UPON MANNERS

WE perceive that for several ages social conditions have tended to equality, and we discover that in the course of the same period the manners of society have been softened. Are these two things merely contemporaneous, or does any secret link exist between them, so that the one cannot go on without making the other advance? Several causes may concur to render the manners of a people less rude; but, of all these causes, the most powerful appears to me to be the equality of conditions. Equality of conditions and growing civility in manners are then, in my eyes, not only contemporaneous occurrences, but correlative facts. When the fabulists seek to interest us in the actions of beasts, they invest them with human notions and passions; the poets who sing of spirits and angels do the same: there is no wretchedness so deep, nor any happiness so pure, as to fill the human mind and touch the heart, unless we are ourselves held up to our own eyes under other features.

This is strictly applicable to the subject upon which we are at present engaged. When all men are irrevocably marshalled in an aristocratic community, according to their professions, their property, and their birth, the members of each class, considering themselves as children of the same family, cherish a constant and lively sympathy toward each other, which can never be felt in an equal degree by the citizens of a democracy. But the same feeling does not exist between the several classes toward each other. Among an aristocratic people each caste has its own opinions, feelings, rights, manners, and modes of living. Thus the men of whom each caste is composed do not resemble the mass of their fellow-citizens; they do not think or feel in the same manner, and they scarcely believe that they belong to the same human race. They cannot, therefore, thoroughly understand what others feel, nor judge of others by themselves. Yet they are sometimes eager to lend each other mutual aid; but this is not contrary to my previous observation. These aristocratic institutions, which made the beings of one and the same race so different, nevertheless bound them to each other by close political ties. Although the serf had no natural interest in the fate of nobles, he did not the less think himself obliged to devote his person to the service of that noble who happened to be his lord: and although the noble held himself to be of a different nature from that of his serfs, he nevertheless held that his duty and his honour constrained him to defend, at the risk of his own life, those who dwelt upon his domains.

It is evident that these mutual obligations did not originate in the law of Nature, but in the law of society; and that the claim of social duty was more stringent than that of mere humanity. These services were not supposed to be due from man to man, but to the vassal or to the lord. Feudal institutions awakened a lively sympathy for the sufferings of certain men, but none at all for the miseries of mankind. They infused generosity rather than mildness into the manners of the time, and although they prompted men to great acts of self-devotion, they engendered no real sympathies; for real sympathies can only exist between those who are alike; and in aristocratic ages men acknowledge none but the members of their own caste to be like themselves. . . .

When all the ranks of a community are nearly equal, as all men think and feel in nearly the same manner, each of them may judge in a moment of the sensations of all the others: he casts a rapid glance upon himself, and that is enough. There is no wretchedness into which he cannot readily enter, and a secret instinct reveals to him its extent. It signifies not that strangers or foes be the sufferers ; imagination puts him in their place : something like a personal feeling is mingled with his pity, and makes himself suffer while the body of his fellow-creature is in torture. In democratic ages men rarely sacrifice themselves for one another; but they display general compassion for the members of the human race. They inflict no useless ills; and they are happy to relieve the griefs of others, when they can do so without much hurting themselves ; they are not disinterested, but they are humane.

Although the Americans have in a manner reduced egotism to a social and philosophical theory, they are nevertheless extremely open to compassion. In no country is criminal justice administered with more mildness than in the United States. While the English seem disposed carefully to retain the bloody traces of the dark ages in their penal legislation, the Americans have almost expunged capital punishment from their codes. North America is, I think, the only one country upon earth in which the life of no one citizen has been taken for a political offence in the course of the last fifty years. The circumstance which conclusively shows that this singular mildness of the Americans arises chiefly from their social condition, is the manner in which they treat their slaves. Perhaps there is not, upon the whole, a single European colony in the New World in which the physical condition of the blacks is less severe than in the United States ; yet the slaves still endure horrid sufferings there, and are constantly exposed to barbarous punishments. It is easy to perceive that the lot of these unhappy beings inspires their masters with but little compassion, and that they look upon slavery, not only as an institution which is profitable to them, but as an evil which does not affect them. Thus the same man who is full of humanity toward his fellow-creatures when they are at the same time his equals, becomes insensible to their afflictions as soon as that equality ceases. His mildness should, therefore, be attributed to the equality of conditions, rather than to civilization and education.

What I have here remarked of individuals is to a certain extent applicable to nations. When each nation has its distinct opinions, belief, laws, and customs, it looks upon itself as the whole of mankind, and is moved by no sorrows but its own. Should war break out between two nations animated by this feeling, it is sure to be waged with great cruelty. At the time of their highest culture, the Romans slaughtered the generals of their enemies, after having dragged them in triumph behind a car; and they flung their prisoners to the beasts of the Circus for the amusement of the people. Cicero, who declaimed so vehemently at the notion of crucifying a Roman citizen, had not a word to say against these horrible abuses of victory. It is evident that in his eyes a barbarian did not belong to the same human race as a Roman. On the contrary, in proportion as nations become more like each other, they become reciprocally more compassionate, and the law of nations is mitigated.

Democracy does not attach men strongly to each other; but it places their habitual intercourse upon an easier footing. If two Englishmen chance to meet at the Antipodes, where they are surrounded by strangers whose language and manners are almost unknown to them, they will first stare at each other with much curiosity and a kind of secret uneasiness;

they will then turn away, or, if one accosts the other, they will take care only to converse with a constrained and absent air upon very unimportant subjects. Yet there is no enmity between these men; they have never seen each other before, and each believes the other to be a respectable person. Why, then, should they stand so cautiously apart? We must go back to England to learn the reason.

When it is birth alone, independent of wealth, which classes men in society, every one knows exactly what his own position is upon the social scale; he does not seek to rise, he does not fear to sink. In a community thus organized, men of different castes communicate very little with each other; but if accident brings them together, they are ready to converse without hoping or fearing to lose their own position. Their intercourse is not upon a footing of equality, but it is not constrained. When moneyed aristocracy succeeds to aristocracy of birth, the case is altered. The privileges of some are still extremely great, but the possibility of acquiring those privileges is open to all: whence it follows that those who possess them are constantly haunted by the apprehension of losing them, or of other men's sharing them; those who do not yet enjoy them long to possess them at any cost, or, if they fail, to appear at least to possess them—which is not impossible. As the social importance of men is no longer ostensibly and permanently fixed by blood, and is infinitely varied by wealth, ranks still exist, but it is not easy clearly to distinguish at a glance those who respectively belong to them. Secret hostilities then arise in the community; one set of men endeavour by innumerable artifices to penetrate, or to appear to penetrate, among those who are above them; another set are constantly in arms against these usurpers of their rights; or rather the same individual does both at once, and while he seeks to raise himself into a higher circle, he is always on the defensive against the intrusion of those below him.

Such is the condition of England at the present time ; and I am of opinion that the peculiarity before adverted to is principally to be attributed to this cause. An aristocratic pride is still extremely great among the English, and as the limits of aristocracy are ill defined, everybody lives in constant dread lest advantage should be taken of his familiarity. Unable to judge at once of the social position of those he meets, an Englishman prudently avoids all contact with them. Men are afraid lest some slight service rendered should draw them into an unsuitable acquaintance ; they dread civilities, and they avoid the obtrusive gratitude of a stranger quite as much as his hatred. Many people attribute these singular anti-social propensities, and the reserved and taciturn bearing of the English, to purely physical causes. I may admit that there is something of it in their race, but much more of it is attributable to their social condition, as is proved by the contrast of the Americans.

In America, where the privileges of birth never existed, and where riches confer no peculiar rights on their possessors, men unacquainted with each other are very ready to frequent the same places, and find neither peril nor advantage in the free interchange of their thoughts. If they meet by accident, they neither seek nor avoid intercourse ; their manner is therefore natural, frank, and open : it is easy to see that they hardly expect or apprehend anything from each other, and that they do not care to display, any more than to conceal, their position in the world. If their demeanour is often cold and serious, it is never haughty or constrained; and if they do not converse, it is because they are not in a humour to talk, not because they think it their interest to be silent. In a foreign country two Americans are at once friends, simply because they are Americans. They are repulsed by no prejudice; they are attracted by their common country. For two Englishmen the same blood is not enough; they must be brought together by the same rank. The Americans remark this unsociable mood of the English as much as the French do, and they are not less astonished by it. Yet the Americans are connected with England by their origin, their religion, their language, and partially by their manners: they only differ in their social condition. It may therefore be inferred that the reserve of the English proceeds from the constitution of their country much more than from that of its inhabitants.

The temper of the Americans is vindictive, like that of all serious and reflecting nations. They hardly ever forget an offence, but it is not easy to offend them; and their resentment is as slow to kindle as it is to abate. In aristocratic communities where a small number of persons manage everything, the outward intercourse of men is subject to settled conventional rules. Every one then thinks he knows exactly what marks of respect or of condescension he ought to display, and none are presumed to be ignorant of the science of etiquette. These usages of the first class in society afterward serve as a model to all the others; besides which each of the latter lays down a code of its own, to which all its members are bound to conform. Thus the rules of politeness form a complex system of legislation, which it is difficult to be perfectly master of, but from which it is dangerous for any one to deviate; so that men are constantly exposed involuntarily to inflict or to receive bitter affronts. But as the distinctions of rank are obliterated, as men differing in education and in birth meet and mingle in the same places of resort, it is almost impossible to agree upon the rules of good breeding. As its laws are uncertain, to disobey them is not a crime, even in the eyes of those who know what they are; men attach more importance to intentions than to forms, and they grow less civil, but at the same time less quarrelsome. There are many little attentions which an American does not care about; he thinks they are not due to him, or he presumes that they are not known to be due: he therefore either does not perceive a rudeness or he forgives it; his manners become less courteous, and his character more plain and masculine.

The mutual indulgence which the Americans display, and the manly confidence with which they treat each other, also result from another deeper and more general cause, which I have already adverted to in the preceding chapter. In the United States the distinctions of rank in civil society are slight, in political society they are null; an American, therefore, does not think himself bound to pay particular attentions to any of his fellow-citizens, nor does he require such attentions from them toward himself. As he does not see that it is his interest eagerly to seek the company of any of his countrymen, he is slow to fancy that his own company is declined: despising no one on account of his station, he does not imagine that any one can despise him for that cause; and until he has clearly perceived an insult, he does not suppose that an affront was intended. The social condition of the Americans naturally accustoms them not to take offence in small matters; and, on the other hand, the democratic freedom which they enjoy transfuses this same mildness of temper into the character of the nation. The political institutions of the United States constantly bring citizens of all ranks into contact, and compel them to pursue great undertakings in concert. People thus engaged have scarcely time to attend to the details of etiquette, and they are, besides, too strongly interested in living harmoniously for them to stick at such things. They therefore soon acquire a habit of considering the feelings and opinions of those whom they meet more than their manners, and they do not allow themselves to be annoyed by trifles.

I have often remarked in the United States that it is not easy to make a man understand that his presence may be dispensed with ; hints will not always suffice to shake him off. I contradict an American at every word he says, to show him that his conversation bores me ; he instantly labours with fresh pertinacity to convince me ; I preserve a dogged silence, and he thinks I am meditating deeply on the truths which he is uttering ; at last I rush from his company, and he supposes that some urgent business hurries me elsewhere. This man will never understand that he wearies me to extinction unless I tell him so : and the only way to get rid of him is to make him my enemy for life.

It appears surprising at first sight that the same man transported to Europe suddenly becomes so sensitive and captious, that I often find it as difficult to avoid offending him here as it was to put him out of countenance. These two opposite effects proceed from the same cause. Democratic institutions generally give men a lofty notion of their country and of themselves. An American leaves his country with a heart swollen with pride ; on arriving in Europe he at once finds out that we are not so engrossed by the United States and the great people which inhabits them as he had supposed, and this begins to annoy him. He has been informed that the conditions of society are not equal in our part of the globe, and he observes that among the nations of Europe the traces of rank are not wholly obliterated; that wealth and birth still retain some indeterminate privileges, which force themselves upon his notice while they elude definition. He is, therefore, profoundly ignorant of the place which he ought to occupy in this half-ruined scale of classes, which are sufficiently distinct to hate and despise each other, yet sufficiently alike for him to be always confounding them. He is afraid of ranging himself too high—still more is he afraid of being ranged too low; this twofold peril keeps his mind constantly on the stretch, and embarrasses all he says and does. He learns from tradition that in Europe ceremonial observances were infinitely varied according to different ranks; this recollection of former times completes his perplexity, and he is the more afraid of not obtaining those marks of respect which are due to him, as he does not exactly know in what they consist. He is like a man surrounded by traps: society is not a recreation for him, but a serious toil: he weighs your least actions, interrogates your looks, and scrutinizes all you say, lest there should be some hidden allusion to affront him. I doubt whether there was ever a provincial man of quality so punctilious in breeding as he is: he endeavours to attend to the slightest rules of etiquette, and does not allow one of them to be waived toward himself: he is full of scruples and at the same time of pretensions; he wishes to do enough, but fears to do too much; and as he does not very well know the limits of the one or of the other, he keeps up a haughty and embarrassed air of reserve.

But this is not all : here is yet another double of the human heart. An American is for ever talking of the admirable equality which prevails in the United States : aloud he makes it the boast of his country, but in secret he deplores it for himself ; and he aspires to show that, for his part, he is an exception to the general state of things which he vaunts. There is hardly an American to be met with who does not claim some remote kindred with the first founders of the colonies ; and as for the scions of the noble families of England, America seemed to me to be covered with them. When an opulent American arrives in Europe, his first care is to surround himself with all the luxuries of wealth : he is so afraid of being taken for the plain citizen of a democracy that he adopts a hundred distorted ways of bringing some new instance of his wealth before you every day. His house will be in the most fashionable part of the town : he will always be surrounded by a host of servants. I have heard an American complain that in the best houses of Paris the society was rather mixed ; the taste which prevails there was not pure enough for him ; and he ventured to hint that, in his opinion, there was a want of elegance of manner ; he could not accustom himself to see wit concealed under such unpretending forms.

These contrasts ought not to surprise us. If the vestiges of former aristocratic distinctions were not so completely effaced in the United States, the Americans would be less simple and less tolerant in their own country—they would require less, and be less fond of borrowed manners in ours.

When men feel a natural compassion for their mutual sufferings—when they are brought together by easy and frequent intercourse, and no sensitive feelings keep them asunder, it may readily be supposed that they will lend assistance to one another whenever it is needed. When an American asks for the co-operation of his fellow-citizens it is seldom refused, and I have often seen it afforded spontaneously and with great good-will. If an accident happens on the highway, everybody hastens to help the sufferer; if some great and sudden calamity befalls a family, the purses of a thousand strangers are at once willingly opened, and small but numerous donations pour in to relieve their distress. It often happens among the most civilized nations of the globe that a poor wretch is as friendless in the midst of a crowd as the savage in his wilds: this is hardly ever the case in the United States. The Americans, who are always cold and often coarse in their manners, seldom show insensibility; and if they do not proffer services eagerly, yet they do not refuse to render them.

All this is not in contradiction to what I have said before on the subject of individualism. The two things are so far from combating each other that I can see how they agree. Equality of conditions, while it makes men feel their independence, shows them their own weakness: they are free, but exposed to a thousand accidents; and experience soon teaches them that, although they do not habitually require the assistance of others, a time almost always comes when they cannot do without it. We constantly see in Europe that men of the same profession are ever ready to assist each other; they are all exposed to the same ills, and that is enough to teach them to seek mutual preservatives, however hard-hearted and selfish they may otherwise be. When one of them falls into danger, from which the others may save him by a slight transient sacrifice or a sudden effort, they do not fail to make the attempt. Not that they are deeply interested in his fate; for if, by chance, their exertions are unavailing, they immediately forget the object of them, and return to their own business ; but a sort of tacit and almost involuntary agreement has been passed between them, by which each one owes to the others a temporary support which he may claim for himself in turn. Extend to a people the remark here applied to a class, and you will understand my meaning. A similar covenant exists, in fact, between all the citizens of a democracy : they all feel themselves subject to the same weakness and the same dangers ; and their interest, as well as their sympathy, makes it a rule with them to lend each other mutual assistance when required. The more equal social conditions become, the more do men display this reciprocal disposition to oblige each other. In democracies no great benefits are conferred, but good offices are constantly rendered : a man seldom displays self-devotion, but all men are ready to be of service to one another.

Chapter XXX

. . . I HAVE always considered England as the country
in the world where, in our time, the bond of domestic
service is drawn most tightly, and France as the
country where it is most relaxed. Nowhere have I
seen masters stand so high or so low as in these two
countries. Between these two extremes the Americans
are to be placed. Such is the fact as it appears upon
the surface of things : to discover the causes of that
fact, it is necessary to search the matter thoroughly.

No communities have ever yet existed in which
social conditions have been so equal that there were
neither rich nor poor, and consequently neither
masters nor servants. Democracy does not prevent
the existence of these two classes, but it changes their
dispositions and modifies their mutual relations.
Among aristocratic nations servants form a distinct
class, not more variously composed than that of
masters. A settled order is soon established ; in the
former as well as in the latter class a scale is formed,
with numerous distinctions or marked gradations of
rank, and generations succeed each other thus without any change of position. . . . In the society of
servants, as in that of masters, men exercise a great
influence over each other : they acknowledge settled
rules, and in the absence of law they are guided by a
sort of public opinion : their habits are settled, and
their conduct is placed under a certain control. . . .

Equality of conditions turns servants and masters
into new beings, and places them in new relative
positions. When social conditions are nearly equal,
men are constantly changing their situations in life :
there is still a class of menials and a class of masters,

but these classes are not always composed of the same individuals, still less of the same families; and those who command are not more secure of perpetuity than those who obey. As servants do not form a separate people, they have no habits, prejudices, or manners peculiar to themselves; they are not remarkable for any particular turn of mind or moods of feeling. They know no vices or virtues of their condition, but they partake of the education, the opinions, the feelings, the virtues and the vices of their contemporaries; and they are honest men or scoundrels in the same way as their masters are. The conditions of servants are not less equal than those of masters. As no marked ranks or fixed subordination are to be found among them, they will not display either the meanness or the greatness which characterize the aristocracy of menials as well as all other aristocracies. I never saw a man in the United States who reminded me of that class of confidential servants of which we still retain a reminiscence in Europe, neither did I ever meet with such a thing as a lackey: all traces of the one and of the other have disappeared.

In democracies servants are not only equal among themselves, but it may be said that they are in some sort the equals of their masters. This requires explanation in order to be rightly understood. At any moment, a servant may become a master, and he aspires to rise to that condition: the servant is therefore not a different man from the master. Why, then, has the former a right to command, and what compels the latter to obey?—the free and temporary consent of both their wills. Neither of them is by nature inferior to the other; they only become so for a time by covenant. Within the terms of this covenant, the one is a servant, the other a master; beyond it they are two citizens of the commonwealth—two men. I

beg the reader particularly to observe that this is not
only the notion which servants themselves entertain
of their own condition; domestic service is looked
upon by masters in the same light; and the precise
limits of authority and obedience are as clearly
settled in the mind of the one as in that of the other.

When the greater part of the community have long
attained a condition nearly alike, and when equality
is an old and acknowledged fact, the public mind,
which is never affected by exceptions, assigns certain
general limits to the value of man, above or below
which no man can long remain placed. It is in vain
that wealth and poverty, authority and obedience,
accidentally interpose great distances between two
men; public opinion, founded upon the usual order
of things, draws them to a common level, and creates
a species of imaginary equality between them, in
spite of the real inequality of their conditions. This
all-powerful opinion penetrates at length even into
the hearts of those whose interest might arm them to
resist it; it affects their judgment while it subdues
their will. In their inmost convictions the master
and the servant no longer perceive any deep-seated
difference between them, and they neither hope nor
fear to meet with any such at any time. They are,
therefore, neither subject to disdain nor to anger, and
they discern in each other neither humility nor pride.
The master holds the contract of service to be the only
source of his power, and the servant regards it as the
only cause of his obedience. They do not quarrel
about their reciprocal situations, but each knows his
own and keeps it. . . .

It would be preposterous to suppose that those
warm and deep-seated affections, which are sometimes kindled in the domestic service of aristocracy,
will ever spring up between these two men, or that

they will exhibit strong instances of self-sacrifice. In aristocracies masters and servants live apart, and frequently their only intercourse is through a third person; yet they commonly stand firmly by one another. In democratic countries the master and the servant are close together; they are in daily personal contact, but their minds do not intermingle; they have common occupations, hardly ever common interests. Among such a people the servant always considers himself as a sojourner in the dwelling of his masters. He knew nothing of their forefathers—he will see nothing of their descendants—he has nothing lasting to expect from their hand. Why, then, should he confound his life with theirs, and whence should so strange a surrender of himself proceed? The reciprocal position of the two men is changed—their mutual relations must be so too.

I would fain illustrate all these reflections by the example of the Americans; but for this purpose the distinctions of persons and places must be accurately traced. In the South of the Union, slavery exists; all that I have just said is consequently inapplicable there. In the North, the majority of servants are either freed-men or the children of freed-men; these persons occupy a contested position in the public estimation; by the laws they are brought up to the level of their masters—by the manners of the country they are obstinately detruded from it. They do not themselves clearly know their proper place, and they are almost always either insolent or craven. But in the Northern States, especially in New England, there are a certain number of whites, who agree, for wages, to yield a temporary obedience to the will of their fellow-citizens. I have heard that these servants commonly perform the duties of their situation with punctuality and intelligence; and that without thinking themselves naturally inferior to the person who orders them, they submit without reluctance to obey him. They appear to me to carry into service some of those manly habits which independence and equality engender. Having once selected a hard way of life, they do not seek to escape from it by indirect means; and they have sufficient respect for themselves not to refuse to their masters that obedience which they have freely promised. On their part, masters require nothing of their servants but the faithful and rigorous performance of the covenant: they do not ask for marks of respect, they do not claim their love or devoted attachment; it is enough that, as servants, they are exact and honest. It would not then be true to assert that, in democratic society, the relation of servants and masters is disorganized: it is organized on another footing; the rule is different, but there is a rule.

It is not my purpose to inquire whether the new state of things which I have just described is inferior to that which preceded it, or simply different. Enough for me that it is fixed and determined: for what is most important to meet with among men is not any given ordering, but order. But what shall I say of those sad and troubled times at which equality is established in the midst of the tumult of revolution—when democracy, after having been introduced into the state of society, still struggles with difficulty against the prejudices and manners of the country? The laws, and partially public opinion, already declare that no natural or permanent inferiority exists between the servant and the master. But this new belief has not yet reached the innermost convictions of the latter, or rather his heart rejects it; in the secret persuasion of his mind the master thinks that he belongs to a peculiar and superior race; he dares not say so, but he shudders while he allows himself to be dragged to the same level. His authority over his servants becomes timid and at the same time harsh : he has already ceased to entertain for them the feelings of patronizing kindness which long un-contested power always engenders, and he is surprised that, being changed himself, his servant changes also. He wants his attendants to form regular and permanent habits, in a condition of domestic service which is only temporary : he requires that they should appear contented with and proud of a servile condi-tion, which they will one day shake off—that they should sacrifice themselves to a man who can neither protect nor ruin them—and, in short, that they should contract an indissoluble engagement to a being like themselves, and one who will last no longer than they will.

Among aristocratic nations it often happens that the condition of domestic service does not degrade the character of those who enter upon it, because they neither know nor imagine any other ; and the amazing inequality which is manifest between them and their master appears to be the necessary and unavoidable consequence of some hidden law of Providence. In democracies the condition of domestic service does not degrade the character of those who enter upon it, because it is freely chosen, and adopted for a time only ; because it is not stigmatized by public opinion, and creates no permanent inequality between the servant and the master. But while the transition from one social condition to another is going on, there is almost always a time when men's minds fluctuate between the aristocratic notion of subjection and the democratic notion of obedience. Obedience then loses its moral importance in the eyes of him who obeys ; he no longer considers it as a species of divine obligation, and he does not yet view it under its purely human aspect; it has to him no character of sanctity or of justice, and he submits to it as to a degrading but profitable condition. At that moment a confused and imperfect phantom of equality haunts the minds of servants; they do not at once perceive whether the equality to which they are entitled is to be found within or without the pale of domestic service; and they rebel in their hearts against a subordination to which they have subjected themselves, and from which they derive actual profit. They consent to serve, and they blush to obey; they like the advantages of service, but not the master; or rather, they are not sure that they ought not themselves to be masters, and they are inclined to consider him who orders them as an unjust usurper of their own rights. . . .

What has been said of servants and masters is applicable, to a certain extent, to land-owners and farming tenants; but this subject deserves to be considered by itself. In America there are, properly speaking, no tenant farmers; every man owns the ground he tills.[1] It must be admitted that democratic laws tend greatly to increase the number of land-owners, and to diminish that of farming tenants. Yet what takes place in the United States is much less attributable to the institutions of the country than to the country itself. In America land is cheap, and any one may easily become a land-owner; its returns are small, and its produce cannot well be divided between a land-owner and a farmer. America, therefore, stands alone in this as well as in many other respects, and it would be a mistake to take it as an example.

[1] A century after Tocqueville wrote forty-two per cent of American farmers were tenants.—H. S. C.

I believe that in democratic as well as in aristocratic countries there will be land-owners and tenants, but the connection existing between them will be of a different kind. In aristocracies the hire of a farm is paid to the landlord, not only in rent, but in respect, regard, and duty; in democracies the whole is paid in cash. When estates are divided and passed from hand to hand, and the permanent connection which existed between families and the soil is dissolved, the land-owner and the tenant are only casually brought into contact. They meet for a moment to settle the conditions of the agreement, and then lose sight of each other; they are two strangers brought together by a common interest, and who keenly talk over a matter of business, the sole object of which is to make money.

In proportion as property is subdivided and wealth distributed over the country, the community is filled with people whose former opulence is declining, and with others whose fortunes are of recent growth and whose wants increase more rapidly than their resources. For all such persons the smallest pecuniary profit is a matter of importance, and none of them feel disposed to waive any of their claims, or to lose any portion of their income. As ranks are intermingled, and as very large as well as very scanty fortunes become more rare, every day brings the social condition of the land-owner nearer to that of the farmer; the one has not naturally any uncontested superiority over the other; between two men who are equal, and not at ease in their circumstances, the contract of hire is exclusively an affair of money. A man whose estate extends over a whole district, and who owns a hundred farms, is well aware of the importance of gaining at the same time the affections of some thousands of men; this object appears to call for his exertions, and to attain it he will readily make considerable sacrifices. But he who owns a hundred acres is insensible to similar considerations, and he cares but little to win the private regard of his tenant. . . .

There is yet another sign by which it is easy to know that a great democratic revolution is going on or approaching. In the Middle Ages almost all lands were leased for lives, or for very long terms ; the domestic economy of that period shows that leases for ninety-nine years were more frequent then than leases for twelve years are now. Men then believed that families were immortal ; men's conditions seemed settled for ever, and the whole of society appeared to be so fixed that it was not supposed that anything would ever be stirred or shaken in its structure. In ages of equality, the human mind takes a different bent ; the prevailing notion is that nothing abides, and man is haunted by the thought of mutability. Under this impression the land-owner and the tenant himself are instinctively averse to protracted terms of obligation ; they are afraid of being tied up to-morrow by the contract which benefits them to-day. They have vague anticipations of some sudden and unforeseen change in their conditions ; they mistrust themselves ; they fear lest their taste should change, and lest they should lament that they cannot rid themselves of what they coveted ; nor are such fears unfounded, for in democratic ages that which is most fluctuating amid the fluctuation of all around is the heart of man.

Most of the remarks which I have already made in speaking of servants and masters may be applied to masters and workmen. As the gradations of the social scale come to be less observed, while the great sink the humble rise, and as poverty as well as opulence ceases to be hereditary, the distance, both in reality and in opinion, which heretofore separated the workman from the master is lessened every day. The workman conceives a more lofty opinion of his rights, of his future, of himself; he is filled with new ambition and with new desires, he is harassed by new wants. Every instant he views with longing eyes the profits of his employer; and in order to share them, he strives to dispose of his labour at a higher rate, and he generally succeeds at length in the attempt. In democratic countries, as well as elsewhere, most of the branches of productive industry are carried on at a small cost by men little removed by their wealth or education above the level of those whom they employ. These manufacturing speculators are extremely numerous; their interests differ; they cannot, therefore, easily concert or combine their exertions. On the other hand, the workmen have almost always some sure resources, which enable them to refuse to work when they cannot get what they conceive to be the fair price of their labour. In the constant struggle for wages which is going on between these two classes, their strength is divided, and success alternates from one to the other. It is even probable that in the end the interest of the working class must prevail; for the high wages which they have already obtained make them every day less dependent on their masters; and as they grow more independent, they have greater facilities for obtaining a further increase of wages. . . .

I think that, upon the whole, it may be asserted that a slow and gradual rise of wages is one of the general laws of democratic communities. In proportion as social conditions become more equal, wages rise; and as wages are higher, social conditions become more equal. But a great and gloomy exception occurs in our own time. I have shown in a preceding chapter that aristocracy, expelled from political society, has taken refuge in certain departments of productive industry, and has established its sway there under another form; this powerfully affects the rate of wages. As a large capital is required to embark in the great manufacturing speculations to which I allude, the number of persons who enter upon them is exceedingly limited : as their number is small, they can easily concert together, and fix the rate of wages as they please. Their workmen, on the contrary, are exceedingly numerous, and the number of them is always increasing; for, from time to time, an extraordinary run of business takes place, during which wages are inordinately high, and they attract the surrounding population to the factories. But, when once men have embraced that line of life, we have already seen that they cannot quit it again, because they soon contract habits of body and mind which unfit them for any other sort of toil. These men have generally but little education and industry, with but few resources; they stand, therefore, almost at the mercy of the master. When competition, or other fortuitous circumstances, lessen his profits, he can reduce the wages of his workmen almost at pleasure, and make from them what he loses by the chances of business. Should the workmen strike, the master, who is a rich man, can very well wait without being ruined until necessity brings them back to him; but they must work day by day or they die, for their only property is in their hands. They have long been impoverished by oppression, and the poorer they become the more easily may they be oppressed : they can never escape from this fatal circle of cause and consequence. It is not then surprising that wages, after having sometimes suddenly risen, are permanently lowered in this branch of industry; whereas in other callings the price of labour, which generally increases but little, is nevertheless constantly augmented.

This state of dependence and wretchedness, in which a part of the manufacturing population of our time lives, forms an exception to the general rule, contrary to the state of all the rest of the community; but, for this very reason, no circumstance is more important or more deserving of the especial consideration of the legislator; for when the whole of society is in motion, it is difficult to keep any one class stationary; and when the greater number of men are opening new paths to fortune, it is no less difficult to make the few support in peace their wants and their desires.

I have just examined the changes which the equality of conditions produces in the mutual relations of the several members of the community among democratic nations, and among the Americans in particular. I would now go deeper, and inquire into the closer ties of kindred: my object here is not to seek for new truths, but to show in what manner facts already known are connected with my subject.

It has been universally remarked that in our time the several members of a family stand upon an entirely new footing toward each other; that the distance which formerly separated a father from his sons has been lessened; and that paternal authority, if not destroyed, is at least impaired. Something analogous to this, but even more striking, may be observed in the United States. In America the family, in the Roman and aristocratic signification of the word, does not exist. All that remains of it are a few vestiges in the first years of childhood, when the father exercises, without opposition, that absolute domestic authority which the feebleness of his children renders necessary, and which their interest, as well as his own incontestable superiority, warrants. But as soon as the young American approaches manhood, the ties of filial obedience are relaxed day by day : master of his thoughts, he is soon master of his conduct. In America there is, strictly speaking, no adolescence : at the close of boyhood the man appears, and begins to trace out his own path. It would be an error to suppose that this is preceded by a domestic struggle, in which the son has obtained by a sort of moral violence the liberty that his father refused him. The same habits, the same principles which impel the one to assert his independence, predispose the other to consider the use of that independence as an incontestable right. The former does not exhibit any of those rancorous or irregular passions which disturb men long after they have shaken off an established authority ; the latter feels none of that bitter and angry regret which is apt to survive a bygone power. The father foresees the limits of his authority long beforehand, and when the time arrives he surrenders it without a struggle : the son looks forward to the exact period at which he will be his own master ; and he enters upon his freedom without precipitation and without effort, as a possession which is his own and which no one seeks to wrest from him. . . .

When men live more for the remembrance of what has been than for the care of what is, and when they are more given to attend to what their ancestors thought than to think themselves, the father is the natural and necessary tie between the past and the present—the link by which the ends of these two chains are connected. In aristocracies, then, the father is not only the civil head of the family, but the oracle of its traditions, the expounder of its customs, the arbiter of its manners. He is listened to with deference, he is addressed with respect, and the love which is felt for him is always tempered with fear. When the condition of society becomes democratic, and men adopt as their general principle that it is good and lawful to judge of all things for one's self, using former points of belief not as a rule of faith but simply as a means of information, the power which the opinions of a father exercise over those of his sons diminishes as well as his legal power.

Perhaps the subdivision of estates which democracy brings with it contributes more than anything else to change the relations existing between a father and his children. When the property of the father of a family is scanty, his son and himself constantly live in the same place, and share the same occupations : habit and necessity bring them together, and force them to hold constant communication : the inevitable consequence is a sort of familiar intimacy, which renders authority less absolute, and which can ill be reconciled with the external forms of respect. Now in democratic countries the class of those who are possessed of small fortunes is precisely that which gives strength to the notions, and a particular direction to the manners, of the community. That class makes its opinions preponderate as universally as its will, and even those who are most inclined to resist its commands are carried away in the end by its example. I have known eager opponents of democracy who allowed their children to address them with perfect colloquial equality.

Thus, at the same time that the power of aristocracy is declining, the austere, the conventional, and the legal part of parental authority vanishes, and a species of equality prevails around the domestic hearth. I know not, upon the whole, whether society loses by the change, but I am inclined to believe that man individually is a gainer by it. I think that, in proportion as manners and laws become more democratic, the relation of father and son becomes more intimate and more affectionate; rules and authority are less talked of; confidence and tenderness are oftentimes increased, and it would seem that the natural bond is drawn closer in proportion as the social bond is loosened. In a democratic family the father exercises no other power than that with which men love to invest the affection and the experience of age; his orders would perhaps be disobeyed, but his advice is for the most part authoritative. Though he be not hedged in with ceremonial respect, his sons at least accost him with confidence; no settled form of speech is appropriated to the mode of addressing him, but they speak to him constantly, and are ready to consult him day by day; the master and the constituted ruler have vanished—the father remains. Nothing more is needed, in order to judge of the difference between the two states of society in this respect, than to peruse the family correspondence of aristocratic ages. The style is always correct, ceremonious, stiff, and so cold that the natural warmth of the heart can hardly be felt in the language. The language, on the contrary, addressed by a son to his father in democratic countries is always marked by mingled freedom, familiarity, and affection, which at once show that new relations have sprung up in the bosom of the family.

A similar revolution takes place in the mutual relations of children. In aristocratic families, as well as in aristocratic society, every place is marked out beforehand. Not only does the father occupy a separate rank, in which he enjoys extensive privileges, but even the children are not equal among themselves. The age and sex of each irrevocably determine his rank, and secure to him certain privileges : most of these distinctions are abolished or diminished by democracy. In aristocratic families the eldest son, inheriting the greater part of the property, and almost all the rights of the family, becomes the chief, and, to a certain extent, the master, of his brothers. Greatness and power are for him—for them, mediocrity and dependence. Nevertheless, it would be wrong to suppose that, among aristocratic nations, the privileges of the eldest son are advantageous to himself alone, or that they excite nothing but envy and hatred in those around him. The eldest son commonly endeavours to procure wealth and power for his brothers, because the general splendour of the house is reflected back on him who represents it ; the younger sons seek to back the elder brother in all his undertakings, because the greatness and power of the head of the family better enable him to provide for all its branches. The different members of an aristocratic family are therefore very closely bound together ; their interests are connected, their minds agree, but their hearts are seldom in harmony.

Democracy also binds brothers to each other, but by very different means. Under democratic laws all the children are perfectly equal, and consequently independent : nothing brings them forcibly together, but nothing keeps them apart ; and as they have the same origin, as they are trained under the same roof, as they are treated with the same care, and as no peculiar privilege distinguishes or divides them, the affectionate and youthful intimacy of early years easily springs up between them. Scarcely any opportunities occur to break the tie thus formed at the outset of life ; for their brotherhood brings them daily together, without embarrassing them. It is not, then, by interest, but by common associations and by the free sympathy of opinion and of taste, that democracy unites brothers to each other. It divides their inheritance, but it allows their hearts and minds to mingle together. Such is the charm of these democratic manners, that even the partisans of aristocracy are caught by it; and after having experienced it for some time, they are by no means tempted to revert to the respectful and frigid observances of aristocratic families. They would be glad to retain the domestic habits of democracy if they might throw off its social conditions and its laws; but these elements are indissolubly united, and it is impossible to enjoy the former without enduring the latter.

The remarks I have made on filial love and fraternal affection are applicable to all the passions which emanate spontaneously from human nature itself. If a certain mode of thought or feeling is the result of some peculiar condition of life, when that condition is altered nothing whatever remains of the thought or feeling. Thus a law may bind two members of the community very closely to one another; but that law being abolished, they stand asunder. Nothing was more strict than the tie which united the vassal to the lord under the feudal system: at the present day the two men know not each other; the fear, the gratitude, and the affection which formerly connected them have vanished, and not a vestige of the tie remains. Such, however, is not the case with those feelings which are natural to mankind. Whenever a law attempts to tutor these feelings in any particular manner, it seldom fails to weaken them; by attempting to add to their intensity, it robs them of some of their elements, for they are never stronger than when left to themselves.

Democracy, which destroys or obscures almost all the old conventional rules of society, and which prevents men from readily assenting to new ones, entirely effaces most of the feelings to which these conventional rules have given rise; but it only modifies some others, and frequently imparts to them a degree of energy and sweetness unknown before. Perhaps it is not impossible to condense into a single proposition the whole meaning of this chapter, and of several others that preceded it. Democracy loosens social ties, but it draws the ties of Nature more tight; it brings kindred more closely together, while it places the various members of the community more widely apart.

No free communities ever existed without morals; and, as I observed in the former part of this work, morals are the work of woman. Consequently, whatever affects the condition of women, their habits, and their opinions, has great political importance in my eyes. Among almost all Protestant nations young women are far more the mistresses of their own actions than they are in Catholic countries. This independence is still greater in Protestant countries like England, which have retained or acquired the right of self-government; the spirit of freedom is then infused into the domestic circle by political habits and by religious opinions. In the United States the doctrines of Protestantism are combined with great political freedom and a most democratic state of society; and nowhere are young women surrendered so early or so completely to their own guidance. Long before an American girl arrives at the age of marriage, her emancipation from maternal control begins: she has scarcely ceased to be a child when she already thinks for herself, speaks with freedom, and acts on her own impulse. The great scene of the world is constantly open to her view: far from seeking concealment, it is every day disclosed to her more completely, and she is taught to survey it with a firm and calm gaze. Thus the vices and dangers of society are early revealed to her; as she sees them clearly, she views them without illusions, and braves them without fear; for she is full of reliance on her own strength, and her reliance seems to be shared by all who are about her. An American girl scarcely ever displays that virginal bloom in the midst of young desires, or that innocent and ingenuous grace which usually attend the European woman in the transition from girlhood to youth. It is rarely that an American woman at any age displays childish timidity or ignorance. Like the young women of Europe, she seeks to please, but she knows precisely the cost of pleasing. If she does not abandon herself to evil, at least she knows that it exists; and she is remarkable rather for purity of manners than for chastity of mind. I have been frequently surprised, and almost frightened, at the singular address and happy boldness with which young women in America contrive to manage their thoughts and their language amid all the difficulties of stimulating conversation; a philosopher would have stumbled at every step along the narrow path which they trod without accidents and without effort. It is easy, indeed, to perceive that, even amid the independence of early youth, an American woman is always mistress of herself: she indulges in all permitted pleasures, without yielding herself up to any of them; and her reason never allows the reins of self-guidance to drop, though it often seems to hold them loosely.

In France, where remnants of every age are still so strangely mingled in the opinions and tastes of the people, women commonly receive a reserved, retired, and almost conventional education, as they did in aristocratic times; and then they are suddenly abandoned, without a guide and without assistance, in the midst of all the irregularities inseparable from democratic society. The Americans are more consistent. They have found out that in a democracy the independence of individuals cannot fail to be very great, youth premature, tastes ill-restrained, customs fleeting, public opinion often unsettled and powerless, paternal authority weak, and marital authority contested. Under these circumstances, believing that they had little chance of repressing in woman the most vehement passions of the human heart, they held that the surer way was to teach her the art of combating those passions for herself. As they could not prevent her virtue from being exposed to frequent danger, they determined that she should know how best to defend it; and more reliance was placed on the free vigour of her will than on safeguards which have been shaken or overthrown. Instead, then, of inculcating mistrust of herself, they contantly seek to enhance their confidence in her own strength of character. As it is neither possible nor desirable to keep a young woman in perpetual or complete ignorance, they hasten to give her a precocious knowledge on all subjects. Far from hiding the corruptions of the world from her, they prefer that she should see them at once and train herself to shun them; and they hold it of more importance to protect her conduct than to be over-scrupulous of her innocence.

Although the Americans are a very religious people, they do not rely on religion alone to defend the virtue of woman; they seek to arm her reason also. In this they have followed the same method as in several other respects; they first make the most vigorous efforts to bring individual independence to exercise a proper control over itself, and they do not call in the aid of religion until they have reached the utmost limits of human strength. I am aware that an education of this kind is not without danger; I am sensible that it tends to invigorate the judgment at the expense of the imagination, and to make cold and virtuous women instead of affectionate wives and agreeable companions to man. Society may be more tranquil and better regulated, but domestic life has often fewer charms. These, however, are secondary evils, which may be braved for the sake of higher interests. At the stage at which we are now arrived the time for choosing is no longer within our control; a democratic education is indispensable to protect women from the dangers with which democratic institutions and manners surround them. . . .

The same strength of purpose which the young wives of America display, in bending themselves at once and without repining to the austere duties of their new condition, is no less manifest in all the great trials of their lives. In no country in the world are private fortunes more precarious than in the United States. It is not uncommon for the same man, in the course of his life, to rise and sink again through all the grades which lead from opulence to poverty. American women support these vicissitudes with calm and unquenchable energy: it would seem that their desires contract, as easily as they expand, with their fortunes.

The greater part of the adventurers who migrate every year to people the Western wilds, belong, as I observed in the former part of this work, to the old Anglo-American race of the Northern States. Many of these men, who rush so boldly onward in pursuit of wealth, were already in the enjoyment of a competency in their own part of the country. They take their wives along with them, and make them share the countless perils and privations which always attend the commencement of these expeditions. I have often met, even on the verge of the wilderness, with young women who, after having been brought up amid all the comforts of the large towns of New England, had passed, almost without any intermediate stage, from the wealthy abode of their parents to a comfortless hovel in a forest. Fever, solitude, and a tedious life had not broken the springs of their courage. Their features were impaired and faded, but their looks were firm : they appeared to be at once sad and resolute. I do not doubt that these young American women had amassed, in the education of their early years, that inward strength which they displayed under these circumstances. The early culture of the girl may still, therefore, be traced, in the United States, under the aspect of marriage : her part is changed, her habits are different, but her character is the same. . . . .

Although the travellers who have visited North America differ on a great number of points, they all agree in remarking that morals are far more strict there than elsewhere. It is evident that on this point the Americans are very superior to their progenitors the English. A superficial glance at the two nations will establish the fact. In England, as in all other countries of Europe, public malice is constantly attacking the frailties of women. Philosophers and statesmen are heard to deplore that morals are not sufficiently strict, and the literary productions of the country constantly lead one to suppose so. In America all books, novels not excepted, suppose women to be chaste, and no one thinks of relating affairs of gallantry. No doubt this great regularity of American morals originates partly in the country, in the race of the people, and in their religion : but all these causes, which operate elsewhere, do not suffice to account for it ; recourse must be had to some special reason. This reason appears to me to be the principle of equality and the institutions derived from it. Equality of conditions does not of itself engender regularity of morals, but it unquestionably facilitates and increases it.

Among aristocratic nations birth and fortune frequently make two such different beings of man and woman that they can never be united to each other. Their passions draw them together, but the condition of society, and the notions suggested by it, prevent them from contracting a permanent and ostensible tie. The necessary consequence is a great number of transient and clandestine connections. Nature secretly avenges herself for the constraint imposed upon her by the laws of man. This is not so much the case when the equality of conditions has swept away all the imaginary, or the real, barriers which separated man from woman. No girl then believes that she cannot become the wife of the man who loves her ; and this renders all breaches of morality before marriage very uncommon : for, whatever be the credulity of the passions, a woman will hardly be able to persuade herself that she is beloved when her lover is perfectly free to marry her and does not.

The same cause operates, though more indirectly, on married life. Nothing better serves to justify an illicit passion, either to the minds of those who have conceived it or to the world which looks on, than compulsory or accidental marriages. In a country in which a woman is always free to exercise her power of choosing, and in which education has prepared her to choose rightly, public opinion is inexorable to her faults. The rigour of the Americans arises in part from this cause. They consider marriage as a covenant which is often onerous, but every condition of which the parties are strictly bound to fulfil, because they knew all those conditions beforehand, and were perfectly free not to have contracted them.

The very circumstances which render matrimonial fidelity more obligatory also render it more easy. In aristocratic countries the object of marriage is rather to unite property than persons; hence the husband is sometimes at school and the wife at nurse when they are betrothed. It cannot be wondered at if the conjugal tie which holds the fortunes of the pair united allows their hearts to rove; this is the natural result of the nature of the contract. When, on the contrary, a man always chooses a wife for himself, without any external coercion or even guidance, it is generally a conformity of tastes and opinions which brings a man and a woman together, and this same conformity keeps and fixes them in close habits of intimacy.

Our forefathers had conceived a very strange notion on the subject of marriage: as they had remarked that the small number of love-matches which occurred in their time almost always turned out ill, they resolutely inferred that it was exceedingly dangerous to listen to the dictates of the heart on the subject. Accident appeared to them to be a better guide than choice. Yet it was not very difficult to perceive that the examples which they witnessed did, in fact, prove nothing at all. For, in the first place, if democratic nations leave a woman at liberty to choose her husband, they take care to give her mind sufficient knowledge, and her will sufficient strength, to make so important a choice: whereas the young women who, among aristocratic nations, furtively elope from the authority of their parents to throw themselves of their own accord into the arms of men whom they have had neither time to know, nor ability to judge of, are totally without those securities. It is not surprising that they make a bad use of their freedom of action the first time they avail themselves of it ; nor that they fall into such cruel mistakes, when, not having received a democratic education, they choose to marry in conformity to democratic customs. But this is not all. When a man and woman are bent upon marriage in spite of the differences of an aristocratic state of society, the difficulties to be overcome are enormous. Having broken or relaxed the bonds of filial obedience, they have then to emancipate themselves by a final effort from the sway of custom and the tyranny of opinion ; and when at length they have succeeded in this arduous task, they stand estranged from their natural friends and kinsmen : the prejudice they have crossed separates them from all, and places them in a situation which soon breaks their courage and sours their hearts. If, then, a couple married in this manner are first unhappy and afterward criminal, it ought not to be attributed to the freedom of their choice, but rather to their living in a community in which this freedom of choice is not admitted.

Moreover, it should not be forgotten that the same effort which makes a man violently shake off a prevailing error, commonly impels him beyond the bounds of reason ; that, to dare to declare war, in however just a cause, against the opinion of one's age and country, a violent and adventurous spirit is required, and that men of this character seldom arrive at happiness or virtue, whatever be the path they follow. And this, it may be observed by the way, is the reason why, in the most necessary and righteous revolutions, it is so rare to meet with virtuous or moderate revolutionary characters. There is, then, no just ground for surprise if a man, who in an age of aristocracy chooses to consult nothing but his own opinion and his own taste in the choice of a wife, soon finds that infractions of morality and domestic wretchedness invade his household : but when this same line of action is in the natural and ordinary course of things, when it is sanctioned by parental authority and backed by public opinion, it cannot be doubted that the internal peace of families will be increased by it, and conjugal fidelity more rigidly observed.

Almost all men in democracies are engaged in public or professional life ; and, on the other hand, the limited extent of common incomes obliges a wife to confine herself to the house, in order to watch in person and very closely over the details of domestic economy. All these distinct and compulsory occupations are so many natural barriers, which, by keeping the two sexes asunder, render the solicitations of the one less frequent and less ardent—the resistance of the other more easy.

Not, indeed, that the equality of conditions can ever succeed in making men chaste, but it may impart a less dangerous character to their breaches of morality. As no one has, then, either sufficient time or opportunity to assail a virtue armed in self-defence, there will be at the same time a great number of courtesans and a great number of virtuous women. This state of things causes lamentable cases of individual hardship, but it does not prevent the body of society from being strong and alert : it does not destroy family ties, or enervate the morals of the nation. Society is endangered not by the great profligacy of a few, but by laxity of morals among all. In the eyes of a legislator, prostitution is less to be dreaded than intrigue.

The tumultuous and constantly harassed life which equality makes men lead, not only distracts them from the passion of love, by denying them time to indulge in it, but it diverts them from it by another more secret but more certain road. All men who live in democratic ages more or less contract the ways of thinking of the manufacturing and trading classes; their minds take a serious, deliberate, and positive turn; they are apt to relinquish the ideal, in order to pursue some visible and proximate object, which appears to be the natural and necessary aim of their desires. Thus the principle of equality does not destroy the imagination, but lowers its flight to the level of the earth. No men are less addicted to reverie than the citizens of a democracy; and few of them are ever known to give way to those idle and solitary meditations which commonly precede and produce the great emotions of the heart. It is true they attach great importance to procuring for themselves that sort of deep, regular, and quiet affection which constitutes the charm and safeguard of life, but they are not apt to run after those violent and capricious sources of excitement which disturb and abridge it. . . .

I have shown how democracy destroys or modifies the different inequalities which originate in society; but is this all? or does it not ultimately affect that great inequality of man and woman which has seemed, up to the present day, to be eternally based in human nature? I believe that the social changes which bring nearer to the same level the father and son, the master and servant, and superiors and inferiors generally speaking, will raise woman and make her more and more the equal of man. But here, more than ever, I feel the necessity of making myself clearly understood; for there is no subject on which the coarse and lawless fancies of our age have taken a freer range.

There are people in Europe who, confounding together the different characteristics of the sexes, would make of man and woman beings not only equal but alike. They would give to both the same functions, impose on both the same duties, and grant to both the same rights; they would mix them in all things—their occupations, their pleasures, their business. It may readily be conceived that by thus attempting to make one sex equal to the other, both are degraded; and from so preposterous a medley of the works of Nature nothing could ever result but weak men and disorderly women.

It is not thus that the Americans understand that species of democratic equality which may be established between the sexes. They admit that as Nature has appointed such wide differences between the physical and moral constitution of man and woman, her manifest design was to give a distinct employment to their various faculties; and they hold that improvement does not consist in making beings so dissimilar do pretty nearly the same things, but in getting each of them to fulfil their respective tasks in the best possible manner. The Americans have applied to the sexes the great principle of political economy which governs the manufactures of our age, by carefully dividing the duties of man from those of woman, in order that the great work of society may be the better carried on.

In no country has such constant care been taken as in America to trace two clearly distinct lines of action for the two sexes, and to make them keep pace one with the other, but in two pathways which are always different. American women never manage the outward concerns of the family, or conduct a business, or take a part in political life; nor are they, on the other hand, ever compelled to perform the rough labour of the fields, or to make any of those laborious exertions which demand the exertion of physical strength. No families are so poor as to form an exception to this rule. If, on the one hand, an American woman cannot escape from the quiet circle of domestic employments, on the other hand she is never forced to go beyond it. Hence it is that the women of America, who often exhibit a masculine strength of understanding and a manly energy, generally preserve great delicacy of personal appearance and always retain the manners of women, although they sometimes show that they have the hearts and minds of men.

Nor have the Americans ever supposed that one consequence of democratic principles is the subversion of marital power, or the confusion of the natural authorities in families. They hold that every association must have a head in order to accomplish its object, and that the natural head of the conjugal association is man. They do not, therefore, deny him the right of directing his partner; and they maintain, that in the smaller association of husband and wife, as well as in the great social community, the object of democracy is to regulate and legalize the powers which are necessary, not to subvert all power. This opinion is not peculiar to one sex, and contested by the other: I never observed that the women of America consider conjugal authority as a fortunate usurpation of their rights, nor that they thought themselves degraded by submitting to it. It appeared to me, on the contrary, that they attach a sort of pride to the voluntary surrender of their own will, and make it their boast to bend themselves to the yoke, not to shake it off. Such at least is the feeling expressed by the most virtuous of their sex; the others are silent; and in the United States it is not the practice for a guilty wife to clamour for the rights of women, while she is trampling on her holiest duties.

It has often been remarked that in Europe a certain degree of contempt lurks even in the flattery which men lavish upon women: although a European frequently affects to be the slave of woman, it may be seen that he never sincerely thinks her his equal. In the United States men seldom compliment women, but they daily show how much they esteem them. They constantly display an entire confidence in the understanding of a wife, and a profound respect for her freedom; they have decided that her mind is just as fitted as that of a man to discover the plain truth, and her heart as firm to embrace it; and they have never sought to place her virtue, any more than his, under the shelter of prejudice, ignorance, and fear. It would seem that in Europe, where man so easily submits to the despotic sway of women, they are nevertheless curtailed of some of the greatest qualities of the human species, and considered as seductive but imperfect beings; and (what may well provoke astonishment) women ultimately look upon themselves in the same light, and almost consider it as a privilege that they are entitled to show themselves futile, feeble, and timid. The women of America claim no such privileges.

Again, it may be said that in our morals we have reserved strange immunities to man; so that there is, as it were, one virtue for his use, and another for the guidance of his partner; and that, according to the opinion of the public, the very same act may be punished alternately as a crime or only as a fault.

The Americans know not this iniquitous division of duties and rights ; among them the seducer is as much dishonoured as his victim. It is true that the Americans rarely lavish upon women those eager attentions which are commonly paid them in Europe ; but their conduct to women always implies that they suppose them to be virtuous and refined ; and such is the respect entertained for the moral freedom of the sex, that in the presence of a woman the most guarded language is used, lest her ear should be offended by an expression. In America a young unmarried woman may, alone and without fear, undertake a long journey.

The legislators of the United States, who have mitigated almost all the penalties of criminal law, still make rape a capital offence, and no crime is visited with more inexorable severity by public opinion. This may be accounted for ; as the Americans can conceive nothing more precious than a woman's honour, and nothing which ought so much to be respected as her independence, they hold that no punishment is too severe for the man who deprives her of them against her will. In France, where the same offence is visited with far milder penalties, it is frequently difficult to get a verdict from a jury against the prisoner. Is this a consequence of contempt of decency or contempt of women ? I cannot but believe that it is a contempt of one and of the other.

Thus the Americans do not think that man and woman have either the duty or the right to perform the same offices, but they show an equal regard for both their respective parts ; and though their lot is different, they consider both of them as being of equal value. They do not give to the courage of woman the same form or the same direction as to that of man ; but they never doubt her courage : and if they hold that man and his partner ought not always to exercise their intellect and understanding in the same manner, they at least believe the understanding of the one to be as sound as that of the other, and her intellect to be as clear. Thus, then, while they have allowed the social inferiority of woman to subsist, they have done all they could to raise her morally and intellectually to the level of man ; and in this respect they appear to me to have excellently understood the true principle of democratic improvement. As for myself, I do not hestitate to avow that, although the women of the United States are confined within the narrow circle of domestic life, and their situation is in some respects one of extreme dependence, I have nowhere seen woman occupying a loftier position ; and if I were asked, now that I am drawing to the close of this work, in which I have spoken of so many important things done by the Americans, to what the singular prosperity and growing strength of that people ought mainly to be attributed, I should reply —to the superiority of their women.

It may probably be supposed that the final consequence and necessary effect of democratic institutions is to confound together all the members of the community in private as well as in public life, and to compel them all to live in common ; but this would be to ascribe a very coarse and oppressive form to the equality which originates in democracy. No state of society or laws can render men so much alike, but that education, fortune, and tastes will interpose some differences between them ; and, though different men may sometimes find it to their interest to combine for the same purposes, they will never make it their pleasure. They will, therefore, always tend to evade the provisions of legislation, whatever they may be ; and departing in some one respect from the circle within which they were to be bounded, they will set up, close by the great political community, small private circles, united together by the similitude of their conditions, habits, and manners.

In the United States the citizens have no sort of pre-eminence over each other; they owe each other no mutual obedience or respect; they all meet for the administration of justice, for the government of the State, and in general to treat of the affairs which concern their common welfare; but I never heard that attempts have been made to bring them all to follow the same diversions, or to amuse themselves promiscuously in the same places of recreation. The Americans, who mingle so readily in their political assemblies and courts of justice, are wont, on the contrary, carefully to separate into small distinct circles, in order to indulge by themselves in the enjoyments of private life. Each of them is willing to acknowledge all his fellow-citizens as his equals, but he will only receive a very limited number of them among his friends or his guests. This appears to me to be very natural. In proportion as the circle of public society is extended, it may be anticipated that the sphere of private intercourse will be contracted; far from supposing that the members of modern society will ultimately live in common, I am afraid that they may end by forming nothing but small coteries.

Among aristocratic nations the different classes are like vast chambers, out of which it is impossible to get, into which it is impossible to enter. These classes have no communication with each other, but within their pale men necessarily live in daily contact; even though they would not naturally suit, the general conformity of a similar condition brings them nearer together. But when neither law nor custom professes to establish frequent and habitual relations between certain men, their intercourse originates in the accidental analogy of opinions and tastes; hence private society is infinitely varied. In democracies, where the members of the community never differ much from each other, and naturally stand in such propinquity that they may all at any time be confounded in one general mass, numerous artificial and arbitrary distinctions spring up, by means of which every man hopes to keep himself aloof, lest he should be carried away in the crowd against his will. This can never fail to be the case; for human institutions may be changed, but not man: whatever may be the general endeavour of a community to render its members equal and alike, the personal pride of individuals will always seek to rise above the line, and to form somewhere an inequality to their own advantage.

In aristocracies men are separated from each other by lofty stationary barriers; in democracies they are divided by a number of small and almost invisible threads, which are constantly broken or moved from place to place. Thus, whatever may be the progress of equality, in democratic nations a great number of small private communities will always be formed within the general pale of political society; but none of them will bear any resemblance in its manners to the highest class in aristocracies.

Nothing seems at first sight less important than the outward form of human actions, yet there is nothing upon which men set more store: they grow used to everything except to living in a society which has not their own manners. The influence of the social and political state of a country upon manners is therefore deserving of serious examination. Manners are, generally, the product of the very basis of the character of a people, but they are also sometimes the result of an arbitrary convention between certain men ; thus they are at once natural and acquired. When certain men perceive that they are the foremost persons in society, without contestation and without effort—when they are constantly engaged on large objects, leaving the more minute details to others—and when they live in the enjoyment of wealth which they did not amass and which they do not fear to lose, it may be supposed that they feel a kind of haughty disdain of the petty interests and practical cares of life, and that their thoughts assume a natural greatness, which their language and their manners denote.   In democratic countries manners are generally devoid of dignity, because private life is there extremely petty in its character ; and they are frequently low, because the mind has few opportunities of rising above the engrossing cares of domestic interests. True dignity in manners consists in always taking one's proper station, neither too high nor too low ; and this is as much within the reach of a peasant as of a prince.   In democracies all stations appear doubtful ; hence it is that the manners of democracies, though often full of arrogance, are commonly wanting in dignity, and, moreover, they are never either well disciplined or accomplished.

The men who live in democracies are too fluctuating for a certain number of them ever to succeed in laying down a code of good breeding, and in forcing people to follow it.   Every man, therefore, behaves after his own fashion, and there is always a certain incoherence in the manners of such times, because they are moulded upon the feelings and notions of each individual, rather than upon an ideal model proposed for general imitation.   This, however, is much more perceptible at the time when an aristocracy has just been overthrown than after it has long been destroyed. New political institutions and new social elements then bring to the same places of resort, and frequently compel to live in common, men whose education and habits are still amazingly dissimilar, and this renders the motley composition of society peculiarly visible. The existence of a former strict code of good breeding is still remembered, but what it contained or where it is to be found is already forgotten. Men have lost the common law of manners, and they have not yet made up their minds to do without it; but every one endeavours to make to himself some sort of arbitrary and variable rule, from the remnant of former usages; so that manners have neither the regularity and the dignity which they often display among aristocratic nations, nor the simplicity and freedom which they sometimes assume in democracies; they are at once constrained and without constraint.

This, however, is not the normal state of things. When the equality of conditions is long established and complete, as all men entertain nearly the same notions and do nearly the same things, they do not require to agree or to copy from one another in order to speak or act in the same manner: their manners are constantly characterized by a number of lesser diversities, but not by any great differences. They are never perfectly alike, because they do not copy from the same pattern; they are never very unlike, because their social condition is the same. At first sight a traveller would observe that the manners of all the Americans are exactly similar; it is only upon close examination that the peculiarities in which they differ may be detected.

The English make game of the manners of the Americans; but it is singular that most of the writers who have drawn these ludicrous delineations belonged themselves to the middle classes in England, to whom the same delineations are exceedingly applicable : so that these pitiless censors for the most part furnish an example of the very thing they blame in the United States ; they do not perceive that they are deriding themselves, to the great amusement of the aristocracy of their own country.

Nothing is more prejudicial to democracy than its outward forms of behaviour ; many men would willingly endure its vices, who cannot support its manners. I cannot, however, admit that there is nothing commendable in the manners of a democratic people. Among aristocratic nations, all who live within reach of the first class in society commonly strain to be like it, which gives rise to ridiculous and insipid imitations. As a democratic people does not possess any models of high breeding, at least it escapes the daily necessity of seeing wretched copies of them. In democracies manners are never so refined as among aristocratic nations, but, on the other hand, they are never so coarse. Neither the coarse oaths of the populace, nor the elegant and choice expressions of the nobility, are to be heard there : the manners of such a people are often vulgar, but they are neither brutal nor mean. I have already observed that in democracies no such thing as a regular code of good breeding can be laid down ; this has some inconveniences and some advantages. In aristocracies the rules of propriety impose the same demeanour on every one ; they make all the members of the same class appear alike, in spite of their private inclinations ; they adorn and they conceal the natural man. Among a democratic people manners are neither so tutored nor so uniform, but they are frequently more sincere. They form, as it were, a light and looselywoven veil, through which the real feelings and private opinions of each individual are easily discernible. The form and the substance of human actions often, therefore, stand in closer relation ; and if the great picture of human life be less embellished, it is more true. Thus it may be said, in one sense, that the effect of democracy is not exactly to give men any particular manners, but to prevent them from having manners at all.

The feelings, the passions, the virtues, and the vices of an aristocracy may sometimes reappear in a democracy, but not its manners ; they are lost, and vanish for ever, as soon as the democratic revolution is completed. It would seem that nothing is more lasting than the manners of an aristocratic class, for they are preserved by that class for some time after it has lost its wealth and its power—nor so fleeting, for no sooner have they disappeared than not a trace of them is to be found ; and it is scarcely possible to say what they have been as soon as they have ceased to be. A change in the state of society works this miracle, and a few generations suffice to consummate it. The principal characteristics of aristocracy are handed down by history after an aristocracy is destroyed, but the light and exquisite touches of manners are effaced from men's memories almost immediately after its fall. Men can no longer conceive what these manners were when they have ceased to witness them ; they are gone, and their departure was unseen, unfelt ; for in order to feel that refined enjoyment which is derived from choice and distinguished manners, habit and education must have prepared the heart, and the taste for them is lost almost as easily as the practice of them. Thus not only a democratic people cannot have aristocratic manners, but they neither comprehend nor desire them ; and as they never have thought of them, it is to their minds as if such things had never been. Too much importance should not be attached to this loss, but it may well be regretted.

I am aware that it has not infrequently happened that the same men have had very high-bred manners and very low-born feelings : the interior of courts has sufficiently shown what imposing externals may conceal the meanest hearts. But though the manners of aristocracy did not constitute virtue, they sometimes embellish virtue itself. It was no ordinary sight to see a numerous and powerful class of men, whose every outward action seemed constantly to be dictated by a natural elevation of thought and feeling, by delicacy and regularity of taste, and by urbanity of manners. Those manners threw a pleasing illusory charm over human nature ; and though the picture was often a false one, it could not be viewed without a noble satisfaction.

Chapter XXXI

INFLUENCE OF DEMOCRACY UPON PUBLIC RELATIONS

MEN who live in democratic countries do not value the simple, turbulent, or coarse diversions in which the people indulge in aristocratic communities : such diversions are thought by them to be puerile or insipid. Nor have they a greater inclination for the intellectual and refined amusements of the aristocratic classes. They want something productive and substantial in their pleasures; they want to mix actual fruition with their joy. In aristocratic communities the people readily give themselves up to bursts of tumultuous and boisterous gaiety, which shake off at once the recollection of their privations : the natives of democracies are not fond of being thus violently broken in upon, and they never lose sight of their own selves without regret. They prefer to these frivolous delights those more serious and silent amusements which are like business, and which do not drive business wholly from their minds. An American, instead of going in a leisure hour to dance merrily at some place of public resort, as the fellows of his calling continue to do throughout the greater part of Europe, shuts himself up at home to drink. He thus enjoys two pleasures : he can go on thinking of his business, and he can get drunk decently by his own fireside.

I thought that the English constituted the most serious nation on the face of the earth, but I have since seen the Americans and have changed my opinion. I do not mean to say that temperament has not a great deal to do with the character of the inhabitants of the United States, but I think that their political institutions are a still more influential cause. I believe the seriousness of the Americans arises partly from their pride. In democratic countries even poor men entertain a lofty notion of their personal importance : they look upon themselves with complacency, and are apt to suppose that others are looking at them too. With this disposition they watch their language and their actions with care, and do not lay themselves open so as to betray their deficiencies ; to preserve their dignity they think it necessary to retain their gravity.

But I detect another more deep-seated and powerful cause which instinctively produces among the Americans this astonishing gravity. Under a despotism communities give way at times to bursts of vehement joy; but they are generally gloomy and moody, because they are afraid. Under absolute monarchies tempered by the customs and manners of the country, their spirits are often cheerful and even, because as they have some freedom and a good deal of security, they are exempted from the most important cares of life ; but all free peoples are serious, because their minds are habitually absorbed by the contemplation of some dangerous or difficult purpose. This is more especially the case among those free nations which form democratic communities. Then there are in all classes a very large number of men constantly occupied with the serious affairs of the government ; and those whose thoughts are not engaged in the direction of the commonwealth are wholly engrossed by the acquisition of a private fortune. Among such a people a serious demeanour ceases to be peculiar to certain men, and becomes a habit of the nation.

We are told of small democracies in the days of antiquity, in which the citizens met upon the public places with garlands of roses, and spent almost all their time in dancing and theatrical amusements. I do not believe in such republics any more than in that of Plato ; or, if the things we read of really happened, I do not hesitate to affirm that these supposed democracies were composed of very different elements from ours, and that they had nothing in common with the latter except their name. But it must not be supposed that, in the midst of all their toils, the people who live in democracies think themselves to be pitied ; the contrary is remarked to be the case. No men are fonder of their own condition. Life would have no relish for them if they were delivered from the anxieties which harass them, and they show more attachment to their cares than aristocratic nations to their pleasures.

I am next led to inquire how it is that these same democratic nations, which are so serious, sometimes act in so inconsiderate a manner. The Americans, who almost always preserve a staid demeanour and a frigid air, nevertheless frequently allow themselves to be borne away, far beyond the bounds of reason, by a sudden passion or a hasty opinion, and they sometimes gravely commit strange absurdities. This contrast ought not to surprise us. There is one sort of ignorance which originates in extreme publicity. In despotic states men know not how to act, because they are told nothing ; in democratic nations they often act at random, because nothing is to be left untold. The former do not know—the latter forget ; and the chief features of each picture are lost to them in a bewilderment of details.

It is astonishing what imprudent language a public man may sometimes use in free countries, and especially in democratic states, without being compromised ; whereas in absolute monarchies a few words dropped by accident are enough to unmask him for ever, and ruin him without hope of redemption.

This is explained by what goes before. When a man speaks in the midst of a great crowd, many of his words are not heard, or are forthwith obliterated from the memories of those who hear them; but amid the silence of a mute and motionless throng the slightest whisper strikes the ear.

In democracies men are never stationary; a thousand chances waft them to and fro, and their life is always the sport of unforeseen or (so to speak) extemporaneous circumstances. Thus they are often obliged to do things which they have imperfectly learned, to say things they imperfectly understand, and to devote themselves to work for which they are unprepared by long apprenticeship. In aristocracies every man has one sole object which he unceasingly pursues, but among democratic nations the existence of man is more complex; the same mind will almost always embrace several objects at the same time, and these objects are frequently wholly foreign to each other: as it cannot know them all well, the mind is readily satisfied with imperfect notions of each.

When the inhabitant of democracies is not urged by his wants, he is so at least by his desires; for of all the possessions which he sees around him, none are wholly beyond his reach. He therefore does everything in a hurry, he is always satisfied with " pretty well," and never pauses more than an instant to consider what he has been doing. His curiosity is at once insatiable and cheaply satisfied; for he cares more to know a great deal quickly than to know anything well: he has no time and but little taste to search things to the bottom.

Thus, then, democratic peoples are grave, because their social and political condition constantly leads them to engage in serious occupations; and they act inconsiderately, because they give but little time and attention to each of these occupations. The habit of inattention must be considered as the greatest bane of the democratic character.

All free nations are vainglorious, but national pride is not displayed by all in the same manner. The Americans in their intercourse with strangers appear impatient of the smallest censure and insatiable of praise. The most slender eulogium is acceptable to them; the most exalted seldom contents them; they unceasingly harass you to extort praise, and if you resist their entreaties they fall to praising themselves. It would seem as if, doubting their own merit, they wished to have it constantly exhibited before their eyes. Their vanity is not only greedy, but restless and jealous; it will grant nothing, while it demands everything, but is ready to beg and to quarrel at the same time. If I say to an American that the country he lives in is a fine one, 'Ay,' he replies, 'there is not its fellow in the world.' If I applaud the freedom which its inhabitants enjoy, he answers, 'Freedom is a fine thing, but few nations are worthy to enjoy it.' If I remark the purity of morals which distinguishes the United States, 'I can imagine,' says he, 'that a stranger, who has been struck by the corruption of all other nations, is astonished at the difference.' At length I leave him to the contemplation of himself; but he returns to the charge, and does not desist till he has got me to repeat all I had just been saying. It is impossible to conceive a more troublesome or more garrulous patriotism; it wearies even those who are disposed to respect it.

Such is not the case with the English. An Englishman calmly enjoys the real or imaginary advantages which in his opinion his country possesses. If he grants nothing to other nations, neither does he solicit anything for his own. The censure of foreigners does not affect him, and their praise hardly flatters him; his position with regard to the rest of the world is one of disdainful and ignorant reserve: his pride requires no sustenance, it nourishes itself. It is remarkable that two nations, so recently sprung from the same stock, should be so opposite to one another in their manner of feeling and conversing.

In aristocratic countries the great possess immense privileges, upon which their pride rests, without seeking to rely upon the lesser advantages which accrue to them. As these privileges came to them by inheritance, they regard them in some sort as a portion of themselves, or at least as a natural right inherent in their own persons. They therefore entertain a calm sense of their superiority; they do not dream of vaunting privileges which every one perceives and no one contests, and these things are not sufficiently new to them to be made topics of conversation. They stand unmoved in their solitary greatness, well assured that they are seen of all the world without any effort to show themselves off, and that no one will attempt to drive them from that position. When an aristocracy carries on the public affairs, its national pride naturally assumes this reserved, indifferent, and haughty form, which is imitated by all the other classes of the nation.

When, on the contrary, social conditions differ but little, the slightest privileges are of some importance; as every man sees around himself a million of people enjoying precisely similar or analogous advantages, his pride becomes craving and jealous, he clings to mere trifles, and doggedly defends them. In democracies, as the conditions of life are very fluctuating, men have almost always recently acquired the advantages which they possess; the consequence is that they feel extreme pleasure in exhibiting them, to show others and convince themselves that they really enjoy them. As at any instant these same advantages may be lost, their possessors are constantly on the alert, and make a point of showing that they still retain them. Men living in democracies love their country just as they love themselves, and they transfer the habits of their private vanity to their vanity as a nation. The restless and insatiable vanity of a democratic people originates so entirely in the equality and precariousness of social conditions, that the members of the haughtiest nobility display the very same passion in those lesser portions of their existence in which there is anything fluctuating or contested. An aristocratic class always differs greatly from the other classes of the nation, by the extent and perpetuity of its privileges ; but it often happens that the only differences between the members who belong to it consist in small transient advantages, which may any day be lost or acquired. . . .

It would seem that nothing can be more adapted to stimulate and to feed curiosity than the aspect of the United States. Fortunes, opinions, and laws are there in ceaseless variation : it is as if immutable Nature herself were mutable, such are the changes worked upon her by the hand of man. Yet in the end the sight of this excited community becomes monotonous, and after having watched the moving pageant for a time the spectator is tired of it. Among aristocratic nations every man is pretty nearly stationary in his own sphere ; but men are astonishingly unlike each other—their passions, their notions, their habits, and their tastes are essentially different : nothing changes, but everything differs. In democracies, on the contrary, all men are alike and do things pretty nearly alike. It is true that they are subject to great and frequent vicissitudes ; but as the same events of good or adverse fortune are continually recurring, the name of the actors only is changed, the piece is always the same. The aspect of American society is animated, because men and things are always changing; but it is monotonous, because all these changes are alike.

Men living in democratic ages have many passions, but most of their passions either end in the love of riches or proceed from it. The cause of this is, not that their souls are narrower, but that the importance of money is really greater at such times. When all the members of a community are independent of or indifferent to each other, the co-operation of each of them can only be obtained by paying for it: this infinitely multiplies the purposes to which wealth may be applied, and increases its value. When the reverence that belonged to what is old has vanished, birth, condition, and profession no longer distinguish men, or scarcely distinguish them at all: hardly anything remains but money to create strongly marked differences between them, and to raise some of them above the common level. The distinction originating in wealth is increased by the disappearance and diminution of all other distinctions. Among aristocratic nations money only reaches to a few points on the vast circle of man's desires—in democracies it seems to lead to all. The love of wealth is therefore to be traced, either as a principal or an accessory motive, at the bottom of all that the Americans do: this gives to all their passions a sort of family likeness, and soon renders the survey of them exceedingly wearisome. This perpetual recurrence of the same passion is monotonous; the peculiar methods by which this passion seeks its own gratification are no less so.

In an orderly and constituted democracy like the United States, where men cannot enrich themselves by war, by public office, or by political confiscation, the love of wealth mainly drives them into business and manufactures. Although these pursuits often bring about great commotions and disasters, they cannot prosper without strictly regular habits and a long routine of petty uniform acts. The stronger the passion is, the more regular are these habits, and the more uniform are these acts. It may be said that it is the vehemence of their desires which makes the Americans so methodical; it perturbs their minds, but it disciplines their lives. . . .

It would seem that men employ two very distinct methods in the public estimation of the actions of their fellow-men; at one time they judge them by those simple notions of right and wrong which are diffused all over the world; at another they refer their decision to a few very special notions which belong exclusively to some particular age and country. It often happens that these two rules differ; they sometimes conflict: but they are never either entirely identified or entirely annulled by one another. Honour, at the periods of its greatest power, sways the will more than the belief of men; and even while they yield without hesitation and without a murmur to its dictates, they feel notwithstanding, by a dim but mighty instinct, the existence of a more general, more ancient, and more holy law, which they sometimes disobey although they cease not to acknowledge it. Some actions have been held to be at the same time virtuous and dishonourable—a refusal to fight a duel is a case in point. . . .

Honour is simply that peculiar rule, founded upon a peculiar state of society, by the application of which a people or a class allot praise or blame. . . .

Whenever men collect together as a distinct community, the notion of honour instantly grows up among them; that is to say, a system of opinions peculiar to themselves as to what is blameable or commendable; and these peculiar rules always originate in the special habits and special interests of the community. This is applicable to a certain extent to democratic communities as well as to others, as we shall now proceed to prove by the example of the Americans. Some loose notions of the old aristocratic honour of Europe are still to be found scattered among the opinions of the Americans; but these traditional opinions are few in number, they have but little root in the country, and but little power. They are like a religion which has still some temples left standing, though men have ceased to believe in it. But amid these half-obliterated notions of exotic honour some new opinions have sprung up, which constitute what may be termed in our days American honour. I have shown how the Americans are constantly driven to engage in commerce and industry. Their origin, their social condition, their political institutions, and even the spot they inhabit, urge them irresistibly in this direction. Their present condition is, then, that of an almost exclusively manufacturing and commercial association, placed in the midst of a new and boundless country, which their principal object is to explore for purposes of profit. This is the characteristic which most peculiarly distinguishes the American people from all others at the present time. All those quiet virtues which tend to give a regular movement to the community, and to encourage business, will therefore be held in peculiar honour by that people, and to neglect those virtues will be to incur public contempt. All the more turbulent virtues, which often dazzle, but more frequently disturb society, will on the contrary occupy a subordinate rank in the estimation of this same people: they may be neglected without forfeiting the esteem of the community—to acquire them would perhaps be to run a risk of losing it.

The Americans make a no less arbitrary classification of men's vices. There are certain propensities which appear censurable to the general reason and the universal conscience of mankind, but which happen to agree with the peculiar and temporary wants of the American community : these propensities are lightly reproved, sometimes even encouraged ; for instance, the love of wealth and the secondary propensities connected with it may be more particularly cited. To clear, to till, and to transform the vast uninhabitable continent which is his domain, the American requires the daily support of an energetic passion ; that passion can only be the love of wealth ; the passion for wealth is therefore not reprobated in America, and, provided it does not go beyond the bounds assigned to it for public security, it is held in honour. The American lauds as a noble and praiseworthy ambition what our own forefathers in the Middle Ages stigmatized as servile cupidity, just as he treats as a blind and barbarous frenzy that ardour of conquest and martial temper which bore them to battle. In the United States fortunes are lost and regained without difficulty ; the country is boundless, and its resources inexhaustible. The people have all the wants and cravings of a growing creature ; and whatever be their efforts, they are always surrounded by more than they can appropriate. It is not the ruin of a few individuals which may be soon repaired, but the inactivity and sloth of the community at large which would be fatal to such a people. Boldness of enterprise is the foremost cause of its rapid progress, its strength, and its greatness. Commercial business is there like a vast lottery, by which a small number of men continually lose, but the State is always a gainer; such a people ought, therefore, to encourage and do honour to boldness in commercial specula- tions. But any bold speculation risks the fortune of the speculator and of all those who put their trust in him. The Americans, who make a virtue of com- mercial temerity, have no right in any case to brand with disgrace those who practise it. Hence arises the strange indulgence which is shown to bankrupts in the United States; their honour does not suffer by such an accident. In this respect the Americans differ, not only from the nations of Europe, but from all the commercial nations of our time, and accord- ingly they resemble none of them in their position or their wants.

In America all those vices which tend to impair the purity of morals, and to destroy the conjugal tie, are treated with a degree of severity which is unknown in the rest of the world. At first sight this seems strangely at variance with the tolerance shown there on other subjects, and one is surprised to meet with a morality so relaxed and so austere among the selfsame people. But these things are less incoherent than they seem to be. Public opinion in the United States very gently represses that love of wealth which promotes the com- mercial greatness and the prosperity of the nation, and it especially condemns that laxity of morals which diverts the human mind from the pursuit of well- being, and disturbs the internal order of domestic life which is so necessary to success in business. To earn the esteem of their countrymen, the Americans are therefore constrained to adapt themselves to orderly habits—and it may be said in this sense that they make it a matter of honour to live chastely.

On one point American honour accords with the notions of honour acknowledged in Europe; it places courage as the highest virtue, and treats it as the greatest of the moral necessities of man; but the notion of courage itself assumes a different aspect. In the United States martial valour is but little prized; the courage which is best known and most esteemed is that which emboldens men to brave the dangers of the ocean, in order to arrive earlier in port —to support the privations of the wilderness without complaint, and solitude more cruel than privations —the courage which renders them almost insensible to the loss of a fortune laboriously acquired, and instantly prompts to fresh exertions to make another. Courage of this kind is peculiarly necessary to the maintenance and prosperity of the American communities, and it is held by them in peculiar honour and estimation; to betray a want of it is to incur certain disgrace.

I have yet another characteristic point which may serve to place the idea of this chapter in stronger relief. In a democratic society like that of the United States, where fortunes are scanty and insecure, everybody works, and work opens a way to everything: this has changed the point of honour quite round, and has turned it against idleness. I have sometimes met in America with young men of wealth, personally disinclined to all laborious exertion, but who had been compelled to embrace a profession. Their disposition and their fortune allowed them to remain without employment; public opinion forbade it, too imperiously to be disobeyed. In the European countries, on the contrary, where aristocracy is still struggling with the flood which overwhelms it, I have often seen men, constantly spurred on by their wants and desires, remain in idleness, in order not to lose the esteem of their equals; and I have known them to submit to ennui and privation rather than to work. No one can fail to perceive that these opposite obligations are two different rules of conduct, both nevertheless originating in the notion of honour.

What our forefathers designated as honour absolutely was in reality only one of its forms; they gave a generic name to what was only a species. Honour, therefore, is to be found in democratic as well as in aristocratic ages, but it will not be difficult to show that it assumes a different aspect in the former. Not only are its injunctions different, but we shall shortly see that they are less numerous, less precise, and that its dictates are less rigorously obeyed. The position of a caste is always much more peculiar than that of a people. Nothing is so much out of the way of the world as a small community invariably composed of the same families (as was, for instance, the aristocracy of the Middle Ages), whose object is to concentrate and to retain, exclusively and hereditarily, education, wealth, and power among its own members. But the more out of the way the position of a community happens to be, the more numerous are its special wants, and the more extensive are its notions of honour corresponding to those wants. The rules of honour will therefore always be less numerous among a people not divided into castes than among any other. If ever any nations are constituted in which it may even be difficult to find any peculiar classes of society, the notion of honour will be confined to a small number of precepts, which will be more and more in accordance with the moral laws adopted by the mass of mankind. Thus the laws of honour will be less peculiar and less multifarious among a democratic people than in an aristocracy. They will also be more obscure; and this is a necessary consequence of what goes before; for as the distinguishing marks of honour are less numerous and less peculiar, it must often be difficult to distinguish them. To this other reasons may be added. Among the aristocratic nations of the Middle Ages, generation succeeded generation in vain ; each family was like a never-dying, ever-stationary man, and the state of opinions was hardly more changeable than that of conditions. Every one of them had always the same objects before his eyes, which he contemplated from the same point ; his eyes gradually detected the smallest details, and his discernment could not fail to become in the end clear and accurate. Thus not only had the men of feudal times very extraordinary opinions in matters of honour, but each of those opinions was present to their minds under a clear and precise form.

This can never be the case in America, where all men are in constant motion ; and where society, transformed daily by its own operations, changes its opinions together with its wants. In such a country men have glimpses of the rules of honour, but they have seldom time to fix attention upon them.

But even if society were motionless, it would still be difficult to determine the meaning which ought to be attached to the word honour. In the Middle Ages, as each class had its own honour, the same opinions were never received at the same time by a large number of men ; and this rendered it possible to give it a deter- mined and accurate form, which was the more easy, as all those by whom it was received, having a per- fectly identical and most peculiar position, were naturally disposed to agree upon the points of a law which was made for themselves alone. Thus the code of honour became a complete and detailed system, in which everything was anticipated and provided for beforehand, and a fixed and always palpable standard was applied to human actions. Among a democratic nation, like the Americans, in which ranks are identified, and the whole of society forms one single mass, composed of elements which are all analogous though not entirely similar, it is impossible ever to agree beforehand on what shall or shall not be allowed by the laws of honour. Among that people, indeed, some national wants do exist which give rise to opinions common to the whole nation on points of honour; but these opinions never occur at the same time, in the same manner, or with the same intensity to the minds of the whole community; the law of honour exists, but it has no organs to promulgate it.

The confusion is far greater still in a democratic country like France, where the different classes of which the former fabric of society was composed, being brought together but not yet mingled, import day by day into each other's circles various and sometimes conflicting notions of honour—where every man, at his own will and pleasure, forsakes one portion of his forefathers' creed, and retains another; so that, amid so many arbitrary measures, no common rule can ever be established, and it is almost impossible to predict which actions will be held in honour and which will be thought disgraceful. Such times are wretched, but they are of short duration.

As honour, among democratic nations, is imperfectly defined, its influence is of course less powerful; for it is difficult to apply with certainty and firmness a law which is not distinctly known. Public opinion, the natural and supreme interpreter of the laws of honour, not clearly discerning to which side censure or approval ought to lean, can only pronounce a hesitating judgment. Sometimes the opinion of the public may contradict itself; more frequently it does not act, and lets things pass.

The weakness of the sense of honour in democracies

also arises from several other causes. In aristocratic countries, the same notions of honour are always entertained by only a few persons, always limited in number, often separated from the rest of their fellow-citizens. Honour is easily mingled and identified in their minds with the idea of all that distinguishes their own position; it appears to them as the chief characteristic of their own rank; they apply its different rules with all the warmth of personal interest, and they feel (if I may use the expression) a passion for complying with its dictates. This truth is extremely obvious in the old black-letter law books on the subject of trial by battle. The nobles, in their disputes, were bound to use the lance and sword; whereas the villains used only sticks among themselves 'inasmuch as', to use the words of the old books, 'villains have no honour'. This did not mean, as it may be imagined at the present day, that these people were contemptible; but simply that their actions were not to be judged by the same rules which were applied to the actions of the aristocracy.

It is surprising, at first sight, that when the sense of honour is most predominant, its injunctions are usually most strange; so that the further it is removed from common reason the better it is obeyed; whence it has sometimes been inferred that the laws of honour were strengthened by their own extravagance. The two things, indeed, originate from the same source, but the one is not derived from the other. Honour becomes fantastical in proportion to the peculiarity of the wants which it denotes, and the paucity of the men by whom those wants are felt; and it is because it denotes wants of this kind that its influence is great. Thus the notion of honour is not the stronger for being fantastical, but it is fantastical and strong from the selfsame cause.

Further, among aristocratic nations each rank is different, but all ranks are fixed; every man occupies a place in his own sphere which he cannot relinquish, and he lives there amid other men who are bound by the same ties. Among these nations no man can either hope or fear to escape being seen; no man is placed so low but that he has a stage of his own, and none can avoid censure or applause by his obscurity. In democratic states, on the contrary, where all the members of the community are mingled in the same crowd and in constant agitation, public opinion has no hold on men; they disappear at every instant, and elude its power. Consequently the dictates of honour will be there less imperious and less stringent; for honour acts solely for the public eye—differing in this respect from mere virtue, which lives upon itself contented with its own approval. . . .

When ranks are commingled and privileges abolished, the men of whom a nation is composed being once more equal and alike, their interests and wants become identical, and all the peculiar notions which each caste styled honour successively disappear: the notion of honour no longer proceeds from any other source than the wants peculiar to the nation at large, and it denotes the individual character of that nation to the world. Lastly, if it be allowable to suppose that all the races of mankind should be commingled, and that all the peoples of earth should ultimately come to have the same interests, the same wants, undistinguished from each other by any characteristic peculiarities, no conventional value whatever would then be attached to men's actions; they would all be regarded by all in the same light; the general necessities of mankind, revealed by conscience to every man, would become the common standard. The simple and general notions of right and wrong only would then be recognized in the world, to which, by a natural and necessary tie, the idea of censure or approbation would be attached. Thus, to comprise all my meaning in a single proposition, the dissimilarities and inequalities of men gave rise to the notion of honour ; that notion is weakened in proportion as these differences are obliterated, and with them it would disappear.

The first thing which strikes a traveller in the United States is the innumerable multitude of those who seek to throw off their original condition ; and the second is the rarity of lofty ambition to be observed in the midst of the universally ambitious stir of society. No Americans are devoid of a yearning desire to rise ; but hardly any appear to entertain hopes of great magnitude, or to drive at very lofty aims. All are constantly seeking to acquire property, power, and reputation—few contemplate these things upon a great scale ; and this is the more surprising, as nothing is to be discerned in the manners or laws of America to limit desire, or to prevent it from spreading its impulses in every direction. It seems difficult to attribute this singular state of things to the equality of social conditions ; for at the instant when that same equality was established in France, the flight of ambition became unbounded. Nevertheless, I think that the principal cause which may be assigned to this fact is to be found in the social condition and democratic manners of the Americans. . . .

If ambition becomes great while the conditions of society are growing equal, it loses that quality when they have grown so. As wealth is subdivided and knowledge diffused, no one is entirely destitute of education or of property ; the privileges and disqualifications of caste being abolished, and men having shattered the bonds which held them fixed, the notion of advancement suggests itself to every mind, the desire to rise swells in every heart, and all men want to mount above their station: ambition is the universal feeling.

But if the equality of conditions gives some resources to all the members of the community, it also prevents any of them from having resources of great extent, which necessarily circumscribes their desires within somewhat narrow limits. Thus among democratic nations ambition is ardent and continual, but its aim is not habitually lofty; and life is generally spent in eagerly coveting small objects which are within reach. What chiefly diverts the men of democracies from lofty ambition is not the scantiness of their fortunes, but the vehemence of the exertions they daily make to improve them. They strain their faculties to the utmost to achieve paltry results, and this cannot fail speedily to limit their discernment and to circumscribe their powers. They might be much poorer and still be greater. The small number of opulent citizens who are to be found amid a democracy do not constitute an exception to this rule. A man who raises himself by degrees to wealth and power, contracts, in the course of this protracted labour, habits of prudence and restraint which he cannot afterward shake off. A man cannot enlarge his mind as he would his house. The same observation is applicable to the sons of such a man; they are born, it is true, in a lofty position, but their parents were humble; they have grown up amid feelings and notions which they cannot afterward easily get rid of; and it may be presumed that they will inherit the propensities of their father as well as his wealth. It may happen, on the contrary, that the poorest scion of a powerful aristocracy may display vast ambition, because the traditional opinions of his race and the general spirit of his order still buoy him up for some time above his fortune.

Another thing which prevents the men of democratic periods from easily indulging in the pursuit of lofty objects is the lapse of time which they foresee must take place before they can be ready to approach them. " It is a great advantage," says Pascal, " to be a man of quality, since it brings one man as forward at eighteen or twenty as another man would be at fifty, which is a clear gain of thirty years." Those thirty years are commonly wanting to the ambitious characters of democracies. The principle of equality, which allows every man to arrive at everything, prevents all men from rapid advancement.

In a democratic society, as well as elsewhere, there are only a certain number of great fortunes to be made; and as the paths which lead to them are indiscriminately open to all, the progress of all must necessarily be slackened. As the candidates appear to be nearly alike, and as it is difficult to make a selection without infringing the principle of equality, which is the supreme law of democratic societies, the first idea which suggests itself is to make them all advance at the same rate and submit to the same probation. Thus in proportion as men become more alike, and the principle of equality is more peaceably and deeply infused into the institutions and manners of the country, the rules of advancement become more inflexible, advancement itself slower, the difficulty of arriving quickly at a certain height far greater. From hatred of privilege and from the embarrassment of choosing, all men are at last constrained, whatever may be their standard, to pass the same ordeal; all are indiscriminately subjected to a multitude of petty preliminary exercises, in which their youth is wasted and their imagination quenched, so that they despair

of ever fully attaining what is held out to them; and
when at length they are in a condition to perform any
extraordinary acts, the taste for such things has
forsaken them.

In China, where the equality of conditions is
exceedingly great and very ancient, no man passes
from one public office to another without undergoing
a probationary trial. This probation occurs afresh at
every stage of his career; and the notion is now so
rooted in the manners of the people that I remember
to have read a Chinese novel in which the hero, after
numberless crosses, succeeds at length in touching the
heart of his mistress by taking honours. A lofty
ambition breathes with difficulty in such an atmosphere.

The remark I apply to politics extends to everything; equality everywhere produces the same effects;
where the laws of a country do not regulate and retard
the advancement of men by positive enactment,
competition attains the same end. In a well-established democratic community great and rapid elevation is therefore rare; it forms an exception to the
common rule; and it is the singularity of such occurrences that makes men forget how rarely they happen.
Men living in democracies ultimately discover these
things; they find out at last that the laws of their
country open a boundless field of action before them,
but that no one can hope to hasten across it. Between
them and the final object of their desires, they perceive a multitude of small intermediate impediments,
which must be slowly surmounted: this prospect
wearies and discourages their ambition at once. They
therefore give up hopes so doubtful and remote, to
search nearer to themselves for less lofty and more easy
enjoyments. Their horizon is not bounded by the
laws but narrowed by themselves.

I have remarked that lofty ambitions are more rare in the ages of democracy than in times of aristocracy : I may add that when, in spite of these natural obstacles, they do spring into existence, their character is different. In aristocracies the career of ambition is often wide, but its boundaries are determined. In democracies ambition commonly ranges in a narrower field, but if once it gets beyond that, hardly any limits can be assigned to it. As men are individually weak—as they live asunder, and in constant motion—as precedents are of little authority and laws but of short duration, resistance to novelty is languid, and the fabric of society never appears perfectly erect or firmly consolidated. So that, when once an ambitious man has the power in his grasp, there is nothing he may not dare ; and when it is gone from him, he meditates the overthrow of the State to regain it. This gives to great political ambition a character of revolutionary violence, which it seldom exhibits to an equal degree in aristocratic communities. The common aspect of democratic nations will present a great number of small and very rational objects of ambition, from among which a few ill-controlled desires of a larger growth will at intervals break out : but no such a thing as ambition conceived and contrived on a vast scale is to be met with there.

I have shown elsewhere by what secret influence the principle of equality makes the passion for physical gratifications and the exclusive love of the present predominate in the human heart : these different propensities mingle with the sentiment of ambition, and tinge it, as it were, with their hues. I believe that ambitious men in democracies are less engrossed than any others with the interests and the judgement of posterity ; the present moment alone engages and absorbs them. They are more apt to complete a number of undertakings with rapidity than to raise lasting monuments of their achievements; and they care much more for success than for fame. What they most ask of men is obedience—what they most covet is empire. Their manners have in almost all cases remained below the height of their station; the consequence is that they frequently carry very low tastes into their extraordinary fortunes, and that they seem to have acquired the supreme power only to minister to their coarse or paltry pleasures.

I think that in our time it is very necessary to cleanse, to regulate, and to adapt the feeling of ambition, but that it would be extremely dangerous to seek to impoverish and to repress it over-much. We should attempt to lay down certain extreme limits, which it should never be allowed to outstep; but its range within those established limits should not be too much checked. I confess that I apprehend much less for democratic society from the boldness than from the mediocrity of desires. What appears to me most to be dreaded is that, in the midst of the small incessant occupations of private life, ambition should lose its vigour and its greatness—that the passions of man should abate, but at the same time be lowered, so that the march of society should every day become more tranquil and less aspiring. I think then that the leaders of modern society would be wrong to seek to lull the community by a state of too uniform and too peaceful happiness; and that it is well to expose it from time to time to matters of difficulty and danger, in order to raise ambition and to give it a field of action. Moralists are constantly complaining that the ruling vice of the present time is pride. This is true in one sense, for indeed no one thinks that he is not better than his neighbour, or consents to obey his superior; but it is extremely false in another; for the same man who cannot endure subordination or equality has so contemptible an opinion of himself that he thinks he is only born to indulge in vulgar pleasures. He willingly takes up with low desires, without daring to embark in lofty enterprises, of which he scarcely dreams. Thus, far from thinking that humility ought to be preached to our contemporaries, I would have endeavours made to give them a more enlarged idea of themselves and of their kind. Humility is unwholesome to them; what they most want is, in my opinion, pride. I would willingly exchange several of our small virtues for this one vice.

In the United States as soon as a man has acquired some education and pecuniary resources, he either endeavours to get rich by commerce or industry, or he buys land in the bush and turns pioneer. All that he asks of the State is not to be disturbed in his toil, and to be secure of his earnings. Among the greater part of European nations, when a man begins to feel his strength and to extend his desires, the first thing that occurs to him is to get some public employment. These opposite effects, originating in the same cause, deserve our passing notice.

When public employments are few in number, ill-paid and precarious, while the different lines of business are numerous and lucrative, it is to business, and not to official duties, that the new and eager desires engendered by the principle of equality turn from every side. But if, while the ranks of society are becoming more equal, the education of the people remains incomplete, or their spirit the reverse of bold —if commerce and industry, checked in their growth, afford only slow and arduous means of making a fortune—the various members of the community, despairing of ameliorating their own condition, rush to the head of the State and demand its assistance. To relieve their own necessities at the cost of the public treasury appears to them to be the easiest and most open, if not the only, way they have to rise above a condition which no longer contents them ; place-hunting becomes the most generally followed of all trades. This must especially be the case in those great centralized monarchies in which the number of paid offices is immense, and the tenure of them toler-ably secure, so that no one despairs of obtaining a place, and of enjoying it as undisturbedly as an hereditary fortune. . . .

Among democratic nations, as well as elsewhere, the number of official appointments has in the end some limits ; but among those nations, the number of aspirants is unlimited ; it perpetually increases, with a gradual and irresistible rise in proportion as social conditions become more equal, and is only checked by the limits of the population. Thus, when public employments afford the only outlet for ambition, the government necessarily meets with a permanent opposition at last ; for it is tasked to satisfy with limited means unlimited desires. It is very certain that of all people in the world the most difficult to restrain and to manage are a people of solicitants. Whatever endeavours are made by rulers, such a people can never be contented ; and it is always to be apprehended that they will ultimately overturn the constitution of the country, and change the aspect of the State, for the sole purpose of making a clearance of places. The sovereigns of the present age, who strive to fix upon themselves alone all those novel desires which are aroused by equality, and to satisfy them, will repent in the end, if I am not mistaken, that they ever embarked in this policy : they will one day discover that they have hazarded their own power, by making it so necessary ; and that the more safe and honest course would have been to teach their subjects the art of providing for themselves.

Chapter XXXII

REVOLUTIONS AMONG DEMOCRATIC PEOPLES

A PEOPLE which has existed for centuries under a system of castes and classes can only arrive at a democratic state of society by passing through a long series of more or less critical transformations, accomplished by violent efforts, and after numerous vicissitudes; in the course of which, property, opinions, and power are rapidly transferred from one hand to another. Even after this great revolution is consummated, the revolutionary habits engendered by it may long be traced, and it will be followed by deep commotion. As all this takes place at the very time at which social conditions are becoming more equal, it is inferred that some concealed relation and secret tie exists between the principle of equality itself and revolution, insomuch that the one cannot exist without giving rise to the other.

On this point reasoning may seem to lead to the same result as experience. Among a people whose ranks are nearly equal, no ostensible bond connects men together, or keeps them settled in their station. None of them have either a permanent right or power to command—none are forced by their condition to obey; but every man, finding himself possessed of some education and some resources, may choose his own path and proceed apart from all his fellow-men. The same causes which make the members of the community independent of each other, continually impel them to new and restless desires, and constantly spur them onward. It therefore seems natural that, in a democratic community, men, things, and opinions should be for ever changing their form and place, and that democratic ages should be times of rapid and incessant transformation.

But is this really the case? does the equality of social conditions habitually and permanently lead men to revolution? does that state of society contain some perturbing principle which prevents the community from ever subsiding into calm, and disposes the citizens to alter incessantly their laws, their principles, and their manners? I do not believe it; and as the subject is important, I beg for the reader's close attention. Almost all the revolutions which have changed the aspect of nations have been made to consolidate or to destroy social inequality. Remove the secondary causes which have produced the great convulsions of the world, and you will almost always find the principle of inequality at the bottom. Either the poor have attempted to plunder the rich, or the rich to enslave the poor. If, then, a state of society can ever be founded in which every man shall have something to keep, and little to take from others, much will have been done for the peace of the world. I am aware that among a great democratic people there will always be some members of the community in great poverty, and others in great opulence; but the poor, instead of forming the immense majority of the nation, as is always the case in aristocratic communities, are comparatively few in number, and the laws do not bind them together by the ties of irremediable and hereditary penury. The wealthy, on their side, are scarce and powerless; they have no privileges which attract public observation; even their wealth, as it is no longer incorporated and bound up with the soil, is impalpable, and as it were invisible. As there is no longer a race of poor men, so there is no longer a race of rich men; the latter spring up daily from the multitude, and relapse into it again. Hence they do not form a distinct class, which may be easily marked out and plundered; and, moreover, as they are connected with the mass of their fellow-citizens by a thousand secret ties, the people cannot assail them without inflicting an injury upon itself. Between these two extremes of democratic communities stands an innumerable multitude of men almost alike, who, without being exactly either rich or poor, are possessed of sufficient property to desire the maintenance of order, yet not enough to excite envy. Such men are the natural enemies of violent commotions : their stillness keeps all beneath them and above them still, and secures the balance of the fabric of society. Not, indeed, that even these men are contented with what they have got, or that they feel a natural abhorrence for a revolution in which they might share the spoil without sharing the calamity ; on the contrary, they desire, with unexampled ardour, to get rich, but the difficulty is to know from whom riches can be taken. The same state of society which constantly prompts desires, restrains these desires within necessary limits : it gives men more liberty of changing and less interest in change.

Not only are the men of democracies not naturally desirous of revolutions, but they are afraid of them. All revolutions more or less threaten the tenure of property : but most of those who live in democratic countries are possessed of property—not only are they possessed of property, but they live in the condition of men who set the greatest store upon their property. If we attentively consider each of the classes of which society is composed, it is easy to see that the passions engendered by property are keenest and most tenacious among the middle classes. The poor often care but little for what they possess, because they suffer much more from the want of what they have not than they enjoy the little they have. The rich have many other passions besides that of riches to satisfy; and, besides, the long and arduous enjoyment of a great fortune sometimes makes them in the end insensible to its charms. But the men who have a competency, alike removed from opulence and from penury, attach an enormous value to their possessions. As they are still almost within the reach of poverty, they see its privations near at hand, and dread them; between poverty and themselves there is nothing but a scanty fortune, upon which they immediately fix their apprehensions and their hopes. Every day increases the interest they take in it, by the constant cares which it occasions; and they are the more attached to it by their continual exertions to increase the amount. The notion of surrendering the smallest part of it is insupportable to them, and they consider its total loss as the worst of misfortunes. Now these eager and apprehensive men of small property constitute the class which is constantly increased by the equality of conditions. Hence, in democratic communities, the majority of the people do not clearly see what they have to gain by a revolution, but they continually and in a thousand ways feel that they might lose by one.

I have shown in another part of this work that the equality of conditions naturally urges men to embark in commercial and industrial pursuits, and that it tends to increase and to distribute real property: I have also pointed out the means by which it inspires every man with an eager and constant desire to increase his welfare. Nothing is more opposed to revolutionary passions than these things. It may happen that the final result of a revolution is favourable to commerce and manufactures; but its first consequence will almost always be the ruin of manufactures and mercantile men, because it must always change at once the general principles of consumption, and temporarily upset the existing proportion between supply and demand. I know of nothing more opposite to revolutionary manners than commercial manners. Commerce is naturally adverse to all the violent passions; it loves to temporize, takes delight in compromise, and studiously avoids irritation. It is patient, insinuating, flexible, and never has recourse to extreme measures until obliged by the most absolute necessity. Commerce renders men independent of each other, gives them a lofty notion of their personal importance, leads them to seek to conduct their own affairs, and teaches how to conduct them well; it therefore prepares men for freedom, but preserves them from revolutions. In a revolution the owners of personal property have more to fear than all others; for on the one hand their property is often easy to seize, and on the other it may totally disappear at any moment—a subject of alarm to which the owners of real property are less exposed, since, although they may lose the income of their estates, they may hope to preserve the land itself through the greatest vicissitudes. Hence the former are much more alarmed at the symptoms of revolutionary commotion than the latter. Thus nations are less disposed to make revolutions in proportion as personal property is augmented and distributed among them, and as the number of those possessing it increases. Moreover, whatever profession men may embrace, and whatever species of property they may possess, one characteristic is common to them all. No one is fully contented with his present fortune—all are perpetually striving in a thousand ways to improve it. Consider any one of them at any period of his life, and he will be found engaged with some new project for the purpose of increasing what he has; talk not to him of the interests and the rights of mankind, this small domestic concern absorbs for the time all his thoughts, and inclines him to defer political excitement to some other season. This not only prevents men from making revolutions, but deters men from desiring them. Violent political passions have but little hold on those who have devoted all their faculties to the pursuit of their well-being. The ardour which they display in small matters calms their zeal for momentous undertakings.

From time to time, indeed, enterprising and ambitious men will arise in democratic communities, whose unbounded aspirations cannot be contented by following the beaten track. Such men like revolutions and hail their approach; but they have great difficulty in bringing them about, unless unwonted events come to their assistance. No man can struggle with advantage against the spirit of his age and country; and, however powerful he may be supposed to be, he will find it difficult to make his contemporaries share in feelings and opinions which are repugnant to all their feelings and desires.

It is a mistake to believe that, when once the equality of conditions has become the old and uncontested state of society, and has imparted its characteristics to the manners of a nation, men will easily allow themselves to be thrust into perilous risks by an imprudent leader or a bold innovator. Not, indeed, that they will resist him openly, by well-contrived schemes, or even by a premeditated plan of resistance. They will not struggle energetically against him, sometimes they will even applaud him—but they do not follow him. To his vehemence they secretly oppose their inertia—to his revolutionary tendencies their conservative interests—their homely tastes to his adventurous passions—their good sense to the flights of his genius—to his poetry their prose.

With immense exertion he raises them for an instant, but they speedily escape from him, and fall back, as it were, by their own weight. He strains himself to rouse the indifferent and distracted multitude, and finds at last that he is reduced to impotence, not because he is conquered, but because he is alone.

I do not assert that men living in democratic communities are naturally stationary; I think, on the contrary, that a perpetual stir prevails in the bosom of those societies, and that rest is unknown there; but I think that men bestir themselves within certain limits beyond which they hardly ever go. They are for ever varying, altering, and restoring secondary matters; but they carefully abstain from touching what is fundamental. They love change, but they dread revolutions. Although the Americans are constantly modifying or abrogating some of their laws, they by no means display revolutionary passions. It may be easily seen, from the promptitude with which they check and calm themselves when public excitement begins to grow alarming, and at the very moment when passions seem most roused, that they dread a revolution as the worst of misfortunes, and that every one of them is inwardly resolved to make great sacrifices to avoid such a catastrophe. In no country in the world is the love of property more active and more anxious than in the United States; nowhere does the majority display less inclination for those principles which threaten to alter, in whatever manner, the laws of property. I have often remarked that theories which are of a revolutionary nature, since they cannot be put in practice without a complete and sometimes a sudden change in the state of property and persons, are much less favourably viewed in the United States than in the great monarchical countries of Europe: if some men profess them, the bulk of the people reject them with instinctive abhorrence. I do not hesitate to say that most of the maxims commonly called democratic in France would be proscribed by the democracy of the United States. This may easily be understood; in America men have the opinions and passions of democracy, in Europe we have still the passions and opinions of revolution. If ever America undergoes great revolutions, they will be brought about by the presence of the black race on the soil of the United States—that is to say, they will owe their origin, not to the equality, but to the inequality, of conditions.

When social conditions are equal, every man is apt to live apart, centred in himself and forgetful of the public. If the rulers of democratic nations were either to neglect to correct this fatal tendency, or to encourage it from a notion that it weans men from political passions and thus wards off revolutions, they might eventually produce the evil they seek to avoid, and a time might come when the inordinate passions of a few men, aided by the unintelligent selfishness or the pusillanimity of the greater number, would ultimately compel society to pass through strange vicissitudes. In democratic communities revolutions are seldom desired except by a minority; but a minority may sometimes effect them. I do not assert that democratic nations are secure from revolutions; I merely say that the state of society in those nations does not lead to revolutions, but rather wards them off. A democratic people left to itself will not easily embark in great hazards; it is only led to revolutions unawares; it may sometimes undergo them, but it does not make them; and I will add that, when such a people has been allowed to acquire sufficient knowledge and experience, it will not suffer them to be made. I am well aware that in this respect public institutions may themselves do much; they may encourage or repress the tendencies which originate in the state of society. I therefore do not maintain, I repeat, that a people is secure from revolutions simply because conditions are equal in the community; but I think that, whatever the institutions of such a people may be, great revolutions will always be far less violent and less frequent than is supposed; and I can easily discern a state of polity which, when combined with the principle of equality, would render society more stationary than it has ever been in our western part of the world.

The observations I have here made on events may also be applied in part to opinions. Two things are surprising in the United States—the mutability of the greater part of human actions, and the singular stability of certain principles. Men are in constant motion; the mind of man appears almost unmoved. When once an opinion has spread over the country and struck root there, it would seem that no power on earth is strong enough to eradicate it. In the United States, general principles in religion, philosophy, morality, and even politics, do not vary, or at least are only modified by a hidden and often an imperceptible process: even the grossest prejudices are obliterated with incredible slowness, amid the continual friction of men and things.

I hear it said that it is in the nature and the habits of democracies to be constantly changing their opinions and feelings. This may be true of small democratic nations, like those of the ancient world, in which the whole community could be assembled in a public place and then excited at will by an orator. But I saw nothing of the kind among the great democratic people which dwells upon the opposite shores of the Atlantic Ocean. What struck me in the United

States was the difficulty of shaking the majority in an opinion once conceived, or of drawing it off from a leader once adopted. Neither speaking nor writing can accomplish it; nothing but experience will avail, and even experience must be repeated. This is surprising at first sight, but a more attentive investigation explains the fact. I do not think that it is as easy as is supposed to uproot the prejudices of a democratic people—to change its belief—to supersede principles once established, by new principles in religion, politics, and morals—in a word, to make great and frequent changes in men's minds. Not that the human mind is there at rest—it is in constant agitation; but it is engaged in infinitely varying the consequences of known principles, and in seeking for new consequences, rather than in seeking for new principles. Its motion is one of rapid circumvolution, rather than of straightforward impulse by rapid and direct effort; it extends its orbit by small continual and hasty movements, but it does not suddenly alter its position.

Men who are equal in rights, in education, in fortune, or, to comprise all in one word, in their social condition, have necessarily wants, habits, and tastes which are hardly dissimilar. As they look at objects under the same aspect, their minds naturally tend to analogous conclusions; and, though each of them may deviate from his contemporaries and form opinions of his own, they will involuntarily and unconsciously concur in a certain number of received opinions. The more attentively I consider the effects of equality upon the mind, the more am I persuaded that the intellectual anarchy which we witness about us is not, as many men suppose, the natural state of democratic nations. I think it is rather to be regarded as an accident peculiar to their youth, and that it only breaks out at that period of transition when men have already snapped the former ties which bound them together, but are still amazingly different in origin, education, and manners; so that, having retained opinions, propensities, and tastes of great diversity, nothing any longer prevents men from avowing them openly. The leading opinions of men become similar in proportion as their conditions assimilate; such appears to me to be the general and permanent law—the rest is casual and transient.

I believe that it will rarely happen to any man among a democratic community, suddenly to frame a system of notions very remote from that which his contemporaries have adopted; and if some such innovator appeared, I apprehend that he would have great difficulty in finding listeners, still more in finding believers. When the conditions of men are almost equal, they do not easily allow themselves to be persuaded by each other. As they all live in close intercourse, as they have learned the same things together, and as they lead the same life, they are not naturally disposed to take one of themselves for a guide, and to follow him implicitly. Men seldom take the opinion of their equal, or of a man like themselves, upon trust. Not only is confidence in the superior attainments of certain individuals weakened among democratic nations, as I have elsewhere remarked, but the general notion of the intellectual superiority which any man whatsoever may acquire in relation to the rest of the community is soon overshadowed. As men grow more like each other, the doctrine of the equality of the intellect gradually infuses itself into their opinions; and it becomes more difficult for any innovator to acquire or to exert much influence over the minds of a people. In such communities sudden intellectual revolutions will therefore be rare ; for, if we read aright the history of the world, we shall find that great and rapid changes in human opinions have been produced far less by the force of reasoning than by the authority of a name. Observe, too, that as the men who live in democratic societies are not connected with each other by any tie, each of them must be convinced individually ; while in aristocratic society it is enough to convince a few—the rest follow. If Luther had lived in an age of equality, and had not had princes and potentates for his audience, he would perhaps have found it more difficult to change the aspect of Europe. Not, indeed, that the men of democracies are naturally strongly persuaded of the certainty of their opinions, or are unwavering in belief ; they frequently entertain doubts which no one, in their eyes, can remove. It sometimes happens at such times that the human mind would willingly change its position ; but as nothing urges or guides it forward, it oscillates to and fro without progressive motion.

Even when the reliance of a democratic people has been won, it is still no easy matter to gain their attention. It is extremely difficult to obtain a hearing from men living in democracies, unless it be to speak to them of themselves. They do not attend to the things said to them, because they are always fully engrossed with the things they are doing. For indeed few men are idle in democratic nations ; life is passed in the midst of noise and excitement, and men are so engaged in acting that little time remains to them for thinking. I would especially remark that they are not only employed, but that they are passionately devoted to their employments. They are always in action, and each of their actions absorbs their faculties : the zeal which they display in business puts out the enthusiasm they might otherwise entertain for ideas. I think that it is extremely difficult to excite the enthusiasm of a democratic people for any theory which has not a palpable, direct, and immediate connection with the daily occupations of life : therefore they will not easily forsake their old opinions ; for it is enthusiasm which flings the minds of men out of the beaten track, and effects the great revolutions of the intellect as well as the great revolutions of the political world. Thus democratic nations have neither time nor taste to go in search of novel opinions. Even when those they possess become doubtful, they still retain them, because it would take too much time and inquiry to change them—they retain them, not as certain, but as established.

There are yet other and more cogent reasons that prevent any great change from being easily effected in the principles of a democratic people. . . . If the influence of individuals is weak and hardly perceptible among such a people, the power exercised by the mass upon the mind of each individual is extremely great. . . . It is wrong to suppose that this depends solely upon the form of government, and that the majority would lose its intellectual supremacy if it were to lose its political power. In aristocracies men have often much greatness and strength of their own : when they find themselves at variance with the greater number of their fellow-countrymen, they withdraw to their own circle, where they support and console themselves. Such is not the case in a democratic country ; there public favour seems as necessary as the air we breathe, and to live at variance with the multitude is, as it were, not to live. The multitude requires no laws to coerce those who think not like itself : public disapprobation is enough ; a sense of their loneliness and impotence overtakes them and drives them to despair.

Whenever social conditions are equal, public

opinion presses with enormous weight upon the mind of each individual; it surrounds, directs, and oppresses him; and this arises from the very constitution of society, much more than from its political laws. As men grow more alike, each man feels himself weaker in regard to all the rest; as he discerns nothing by which he is considerably raised above them, or distinguished from them, he mistrusts himself as soon as they assail him. Not only does he mistrust his strength, but he even doubts of his right; and he is very near acknowledging that he is in the wrong, when the greater number of his countrymen assert that he is so. The majority do not need to constrain him—they convince him. In whatever way, then, the powers of a democratic community may be organized and balanced, it will always be extremely difficult to believe what the bulk of the people reject, or to profess what they condemn.

This circumstance is extraordinarily favourable to the stability of opinions. When an opinion has taken root among a democratic people, and established itself in the minds of the bulk of the community, it afterward subsists by itself and is maintained without effort, because no one attacks it. Those who at first rejected it as false, ultimately receive it as the general impression; and those who still dispute it in their hearts, conceal their dissent; they are careful not to engage in a dangerous and useless conflict. It is true that when the majority of a democratic people change their opinions they may suddenly and arbitrarily effect strange revolutions in men's minds; but their opinions do not change without much difficulty, and it is almost as difficult to show that they are changed.

Time, events, or the unaided individual action of the mind, will sometimes undermine or destroy an opinion, without any outward sign of the change. It has not been openly assailed, no conspiracy has been formed to make war on it, but its followers one by one noiselessly secede—day by day a few of them abandon it, until at last it is only professed by a minority. In this state it will still continue to prevail. As its enemies remain mute, or only interchange their thoughts by stealth, they are themselves unaware for a long period that a great revolution has actually been effected ; and in this state of uncertainty they take no steps—they observe each other and are silent. The majority have ceased to believe what they believed before ; but they still affect to believe, and this empty phantom of public opinion is strong enough to chill innovators, and to keep them silent and at a respectful distance. We live at a time which has witnessed the most rapid changes of opinion in the minds of men ; nevertheless it may be that the leading opinions of society will ere long be more settled than they have been for several centuries in our history : that time is not yet come, but it may perhaps be approaching. As I examine more closely the natural wants and tendencies of democratic nations, I grow persuaded that if ever social equality is generally and permanently established in the world, great intellectual and political revolutions will become more difficult and less frequent than is supposed. Because the men of democracies appear always excited, uncertain, eager, changeable in their wills and in their positions, it is imagined that they are suddenly to abrogate their laws, to adopt new opinions, and to assume new manners. But if the principle of equality predisposes men to change, it also suggests to them certain interests and tastes which cannotbe satisfied without a settled order of things ; equality urges them on, but at the same time it holds them back ; it spurs them, but fastens them to earth—it kindles their desires, but limits their powers. This, however, is not perceived at first; the passions which tend to sever the citizens of a democracy are obvious enough; but the hidden force which restrains and unites them is not discernible at a glance.

Amid the ruins which surround me, shall I dare to say that revolutions are not what I most fear for coming generations? If men continue to shut themselves more closely within the narrow circle of domestic interests and to live upon that kind of excitement, it is to be apprehended that they may ultimately become inaccessible to those great and powerful public emotions which perturb nations—but which enlarge them and recruit them. When property becomes so fluctuating, and the love of property so restless and so ardent, I cannot but fear that men may arrive at such a state as to regard every new theory as a peril, every innovation as an irksome toil, every social improvement as a stepping-stone to revolution, and so refuse to move altogether for fear of being moved too far. I dread, and I confess it, lest they should at last so entirely give way to a cowardly love of present enjoyment, as to lose sight of the interests of their future selves and of those of their descendants; and to prefer to glide along the easy current of life, rather than to make, when it is necessary, a strong and sudden effort to a higher purpose. It is believed by some that modern society will be ever changing its aspect; for myself, I fear that it will ultimately be too invariably fixed in the same institutions, the same prejudices, the same manners, so that mankind will be stopped and circumscribed; that the mind will swing backward and forward for ever, without begetting fresh ideas; that man will waste his strength in bootless and solitary trifling; and, though in continual motion, that humanity will cease to advance.

Chapter XXXIII

WARFARE AMONG DEMOCRATIC PEOPLES

THE same interests, the same fears, the same passions which deter democratic nations from revolutions, deter them also from war; the spirit of military glory and the spirit of revolution are weakened at the same time and by the same causes. The ever-increasing numbers of men of property—lovers of peace, the growth of personal wealth which war so rapidly consumes, the mildness of manners, the gentleness of heart, those tendencies to pity which are engendered by the equality of conditions, that coolness of understanding which renders men comparatively insensible to the violent and poetical excitement of arms—all these causes concur to quench the military spirit. I think it may be admitted as a general and constant rule that, among civilized nations, the warlike passions will become more rare and less intense in proportion as social conditions shall be more equal. War is nevertheless an occurrence to which all nations are subject, democratic nations as well as others. Whatever taste they may have for peace, they must hold themselves in readiness to repel aggression, or, in other words, they must have an army.

Fortune, which has conferred so many peculiar benefits upon the inhabitants of the United States, has placed them in the midst of a wilderness, where they have, so to speak, no neighbours: a few thousand soldiers are sufficient for their wants; but this is peculiar to America, not to democracy. The equality of conditions, and the manners as well as the institutions resulting from it, do not exempt a democratic people from the necessity of standing armies, and their armies always exercise a powerful influence over their fate. It is therefore of singular importance to inquire what are the natural propensities of the men of whom these armies are composed.

Among aristocratic nations, especially among those in which birth is the only source of rank, the same inequality exists in the army as in the nation ; the officer is noble, the soldier is a serf; the one is naturally called upon to command, the other to obey. In aristocratic armies, the private soldier's ambition is therefore circumscribed within very narrow limits. Nor has the ambition of the officer an unlimited range. An aristocratic body not only forms a part of the scale of ranks in the nation, but it contains a scale of ranks within itself: the members of whom it is composed are placed one above another, in a particular and unvarying manner. Thus one man is born to the command of a regiment, another to that of a company ; when once they have reached the utmost object of their hopes, they stop of their own accord, and remain contented with their lot. There is, besides, a strong cause, which, in aristocracies, weakens the officer's desire of promotion. Among aristocratic nations, an officer, independently of his rank in the army, also occupies an elevated rank in society ; the former is almost always in his eyes only an appendage to the latter. A nobleman who embraces the profession of arms follows it less from motives of ambition than from a sense of the duties imposed on him by his birth. He enters the army in order to find an honourable employment for the idle years of his youth, and to be able to bring back to his home and his peers some honourable recollections of military life ; but his principal object is not to obtain by that profession either property, distinction, or power, for he possesses these advantages in his own right, and enjoys them without leaving his home.

In democratic armies all the soldiers may become

officers, which makes the desire of promotion general, and immeasurably extends the bounds of military ambition. The officer, on his part, sees nothing which naturally and necessarily stops him at one grade more than at another; and each grade has immense importance in his eyes, because his rank in society almost always depends on his rank in the army. Among democratic nations it often happens that an officer has no property but his pay, and no distinction but that of military honours: consequently as often as his duties change, his fortune changes, and he becomes, as it were, a new man. What was only an appendage to his position in aristocratic armies has thus become the main point, the basis of his whole condition. Under the old French monarchy officers were always called by their titles of nobility; they are now always called by the title of their military rank. This little change in the forms of language suffices to show that a great revolution has taken place in the constitution of society and in that of the army. In democratic armies the desire of advancement is almost universal: it is ardent, tenacious, perpetual; it is strengthened by all other desires, and only extinguished with life itself. But it is easy to see that, of all armies in the world, those in which advancement must be slowest in time of peace are the armies of democratic countries. As the number of commissions is naturally limited, while the number of competitors is almost unlimited, and as the strict law of equality is over all alike, none can make rapid progress— many can make no progress at all. Thus the desire of advancement is greater, and the opportunities of advancement fewer, there than elsewhere. All the ambitious spirits of a democratic army are conse- quently ardently desirous of war, because war makes vacancies, and warrants the violation of that law of seniority which is the sole privilege natural to democracy.

We thus arrive at this singular consequence, that of all armies those most ardently desirous of war are democratic armies, and of all nations those most fond of peace are democratic nations : and, what makes these facts still more extraordinary, is that these contrary effects are produced at the same time by the principle of equality.

All the members of the community, being alike, constantly harbour the wish, and discover the possibility, of changing their condition and improving their welfare : this makes them fond of peace, which is favourable to industry, and allows every man to pursue his own little undertakings to their completion. On the other hand, this same equality makes soldiers dream of fields of battle, by increasing the value of military honours in the eyes of those who follow the profession of arms, and by rendering those honours accessible to all. In either case the inquietude of the heart is the same, the taste for enjoyment as insatiable, the ambition of success as great—the means of gratifying it are alone different.

These opposite tendencies of the nation and the army expose democratic communities to great dangers. When a military spirit forsakes a people, the profession of arms immediately ceases to be held in honour, and military men fall to the lowest rank of the public servants : they are little esteemed, and no longer understood. The reverse of what takes place in aristocratic ages then occurs ; the men who enter the army are no longer those of the highest, but of the lowest rank. Military ambition is only indulged in when no other is possible. Hence arises a circle of cause and consequence from which it is difficult to escape : the best part of the nation shuns the military profession because that profession is not honoured, and the profession is not honoured because the best part of the nation has ceased to follow it. It is then no matter of surprise that democratic armies are often restless, ill-tempered, and dissatisfied with their lot, although their physical condition is commonly far better and their discipline less strict than in other countries. The soldier feels that he occupies an inferior position, and his wounded pride either stimulates his taste for hostilities which would render his services necessary, or gives him a turn for revolutions, during which he may hope to win by force of arms the political influence and personal importance now denied him. The composition of democratic armies makes this last-mentioned danger much to be feared. In democratic communities almost every man has some property to preserve; but democratic armies are generally led by men without property, most of whom have little to lose in civil broils. The bulk of the nation is naturally much more afraid of revolutions than in the ages of aristocracy, but the leaders of the army much less so.

Moreover, as among democratic nations . . . the wealthiest, the best educated, and the most able men seldom adopt the military profession, the army, taken collectively, eventually forms a small nation by itself, where the mind is less enlarged, and habits are more rude than in the nation at large. Now, this small uncivilized nation has arms in its possession, and alone knows how to use them : for, indeed, the pacific temper of the community increases the danger to which a democratic people is exposed from the military and turbulent spirit of the army. Nothing is so dangerous as an army amid an unwarlike nation ; the excessive love of the whole community for quiet continually puts its constitution at the mercy of the soldiery.

It may, therefore, be asserted, generally speaking, that if democratic nations are naturally prone to peace from their interests and their propensities, they are constantly drawn to war and revolutions by their armies. Military revolutions, which are scarcely ever to be apprehended in aristocracies, are always to be dreaded among democratic nations. These perils must be reckoned among the most formidable which beset their future fate, and the attention of statesmen should be sedulously applied to find a remedy for the evil.

When a nation perceives that it is inwardly affected by the restless ambition of its army, the first thought which occurs is to give this inconvenient ambition an object by going to war. I speak no ill of war: war almost always enlarges the mind of a people, and raises their character. In some cases it is the only check to the excessive growth of certain propensities which naturally spring out of the equality of conditions, and it must be considered as a necessary corrective to certain inveterate diseases to which democratic communities are liable. War has great advantages, but we must not flatter ourselves that it can diminish the danger I have just pointed out. That peril is only suspended by it, to return more fiercely when the war is over; for armies are much more impatient of peace after having tasted military exploits. War could only be a remedy for a people which should always be athirst for military glory. I foresee that all the military rulers who may rise up in great democratic nations will find it easier to conquer with their armies than to make their armies live at peace after conquest. There are two things which a democratic people will always find very difficult—to begin a war, and to end it.

Again, if war has some peculiar advantages for

democratic nations, on the other hand it exposes them to certain dangers which aristocracies have no cause to dread to an equal extent. I shall only point out two of these. Although war gratifies the army, it embarrasses and often exasperates that countless multitude of men whose minor passions every day require peace in order to be satisfied. Thus there is some risk of its causing, under another form, the disturbance it is intended to prevent. No protracted war can fail to endanger the freedom of a democratic country. Not, indeed, that after every victory it is to be apprehended that the victorious generals will possess themselves by force of the supreme power, after the manner of Sylla and Cæsar : the danger is of another kind. War does not always give over democratic communities to military government, but it must invariably and immeasurably increase the powers of civil government; it must almost compulsorily concentrate the direction of all men and the management of all things in the hands of the administration. If it lead not to despotism by sudden violence, it prepares men for it more gently by their habits. All those who seek to destroy the liberties of a democratic nation ought to know that war is the surest and the shortest means to accomplish it. This is the first axiom of the science.

One remedy, which appears to be obvious when the ambition of soldiers and officers becomes the subject of alarm, is to augment the number of commissions to be distributed by increasing the army. This affords temporary relief, but it plunges the country into deeper difficulties at some future period. To increase the army may produce a lasting effect in an aristocratic community, because military ambition is there confined to one class of men, and the ambition of each individual stops, as it were, at a certain limit ; so that it may be possible to satisfy all who feel its influence. But nothing is gained by increasing the army among a democratic people, because the number of aspirants always rises in exactly the same ratio as the army itself. Those whose claims have been satisfied by the creation of new commissions are instantly succeeded by a fresh multitude beyond all power of satisfaction ; and even those who were but now satisfied soon begin to crave more advancement ; for the same excitement prevails in the ranks of the army as in the civil classes of democratic society, and what men want is not to reach a certain grade, but to have constant promotion. Though these wants may not be very vast, they are perpetually recurring. Thus a democratic nation, by augmenting its army, only allays for a time the ambition of the military profession, which soon becomes even more formidable, because the number of those who feel it is increased. I am of opinion that a restless and turbulent spirit is an evil inherent in the very constitution of democratic armies, and beyond hope of cure. The legislators of democracies must not expect to devise any military organization capable by its influence of calming and restraining the military profession : their efforts would exhaust their powers before the object is attained.

The remedy for the vices of the army is not to be found in the army itself, but in the country. Democratic nations are naturally afraid of disturbance and of despotism ; the object is to turn these natural instincts into well-digested, deliberate, and lasting tastes. When men have at last learned to make a peaceful and profitable use of freedom, and have felt its blessing—when they have conceived a manly love of order, and have freely submitted themselves to discipline—these same men, if they follow the profession of arms, bring into it, unconsciously and almost against their will, these same habits and manners. The general spirit of the nation being infused into the spirit peculiar to the army, tempers the opinions and desires engendered by military life, or represses them by the mighty force of public opinion. Teach but the citizens to be educated, orderly, firm, and free, the soldiers will be disciplined and obedient. Any law which, in repressing the turbulent spirit of the army, should tend to diminish the spirit of freedom in the nation, and to overshadow the notion of law and right, would defeat its object : it would do much more to favour, than to defeat, the establishment of military tyranny.

After all, and in spite of all precautions, a large army amid a democratic people will always be a source of great danger ; the most effectual means of diminishing that danger would be to reduce the army, but this is a remedy which all nations have it not in their power to use.

It is a part of the essence of a democratic army to be very numerous in proportion to the people to which it belongs, as I shall hereafter show. On the other hand, men living in democratic times seldom choose a military life. Democratic nations are therefore soon led to give up the system of voluntary recruiting for that of compulsory enlistment. The necessity of their social condition compels them to resort to the latter means, and it may easily be foreseen that they will all eventually adopt it. When military service is compulsory, the burden is indiscriminately and equally borne by the whole community. This is another necessary consequence of the social condition of these nations, and of their notions. The government may do almost whatever it pleases, provided it appeals to the whole community at once : it is the unequal distribution of the weight, not the weight itself, which commonly occasions resistance. But as military service is common to all the citizens, the evident consequence is that each of them remains but for a few years on active duty. Thus it is in the nature of things that the soldier in democracies only passes through the army, while among most aristocratic nations the military profession is one which the soldier adopts, or which is imposed upon him, for life.

This has important consequences. Among the soldiers of a democratic army, some acquire a taste for military life, but the majority being enlisted against their will, and ever ready to go back to their homes, do not consider themselves as seriously engaged in the military profession, and are always thinking of quitting it. Such men do not contract the wants, and only half partake in the passions, which that mode of life engenders. They adapt themselves to their military duties, but their minds are still attached to the interests and the duties which engaged them in civil life. They do not, therefore, imbibe the spirit of the army—or rather, they infuse the spirit of the community at large into the army, and retain it there. Among democratic nations the private soldiers remain most like civilians : upon them the habits of the nation have the firmest hold, and public opinion most influence. It is by the instrumentality of the private soldiers especially that it may be possible to infuse into a democratic army the love of freedom and the respect of rights, if these principles have once been successfully inculcated on the people at large. The reverse happens among aristocratic nations, where the soldiery have eventually nothing in common with their fellow-citizens, and where they live among them as strangers, and often as enemies. In aristocratic armies the officers are the conservative element, because the officers alone have retained a strict con-

nection with civil society, and never forego their
purpose of resuming their place in it sooner or later :
in democratic armies the private soldiers stand in
this position, and from the same cause. . . .

Any army is in danger of being conquered at the
outset of a campaign, after a long peace ; any army
which has long been engaged in warfare has strong
chances of victory : this truth is peculiarly applicable
to democratic armies. In aristocracies the military
profession, being a privileged career, is held in honour
even in time of peace. Men of great talents, great
attainments, and great ambition embrace it ; the
army is in all respects on a level with the nation, and
frequently above it. We have seen, on the contrary,
that among a democratic people the choicer minds
of the nation are gradually drawn away from the
military profession, to seek by other paths distinction,
power, and especially wealth. After a long peace—
and in democratic ages the periods of peace are long—
the army is always inferior to the country itself. In
this state it is called into active service ; and until war
has altered it, there is danger for the country as well
as for the army.

I have shown that in democratic armies, and in
time of peace, the rule of seniority is the supreme and
inflexible law of advancement. This is not only a
consequence, as I have before observed, of the constitution of these armies, but of the constitution of the
people, and it will always occur. Again, as among
these nations the officer derives his position in the
country solely from his position in the army, and as
he draws all the distinction and the competency he
enjoys from the same source, he does not retire from
his profession, or is not superannuated, till toward the
extreme close of life. The consequence of these two
causes is, that when a democratic people goes to war

after a long interval of peace all the leading officers of the army are old men. I speak not only of the generals, but of the non-commissioned officers, who have most of them been stationary, or have only advanced step by step. It may be remarked with surprise, that in a democratic army after a long peace all the soldiers are mere boys, and all the superior officers in declining years; so that the former are wanting in experience, the latter in vigour. This is a strong element of defeat, for the first condition of successful generalship is youth: I should not have ventured to say so if the greatest captain of modern times had not made the observation. . . .

A long peace not only fills democratic armies with elderly officers, but it also gives to all the officers habits both of body and mind which render them unfit for actual service. The man who has long lived amid the calm and lukewarm atmosphere of democratic manners can at first ill adapt himself to the harder toils and sterner duties of warfare; and if he has not absolutely lost the taste for arms, at least he has assumed a mode of life which unfits him for conquest.

Among aristocratic nations, the ease of civil life exercises less influence on the manners of the army, because among those nations the aristocracy commands the army: and an aristocracy, however plunged in luxurious pleasures, has always many other passions besides that of its own well-being, and to satisfy those passions more thoroughly its well-being will be readily sacrificed.

I have shown that in democratic armies, in time of peace, promotion is extremely slow. The officers at first support this state of things with impatience, they grow excited, restless, exasperated, but in the end most of them make up their minds to it. Those who have the largest share of ambition and of resources quit the army; others, adapting their tastes and their desires to their scanty fortunes, ultimately look upon the military profession in a civil point of view. The quality they value most in it is the competency and security which attend it: their whole notion of the future rests upon the certainty of this little provision, and all they require is peaceably to enjoy it. Thus not only does a long peace fill an army with old men, but it frequently imparts the views of old men to those who are still in the prime of life.

I have also shown that among democratic nations in time of peace the military profession is held in little honour and indifferently followed. This want of public favour is a heavy discouragement to the army; it weighs down the minds of the troops, and when war breaks out at last, they cannot immediately resume their spring and vigour. No similar cause of moral weakness occurs in aristocratic armies: there the officers are never lowered either in their own eyes or in those of their countrymen, because, independently of their military greatness, they are personally great. But even if the influence of peace operated on the two kinds of armies in the same manner, the results would still be different. When the officers of an aristocratic army have lost their warlike spirit and the desire of raising themselves by service, they still retain a certain respect for the honour of their class, and an old habit of being foremost to set an example. But when the officers of a democratic army have no longer the love of war and the ambition of arms, nothing whatever remains to them.

I am therefore of opinion that, when a democratic people engages in a war after a long peace, it incurs much more risk of defeat than any other nation; but it ought not easily to be cast down by its reverses, for the chances of success for such an army are increased by the duration of the war. When a war has at length, by its long continuance, roused the whole community from their peaceful occupations and ruined their minor undertakings, the same passions which made them attach so much importance to the maintenance of peace will be turned to arms. War, after it has destroyed all modes of speculation, becomes itself the great and sole speculation, to which all the ardent and ambitious desires which equality engenders are exclusively directed. Hence it is that the self-same democratic nations which are so reluctant to engage in hostilities sometimes perform prodigious achievements when once they have taken the field. As the war attracts more and more of public attention, and is seen to create high reputations and great fortunes in a short space of time, the choicest spirits of the nation enter the military profession : all the enterprising, proud, and martial minds, no longer of the aristocracy solely, but of the whole country, are drawn in this direction. As the number of competitors for military honours is immense, and war drives every man to his proper level, great generals are always sure to spring up. A long war produces upon a democratic army the same effects that a revolution produces upon a people ; it breaks through regulations, and allows extraordinary men to rise above the common level. Those officers whose bodies and minds have grown old in peace, are removed, or superannuated, or they die. In their stead a host of young men are pressing on, whose frames are already hardened, whose desires are extended and inflamed by active service. They are bent on advancement at all hazards, and perpetual advancement ; they are followed by others with the same passions and desires, and after these are others yet unlimited by aught but the size of the army. The principle of equality opens the door of ambition to all, and death provides chances for ambition. Death is constantly thinning the ranks, making vacancies, closing and opening the career of arms.

There is, moreover, a secret connection between the military character and the character of democracies, which war brings to light. The men of democracies are naturally passionately eager to acquire what they covet, and to enjoy it on easy conditions. They for the most part worship chance, and are much less afraid of death than of difficulty. This is the spirit which they bring to commerce and manufactures; and this same spirit, carried with them to the field of battle, induces them willingly to expose their lives in order to secure in a moment the rewards of victory. No kind of greatness is more pleasing to the imagination of a democratic people than military greatness—a greatness of vivid and sudden lustre, obtained without toil, by nothing but the risk of life. Thus, while the interests and the tastes of the members of a democratic community divert them from war, their habits of mind fit them for carrying on war well; they soon make good soldiers, when they are roused from their business and their enjoyments. If peace is peculiarly hurtful to democratic armies, war secures to them advantages which no other armies ever possess: and these advantages, however little felt at first, cannot fail in the end to give them the victory. An aristocratic nation, which in a contest with a democratic people does not succeed in ruining the latter at the outset of the war, always runs a great risk of being conquered by it.

It is a very general opinion, especially in aristocratic countries, that the great social equality which prevails in democracies ultimately renders the private soldier independent of the officer, and thus destroys the bond of discipline. This is a mistake, for there are two kinds of discipline, which it is important not to confound. When the officer is noble and the soldier is a serf—one rich, the other poor—the former educated and strong, the latter ignorant and weak—the strictest bond of obedience may easily be established between the two men. The soldier is broken in to military discipline, as it were, before he enters the army; or rather, military discipline is nothing but an enhancement of social servitude. In aristocratic armies the soldier will soon become insensible to everything but the orders of his superior officers; he acts without reflection, triumphs without enthusiasm, and dies without complaint : in this state he is no longer a man, but he is still a most formidable animal trained for war.

A democratic people must despair of ever obtaining from soldiers that blind, minute, submissive, and invariable obedience which an aristocratic people may impose on them without difficulty. The state of society does not prepare them for it, and the nation might be in danger of losing its natural advantages if it sought artificially to acquire advantages of this particular kind. Among democratic communities, military discipline ought not to attempt to annihilate the free spring of the faculties ; all that can be done by discipline is to direct it ; the obedience thus inculcated is less exact, but it is more eager and more intelligent. It has its root in the will of him who obeys : it rests not only on his instinct, but on his reason ; and consequently it will often spontaneously become more strict as danger requires it. The discipline of an aristocratic army is apt to be relaxed in war, because that discipline is founded upon habits, and war disturbs those habits. The discipline of a democratic army, on the contrary, is strengthened in sight of the enemy, because every soldier then clearly perceives that he must be silent and obedient in order to conquer.

The nations which have performed the greatest warlike achievements knew no other discipline than that which I speak of. Among the ancients none were admitted into the armies but freemen and citizens, who differed but little from one another, and were accustomed to treat each other as equals. In this respect it may be said that the armies of antiquity were democratic, although they came out of the bosom of aristocracy; the consequence was that in those armies a sort of fraternal familiarity prevailed between the officers and the men. Plutarch's lives of great commanders furnish convincing instances of the fact: the soldiers were in the constant habit of freely addressing their general, and the general listened to and answered whatever the soldiers had to say: they were kept in order by language and by example, far more than by constraint or punishment; the general was as much their companion as their chief. I know not whether the soldiers of Greece and Rome ever carried the minutiæ of military discipline to the same degree of perfection as the Russians have done; but this did not prevent Alexander from conquering Asia—and Rome, the world.

When the principle of equality is in growth, not only among a single nation, but among several neighbouring nations at the same time, as is now the case in Europe, the inhabitants of these different countries, notwithstanding the dissimilarity of language, of customs, and of laws, nevertheless resemble each other in their equal dread of war and their common love of peace. It is in vain that ambition or anger puts arms in the hands of princes; they are appeased in spite of themselves by a species of general apathy, and good-will, which makes the sword drop from their grasp, and wars become more rare. As the spread of equality, taking place in several countries at once, simultaneously impels their various inhabitants to follow manufactures and commerce, not only do their tastes grow alike, but their interests are so mixed and entangled with one another that no nation can inflict evils on other nations without those evils falling back upon itself; and all nations ultimately regard war as a calamity, almost as severe to the conqueror as to the conquered. Thus, on the one hand, it is extremely difficult in democratic ages to draw nations into hostilities; but, on the other hand, it is almost impossible that any two of them should go to war without embroiling the rest. The interests of all are so interlaced, their opinions and their wants so much alike, that none can remain quiet when the others stir. Wars, therefore, become more rare, but when they break out they spread over a larger field. Neighbouring democratic nations not only become alike in some respects, but they eventually grow to resemble each other in almost all. This similitude of nations has consequences of great importance in relation to war. . . .

A great aristocratic people cannot either conquer its neighbours, or be conquered by them, without great difficulty. It cannot conquer them, because all its forces can never be collected and held together for a considerable period: it cannot be conquered, because an enemy meets at every step small centres of resistance by which invasion is arrested. War against an aristocracy may be compared to war in a mountainous country; the defeated party has constant opportunities of rallying its forces to make a stand in a new position. Exactly the reverse occurs among democratic nations: they easily bring their whole disposable force into the field, and when the nation is wealthy and populous it soon becomes victorious; but if ever it is conquered, and its territory invaded, it has few resources at command; and if the enemy takes the capital, the nation is lost. This may very well be explained: as each member of the community is individually isolated and extremely powerless, no one of the whole body can either defend himself or present a rallying-point to others. Nothing is strong in a democratic country except the State; as the military strength of the State is destroyed by the destruction of the army, and its civil power paralysed by the capture of the chief city, all that remains is only a multitude without strength or government, unable to resist the organized power by which it is assailed. I am aware that this danger may be lessened by the creation of provincial liberties, and consequently of provincial powers, but this remedy will always be insufficient. For after such a catastrophe not only is the population unable to carry on hostilities, but it may be apprehended that they will not be inclined to attempt it.

In accordance with the law of nations adopted in civilized countries, the object of wars is not to seize the property of private individuals, but simply to get possession of political power. The destruction of private property is only occasionally resorted to for the purpose of attaining the latter object. When an aristocratic country is invaded after the defeat of its army, the nobles, although they are at the same time the wealthiest members of the community, will continue to defend themselves individually rather than submit; for if the conqueror remained master of the country, he would deprive them of their political power, to which they cling even more closely than to their property. They therefore prefer fighting to subjection, which is to them the greatest of all misfortunes; and they readily carry the people along with them because the people has long been used to follow and obey them, and besides has but little to risk in the war. Among a nation in which equality of conditions prevails, each citizen, on the contrary, has but a slender share of political power, and often has no share at all; on the other hand, all are independent, and all have something to lose; so that they are much less afraid of being conquered, and much more afraid of war, than an aristocratic people. It will always be extremely difficult to decide a democratic population to take up arms, when hostilities have reached its own territory. Hence the necessity of giving to such a people the rights and the political character which may impart to every citizen some of those interests that cause the nobles to act for the public welfare in aristocratic countries.

It should never be forgotten by the princes and other leaders of democratic nations that nothing but the passion and the habit of freedom can maintain an advantageous contest with the passion and the habit of physical well-being. I can conceive nothing better prepared for subjection, in case of defeat, than a democratic people without free institutions. . . .

I shall add but a few words on civil wars, for fear of exhausting the patience of the reader. Most of the remarks which I have made respecting foreign wars are applicable *a fortiori* to civil wars. Men living in democracies are not naturally prone to the military character; they sometimes assume it, when they have been dragged by compulsion to the field; but to rise in a body and voluntarily to expose themselves to the horrors of war, and especially of civil war, is a course which the men of democracies are not apt to adopt. None but the most adventurous members of the community consent to run into such risks; the bulk of the population remains motionless. But even if the population were inclined to act, considerable obstacles would stand in their way ; for they can resort to no old and well-established influence which they are willing to obey—no well-known leaders to rally the discontented, as well as to discipline and to lead them —no political powers subordinate to the supreme power of the nation, which afford an effectual support to the resistance directed against the government. In democratic countries the moral power of the majority is immense, and the physical resources which it has at its command are out of all proportion to the physical resources which may be combined against it. Therefore the party which occupies the seat of the majority, which speaks in its name and wields its power, triumphs instantaneously and irresistibly over all private resistance; it does not even give such opposition time to exist, but nips it in the bud. Those who in such nations seek to effect a revolution by force of arms have no other resource than suddenly to seize upon the whole engine of government as it stands, which can better be done by a single blow than by a war ; for as soon as there is a regular war, the party which represents the State is always certain to conquer. The only case in which a civil war could arise is, if the army should divide itself into two factions, the one raising the standard of rebellion, the other remaining true to its allegiance. An army constitutes a small community, very closely united together, endowed with great powers of vitality, and able to supply its own wants for some time. Such a war might be bloody, but it could not be long ; for either the rebellious army would gain over the government by the sole display of its resources, or by its first victory, and then the war would be over ; or the struggle would take place, and then that portion of the army

which should not be supported by the organized
powers of the State would speedily either disband
itself or be destroyed. It may, therefore, be admitted
as a general truth, that in ages of equality civil wars
will become much less frequent and less protracted.

Chapter XXXIV

INFLUENCE OF DEMOCRATIC OPINIONS AND
SENTIMENTS UPON POLITICAL SOCIETY

I SHOULD imperfectly fulfil the purpose of this book if,
after having shown what opinions and sentiments are
suggested by the principle of equality, I did not point
out, ere I conclude, the general influence which these
same opinions and sentiments may exercise upon the
government of human societies. To succeed in this
object I shall frequently have to retrace my steps;
but I trust the reader will not refuse to follow me
through paths already known to him, which may lead
to some new truth.

The principle of equality, which makes men independent of each other, gives them a habit and a taste
for following, in their private actions, no other guide
but their own will. This complete independence,
which they constantly enjoy toward their equals and
in the intercourse of private life, tends to make them
look upon all authority with a jealous eye, and speedily
suggests to them the notion and the love of political
freedom. Men living at such times have a natural
bias to free institutions. Take any one of them at a
venture, and search if you can his most deep-seated
instincts; you will find that of all governments he will
soonest conceive and most highly value that government whose head he has himself elected, and whose
administration he may control. Of all the political
effects produced by the equality of conditions, this
love of independence is the first to strike the observing,
and to alarm the timid; nor can it be said that their
alarm is wholly misplaced, for anarchy has a more
formidable aspect in democratic countries than elsewhere. As the citizens have no direct influence on
each other, as soon as the supreme power of the

nation fails, which kept them all in their several stations, it would seem that disorder must instantly reach its utmost pitch, and that, every man drawing aside in a different direction, the fabric of society must at once crumble away.

I am, however, persuaded that anarchy is not the principal evil that democratic ages have to fear, but the least. For the principle of equality begets two tendencies : the one leads men straight to independence, and may suddenly drive them into anarchy ; the other conducts them by a longer, more secret, but more certain road, to servitude. Nations readily discern the former tendency, and are prepared to resist it ; they are led away by the latter, without perceiving its drift ; hence it is peculiarly important to point it out. For myself, I am so far from urging as a reproach to the principle of equality that it renders men untractable, that this very circumstance principally calls forth my approbation. I admire to see how it deposits in the mind and heart of man the dim conception and instinctive love of political independence, thus preparing the remedy for the evil which it engenders ; it is on this very account that I am attached to it.

The notion of secondary powers, placed between the sovereign and his subjects, occurred naturally to the imagination of aristocratic nations, because those communities contained individuals or families raised above the common level, and apparently destined to command by their birth, their education, and their wealth. This same notion is naturally wanting in the minds of men in democratic ages, for converse reasons : it can only be introduced artificially, it can only be kept there with difficulty ; whereas they conceive, as it were, without thinking upon the subject, the notion of a sole and central power which governs the whole community by its direct influence. Moreover, in politics, as well as in philosophy and in religion, the intellect of democratic nations is peculiarly open to simple and general notions. Complicated systems are repugnant to it, and its favourite conception is that of a great nation composed of citizens all resembling the same pattern, and all governed by a single power.

The very next notion to that of a sole and central power, which presents itself to the minds of men in the ages of equality, is the notion of uniformity of legislation. As every man sees that he differs but little from those about him, he cannot understand why a rule which is applicable to one man should not be equally applicable to all others. Hence the slightest privileges are repugnant to his reason ; the faintest dissimilarities in the political institutions of the same people offend him, and uniformity of legislation appears to him to be the first condition of good government. I find, on the contrary, that this same notion of a uniform rule, equally binding on all the members of the community, was almost unknown to the human mind in aristocratic ages ; it was either never entertained, or it was rejected. These contrary tendencies of opinion ultimately turn on either side to such blind instincts and such ungovernable habits that they still direct the actions of men, in spite of particular exceptions. Notwithstanding the immense variety of conditions in the Middle Ages, a certain number of persons existed at that period in precisely similar circumstances ; but this did not prevent the laws then in force from assigning to each of them distinct duties and different rights. On the contrary, at the present time all the powers of government are exerted to impose the same customs and the same laws on populations which have as yet but few points of resemblance. As the conditions of men become equal among a people, individuals seem of less importance, and society of greater dimensions; or rather, every citizen, being assimilated to all the rest, is lost in the crowd, and nothing stands conspicuous but the great and imposing image of the people at large. This naturally gives the men of democratic periods a lofty opinion of the privileges of society, and a very humble notion of the rights of individuals; they are ready to admit that the interests of the former are everything, and those of the latter nothing. They are willing to acknowledge that the power which represents the community has far more information and wisdom than any of the members of that community; and that it is the duty, as well as the right, of that power to guide as well as govern each private citizen.

If we closely scrutinize our contemporaries, and penetrate to the root of their political opinions, we shall detect some of the notions which I have just pointed out, and we shall perhaps be surprised to find so much accordance between men who are so often at variance. The Americans hold that in every State the supreme power ought to emanate from the people; but when once that power is constituted, they can conceive, as it were, no limits to it, and they are ready to admit that it has the right to do whatever it pleases. They have not the slightest notion of peculiar privileges granted to cities, families, or persons: their minds appear never to have foreseen that it might be possible not to apply with strict uniformity the same laws to every part, and to all the inhabitants. These same opinions are more and more diffused in Europe; they even insinuate themselves among those nations which most vehemently reject the principle of the sovereignty of the people. Such nations assign a different origin to the supreme power, but they ascribe to that power the same characteristics. Among them all, the idea of intermediate powers is weakened and obliterated : the idea of rights inherent in certain individuals is rapidly disappearing from the minds of men ; the idea of the omnipotence and sole authority of society at large rises to fill its place. These ideas take root and spread in proportion as social conditions become more equal, and men more alike ; they are engendered by equality, and in turn they hasten the progress of equality. . . .

Our contemporaries are much less divided than is commonly supposed ; they are constantly disputing as to the hands in which supremacy is to be vested, but they readily agree upon the duties and the rights of that supremacy. The notion they all form of government is that of a sole, simple, providential, and creative power. All secondary opinions in politics are unsettled ; this one remains fixed, invariable, and consistent. It is adopted by statesmen and political philosophers ; it is eagerly laid hold of by the multitude ; those who govern and those who are governed agree to pursue it with equal ardour : it is the foremost notion of their minds, it seems connatural with their feelings. It originates, therefore, in no caprice of the human intellect, but it is a necessary condition of the present state of mankind.

If it be true that, in ages of equality, men readily adopt the notion of a great central power, it cannot be doubted, on the other hand, that their habits and sentiments predispose them to recognize such a power and to give it their support. This may be demonstrated in a few words, as the greater part of the reasons, to which the fact may be attributed, have been previously stated. As the men who inhabit democratic countries have no superiors, no inferiors, and no habitual or necessary partners in their undertakings, they readily fall back upon themselves and consider themselves as beings apart. I had occasion to point this out at considerable length in treating of individualism. Hence such men can never, without an effort, tear themselves from their private affairs to engage in public business; their natural bias leads them to abandon the latter to the sole visible and permanent representative of the interests of the community—that is to say, to the State. Not only are they naturally wanting in a taste for public business, but they have frequently no time to attend to it. Private life is so busy in democratic periods, so excited, so full of wishes and of work, that hardly any energy or leisure remains to each individual for public life. I am the last man to contend that these propensities are unconquerable, since my chief object in writing this book has been to combat them. I only maintain that at the present day a secret power is fostering them in the human heart, and that if they are not checked they will wholly overgrow it.

I have also had occasion to show how the increasing love of well-being, and the fluctuating character of property, cause democratic nations to dread all violent disturbance. The love of public tranquillity is frequently the only passion which these nations retain, and it becomes more active and powerful among them in proportion as all other passions droop and die. This naturally disposes the members of the community constantly to give or to surrender additional rights to the central power, which alone seems to be interested in defending them by the same means that it uses to defend itself. As in ages of equality no man is compelled to lend his assistance to his fellow-men, and none has any right to expect much support from them, every one is at once independent and powerless. These two conditions, which must never be either separately considered or confounded together, inspire the citizen of a democratic country with very contrary propensities. His independence fills him with self-reliance and pride among his equals; his debility makes him feel from time to time the want of some outward assistance, which he cannot expect from any of them, because they are all impotent and unsympathizing. In this predicament he naturally turns his eyes to that imposing power which alone rises above the level of universal depression. Of that power his wants and especially his desires continually remind him, until he ultimately views it as the sole and necessary support of his own weakness. This may more completely explain what frequently takes place in democratic countries, where the very men who are so impatient of superiors patiently submit to a master, exhibiting at once their pride and their servility.

The hatred which men bear to privilege increases in proportion as privileges become more scarce and less considerable, so that democratic passions would seem to burn most fiercely at the very time when they have least fuel. I have already given the reason of this phenomenon. When all conditions are unequal, no inequality is so great as to offend the eye; whereas the slightest dissimilarity is odious in the midst of general uniformity: the more complete is this uniformity, the more insupportable does the sight of such a difference become. Hence it is natural that the love of equality should constantly increase together with equality itself, and that it should grow by what it feeds upon. This never-dying, ever-kindling hatred, which sets a democratic people against the smallest privileges, is peculiarly favourable to the gradual concentration of all political rights in the hands of the representative of the State alone. The sovereign, being necessarily and incontestably above all the citizens, excites not their envy, and each of them thinks that he strips his equals of the prerogative which he concedes to the crown. The man of a democratic age is extremely reluctant to obey his neighbour who is his equal ; he refuses to acknowledge in such a person ability superior to his own ; he mistrusts his justice, and is jealous of his power ; he fears and he contemns him ; and he loves continually to remind him of the common dependence in which both of them stand to the same master. Every central power which follows its natural tendencies courts and encourages the principle of equality ; for equality singularly facilitates, extends, and secures the influence of a central power.

In like manner it may be said that every central government worships uniformity : uniformity relieves it from inquiry into an infinite number of small details which must be attended to if rules were to be adapted to men, instead of indiscriminately subjecting men to rules : thus the government likes what the citizens like, and naturally hates what they hate. These common sentiments, which, in democratic nations, constantly unite the sovereign and every member of the community in one and the same conviction, establish a secret and lasting sympathy between them. The faults of the government are pardoned for the sake of its tastes ; public confidence is only reluctantly withdrawn in the midst even of its excesses and its errors, and it is restored at the first call. Democratic nations often hate those in whose hands the central power is vested ; but they always love that power itself.

Thus by two separate paths I have reached the same conclusion. I have shown that the principle of equality suggests to men the notion of a sole, uniform, and strong government : I have now shown that the principle of equality imparts to them a taste for it. To governments of this kind the nations of our age are therefore tending. They are drawn thither by the natural inclination of mind and heart; and in order to reach that result, it is enough that they do not check themselves in their course. I am of opinion that, in the democratic ages which are opening upon us, individual independence and local liberties will ever be the produce of artificial contrivance; that centralization will be the natural form of government.

If all democratic nations are instinctively led to the centralization of government, they tend to this result in an unequal manner. This depends on the particular circumstances which may promote or prevent the natural consequences of that state of society—circumstances which are exceedingly numerous; but I shall only advert to a few of them. Among men who have lived free long before they became equal, the tendencies derived from free institutions combat, to a certain extent, the propensities superinduced by the principle of equality; and although the central power may increase its privileges among such a people, the private members of such a community will never entirely forfeit their independence. But when the equality of conditions grows up among a people which has never known, or has long ceased to know, what freedom is (and such is the case upon the continent of Europe), as the former habits of the nation are suddenly combined, by some sort of natural attraction, with the novel habits and principles engendered by the state of society, all powers seem spontaneously to rush to the centre. These powers accumulate there with astonishing rapidity, and the State instantly attains the utmost limits of its strength, while private persons allow themselves to sink as suddenly to the lowest degree of weakness.

The English who emigrated three hundred years

ago to found a democratic commonwealth on the shores of the New World, had all learned to take a part in public affairs in their mother-country; they were conversant with trial by jury; they were accustomed to liberty of speech and of the press—to personal freedom, to the notion of rights, and the practice of asserting them. They carried with them to America these free institutions and manly customs, and these institutions preserved them against the encroachments of the State. Thus among the Americans it is freedom which is old—equality is of comparatively modern date. The reverse is occurring in Europe, where equality, introduced by absolute power and under the rule of kings, was already infused into the habits of nations long before freedom had entered into their conceptions.

I have said that among democratic nations the notion of government naturally presents itself to the mind under the form of a sole and central power, and that the notion of intermediate powers is not familiar to them. This is peculiarly applicable to the democratic nations which have witnessed the triumph of the principle of equality by means of a violent revolution. As the classes which managed local affairs have been suddenly swept away by the storm, and as the confused mass which remains has as yet neither the organization nor the habits which fit it to assume the administration of these same affairs, the State alone seems capable of taking upon itself all the details of government, and centralization becomes, as it were, the unavoidable state of the country. Napoleon deserves neither praise nor censure for having centred in his own hands almost all the administrative power of France; for, after the abrupt disappearance of the nobility and the higher rank of the middle classes, these powers devolved on him of course: it would have been almost as difficult for him to reject as to assume them. But no necessity of this kind has ever been felt by the Americans, who, having passed through no revolution, and having governed themselves from the first, never had to call upon the State to act for a time as their guardian. Thus the progress of centralization among a democratic people depends not only on the progress of equality, but on the manner in which this equality has been established.

At the commencement of a great democratic revolution, when hostilities have but just broken out between the different classes of society, the people endeavours to centralize the public administration in the hands of the government, in order to wrest the management of local affairs from the aristocracy. Toward the close of such a revolution, on the contrary, it is usually the conquered aristocracy that endeavours to make over the management of all affairs to the State, because such an aristocracy dreads the tyranny of a people which has become its equal, and not infrequently its master. Thus it is not always the same class of the community which strives to increase the prerogative of the government; but as long as the democratic revolution lasts there is always one class in the nation, powerful in numbers or in wealth, which is induced, by peculiar passions or interests, to centralize the public administration, independently of that hatred of being governed by one's neighbour, which is a general and permanent feeling among democratic nations. It may be remarked that at the present day the lower orders in England are striving with all their might to destroy local independence, and to transfer the administration from all points of the circumference to the centre; whereas the higher classes are endeavouring to retain this administration within its ancient boundaries. I venture to predict that a time will come when the very reverse will happen.

These observations explain why the supreme power is always stronger, and private individuals weaker, among a democratic people which has passed through a long and arduous struggle to reach a state of equality than among a democratic community in which the citizens have been equal from the first. The example of the Americans completely demonstrates the fact. The inhabitants of the United States were never divided by any privileges; they have never known the mutual relation of master and inferior, and as they neither dread nor hate each other, they have never known the necessity of calling in the supreme power to manage their affairs. The lot of the Americans is singular: they have derived from the aristocracy of England the notion of private rights and the taste for local freedom; and they have been able to retain both the one and the other, because they have had no aristocracy to combat.

If at all times education enables men to defend their independence, this is most especially true in democratic ages. When all men are alike, it is easy to found a sole and all-powerful government, by the aid of mere instinct. But men require much intelligence, knowledge, and art to organize and to maintain secondary powers under similar circumstances, and to create amid the independence and individual weakness of the citizens such free associations as may be in a condition to struggle against tyranny without destroying public order.

Hence the concentration of power and the subjection of individuals will increase among democratic nations, not only in the same proportion as their equality, but in the same proportion as their ignorance. It is true, that in ages of imperfect civilization the government is frequently as wanting in the knowledge required to impose a despotism upon the people as the people are wanting in the knowledge required to shake it off; but the effect is not the same on both sides. However rude a democratic people may be, the central power which rules it is never completely devoid of cultivation, because it readily draws to its own uses what little cultivation is to be found in the country, and, if necessary, may seek assistance elsewhere. Hence, among a nation which is ignorant as well as democratic, an amazing difference cannot fail speedily to arise between the intellectual capacity of the ruler and that of each of his subjects. This completes the easy concentration of all power in his hands : the administrative function of the State is perpetually extended, because the State alone is competent to administer the affairs of the country. Aristocratic nations, however unenlightened they may be, never afford the same spectacle, because in them instruction is nearly equally diffused between the monarch and the leading members of the community. . . .

I think that extreme centralization of government ultimately enervates society, and thus after a length of time weakens the government itself; but I do not deny that a centralized social power may be able to execute great undertakings with facility in a given time and on a particular point. This is more especially true of war, in which success depends much more on the means of transferring all the resources of a nation to one single point, than on the extent of those resources. Hence it is chiefly in war that nations desire and frequently require to increase the powers of the central government. All men of military genius are fond of centralization, which increases their strength ; and all men of centralizing genius are fond of war, which compels nations to combine all their powers in the hands of the government. Thus the democratic tendency which leads men unceasingly to multiply the privileges of the State, and to circumscribe the rights of private persons, is much more rapid and constant among those democratic nations which are exposed by their position to great and frequent wars, than among all others.

I have shown how the dread of disturbance and the love of well-being insensibly lead democratic nations to increase the functions of central government, as the only power which appears to be intrinsically sufficiently strong, enlightened, and secure, to protect them from anarchy. I would now add that all the particular circumstances which tend to make the state of a democratic community agitated and precarious, enhance this general propensity, and lead private persons more and more to sacrifice their rights to their tranquillity. A people is therefore never so disposed to increase the functions of central government as at the close of a long and bloody revolution, which, after having wrested property from the hands of its former possessors, has shaken all belief, and filled the nation with fierce hatreds, conflicting interests, and contending factions. The love of public tranquillity becomes at such times an indiscriminating passion, and the members of the community are apt to conceive a most inordinate devotion to order.

I have already examined several of the incidents which may concur to promote the centralization of power, but the principal cause still remains to be noticed. The foremost of the incidental causes which may draw the management of all affairs into the hands of the ruler in democratic countries is the origin of that ruler himself, and his own propensities. Men who live in the ages of equality are naturally fond of central power, and are willing to extend its privileges;

but if it happens that this same power faithfully represents their own interests, and exactly copies their own inclinations, the confidence they place in it knows no bounds, and they think that whatever they bestow upon it is bestowed upon themselves.

The attraction of administrative powers to the centre will always be less easy and less rapid under the reign of kings who are still in some way connected with the old aristocratic order, than under new princes, the children of their own achievements, whose birth, prejudices, propensities, and habits appear to bind them indissolubly to the cause of equality. I do not mean that princes of aristocratic origin who live in democratic ages do not attempt to centralize; I believe they apply themselves to that object as diligently as any others. For them, the sole advantages of equality lie in that direction; but their opportunities are less great, because the community, instead of volunteering compliance with their desires, frequently obeys them with reluctance. In democratic communities the rule is that centralization must increase in proportion as the sovereign is less aristocratic. When an ancient race of kings stands at the head of an aristocracy, as the natural prejudices of the sovereign perfectly accord with the natural prejudices of the nobility, the vices inherent in aristocratic communities have a free course, and meet with no corrective. The reverse is the case when the scion of a feudal stock is placed at the head of a democratic people. The sovereign is constantly led, by his education, his habits, and his associations, to adopt sentiments suggested by the inequality of conditions, and the people tend as constantly, by their social condition, to those manners which are engendered by equality. At such times it often happens that the citizens seek to control the central power far less as a tyrannical than as an aristocratical power, and that they persist in the firm defence of their independence, not only because they would remain free, but especially because they are determined to remain equal. A revolution which overthrows an ancient regal family, in order to place men of more recent growth at the head of a democratic people, may temporarily weaken the central power ; but however anarchical such a revolution may appear at first, we need not hesitate to predict that its final and certain consequence will be to extend and to secure the prerogatives of that power. The foremost or, indeed, the sole condition which is required in order to succeed in centralizing the supreme power in a democratic community, is to love equality, or to get men to believe you love it. Thus the science of despotism, which was once so complex, is simplified, and reduced as it were to a single principle.

On reflecting upon what has already been said, the reader will be startled and alarmed to find that in Europe everything seems to conduce to the indefinite extension of the prerogatives of government, and to render all that enjoyed the rights of private independence more weak, more subordinate, and more precarious. The democratic nations of Europe have all the general and permanent tendencies which urge the Americans to the centralization of government, and they are, moreover, exposed to a number of secondary and incidental causes with which the Americans are unacquainted. It would seem as if every step they make toward equality brings them nearer to despotism. And, indeed, if we do but cast our looks around, we shall be convinced that such is the fact. During the aristocratic ages which preceded the present time, the sovereigns of Europe had been deprived of, or had relinquished, many of the rights inherent in their power. Not a hundred years ago, among the greater part of European nations, numerous private persons and corporations were sufficiently independent to administer justice, to raise and maintain troops, to levy taxes, and frequently even to make or interpret the law. The State has everywhere resumed to itself alone these natural attributes of sovereign power ; in all matters of government the State tolerates no intermediate agent between itself and the people, and in general business it directs the people by its own immediate influence. I am far from blaming this concentration of powers, I simply point it out.

At the same period a great number of secondary powers existed in Europe, which represented local interests and administered local affairs. Most of these local authorities have already disappeared ; all are speedily tending to disappear, or to fall into the most complete dependence. From one end of Europe to the other the privileges of the nobility, the liberties of cities, and the powers of provincial bodies, are either destroyed or upon the verge of destruction. Europe has endured, in the course of the last half century, many revolutions and counter-revolutions which have agitated it in opposite directions : but all these per-turbations resemble each other in one respect—they have all shaken or destroyed the secondary powers of government. The local privileges which the French did not abolish in the countries they conquered, have finally succumbed to the policy of the princes who conquered the French. Those princes rejected all the innovations of the French Revolution except central-ization : that is the only principle they consented to receive from such a source. My object is to remark, that all these various rights, which have been success-ively wrested, in our time, from classes, corporations, and individuals, have not served to raise new secondary powers on a more democratic basis, but have uniformly been concentrated in the hands of the sovereign. Everywhere the State acquires more and more direct control over the humblest members of the community, and a more exclusive power of governing each of them in his smallest concerns. Almost all the charitable establishments of Europe were formerly in the hands of private persons or of corporations; they are now almost all dependent on the supreme government, and in many countries are actually administered by that power. The State almost exclusively undertakes to supply bread to the hungry, assistance and shelter to the sick, work to the idle, and to act as the sole reliever of all kinds of misery. Education, as well as charity, is become in most countries at the present day a national concern. The State receives, and often takes, the child from the arms of the mother, to hand it over to official agents: the State undertakes to train the heart and to instruct the mind of each generation. Uniformity prevails in the courses of public instruction as in everything else; diversity, as well as freedom, are disappearing day by day. Nor do I hesitate to affirm that among almost all the Christian nations of our days, Catholic as well as Protestant, religion is in danger of falling into the hands of the government. Not that rulers are over-jealous of the right of settling points of doctrine, but they get more and more hold upon the will of those by whom doctrines are expounded; they deprive the clergy of their property, and pay them by salaries; they divert to their own use the influence of the priesthood, they make them their own ministers—often their own servants—and by this alliance with religion they reach the inner depths of the soul of man. . . .

The authority of government has not only spread . . . throughout the sphere of all existing powers, till that sphere can no longer contain it, but it goes further, and invades the domain heretofore reserved to private independence. A multitude of actions, which were formerly entirely beyond the control of the public administration, have been subjected to that control in our time, and the number of them is constantly increasing. Among aristocratic nations the supreme government usually contented itself with managing and superintending the community in whatever directly and ostensibly concerned the national honour; but in all other respects the people were left to work out their own free will. Among these nations the government often seemed to forget that there is a point at which the faults and the sufferings of private persons involve the general prosperity, and that to prevent the ruin of a private individual must sometimes be a matter of public importance. The democratic nations of our time lean to the opposite extreme. It is evident that most of our rulers will not content themselves with governing the people collectively: it would seem as if they thought themselves responsible for the actions and private condition of their subjects— as if they had undertaken to guide and to instruct each of them in the various incidents of life, and to secure their happiness quite independently of their own consent. On the other hand, private individuals grow more and more apt to look upon the supreme power in the same light; they invoke its assistance in all their necessities, and they fix their eyes upon the administration as their mentor or their guide. . . .

In examining the ancient constitution of the judicial power, among most European nations, two things strike the mind—the independence of that power, and the extent of its functions. Not only did the courts of justice decide almost all differences between private persons, but in very many cases they acted as arbiters between private persons and the State. I do not here allude to the political and administrative offices which courts of judicature had in some countries usurped, but the judicial office common to them all. In most of the countries of Europe, there were, and there still are, many private rights, connected for the most part with the general right of property, which stood under the protection of the courts of justice, and which the State could not violate without their sanction. It was this semi-political power which mainly distinguished the European courts of judicature from all others ; for all nations have had judges, but all have not invested their judges with the same privileges. Upon examining what is now occurring among the democratic nations of Europe which are called free, as well as among the others, it will be observed that new and more dependent courts are everywhere springing up by the side of the old ones, for the express purpose of deciding, by an extraordinary jurisdiction, such litigated matters as may arise between the government and private persons. The elder judicial power retains its independence, but its jurisdiction is narrowed ; and there is a growing tendency to reduce it to be exclusively the arbiter between private interests. The number of these special courts of justice is continually increasing, and their functions increase likewise. Thus the government is more and more absolved from the necessity of subjecting its policy and its rights to the sanction of another power. As judges cannot be dispensed with, at least the State is to select them, and always to hold them under its control ; so that, between the government and private individuals, they place the effigy of justice rather than justice itself. The State is not satisfied with drawing all concerns to itself, but it acquires an ever-increasing power of deciding on them all without restriction and without appeal.

There exists among the modern nations of Europe one great cause, independent of all those which have already been pointed out, which perpetually contributes to extend the agency or to strengthen the prerogative of the supreme power, though it has not been sufficiently attended to : I mean the growth of manufactures, which is fostered by the progress of social equality. Manufactures generally collect a multitude of men on the same spot, among whom new and complex relations spring up. These men are exposed by their calling to great and sudden alternations of plenty and want, during which public tranquillity is endangered. It may also happen that these employments sacrifice the health, and even the life, of those who gain by them, or of those who live by them. Thus the manufacturing classes require more regulation, superintendence, and restraint than the other classes of society, and it is natural that the powers of government should increase in the same proportion as those classes.

This is a truth of general application ; what follows more especially concerns the nations of Europe. In the centuries which preceded that in which we live, the aristocracy was in possession of the soil, and was competent to defend it : landed property was therefore surrounded by ample securities, and its possessors enjoyed great independence. This gave rise to laws and customs that have been perpetuated, notwithstanding the subdivision of lands and the ruin of the nobility ; and, at the present time, land-owners and agriculturists are still those among the community who most easily escape from the control of the supreme power. In these same aristocratic ages, in which all the sources of our history are to be traced, personal property was of small importance, and those who possessed it were despised and weak : the manu-

facturing class formed an exception in the midst of
those aristocratic communities; as it had no certain
patronage, it was not outwardly protected, and was
often unable to protect itself. Hence a habit sprang
up of considering manufacturing property as something of a peculiar nature, not entitled to the same
deference, and not worthy of the same securities as
property in general; and manufacturers were looked
upon as a small class in the bulk of the people, whose
independence was of small importance, and who might
with propriety be abandoned to the disciplinary
passions of princes. On glancing over the codes of
the Middle Ages, one is surprised to see, in those
periods of personal independence, with what incessant
royal regulations manufactures were hampered, even
in their smallest details: on this point centralization
was as active and as minute as it can ever be. Since
that time a great revolution has taken place in the
world; manufacturing property, which was then only
in the germ, has spread till it covers Europe: the
manufacturing class has been multiplied and enriched
by the remnants of all other ranks; it has grown and
is still perpetually growing in numbers, in importance,
in wealth. Almost all those who do not belong to it
are connected with it at least on some one point; after
having been an exception in society, it threatens to
become the chief, if not the only, class; nevertheless,
the notions and political precedents engendered by it
of old still cling about it. These notions and these
precedents remain unchanged, because they are old,
and also because they happen to be in perfect accordance with the new notions and general habits of our
contemporaries. Manufacturing property, then, does
not extend its rights in the same ratio as its importance. The manufacturing classes do not become less
dependent, while they become more numerous; but,

on the contrary, it would seem as if despotism lurked within them, and naturally grew with their growth. As a nation becomes more engaged in manufactures, the want of roads, canals, harbours, and other works of a semi-public nature, which facilitate the acquisition of wealth, is more strongly felt; and as a nation becomes more democratic, private individuals are less able, and the State more able, to execute works of such magnitude. I do not hesitate to assert that the manifest tendency of all governments at the present time is to take upon themselves alone the execution of these undertakings; by which means they daily hold in closer dependence the population which they govern.

On the other hand, in proportion as the power of a State increases, and its necessities are augmented, the State consumption of manufactured produce is always growing larger, and these commodities are generally made in the arsenals or establishments of the government. Thus, in every kingdom, the ruler becomes the principal manufacturer; he collects and retains in his service a vast number of engineers, architects, mechanics, and handicraftsmen. Not only is he the principal manufacturer, but he tends more and more to become the chief, or rather the master, of all other manufacturers. As private persons become more powerless by becoming more equal, they can effect nothing in manufactures without combination; but the government naturally seeks to place these combinations under its own control.

It must be admitted that these collective beings, which are called combinations, are stronger and more formidable than a private individual can ever be, and that they have less of the responsibility of their own actions; whence it seems reasonable that they should not be allowed to retain so great an independence of the supreme government as might be conceded to a private individual.

Rulers are the more apt to follow this line of policy, as their own inclinations invite them to it. Among democratic nations it is only by association that the resistance of the people to the government can ever display itself: hence the latter always looks with ill-favour on those associations which are not in its own power; and it is well worthy of remark that, among democratic nations, the people themselves often entertain a secret feeling of fear and jealousy against these very associations, which prevents the citizens from defending the institutions of which they stand so much in need. The power and the duration of these small private bodies, in the midst of the weakness and instability of the whole community, astonish and alarm the people; and the free use which each association makes of its natural powers is almost regarded as a dangerous privilege. All the associations which spring up in our age are, moreover, new corporate powers, whose rights have not been sanctioned by time; they come into existence at a time when the notion of private rights is weak, and when the power of government is unbounded; hence it is not surprising that they lose their freedom at their birth. Among all European nations there are some kinds of associations which cannot be formed until the State has examined their by-laws, and authorized their existence. In several others, attempts are made to extend this rule to all associations; the consequences of such a policy, if it were successful, may easily be foreseen. If once the sovereign had a general right of authorizing associations of all kinds upon certain conditions, he would not be long without claiming the right of superintending and managing them, in order to prevent them from departing from the rules laid down by himself. In this manner, the State, after having reduced all who are desirous of forming associations into dependence, would proceed to reduce into the same condition all who belong to associations already formed—that is to say, almost all the men who are now in existence. Governments thus appropriate to themselves, and convert to their own purposes, the greater part of this new power which manufacturing interests have in our time brought into the world. Manufactures govern us—they govern manufactures.

I attach so much importance to all that I have just been saying that I am tormented by the fear of having impaired my meaning in seeking to render it more clear. If the reader thinks that the examples I have adduced to support my observations are insufficient or ill-chosen—if he imagines that I have anywhere exaggerated the encroachments of the supreme power, and, on the other hand, that I have underrated the extent of the sphere which still remains open to the exertions of individual independence, I entreat him to lay down the book for a moment, and to turn his mind to reflect for himself upon the subjects I have attempted to explain. . . . He will perceive that for the last half-century centralization has everywhere been growing up in a thousand different ways. Wars, revolutions, conquests, have served to promote it : all men have laboured to increase it. In the course of the same period, during which men have succeeded each other with singular rapidity at the head of affairs, their notions, interests, and passions have been infinitely diversified ; but all have by some means or other sought to centralize. This instinctive centralization has been the only settled point amid the extreme mutability of their lives and of their thoughts.

If the reader, after having investigated these details of human affairs, will seek to survey the wide prospect as a whole, he will be struck by the result. On the one hand, the most settled dynasties shaken or overthrown—the people everywhere escaping by violence from the sway of their laws—abolishing or limiting the authority of their rulers or their princes—the nations, which are not in open revolution, restless at least, and excited—all of them animated by the same spirit of revolt : and, on the other hand, at this very period of anarchy, and among these untractable nations, the incessant increase of the prerogative of the supreme government, becoming more centralized, more adventurous, more absolute, more extensive—the people perpetually falling under the control of the public administration—led insensibly to surrender to it some further portion of their individual independence, till the very men, who from time to time upset a throne and trample on a race of kings, bend more and more obsequiously to the slightest dictate of a clerk. Thus, two contrary revolutions appear in our days to be going on ; the one continually weakening the supreme power, the other as continually strengthening it : at no other period in our history has it appeared so weak or so strong.

But upon a more attentive examination of the state of the world, it appears that these two revolutions are intimately connected together, that they originate in the same source, and that after having followed a separate course, they lead men at last to the same result. I may venture once more to repeat what I have already said or implied in several parts of this book : great care must be taken not to confound the principle of equality itself with the revolution which finally establishes that principle in the social condition and the laws of a nation : here lies the reason of almost all the phenomena which occasion our astonishment. All the old political powers of Europe, the greatest as well as the least, were founded in ages of aristocracy, and they more or less represented or defended the principles of inequality and of privilege. To make the novel wants and interests, which the growing principle of equality introduced, preponderate in government, our contemporaries had to overturn or to coerce the established powers. This led them to make revolutions, and breathed into many of them that fierce love of disturbance and independence which all revolutions, whatever be their object, always engender. I do not believe that there is a single country in Europe in which the progress of equality has not been preceded or followed by some violent changes in the state of property and persons ; and almost all these changes have been attended with much anarchy and licence, because they have been made by the least civilized portion of the nation against that which is most civilized. Hence proceeded the twofold contrary tendencies which I have just pointed out. As long as the democratic revolution was glowing with heat, the men who were bent upon the destruction of old aristocratic powers hostile to that revolution displayed a strong spirit of independence ; but as the victory or the principle of equality became more complete, they gradually surrendered themselves to the propensities natural to that condition of equality, and they strengthened and centralized their governments. They had sought to be free in order to make themselves equal ; but in proportion as equality was more established by the aid of freedom, freedom itself was thereby rendered of more difficult attainment.

These two states of a nation have sometimes been contemporaneous : the last generation in France showed how a people might organize a stupendous tyranny in the community, at the very time when they were baffling the authority of the nobility and braving the power of all kings—at once teaching the world the way to win freedom, and the way to lose it. In our days men see that constituted powers are dilapidated on every side—they see all ancient authority gasping away, all ancient barriers tottering to their fall, and the judgement of the wisest is troubled at the sight : they attend only to the amazing revolution which is taking place before their eyes, and they imagine that mankind is about to fall into perpetual anarchy : if they looked to the final consequences of this revolution, their fears would perhaps assume a different shape. For myself, I confess that I put no trust in the spirit of freedom which appears to animate my contemporaries. I see well enough that the nations of this age are turbulent, but I do not clearly perceive that they are liberal ; and I fear lest, at the close of those perturbations which rock the base of thrones, the domination of sovereigns may prove more powerful than it ever was before.

I had remarked during my stay in the United States that a democratic state of society, similar to that of the Americans, might offer singular facilities for the establishment of despotism ; and I perceive, upon my return to Europe, how much use had already been made by most of our rulers of the notions, the sentiments, and the wants engendered by this same social condition, for the purpose of extending the circle of their power. This led me to think that the nations of Christendom would perhaps eventually undergo some sort of oppression like that which hung over several of the nations of the ancient world. A more accurate examination of the subject, and five years of further meditations, have not diminished my apprehensions, but they have changed the object of them. No sovereign ever lived in former ages so absolute or so powerful as to undertake to administer by his own agency, and without the assistance of intermediate powers, all the parts of a great empire : none ever attempted to subject all his subjects indiscriminately to strict uniformity of regulation, and personally to tutor and direct every member of the community. The notion of such an undertaking never occurred to the human mind ; and if any man had conceived it, the want of information, the imperfection of the administrative system, and, above all, the natural obstacles caused by the inequality of conditions, would speedily have checked the execution of so vast a design. When the Roman emperors were at the height of their power, the different nations of the empire still preserved manners and customs of great diversity; although they were subject to the same monarch, most of the provinces were separately administered ; they abounded in powerful and active municipalities ; and although the whole government of the empire was centred in the hands of the emperor alone, and he always remained, upon occasions, the supreme arbiter in all matters, yet the details of social life and private occupations lay for the most part beyond his control. The emperors possessed, it is true, an immense and unchecked power, which allowed them to gratify all their whimsical tastes, and to employ for that purpose the whole strength of the State. They frequently abused that power arbitrarily to deprive their subjects of property or of life : their tyranny was extremely onerous to the few, but it did not reach the greater number ; it was fixed to some few main objects, and neglected the rest ; it was violent, but its range was limited.

But it would seem that if despotism were to be established among the democratic nations of our days, it might assume a different character ; it would be more extensive and more mild ; it would degrade men without tormenting them. I do not question that in an age of instruction and equality like our own, sovereigns might more easily succeed in collecting all political power into their own hands, and might interfere more habitually and decidedly within the circle of private interests, than any sovereign of antiquity could ever do. But this same principle of equality which facilitates despotism tempers its rigour. We have seen how the manners of society become more humane and gentle in proportion as men become more equal and alike. When no member of the community has much power or much wealth, tyranny is, as it were, without opportunities and a field of action. As all fortunes are scanty, the passions of men are naturally circumscribed—their imagination limited, their pleasures simple. This universal moderation moderates the sovereign himself, and checks within certain limits the inordinate stretch of his desires.

Independently of these reasons drawn from the nature of the state of society itself, I might add many others arising from causes beyond my subject; but I shall keep within the limits I have laid down to myself. Democratic governments may become violent and even cruel at certain periods of extreme effervescence or of great danger : but these crises will be rare and brief. When I consider the petty passions of our contemporaries, the mildness of their manners, the extent of their education, the purity of their religion, the gentleness of their morality, their regular and industrious habits, and the restraint which they almost all observe in their vices no less than in their virtues, I have no fear that they will meet with tyrants in their rulers, but rather guardians. I think, then, that the species of oppression by which democratic nations are menaced is unlike anything which ever before existed in the world : our contemporaries will find no prototype of it in their memories. I am trying myself to choose an expression which will accurately convey the whole of the idea I have formed of it, but in vain; the old words despotism and tyranny are inappropriate: the thing itself is new; and since I cannot name it, I must attempt to define it.

I seek to trace the novel features under which despotism may appear in the world. The first thing that strikes the observation is an innumerable multitude of men all equal and alike, incessantly endeavouring to procure the petty and paltry pleasures with which they glut their lives. Each of them, living apart, is as a stranger to the fate of all the rest—his children and his private friends constitute to him the whole of mankind; as for the rest of his fellow-citizens, he is close to them, but he sees them not—he touches them, but he feels them not; he exists but in himself and for himself alone; and if his kindred still remain to him, he may be said at any rate to have lost his country. Above this race of men stands an immense and tutelary power, which takes upon itself alone to secure their gratifications, and to watch over their fate. That power is absolute, minute, regular, provident, and mild. It would be like the authority of a parent, if, like that authority, its object was to prepare men for manhood; but it seeks, on the contrary, to keep them in perpetual childhood: it is well content that the people should rejoice, provided they think of nothing but rejoicing. For their happiness such a government willingly labours, but it chooses to be the sole agent and the only arbiter of that happiness: it provides for their security, foresees and supplies their necessities, facilitates their pleasures, manages their principal concerns, directs their industry, regulates the descent of property, and subdivides their inheritances—what remains, but to spare them all the care of thinking and all the trouble of living? Thus it every day renders the exercise of the free agency of man less useful and less frequent; it circumscribes the will within a narrower range, and gradually robs a man of all the uses of himself. The principle of equality has prepared men for these things: it has predisposed men to endure them, and oftentimes to look on them as benefits.

After having thus successively taken each member of the community in its powerful grasp, and fashioned them at will, the supreme power then extends its arm over the whole community. It covers the surface of society with a network of small complicated rules, minute and uniform, through which the most original minds and the most energetic characters cannot penetrate, to rise above the crowd. The will of man is not shattered, but softened, bent, and guided: men are seldom forced by it to act, but they are constantly restrained from acting: such a power does not destroy, but it prevents existence; it does not tyrannize, but it compresses, enervates, extinguishes, and stupefies a people, till each nation is reduced to be nothing better than a flock of timid and industrious animals, of which the government is the shepherd.

I have always thought that servitude of the regular, quiet, and gentle kind which I have just described might be combined more easily than is commonly believed with some of the outward forms of freedom; and that it might even establish itself under the wing of the sovereignty of the people. Our contemporaries are constantly excited by two conflicting passions; they want to be led, and they wish to remain free: as they cannot destroy either one or the other of these contrary propensities, they strive to satisfy them both at once. They devise a sole, tutelary, and all-powerful form of government, but elected by the people. They

combine the principle of centralization and that of
popular sovereignty; this gives them a respite; they
console themselves for being in tutelage by the reflection that they have chosen their own guardians.
Every man allows himself to be put in leading-strings,
because he sees that it is not a person or a class of
persons, but the people at large, that holds the end of
his chain. By this system the people shake off their
state of dependence just long enough to select their
master, and then relapse into it again. A great many
persons at the present day are quite contented with
this sort of compromise between administrative
despotism and the sovereignty of the people; and
they think they have done enough for the protection
of individual freedom when they have surrendered it
to the power of the nation at large. This does not
satisfy me: the nature of him I am to obey signifies
less to me than the fact of extorted obedience.

I do not, however, deny that a constitution of this
kind appears to me to be infinitely preferable to one
which, after having concentrated all the powers of
government, should vest them in the hands of an
irresponsible person or body of persons. Of all the
forms which democratic despotism could assume, the
latter would assuredly be the worst. When the sovereign is elective, or narrowly watched by a legislature which is really elective and independent, the
oppression which he exercises over individuals is
sometimes greater, but it is always less degrading;
because every man, when he is oppressed and dis-
armed, may still imagine that while he yields obedience it is to himself he yields it, and that it is to one of
his own inclinations that all the rest give way. In like
manner I can understand that when the sovereign
represents the nation, and is dependent upon the
people, the rights and the power of which every

U

citizen is deprived, not only serve the head of the State, but the State itself; and that private persons derive some return from the sacrifice of their independence which they have made to the public. To create a representation of the people in every centralized country is, therefore, to diminish the evil which extreme centralization may produce, but not to get rid of it. I admit that by this means room is left for the intervention of individuals in the more important affairs; but it is not the less suppressed in the smaller and more private ones. It must not be forgotten that it is especially dangerous to enslave men in the minor details of life. For my own part, I should be inclined to think freedom less necessary in great things than in little ones, if it were possible to be secure of the one without possessing the other. Subjection in minor affairs breaks out every day, and is felt by the whole community indiscriminately. It does not drive men to resistance, but it crosses them at every turn, till they are led to surrender the exercise of their will. Thus their spirit is gradually broken and their character enervated; whereas that obedience, which is exacted on a few important but rare occasions, only exhibits servitude at certain intervals, and throws the burden of it upon a small number of men. It is in vain to summon a people, which has been rendered so dependent on the central power, to choose from time to time the representatives of that power; this rare and brief exercise of their free choice, however important it may be, will not prevent them from gradually losing the faculties of thinking, feeling, and acting for themselves, and thus gradually falling below the level of humanity. I add that they will soon become incapable of exercising the great and only privilege which remains to them. The democratic nations which have introduced freedom into their political constitution, at the very time when they were augmenting the despotism of their administrative constitution, have been led into strange paradoxes. To manage those minor affairs in which good sense is all that is wanted—the people are held to be unequal to the task ; but when the government of the country is at stake, the people are invested with immense powers ; they are alternately made the playthings of their ruler, and his masters—more than kings, and less than men. After having exhausted all the different modes of election, without finding one to suit their purpose, they are still amazed, and still bent on seeking further ; as if the evil they remark did not originate in the constitution of the country far more than in that of the electoral body. It is, indeed, difficult to conceive how men who have entirely given up the habit of self-government should succeed in making a proper choice of those by whom they are to be governed ; and no one will ever believe that a liberal, wise, and energetic government can spring from the suffrages of a subservient people. A constitution, which should be republican in its head and ultra-monarchical in all its other parts, has ever appeared to me to be a short-lived monster. The vices of rulers and the ineptitude of the people would speedily bring about its ruin ; and the nation, weary of its representatives and of itself, would create freer institutions, or soon return to stretch itself at the feet of a single master.

I believe that it is easier to establish an absolute and despotic government among a people in which the conditions of society are equal, than among any other ; and I think that if such a government were once established among such a people, it would not only oppress men, but would eventually strip each of them of several of the highest qualities of humanity.

Despotism, therefore, appears to me peculiarly to be dreaded in democratic ages. I should have loved freedom, I believe, at all times, but in the time in which we live I am ready to worship it. On the other hand, I am persuaded that all who shall attempt, in the ages upon which we are entering, to base freedom upon aristocratic privilege, will fail—that all who shall attempt to draw and to retain authority within a single class, will fail. At the present day no ruler is skilful or strong enough to found a despotism, by re-establishing permanent distinctions of rank among his subjects : no legislator is wise or powerful enough to preserve free institutions if he does not take equality for his first principle and his watchword. All those of our contemporaries who would establish or secure the independence and the dignity of their fellow-men, must show themselves the friends of equality ; and the only worthy means of showing themselves as such, is to be so : upon this depends the success of their holy enterprise. Thus the question is not how to reconstruct aristocratic society, but how to make liberty proceed out of that democratic state of society in which God has placed us.

These two truths appear to me simple, clear, and fertile in consequences ; and they naturally lead me to consider what kind of free government can be established among a people in which social conditions are equal.

It results from the very constitution of democratic nations and from their necessities that the power of government among them must be more uniform, more centralized, more extensive, more searching, and more efficient than in other countries. Society at large is naturally stronger and more active, individuals more subordinate and weak ; the former does more, the latter less ; and this is inevitably the case. It is not, therefore, to be expected that the range of private independence will ever be as extensive in democratic as in aristocratic countries—nor is this to be desired ; for, among aristocratic nations, the mass is often sacrificed to the individual, and the prosperity of the greater number to the greatness of the few. It is both necessary and desirable that the government of a democratic people should be active and powerful : and our object should not be to render it weak or indolent, but solely to prevent it from abusing its aptitude and its strength.

The circumstance which most contributed to secure the independence of private persons in aristocratic ages was, that the supreme power did not affect to take upon itself alone the government and administration of the community : those functions were necessarily partially left to the members of the aristocracy : so that as the supreme power was always divided, it never weighed with its whole weight and in the same manner on each individual. Not only did the government not perform everything by its immediate agency ; but as most of the agents who discharged its duties derived their power not from the State, but from the circumstance of their birth, they were not perpetually under its control. The government could not make or unmake them in an instant, at pleasure, nor bend them in strict uniformity to its slightest caprice—this was an additional guarantee of private independence. I readily admit that recourse cannot be had to the same means at the present time : but I discover certain democratic expedients which may be substituted for them. Instead of vesting in the government alone all the administrative powers of which corporations and nobles have been deprived, a portion of them may be intrusted to secondary public bodies, temporarily composed of private citizens : thus the liberty of private persons will be more secure, and their equality will not be diminished.

The Americans, who care less for words than the French, still designate by the name of County the largest of their administrative districts : but the duties of the count or lord-lieutenant are in part performed by a provincial assembly. At a period of equality like our own it would be unjust and unreasonable to institute hereditary officers ; but there is nothing to prevent us from substituting elective public officers to a certain extent. Election is a democratic expedient which insures the independence of the public officer in relation to the government, as much and even more than hereditary rank can insure it among aristocratic nations. Aristocratic countries abound in wealthy and influential persons who are competent to provide for themselves, and who cannot be easily or secretly oppressed : such persons restrain a government within general habits of moderation and reserve. I am very well aware that democratic countries contain no such persons naturally ; but something analogous to them may be created by artificial means. I firmly believe that an aristocracy cannot again be founded in the world ; but I think that private citizens, by combining together, may constitute bodies of great wealth, influence, and strength, corresponding to the persons of an aristocracy. By this means many of the greatest political advantages of aristocracy would be obtained without its injustice or its dangers. An association for political, commercial, or manufacturing purposes, or even for those of science and literature, is a powerful and enlightened member of the community, which cannot be disposed of at pleasure, or oppressed without remonstrance ; and which, by defending its own rights against the encroachments of the government, saves the common liberties of the country.

In periods of aristocracy every man is always bound so closely to many of his fellow-citizens that he cannot be assailed without their coming to his assistance. In ages of equality every man naturally stands alone ; he has no hereditary friends whose co-operation he may demand—no class upon whose sympathy he may rely : he is easily got rid of, and he is trampled on with impunity. At the present time, an oppressed member of the community has therefore only one method of self-defence—he may appeal to the whole nation : and if the whole nation is deaf to his complaint, he may appeal to mankind : the only means he has of making this appeal is by the press. Thus the liberty of the press is infinitely more valuable among democratic nations than among all others ; it is the only cure for the evils which equality may produce. Equality sets men apart and weakens them ; but the press places a powerful weapon within every man's reach, which the weakest and loneliest of them all may use. Equality deprives a man of the support of his connections ; but the press enables him to summon all his fellow-countrymen and all his fellow-men to his assistance. Printing has accelerated the progress of equality, and it is also one of its best correctives.

I think that men living in aristocracies may, strictly speaking, do without the liberty of the press : but such is not the case with those who live in democratic countries. To protect their personal independence I trust not to great political assemblies, to parliamentary privilege, or to the assertion of popular sovereignty. All these things may, to a certain extent, be reconciled with personal servitude—but that servitude cannot be complete if the press is free : the press is the chiefest democratic instrument of freedom.

Something analogous may be said of the judicial power. It is a part of the essence of judicial power to

attend to private interests, and to fix itself with pre-
dilection on minute objects submitted to its observation; another essential quality of judicial power is
never to volunteer its assistance to the oppressed, but
always to be at the disposal of the humblest of those
who solicit it; their complaint, however feeble they
may themselves be, will force itself upon the ear of
justice and claim redress, for this is inherent in the
very constitutions of the court of justice. A power of
this kind is therefore peculiarly adapted to the wants
of freedom, at a time when the eye and finger of the
government are constantly intruding into the minutest
details of human actions, and when private persons
are at once too weak to protect themselves, and too
much isolated for them to reckon upon the assistance
of their fellows. The strength of the courts of law has
ever been the greatest security which can be offered
to personal independence; but this is more especially
the case in democratic ages: private rights and interests are in constant danger, if the judicial power
does not grow more extensive and more strong to keep
pace with the growing equality of conditions.

Equality awakens in men several propensities
extremely dangerous to freedom, to which the attention of the legislator ought constantly to be directed.
I shall only remind the reader of the most important
among them. Men living in democratic ages do not
readily comprehend the utility of forms: they feel
an instinctive contempt for them—I have elsewhere
shown for what reasons. Forms excite their contempt
and often their hatred; as they commonly aspire to
none but easy and present gratifications, they rush
onward to the object of their desires, and the slightest
delay exasperates them. This same temper, carried
with them into political life, renders them hostile to
forms, which perpetually retard or arrest them in some

of their projects. Yet this objection which the men of democracies make to forms is the very thing which renders forms so useful to freedom; for their chief merit is to serve as a barrier between the strong and the weak, the ruler and the people, to retard the one, and give the other time to look about him. Forms become more necessary in proportion as the government becomes more active and more powerful, while private persons are becoming more indolent and more feeble. Thus democratic nations naturally stand more in need of forms than other nations, and they naturally respect them less. This deserves most serious attention. Nothing is more pitiful than the arrogant disdain of most of our contemporaries for questions of form; for the smallest questions of form have acquired in our time an importance which they never had before: many of the greatest interests of mankind depend upon them. I think that if the statesmen of aristocratic ages could sometimes contemn forms with impunity, and frequently rise above them, the statesmen to whom the government of nations is now confided ought to treat the very least among them with respect, and not neglect them without imperious necessity. In aristocracies the observance of forms was superstitious; among us they ought to be kept with a deliberate and enlightened deference.

Another tendency, which is extremely natural to democratic nations and extremely dangerous, is that which leads them to despise and undervalue the rights of private persons. The attachment which men feel to a right, and the respect which they display for it, is generally proportioned to its importance, or to the length of time during which they have enjoyed it. The rights of private persons among democratic nations are commonly of small importance, of recent growth, and extremely precarious—the consequence is that they are often sacrificed without regret, and almost always violated without remorse. But it happens that at the same period and among the same nations in which men conceive a natural contempt for the rights of private persons, the rights of society at large are naturally extended and consolidated : in other words, men become less attached to private rights at the very time at which it would be most necessary to retain and to defend what little remains of them. It is therefore most especially in the present democratic ages that the true friends of the liberty and the greatness of man ought constantly to be on the alert to prevent the power of government from lightly sacrificing the private rights of individuals to the general execution of its designs. At such times no citizen is so obscure that it is not very dangerous to allow him to be oppressed—no private rights are so unimportant that they can be surrendered with impunity to the caprices of a government. The reason is plain : if the private right of an individual is violated at a time when the human mind is fully impressed with the importance and the sanctity of such rights, the injury done is confined to the individual whose right is infringed ; but to violate such a right, at the present day, is deeply to corrupt the manners of the nation and to put the whole community in jeopardy, because the very notion of this kind of right constantly tends among us to be impaired and lost.

There are certain habits, certain notions, and certain vices which are peculiar to a state of revolution, and which a protracted revolution cannot fail to engender and to propagate, whatever be, in other respects, its character, its purpose, and the scene on which it takes place. When any nation has, within a short space of time, repeatedly varied its rulers, its opinions, and its laws, the men of whom it is composed eventually contract a taste for change, and grow accustomed to see all changes effected by sudden violence. Thus they naturally conceive a contempt for forms which daily prove ineffectual ; and they do not support without impatience the dominion of rules which they have so often seen infringed. As the ordinary notions of equity and morality no longer suffice to explain and justify all the innovations daily begotten by a revolution, the principle of public utility is called in, the doctrine of political necessity is conjured up, and men accustom themselves to sacrifice private interests without scruple, and to trample on the rights of individuals in order more speedily to accomplish any public purpose.

These habits and notions, which I shall call revolutionary, because all revolutions produce them, occur in aristocracies just as much as among democratic nations ; but among the former they are often less powerful and always less lasting, because there they meet with habits, notions, defects, and impediments, which counteract them : they consequently disappear as soon as the revolution is terminated, and the nation reverts to its former political courses. This is not always the case in democratic countries, in which it is ever to be feared that revolutionary tendencies, becoming more gentle and more regular, without entirely disappearing from society, will be gradually transformed into habits of subjection to the administrative authority of the government. I know of no countries in which revolutions are more dangerous than in democratic countries ; because, independently of the accidental and transient evils which must always attend them, they may always create some evils which are permanent and unending. I believe that there are such things as justifiable resistance and legitimate rebellion : I do not therefore assert, as an absolute proposition, that the men of democratic ages ought never to make revolutions; but I think that they have especial reason to hesitate before they embark in them, and that it is far better to endure many grievances in their present condition than to have recourse to so perilous a remedy.

I shall conclude by one general idea, which comprises not only all the particular ideas which have been expressed in the present chapter, but also most of those which it is the object of this book to treat of. In the ages of aristocracy which preceded our own, there were private persons of great power, and a social authority of extreme weakness. The outline of society itself was not easily discernible, and constantly confounded with the different powers by which the community was ruled. The principal efforts of the men of those times were required to strengthen, aggrandize, and secure the supreme power; and, on the other hand, to circumscribe individual independence within narrower limits, and to subject private interests to the interests of the public. Other perils and other cares await the men of our age. Among the greater part of modern nations, the government, whatever may be its origin, its constitution, or its name, has become almost omnipotent, and private persons are falling, more and more, into the lowest stage of weakness and dependence. In olden society everything was different; unity and uniformity were nowhere to be met with. In modern society everything threatens to become so much alike, that the peculiar characteristics of each individual will soon be entirely lost in the general aspect of the world. Our forefathers were ever prone to make an improper use of the notion that private rights ought to be respected; and we are naturally prone, on the other hand, to exaggerate the idea that the interest of a private individual ought always to bend to the interest of the many. The political world is metamorphosed: new remedies must henceforth be sought for new disorders. To lay down extensive, but distinct and settled limits, to the action of the government; to confer certain rights on private persons, and to secure to them the undisputed enjoyment of those rights; to enable individual man to maintain whatever independence, strength, and original power he still possesses; to raise him by the side of society at large, and uphold him in that position—these appear to me the main objects of legislators in the ages upon which we are now entering. It would seem as if the rulers of our time sought only to use men in order to make things great; I wish that they would try a little more to make great men; that they would set less value on the work, and more upon the workman; that they would never forget that a nation cannot long remain strong when every man belonging to it is individually weak, and that no form or combination of social polity has yet been devised to make an energetic people out of a community of pusillanimous and enfeebled citizens.

I trace among our contemporaries two contrary notions which are equally injurious. One set of men can perceive nothing in the principle of equality but the anarchical tendencies which it engenders: they dread their own free agency—they fear themselves. Other thinkers, less numerous but more enlightened, take a different view: beside that track which starts from the principle of equality to terminate in anarchy, they have at last discovered the road which seems to lead men to inevitable servitude. They shape their souls beforehand to this necessary condition; and, despairing of remaining free, they already do obeisance in their hearts to the master who is soon to appear. The former abandon freedom, because they think it dangerous; the latter, because they hold it to be impossible. If I had entertained the latter conviction, I should not have written this book, but I should have confined myself to deploring in secret the destiny of mankind. I have sought to point out the dangers to which the principle of equality exposes the independence of man, because I firmly believe that these dangers are the most formidable, as well as the least foreseen, of all those which futurity holds in store : but I do not think that they are insurmountable. The men who live in the democratic ages upon which we are entering have naturally a taste for independence : they are naturally impatient of regulation, and they are wearied by the permanence even of the condition they themselves prefer. They are fond of power ; but they are prone to despise and hate those who wield it, and they easily elude its grasp by their own mobility and insignificance. These propensities will always manifest themselves, because they originate in the groundwork of society, which will undergo no change : for a long time they will prevent the establishment of any despotism, and they will furnish fresh weapons to each succeeding generation which shall struggle in favour of the liberty of mankind. Let us then look forward to the future with that salutary fear which makes men keep watch and ward for freedom, not with that faint and idle terror which depresses and enervates the heart.

Before I close for ever the theme that has detained me so long, I would fain take a parting survey of all the various characteristics of modern society, and appreciate at last the general influence to be exercised by the principle of equality upon the fate of mankind ; but I am stopped by the difficulty of the task, and in presence of so great an object my sight is troubled and my reason fails. The society of the modern world which I have sought to delineate, and which I seek to judge, has but just come into existence. Time has not yet shaped it into perfect form : the great revolution by which it has been created is not yet over : and amid the occurrences of our time, it is almost impossible to discern what will pass away with the revolution itself, and what will survive its close. The world which is rising into existence is still half encumbered by the remains of the world which is waning into decay ; and amid the vast perplexity of human affairs, none can say how much of ancient institutions and former manners will remain, or how much will completely disappear. Although the revolution that is taking place in the social condition, the laws, the opinions, and the feelings of men, is still very far from being terminated, yet its results already admit of no comparison with anything that the world has ever before witnessed. I go back from age to age up to the remotest antiquity ; but I find no parallel to what is occurring before my eyes : as the past has ceased to throw its light upon the future, the mind of man wanders in obscurity.

Nevertheless, in the midst of a prospect so wide, so novel, and so confused, some of the more prominent characteristics may already be discerned and pointed out. The good things and the evils of life are more equally distributed in the world : great wealth tends to disappear, the number of small fortunes to increase ; desires and gratifications are multiplied, but extraordinary prosperity and irremediable penury are alike unknown. The sentiment of ambition is universal, but the scope of ambition is seldom vast. Each individual stands apart in solitary weakness ; but society at large is active, provident, and powerful : the performances of private persons are insignificant, those of the State immense. There is little energy of character ;

but manners are mild, and laws humane. If there be few instances of exalted heroism or of virtues of the highest, brightest, and purest temper, men's habits are regular, violence is rare, and cruelty almost unknown. Human existence becomes longer, and property more secure: life is not adorned with brilliant trophies, but it is extremely easy and tranquil. Few pleasures are either very refined or very coarse; and highly polished manners are as uncommon as great brutality of tastes. Neither men of great learning, nor extremely ignorant communities, are to be met with; genius becomes more rare, information more diffused. The human mind is impelled by the small efforts of all mankind combined together, not by the strenuous activity of certain men. There is less perfection, but more abundance, in all the productions of the arts. The ties of race, of rank, and of country are relaxed; the great bond of humanity is strengthened. If I endeavour to find out the most general and the most prominent of all these different characteristics, I shall have occasion to perceive that what is taking place in men's fortunes manifests itself under a thousand other forms. Almost all extremes are softened or blunted: all that was most prominent is superseded by some mean term, at once less lofty and less low, less brilliant and less obscure, than what before existed in the world.

When I survey this countless multitude of beings, shaped in each other's likeness, amid whom nothing rises and nothing falls, the sight of such universal uniformity saddens and chills me, and I am tempted to regret that state of society which has ceased to be. When the world was full of men of great importance and extreme insignificance, of great wealth and extreme poverty, of great learning and extreme ignorance, I turned aside from the latter to fix my observation on the former alone, who gratified my sympathies. But I admit that this gratification arose from my own weakness : it is because I am unable to see at once all that is around me that I am allowed thus to select and separate the objects of my pre-dilection from among so many others. Such is not the case with that Almighty and Eternal Being, whose gaze necessarily includes the whole of created things, and who surveys distinctly, though at once, mankind and man. We may naturally believe that it is not the singular prosperity of the few, but the greater well-being of all, which is most pleasing in the sight of the Creator and Preserver of men. What appears to me to be man's decline is to his eye advancement ; what afflicts me is acceptable to him. A state of equality is perhaps less elevated, but it is more just ; and its justice constitutes its greatness and its beauty. I would strive, then, to raise myself to this point of the divine contemplation, and thence to view and to judge the concerns of men.

No man, upon the earth, can as yet affirm absolutely and generally that the new state of the world is better than its former one ; but it is already easy to perceive that this state is different. Some vices and some virtues were so inherent in the constitution of an aristocratic nation, and are so opposite to the char-acter of a modern people, that they can never be infused into it ; some good tendencies and some bad propensities which were unknown to the former are natural to the latter ; some ideas suggest themselves spontaneously to the imagination of the one which are utterly repugnant to the mind of the other. They are like two distinct orders of human beings, each of which has its own merits and defects, its own advantages and its own evils. Care must therefore be taken not to judge the state of society, which is now coming into existence, by notions derived from a state of society which no longer exists; for as these states of society are exceedingly different in their structure, they cannot be submitted to a just or fair comparison. It would be scarcely more reasonable to require of our own contemporaries the peculiar virtues which originated in the social condition of their forefathers, since that social condition is itself fallen, and has drawn into one promiscuous ruin the good and evil which belonged to it.

But as yet these things are imperfectly understood. I find that a great number of my contemporaries undertake to make a certain selection from among the institutions, the opinions, and the ideas which originated in the aristocratic constitution of society as it was: a portion of these elements they would willingly relinquish, but they would keep the remainder and transplant them into their new world. I apprehend that such men are wasting their time and their strength in virtuous but unprofitable efforts. The object is not to retain the peculiar advantages which the inequality of conditions bestows upon mankind, but to secure the new benefits which equality may supply. We have not to seek to make ourselves like our progenitors, but to strive to work out that species of greatness and happiness which is our own. For myself, who now look back from this extreme limit of my task, and discover from afar, but at once, the various objects which have attracted my more attentive investigation upon my way, I am full of apprehensions and of hopes. I perceive mighty dangers which it is possible to ward off—mighty evils which may be avoided or alleviated; and I cling with a firmer hold to the belief, that for democratic nations to be virtuous and prosperous they require but to will it. I am aware that many of my contemporaries maintain that nations are never their own masters here below, and that they necessarily obey some insurmountable and unintelligent power, arising from anterior events, from their race, or from the soil and climate of their country. Such principles are false and cowardly; such principles can never produce aught but feeble men and pusillanimous nations. Providence has not created mankind entirely independent or entirely free. It is true that around every man a fatal circle is traced, beyond which he cannot pass; but within the wide verge of that circle he is powerful and free: as it is with man, so with communities. The nations of our time cannot prevent the conditions of men from becoming equal; but it depends upon themselves whether the principle of equality is to lead them to servitude or freedom, to knowledge or barbarism, to prosperity or to wretchedness.

THE END